W9-ANJ-364

WITHDRAWN

ACT POWER
PRACTICE

Other Titles of Interest from LearningExpress

ACT Word Games
501 Reading Comprehension Questions, 4th Edition
Geometry Success in 20 Minutes a Day, 3rd Edition
Reading Comprehension Success in 20 Minutes a Day, 4th Edition
SAT Math Essentials
411 SAT Critical Reading Questions

ACT POWER PRACTICE

LEARNINGEXPRESS ®

NEW YORK

Library of Congress Cataloging-in-Publication Data:
ACT: power practice.—1st ed.
        p.   cm.
   ISBN-13: 978-1-57685-789-2 (pbk. : alk. paper)
   ISBN-10: 1-57685-789-1 (pbk. : alk. paper)
   1. ACT Assessment—Study guides.   I. LearningExpress (Organization)
   LB2353.48.A2915   2011
   378.1'662—dc22

                                        2011005066

Printed in the United States of America

9 8 7 6 5 4 3 2 1

First Edition

ISBN-13: 978-1-57685-789-2
ISBN-10: 1-57685-789-1

For more information or to place an order, contact LearningExpress at:
   2 Rector Street
   26th Floor
   New York, NY 10006

Or visit us at:
   www.learnatest.com

Editor: Marco A. Annunziata
Production Editor: Eric Titner
Assistant Editor: Miranda Pennington

CONTENTS

CONTRIBUTORS ▶

The following individuals contributed to the content of this book.

Stanley Ezrol is an instructor and private tutor in math and science, a freelance writer/editor, and a data processing consultant. His experience as a professional writer and editor spans 40 years, including work in publicity, business writing, and journalism. He has published numerous articles on history, culture, and current events. He also has worked as an electronic data processing (EDP) system designer and management advisor for 30 years.

S.D. Spizer grew up in New York City. After graduating from Yale in 1981, he worked at ABC News. In 1990, he was part of a group that opened Carmine's Restaurant on the Upper West Side of Manhattan. He spent the late 1990s building a cabin near Strasburg, Virginia, and writing a series of children's stories. He returned to New York City in 2000, where he continued to write children's stories and began working in child education. He specializes in high school math and English tutoring and preparing students for college entrance exams. He splits his time between New York City and Pawling, New York, with his partner Michelle and their two daughters, Sasha and Kate.

ABOUT ACT: POWER PRACTICE

LearningExpress understands the importance of achieving top scores on your ACT® college entrance examination, and we strive to publish the most authentic and comprehensive ACT preparation materials available today. Practice does indeed make perfect, and that's why we've created this book composed of four practice ACTs (plus another four online) complete with detailed answer explanations—it offers you all the extra practice you need to get a great score. Whether used on its own or as a powerful companion to other ACT preparation titles, *ACT: Power Practice* is the key to a top score and a brighter future.

C H A P T E R

1 ▶ ACT STUDY SKILLS AND TEST-TAKING STRATEGIES

The advice in this chapter will help you set up an effective learning environment and create a successful study plan. You will also learn important study strategies and test-taking tips.

Part 1: Study Skills

You probably feel as though you have spent practically your entire life studying, so why do you need to learn how to study for the ACT test? The ACT is different from any other test you have ever taken. Not only is it longer and more important, but multisubject, standardized tests require a unique form of preparation.

You certainly do not have to scrap all the good study habits you have already learned, but you will most likely need to adapt them to the specifics of the ACT. You may already be using some of the techniques found in this chapter, but now is a good time to re-evaluate your study habits and tailor them specifically to the ACT.

While studying for the ACT, you will also learn which study habits do not work and be able to eliminate wasted study time. Remember that the more effective your study habits, the less time you will spend studying and the more free time you will have to do what you really enjoy.

Study Environment and Attitude
The Right Mood

It will probably be tough to carve out extra time to study for the ACT on top of your regular schoolwork, your extracurricular activities, and your social life. These reasons may even lead you to procrastinate, but procrastinating can cause lots of trouble at test time. If you procrastinate too much or for too long, you will not be prepared for the exam.

One of the best ways to beat procrastination is to use a reward system. We all like to be rewarded for a job well done. If we know there is going to be a reward at the end of our work, it is easier to get started. So promise yourself a small reward for each study session. For example, you might promise yourself an hour of watching TV or playing video games as a reward for an hour of study. You might promise to treat yourself to a movie or a new CD after you finish a chapter in a test-prep book. Get your parents involved with your reward plan and maybe they will provide some rewards of their own.

Remember, your attitude is important. It can dramatically affect how much you learn and how well you learn it. Make sure that you have a positive attitude. You will study, you will learn, and you will do well. Your study time will be time well spent.

The Right Conditions

You can have the best attitude in the world, but if you are tired or distracted, you are going to have difficulty studying. To be at your best, you need to be focused, alert, and calm. That means you need to study under the right conditions.

Everyone is different, so you need to know what conditions work best for you. Here are eight questions to consider:

1. What time of day do you work best—morning, afternoon, or evening? How early in the day or late in the night can you think clearly?
2. Do you work best in total silence? Or do you prefer music or other noise in the background?

3. If you prefer music, what kind? Classical music often helps people relax because the music is soft and there are no words. But you may prefer music that energizes you. Others work best with music that has special meaning to them and puts them in a positive state of mind.
4. Where do you like to work? Do you feel most comfortable sitting at the kitchen counter? At the dining room table? At a desk in your bedroom? (Try to avoid studying in bed. You will probably be relaxed, but you may be too comfortable and fall asleep.) Or do you prefer to study out of the house, in the library or a local coffee shop?
5. What do you like to have around you when you work? Do you feel most comfortable in your favorite chair? Do you like to have pictures of family and friends around?
6. What kind of lighting do you prefer? Does soft light make you sleepy? Do you need bright light? If it's too bright, you may feel uncomfortable. If it is too dark, you may feel sleepy. Remember that poor lighting can also strain your eyes and give you a headache.
7. How does eating affect you? Do you feel most energized right after a meal? Or does eating tend to make you drowsy? Which foods give you a lot of energy? Which slow you down?
8. Can you put problems or other pressing concerns out of your mind to focus on a different task? How can you minimize distractions so you can fully focus on your work?

Think carefully about each of these questions and be honest with yourself. You may like listening to music, but do you really study better in silence? Do you usually study in your room but are tempted by talking on the phone or using the computer? The more honestly you evaluate your study environment, the more effectively you will use your time, and the less time you will have to spend studying. Write down your answers so you can develop a good study plan.

Study Groups

The majority of your study time should be spent alone in the environment that is best for your study style. However, a good way to get motivated and add some variety to your studying is by forming or joining a study group. Studying with a group will not only be more fun than studying alone, but if you are stuck on a problem, someone in your group may be able to explain it to you. And do not underestimate the value of helping other people in your group. Explaining a difficult concept to someone else is a great way to reinforce what you know or help you decipher what you do not really understand. There are a few things to consider when you form your study group:

- Find an appropriate place with few distractions to study.
- Keep your group small; three or four people is best.
- Include only other students who are as serious about studying for the ACT as you are.
- Set an agenda for your meeting, keep it specific, and decide on one concrete goal for your meeting.

The Right Tools

Help make your study session successful by having the right learning tools. As you study for the ACT, have:

- a good dictionary, such as *Merriam-Webster's Collegiate Dictionary, 11th Edition*
- a calculator
- paper or legal pads
- pencils (and a pencil sharpener) or pens
- a highlighter, or several, in different colors
- index or other note cards
- folders or notebooks
- a calendar

Keep your personal preferences in mind. Perhaps you like to write with a certain kind of pen or on a certain kind of paper. If so, make sure you have that pen or paper with you when you study. It will help you feel more comfortable and relaxed as you work.

Learning How You Learn

Imagine that you need directions to a restaurant you have never been to before. Which of the following would you do?

- Look on a map.
- Ask someone to tell you how to get there.
- Draw a map or copy someone's written directions.
- List step-by-step directions.

Most people learn in a variety of ways. They learn by seeing, hearing, doing, and organizing information from the world around them. But most of us tend to use one of these ways more than the others. That's our *dominant* (strongest) learning style. How you would handle getting directions, for example, suggests which learning style you use most often:

- **Visual.** Visual learners learn best *by seeing*. If you would look at a map for directions, you are probably a visual learner. You understand ideas best when they are in pictures or graphs. You may learn better by using different colors as you take notes. Use a highlighter (or several, in different colors) as you read, to mark important ideas. Mapping and diagramming ideas are good learning strategies for visual learners.
- **Auditory.** Auditory learners learn best *by listening*. If you would ask someone to tell you directions, you are probably an auditory learner. You would probably rather listen to a lecture than read a textbook, and you may learn better by reading aloud. Try recording your notes on a tape player and listening to your tapes.

- **Kinesthetic.** Kinesthetic learners learn best *by doing*. (*Kinesthetic* means *feeling the movements of the body*.) They like to keep their hands and bodies moving. If you would draw a map or copy down directions, you are probably a kinesthetic learner. You will benefit from interacting with the material you are studying. Underline, take notes, and create note cards. Recopying material will help you remember it.

- **Sequential.** Sequential learners learn best *by putting things in order*. If you would create a step-by-step list of driving directions, you are probably a sequential learner. You may learn better by creating outlines and grouping ideas together into categories.

Think carefully about how you learn. Which is your dominant learning style? Keep it in mind as you read about Learning Strategies in Part 2 of this chapter.

Learning Styles and Finding the Methods Right for You

The best way to tackle the preparations involved in studying for the ACT is first to think about the way you study now. Do you set aside a specific time to do your homework? Is there a place that you always go to study? Do you take on all your subjects at once or start with the easiest? Once you have given some thought to your current study habits, it is time to honestly evaluate how well they work.

Creating a Study Plan

You will probably spend more time studying for the ACT than you have spent studying for any other test. So even with the best intentions, if you sit down with this book and say, "I'm going to master the ACT," you will most likely get discouraged and give up before you sharpen your number 2 pencil. But if instead you create a study plan by breaking down your tasks into manageable parts and scheduling time to tackle them, you will almost certainly succeed.

The first step you should take is to make a list of everything you need to study in order to do well on the ACT. Make this list as detailed as possible. Instead of "study English" or "practice math," for example, appropriate tasks should be "take a practice English test" or "go over missed questions on the last math practice test." Make your list long. The smaller the tasks, the faster you will cross them off your list. The effort you put forth at the start will more than pay off in the end by eliminating wasted time.

What You Know and What You Need to Know

In order to make your list, you need to determine what you already know and what you need to learn. To create an effective study plan, you need a good sense of exactly what you need to study. Chances are you already know some of the test material well. Some of it you may need only to review, and some of it you may need to study in detail.

Take the ACT practice tests in each chapter of this book to find out how you would do on the exam. How did you score? What do you seem to know well? What do you need to review? What do you need to study in detail?

Scheduling Study Time

Next, you need to set a time frame. Once you have a good sense of how much studying is ahead, create a detailed study schedule. Use a calendar to set specific deadlines. If deadlines make you nervous, give yourself plenty of time for each task. Otherwise, you might have trouble keeping calm and staying on track.

To create a good schedule, break your studying into small tasks that move toward your learning goals. A study plan that says "Learn everything by May 1" isn't going to be helpful. However, a study plan that sets dates for learning specific material in March and April *will* enable you to learn everything by May 1. For example, if you need to focus on building your reading comprehension skills, you might create a schedule like the following:

Week 1	Review basic reading comprehension strategies.
Week 2	Practice finding the main idea.
Week 3	Practice vocabulary in context questions.
Week 4	Practice specific detail questions.
Week 5	Practice inference questions.
Week 6	Practice finding the references.
Week 7	Take reading practice test.
Week 8	Begin reviewing grammar/usage rules.
Week 9	Continue reviewing grammar/usage rules.
Week 10	Start overall review.
Week 11	Continue overall review.
Every day	Read the editorials in the local newspaper.

As you set your deadlines, consider your day-to-day schedule. How much time can you spend on studying each week? Exactly when can you fit in the time to study? Be sure to be realistic about how much time you have and how much you can accomplish. Give yourself the study time you need to succeed.

Stick to Your Plan

Make sure you have your plan on paper and post your plan where you can see it. Do not just keep it in your head! Look at it regularly so you can remember what and when to study. Checking your plan regularly can also help you see how much progress you have made along the way.

It is important that you do not give up or get discouraged if you fall behind. Unexpected events may interrupt your plans. You may have a big test coming up at school or you may come down with the flu. Or it might just take you longer to complete a task than you planned. That's okay. Stick to your schedule as much as possible, but remember that

sometimes life gets in the way. So, if you miss one of your deadlines, do not despair. Instead, just pick up where you left off. Try to squeeze in a little extra time in the next few weeks to catch up. If that does not seem possible, simply adjust your schedule. Change your deadlines so that they are more realistic. Just be sure you still have enough time to finish everything before the exam.

You will need to revisit your list often, allotting more time to areas with which you feel less comfortable and reducing the time needed on areas you have mastered.

How Do You Know What You Know?

One of the keys to successful studying is knowing what you know and knowing what you don't know. Practice tests are one effective way to measure this. But there are other ways.

One of the best ways to measure how well you know something is by assessing how well you can explain it to someone else. If you *really* know the material, you should be able to help someone else understand it. Use your learning style to explain a difficult question to someone in your study group. For example, if you are an auditory learner, talk it out. If you are a visual learner, create diagrams and tables to demonstrate your knowledge. Rewrite your notes or devise your own quizzes with questions and answers like those on the exam. Provide an explanation along with the correct answer.

How do you know what you *do not* know? If you feel uncertain or uncomfortable during a practice test or when you try to explain it to someone else, you probably need to study more. Write down all of your questions and uncertainties. If you write down what you do not know, you can focus on searching for answers. When you get the answers, you can write them next to the question and review them periodically. And notice how many questions you answer along the way—you will see yourself making steady progress.

If you are avoiding certain topics, it is a sign that you don't know those topics well enough for the exam. Make up your mind to tackle these areas at your next study session. Do not procrastinate!

Part 2: Learning Strategies

How successful you are at studying usually has less to do with how much you know and how much you study than with *how* you study. That is because some study techniques are more effective than others. You can spend hours and hours doing practice tests, but if you do not carefully review your answers, much of your time will be wasted. You need to learn from your mistakes and study what you do not know. The best method is to use several of the following proven study techniques. You may already be using many of these study skills in your normal schoolwork, but they can help you make the most of your learning style and store information in your long-term memory.

Asking Questions

Asking questions is a powerful study strategy because it forces you to get actively involved in the material you want to learn. That, in turn, helps you better understand and remember the material. And there is another important benefit—the process of asking and answering your own questions helps you become comfortable with the exam format.

For example, as you read something, you can ask yourself questions like those you would see on the ACT, such as:

- What is this passage about?
- What is the main idea?
- What is the author's purpose and point of view?
- What is the mood or tone?

- What is the meaning of this word as it is used in the sentence?
- Is this sentence a main idea or a detail?

Highlighting and Underlining

Whenever you read or study, have a pen, pencil, or highlighter in your hand. That way, as you read books, notes, or handouts that belong to you (not the school or library), you can mark the words and ideas that are most important to learn or remember. Highlighting or underlining helps make key ideas stand out. Important information is then easy to find when you need to take notes or review.

The key to effective highlighting or underlining is *to be selective*. Do not highlight or underline indiscriminately. If you highlight every other sentence, nothing will stand out for you on the page. Highlight only the key words and ideas or concepts you do not understand.

Taking Notes

Taking notes helps you understand, organize, and remember information. The secret to taking useful notes is knowing what you should write down. As with highlighting, the key is to be selective. Take notes about the same things you would underline, especially main ideas, rules, and other items you need to learn. Whenever possible, include examples so that you can *see* the concept clearly.

Making Notes

Making notes is often as important as *taking* notes. Making notes means that you *respond* to what you study. There are several ways you can respond (talk back) to the text:

- **Write questions.** If you see something you don't understand, write a question. *What does this mean? Why is this word used this way? Why is this the best title?* Then, answer all of your questions.

- **Make connections.** Any time you make connections between ideas, you improve your chances of remembering that material. For example, if you are trying to learn the definition of the word *demographic*, you may know that *demo*cracy refers to government by the *people*, while *graphic* refers to *information*, written or drawn. From that you can remember that *demographic* has to do with *information* about *people*.
- **Write your reactions.** Your reactions work much like connections, and they can help you remember information.

Outlining and Mapping Information

Outlines are great tools, especially for sequential learners. They help you focus on what is most important by making it easier to review key ideas and see relationships among those ideas. With an outline, you can see how supporting information is related to main ideas.

The basic outline structure is this:

I. Topic
  1. Main idea
    a. Major supporting idea
      i. Minor supporting idea

Mapping information is similar to making an outline. The difference is that maps are less structured. You do not have to organize ideas from top to bottom. Instead, with a map, the ideas can go all over the page. The key is that you still show how the ideas are related.

Making Flash Cards

Flash cards are a simple but effective study tool. First, buy or cut out small pieces of paper (3×5 index cards work well). On one side, put a question or word you need to learn. On the back, put the answer. You can use different colors and pictures, especially if you are a visual learner.

Memorizing versus Remembering

It is true that repetition is the key to mastery. Try repeating a new phone number over and over, for example. Eventually you will remember it. But it may stay only in your *short-term* memory. In a few days (or maybe even a few hours), you are likely to forget the number. You need to use it to really learn it and store the information in your *long-term* memory.

Although there are some tricks you can use to help remember things in the short term, your best bet is to *use* what you are learning as much and as soon as possible. This is especially important when you are studying for the ACT, because much of the test focuses on your reasoning skills and not simple memorization. This means you really have to understand the material, because you will not be given the opportunity simply to recall information. This does not mean that you do not need to know basic information in all of the areas covered. If, for example, you do not know common punctuation rules, you will get answers wrong on the ACT English Test. If you find (through the ACT or practice questions) that you do not remember certain grammar rules or math concepts, you will need to study them.

Here are some general strategies to help you remember information as you prepare for the ACT:

- **Learn information in small chunks.** Our brains process small chunks of information better than large ones. If you have a list of 20 grammar rules, break that list into four lists of five rules each.
- **Spread out your memory work.** Do not try to remember too much at one time. For example, if you break up those 20 rules into four lists, do not try to do all four lists, one after another. Instead, try studying one list each day in several short, spaced-out sessions. For example, spend 20 minutes in the morning getting familiar with the new rules. Review the rules again for 15 minutes at lunchtime. Take another 15 minutes while you are on the bus going home. Add another ten-minute review before bed. This kind of

A rested and relaxed brain learns information best. Whenever possible, study right before you go to sleep or first thing after you awaken. Try not to do anything else in between. If you study for an hour and then watch TV for an hour before bed, you will not remember as much as if you studied for an hour and then went right to bed. Right before and after sleep, you are usually in your most relaxed state—and that makes it easier for you to learn.

distributed practice is very effective. It is also a sneaky way to add more study time to your schedule. And it provides lots of repetition without tiring your brain.

- **Make connections.** You learn best when you make connections to things you already know.
- **Use visual aids,** especially if you are a visual learner. Help yourself see in your mind what you need to learn.
- **Use your voice,** especially if you are an auditory learner. Say aloud what you need to learn; you can even sing it if you like, especially if you can make a rhyme. Any time you are learning grammar and structure, say a sample sentence aloud several times. Try different variations, too.

ACT-Specific Strategies

The amount of material covered in the ACT may seem overwhelming at first. But keep in mind that there should be little new information for you to learn. The most important thing to do is identify your areas of weakness. Once you do that, you will realize that the few grammar rules and math problems you need to learn are entirely manageable.

Learn from Your Mistakes

Spend time reviewing your practice questions to determine exactly why you got an answer wrong. Did you misread the question? Are you unfamiliar with comma usage? Only when you pinpoint exactly why you answered something incorrectly can you learn to get it right.

Access Your Teachers

Talk to your current and past teachers to find out how they can help. They can probably point out the areas they think you need to review and they may offer extra help on subjects that are giving you trouble.

Go through Old Tests and Texts

Some of the material on the ACT will be from subjects you are not currently taking. Go through your old exams (talk to your former teachers if you do not have them), and use your old textbooks to refresh your memory.

Part 3: Test-Taking Strategies

Knowing the material on which you will be tested improves your chances of succeeding. But it does not guarantee that you will do your best on the exam. The ACT does not test just your knowledge of English, math, science, and writing. Like all standardized tests, it also measures your test-taking skills. In this section, you will learn strategies for taking standardized tests like the ACT.

Learn about the Test

One sure way to increase your chances of success is to find out as much as you can about the exam. If you do not know what to expect on the test, you will not know how to study. It is likely that you will be extra anxious about the exam, too. The more you know about the test, the better you can prepare—and the more relaxed you will be when the test comes.

You already know what kind of test the ACT is. You know that there are five separate tests that make up the whole ACT: English, math, reading, science, and the optional writing test. You know that the test questions for the first four tests are all multiple-choice. You know how much time you have to complete each test. But until you look at actual sample questions, you still do not *really* know what to expect. For example, in the reading test, what kind of passages will you be presented with? What kind of questions will you be asked about those passages?

Getting sample tests and working with skill builders like this book can help you in many ways. You will get used to the kind of questions asked and the level of difficulty of those questions. You will also become familiar with the format and comfortable with the length of the exam.

When you take your practice tests, try to re-create the actual testing conditions as closely as possible. Sit in a chair at a desk or table somewhere free from distractions. Time the test and use only the amount of time you would have on the real test. After you score your test, review your answers carefully. Ask yourself why you got the questions wrong that you did and add those concepts to your study schedule.

Timing

The more practice tests you take, the more comfortable you will feel regarding how long you have to answer each question. You should be able to spend less time answering the easier questions, and then come back to the harder ones with the time remaining.

The following list gives you a basic idea of how long you have for each question (remember that some questions will be easier than others and will, therefore, require less time):

- English: 30 seconds
- Math: 1 minute
- Reading: 30 seconds (with about 5 minutes to read each passage)
- Science: 30 seconds

Multiple-Choice Test Strategies

Multiple-choice is the most popular question format for standardized tests like the ACT. Understandably so: multiple-choice questions are easy and fast to grade. They are also popular because they are generally considered *objective*. They are questions based solely on information and do not allow the test taker to express opinions.

Multiple-choice questions have two parts:

1. **Stem:** the question
2. **Options:** the answer choices

The incorrect answers are called **distracters**.

> **stem:** If $a = 10$, then which of the following represents 803?
> **options:**
> **a.** $8a + 3$
> **b.** $80a + 3$
> **c.** $8a^2 + 3$
> **d.** $8a^3 + 3$
> **e.** $8a^4 + 3$

In this question, the correct answer is **b**. The other options are all distracters. Here are six strategies to help you answer multiple-choice questions correctly:

1. **Circle or underline key words in the stem.** These are the words that help you search for the correct answer. For example, in the stem:

   The modern bicycle has all of the following safety features EXCEPT

   the key words are *modern*, *safety features*, and *except*. You need to look in the passage for the safety features of modern bicycles. And you need to select the answer choice that is *not* specifically mentioned in the passage.

2. **Immediately cross out all answers you know are incorrect.** This will help you find the correct

answer. It is an especially important step if you have to guess the answer.

3. **Beware of distracter techniques.** Test developers will often put in look-alike options, easily confused options, and silly options.

4. **Read stems carefully:** Be sure you understand exactly what is being asked. Watch for tricky wording such as "All of the following are true EXCEPT." You will find distracters that seem accurate and may sound right but do not apply to that stem. For example, if you don't notice the *except* on the bicycle question stem, you might choose a distracter that is a safety feature of the modern bicycle. The answer would seem accurate but would be wrong because you did not read the question carefully.

5. **Beware of absolutes.** Read carefully any stem that includes words like *always*, *never*, *none*, or *all*. An answer may sound perfectly correct and the general principle may be correct. However, it may not be true in all circumstances.

6. **Work easiest questions first.** Although the questions on the ACT are not in order of difficulty, you should still quickly read through a question, and if it seems too hard, circle it and come back to it later. Remember that easy questions are worth the same as hard questions.

Almost There: Strategies for the Final Days before the Exam

Your months of preparation will soon pay off. You have worked hard, and the test is just a week or two away. Here are some tips for making sure things go smoothly in the home stretch.

The Week before the Test:

- Be sure you know exactly where you are taking the test. Get detailed directions. Take a practice drive or mass transit trip so you know exactly how long it will take to get there.
- Review everything you have learned.
- Get quality sleep each night.

- Practice visualization—see yourself performing well on the ACT.

The Day before the Test:

- Get light exercise. Do not work out too hard. You do not want to be sore or physically exhausted the day of the exam.
- Get everything you will need ready: pencils/pens, a calculator, admission materials/documentation, and water or any mints or snacks you would like to have along.
- Make a list of everything you need to bring so you don't forget anything in the morning.
- Get to bed early.
- Make sure you set your alarm. Ask a family member to make sure you are up on time.

The Day of the Test:

- Get up early.
- Eat a light, healthy breakfast, such as yogurt and granola or a low-fat, low-sugar cereal and fruit.
- Dress comfortably. Wear layers so that you can take off a sweatshirt or sweater if you are too warm in the test room.
- Do not drastically alter your diet. For example, if you drink coffee every morning, do not skip it—you could get a headache. However, do not drink a second cup or super-sized portion. Too much caffeine can make you jittery during the exam, and you may crash when the caffeine wears off.

At the Test Site:

- Chat with others, but *not* about the test. That might only make you more nervous.
- Think positively. Remember, you are prepared.
- Avoid squeezing in a last-minute review. Instead, visualize your success and plan your reward for after the test is over.

After the Test:

- Celebrate!

WHAT TO BRING TO THE TEST

- picture ID
- admission slip
- calculator
- watch
- three number 2 pencils with erasers
- sweatshirt or sweater
- water
- nutritious snack

Handling and Preventing Test Stress
Handling Test Stress

Test anxiety is like the common cold. Most people suffer from it periodically. It won't kill you, but it can make your life miserable for several days.

Like a cold, test anxiety can be mild or severe. You may just feel an underlying nervousness about the upcoming exam. Or you may be nearly paralyzed with worry, especially if there is a lot riding on the exam. Whatever the case, if you have test anxiety, you need to cope with it. Fortunately, many strategies help prevent and treat test anxiety.

Prevention

The best cure for test anxiety is to *prevent* it from happening in the first place. Test anxiety is often caused by a lack of preparation. If you learn all you can about the test and create and follow a study plan, you should be in good shape when it comes to exam time. Here are some other, more general strategies:

- **Establish and stick to a routine.** Routines help us feel more comfortable and in control. Whenever possible, study at the same time and in the same place. Make your test preparation a habit that is hard to break. Studying for the ACT will become easier as it becomes routine. You will be more likely to avoid distractions, and others will know not to disturb you during your ACT study time.

- **Keep your general stress level low.** If there are a lot of other stresses in your life, chances are a big test will make those other stresses seem more difficult to manage. Remember to keep things in perspective. If something is beyond your control, don't waste your energy worrying about it. Instead, think of how you can handle what is in your control.
- **Stay confident.** Remind yourself that you are smart and capable. You can take this test—and you can do well on it.
- **Stay healthy.** When your body is run down or ill, your brainpower will suffer, too. You are much more likely to be overtaken by worries. Take care of yourself throughout the test-preparation process. (See more information at the end of this chapter.)

Treatment

If it is too late to prevent test anxiety, don't panic. You can still treat it effectively. Here are some strategies to help reduce test stress:

- **Face your fears.** Admit that you are worried about the test, and examine the reasons. Your fears won't change the fact that you have to take the test, but they can paralyze you and keep you from studying and doing well on the exam. Acknowledge your fears, put them in perspective, and refuse to let your fears hurt you.

    One helpful strategy is to write down your fears. When you put your worries on paper, they seem more manageable than when they are bouncing around in your brain and keeping you awake at night. Once you write down your fears, you can then brainstorm solutions. For example, imagine you are worried about not being able to find enough time to get your work done and finish studying. Once you put this fear down on paper, you can begin to determine how to squeeze in the hours you need to get everything done, and you will feel more in control.

■ **Keep things in perspective.** Yes, the ACT is a big deal; it is an important test. But even if you do poorly on the test, is it the end of the world? Will your family stop loving you? Will you be less of a person? Of course not. And if you really blow it, remember that you can take the test again. Perspective is important to performance. Of course you should be serious about succeeding. But don't lose sight of other important aspects of your life.

■ **Be sufficiently prepared.** Anxiety often comes from feeling insecure in a new situation. But if you prepare well, using this and other books, the ACT will not be new to you. And if you follow your study plan, you will know how to answer the questions. If you have fallen behind, remember that it is not too late to catch up.

■ **Stop making excuses.** Excuses may give you some comfort in the short term, but they do not take away test anxiety—and they will not help you do well on the exam. In fact, excuses often make things worse by making you feel guilty and powerless. Do not let yourself feel like a victim. You may have a lot of things happening in your life and many things may interfere with your studies, but you have the power to choose how you deal with your circumstances.

■ **Imagine yourself succeeding.** Highly successful people will often tell you that one of their secrets is visualization. In their mind's eye, they *see* themselves succeeding. They imagine the situations they will face, and then imagine themselves handling those situations beautifully.

Visualization is a powerful tool. It is a way of telling yourself that *you believe you can do it*. The power of this kind of belief is amazing. If you believe you can accomplish something, you are far more likely to accomplish it. Likewise, if you believe you *can't* do something, you are far more likely to *fail*. Positive visualization will make it easier for you to study and manage your entire test-preparation process.

Anyone can use the power of visualization. Picture yourself sitting calmly through the exam, answering one question after another correctly. See yourself getting excellent test results in the mail. Imagine yourself telling family and friends how well you did on the exam. Picture yourself receiving the college acceptance letter you desire.

■ **Stick to your study plan.** Test anxiety can paralyze you if you let it. And before you know it, you have missed several deadlines on your study plan. Guess what? That only makes your test anxiety worse. As soon as you feel your stomach start to flutter with test anxiety, return to your study plan. Make an extra effort to stick to your schedule.

A Healthy Mind and a Healthy Body

It is difficult to do your best on a test when you are not feeling well. Your mind *and* body need to be in good shape for the test. If you let your body get run-down, you may become ill. That, in turn, sets you back on your study schedule. And that may lead to test anxiety, which can make you feel run-down again. You need to avoid this downward spiral. If you do feel run-down, take a day or two to rest and feel better. Maybe you will be two days behind your study schedule, but when you continue, your studying will be more effective. As long as it is not a constant problem for you and as long as you are not using illness to avoid studying, you will do yourself a favor by resting.

Take good care of yourself throughout the entire test-preparation process and especially in the week before the exam. Here are some specific suggestions for staying healthy:

■ **Get enough rest.** Some of us need eight or more hours of sleep each night. Others are happy with just six. You know what your body needs for you to feel clear-headed and energized. Make sleep a priority, so that you are able to concentrate the day of the exam. If you have trouble sleeping, try one of the following strategies:

- Get exercise during the day. A tired body will demand more sleep.
- Get up and study. If you study in the night when you can't sleep, you can cut out study time from the next day so you can take a nap or get to bed earlier. (Of course, sometimes studying will help you fall asleep in the first place.)
- Relax with a hot bath, a good book, or sleep-inducing foods. A glass of warm milk, for example, may help you fall back asleep.
- Do some gentle stretching or seated forward bends. Try to touch your toes with your legs outstretched. This is a relaxing posture. Or practice a few relaxation poses from yoga: child's pose or cat stretch (see a website like www.yoga.com for details).
- Spend a few minutes doing deep breathing. Fill your lungs slowly and completely. Hold for a few seconds and then release slowly and completely. You can practice deep breathing anytime you need to relax or regain focus.
- Write down your worries. Again, putting your fears on paper can help make them more manageable.
- **Eat well.** Keeping a healthy diet is often as hard as getting enough rest when you are busy preparing for a test. But how you eat can have a tremendous impact on how you study and how you perform on the exam. You may think you are saving time by eating fast food. But in reality, you are depriving your body of the nutrition it needs to perform at its best. You may think that a couple of extra cups of coffee a day are a good thing because you can stay up later and study. But in reality, you are tricking your brain into thinking that it's awake and you are making yourself more dependent on caffeine.

Foods to avoid—especially at test time—include high-sugar, high-calorie, low-nutrition foods, such as doughnuts, chips, and cookies. Instead, find healthy substitutes.

INSTEAD OF . . .	EAT . . .
doughnuts	low-sugar, multigrain cereal
chips	carrot sticks
cookies	natural granola bar
ice cream	low-fat yogurt
sugary soda	freshly squeezed fruit juice
giant-sized coffee	green tea

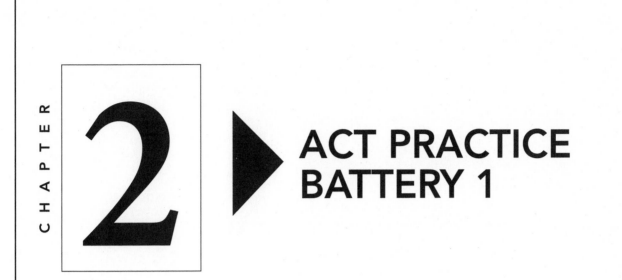

2 ▶ ACT PRACTICE BATTERY 1

This is the first of four complete ACT practice tests in this book. In this chapter you'll find full English, Mathematics, Reading, Science, and Writing tests. Complete answers are at the end of the chapter, and instructions on how to score these practice tests are in Chapter 6. Good luck!

ACT English Practice Test 1

1.	ⓐ	ⓑ	ⓒ	ⓓ	26.	ⓕ	ⓖ	ⓗ	ⓙ	51.	ⓐ	ⓑ	ⓒ	ⓓ
2.	ⓕ	ⓖ	ⓗ	ⓙ	27.	ⓐ	ⓑ	ⓒ	ⓓ	52.	ⓕ	ⓖ	ⓗ	ⓙ
3.	ⓐ	ⓑ	ⓒ	ⓓ	28.	ⓕ	ⓖ	ⓗ	ⓙ	53.	ⓐ	ⓑ	ⓒ	ⓓ
4.	ⓕ	ⓖ	ⓗ	ⓙ	29.	ⓐ	ⓑ	ⓒ	ⓓ	54.	ⓕ	ⓖ	ⓗ	ⓙ
5.	ⓐ	ⓑ	ⓒ	ⓓ	30.	ⓕ	ⓖ	ⓗ	ⓙ	55.	ⓐ	ⓑ	ⓒ	ⓓ
6.	ⓕ	ⓖ	ⓗ	ⓙ	31.	ⓐ	ⓑ	ⓒ	ⓓ	56.	ⓕ	ⓖ	ⓗ	ⓙ
7.	ⓐ	ⓑ	ⓒ	ⓓ	32.	ⓕ	ⓖ	ⓗ	ⓙ	57.	ⓐ	ⓑ	ⓒ	ⓓ
8.	ⓕ	ⓖ	ⓗ	ⓙ	33.	ⓐ	ⓑ	ⓒ	ⓓ	58.	ⓕ	ⓖ	ⓗ	ⓙ
9.	ⓐ	ⓑ	ⓒ	ⓓ	34.	ⓕ	ⓖ	ⓗ	ⓙ	59.	ⓐ	ⓑ	ⓒ	ⓓ
10.	ⓕ	ⓖ	ⓗ	ⓙ	35.	ⓐ	ⓑ	ⓒ	ⓓ	60.	ⓕ	ⓖ	ⓗ	ⓙ
11.	ⓐ	ⓑ	ⓒ	ⓓ	36.	ⓕ	ⓖ	ⓗ	ⓙ	61.	ⓐ	ⓑ	ⓒ	ⓓ
12.	ⓕ	ⓖ	ⓗ	ⓙ	37.	ⓐ	ⓑ	ⓒ	ⓓ	62.	ⓕ	ⓖ	ⓗ	ⓙ
13.	ⓐ	ⓑ	ⓒ	ⓓ	38.	ⓕ	ⓖ	ⓗ	ⓙ	63.	ⓐ	ⓑ	ⓒ	ⓓ
14.	ⓕ	ⓖ	ⓗ	ⓙ	39.	ⓐ	ⓑ	ⓒ	ⓓ	64.	ⓕ	ⓖ	ⓗ	ⓙ
15.	ⓐ	ⓑ	ⓒ	ⓓ	40.	ⓕ	ⓖ	ⓗ	ⓙ	65.	ⓐ	ⓑ	ⓒ	ⓓ
16.	ⓕ	ⓖ	ⓗ	ⓙ	41.	ⓐ	ⓑ	ⓒ	ⓓ	66.	ⓕ	ⓖ	ⓗ	ⓙ
17.	ⓐ	ⓑ	ⓒ	ⓓ	42.	ⓕ	ⓖ	ⓗ	ⓙ	67.	ⓐ	ⓑ	ⓒ	ⓓ
18.	ⓕ	ⓖ	ⓗ	ⓙ	43.	ⓐ	ⓑ	ⓒ	ⓓ	68.	ⓕ	ⓖ	ⓗ	ⓙ
19.	ⓐ	ⓑ	ⓒ	ⓓ	44.	ⓕ	ⓖ	ⓗ	ⓙ	69.	ⓐ	ⓑ	ⓒ	ⓓ
20.	ⓕ	ⓖ	ⓗ	ⓙ	45.	ⓐ	ⓑ	ⓒ	ⓓ	70.	ⓕ	ⓖ	ⓗ	ⓙ
21.	ⓐ	ⓑ	ⓒ	ⓓ	46.	ⓕ	ⓖ	ⓗ	ⓙ	71.	ⓐ	ⓑ	ⓒ	ⓓ
22.	ⓕ	ⓖ	ⓗ	ⓙ	47.	ⓐ	ⓑ	ⓒ	ⓓ	72.	ⓕ	ⓖ	ⓗ	ⓙ
23.	ⓐ	ⓑ	ⓒ	ⓓ	48.	ⓕ	ⓖ	ⓗ	ⓙ	73.	ⓐ	ⓑ	ⓒ	ⓓ
24.	ⓕ	ⓖ	ⓗ	ⓙ	49.	ⓐ	ⓑ	ⓒ	ⓓ	74.	ⓕ	ⓖ	ⓗ	ⓙ
25.	ⓐ	ⓑ	ⓒ	ⓓ	50.	ⓕ	ⓖ	ⓗ	ⓙ	75.	ⓐ	ⓑ	ⓒ	ⓓ

ACT Mathematics Practice Test 1

1.	ⓐ ⓑ ⓒ ⓓ ⓔ	21.	ⓐ ⓑ ⓒ ⓓ ⓔ	41.	ⓐ ⓑ ⓒ ⓓ ⓔ
2.	ⓕ ⓖ ⓗ ⓙ ⓚ	22.	ⓕ ⓖ ⓗ ⓙ ⓚ	42.	ⓕ ⓖ ⓗ ⓙ ⓚ
3.	ⓐ ⓑ ⓒ ⓓ ⓔ	23.	ⓐ ⓑ ⓒ ⓓ ⓔ	43.	ⓐ ⓑ ⓒ ⓓ ⓔ
4.	ⓕ ⓖ ⓗ ⓙ ⓚ	24.	ⓕ ⓖ ⓗ ⓙ ⓚ	44.	ⓕ ⓖ ⓗ ⓙ ⓚ
5.	ⓐ ⓑ ⓒ ⓓ ⓔ	25.	ⓐ ⓑ ⓒ ⓓ ⓔ	45.	ⓐ ⓑ ⓒ ⓓ ⓔ
6.	ⓕ ⓖ ⓗ ⓙ ⓚ	26.	ⓕ ⓖ ⓗ ⓙ ⓚ	46.	ⓕ ⓖ ⓗ ⓙ ⓚ
7.	ⓐ ⓑ ⓒ ⓓ ⓔ	27.	ⓐ ⓑ ⓒ ⓓ ⓔ	47.	ⓐ ⓑ ⓒ ⓓ ⓔ
8.	ⓕ ⓖ ⓗ ⓙ ⓚ	28.	ⓕ ⓖ ⓗ ⓙ ⓚ	48.	ⓕ ⓖ ⓗ ⓙ ⓚ
9.	ⓐ ⓑ ⓒ ⓓ ⓔ	29.	ⓐ ⓑ ⓒ ⓓ ⓔ	49.	ⓐ ⓑ ⓒ ⓓ ⓔ
10.	ⓕ ⓖ ⓗ ⓙ ⓚ	30.	ⓕ ⓖ ⓗ ⓙ ⓚ	50.	ⓕ ⓖ ⓗ ⓙ ⓚ
11.	ⓐ ⓑ ⓒ ⓓ ⓔ	31.	ⓐ ⓑ ⓒ ⓓ ⓔ	51.	ⓐ ⓑ ⓒ ⓓ ⓔ
12.	ⓕ ⓖ ⓗ ⓙ ⓚ	32.	ⓕ ⓖ ⓗ ⓙ ⓚ	52.	ⓕ ⓖ ⓗ ⓙ ⓚ
13.	ⓐ ⓑ ⓒ ⓓ ⓔ	33.	ⓐ ⓑ ⓒ ⓓ ⓔ	53.	ⓐ ⓑ ⓒ ⓓ ⓔ
14.	ⓕ ⓖ ⓗ ⓙ ⓚ	34.	ⓕ ⓖ ⓗ ⓙ ⓚ	54.	ⓕ ⓖ ⓗ ⓙ ⓚ
15.	ⓐ ⓑ ⓒ ⓓ ⓔ	35.	ⓐ ⓑ ⓒ ⓓ ⓔ	55.	ⓐ ⓑ ⓒ ⓓ ⓔ
16.	ⓕ ⓖ ⓗ ⓙ ⓚ	36.	ⓕ ⓖ ⓗ ⓙ ⓚ	56.	ⓕ ⓖ ⓗ ⓙ ⓚ
17.	ⓐ ⓑ ⓒ ⓓ ⓔ	37.	ⓐ ⓑ ⓒ ⓓ ⓔ	57.	ⓐ ⓑ ⓒ ⓓ ⓔ
18.	ⓕ ⓖ ⓗ ⓙ ⓚ	38.	ⓕ ⓖ ⓗ ⓙ ⓚ	58.	ⓕ ⓖ ⓗ ⓙ ⓚ
19.	ⓐ ⓑ ⓒ ⓓ ⓔ	39.	ⓐ ⓑ ⓒ ⓓ ⓔ	59.	ⓐ ⓑ ⓒ ⓓ ⓔ
20.	ⓕ ⓖ ⓗ ⓙ ⓚ	40.	ⓕ ⓖ ⓗ ⓙ ⓚ	60.	ⓕ ⓖ ⓗ ⓙ ⓚ

ACT Reading Practice Test 1

1.	ⓐ ⓑ ⓒ ⓓ	15.	ⓐ ⓑ ⓒ ⓓ	29.	ⓐ ⓑ ⓒ ⓓ
2.	ⓕ ⓖ ⓗ ⓙ	16.	ⓕ ⓖ ⓗ ⓙ	30.	ⓕ ⓖ ⓗ ⓙ
3.	ⓐ ⓑ ⓒ ⓓ	17.	ⓐ ⓑ ⓒ ⓓ	31.	ⓐ ⓑ ⓒ ⓓ
4.	ⓕ ⓖ ⓗ ⓙ	18.	ⓕ ⓖ ⓗ ⓙ	32.	ⓕ ⓖ ⓗ ⓙ
5.	ⓐ ⓑ ⓒ ⓓ	19.	ⓐ ⓑ ⓒ ⓓ	33.	ⓐ ⓑ ⓒ ⓓ
6.	ⓕ ⓖ ⓗ ⓙ	20.	ⓕ ⓖ ⓗ ⓙ	34.	ⓕ ⓖ ⓗ ⓙ
7.	ⓐ ⓑ ⓒ ⓓ	21.	ⓐ ⓑ ⓒ ⓓ	35.	ⓐ ⓑ ⓒ ⓓ
8.	ⓕ ⓖ ⓗ ⓙ	22.	ⓕ ⓖ ⓗ ⓙ	36.	ⓕ ⓖ ⓗ ⓙ
9.	ⓐ ⓑ ⓒ ⓓ	23.	ⓐ ⓑ ⓒ ⓓ	37.	ⓐ ⓑ ⓒ ⓓ
10.	ⓕ ⓖ ⓗ ⓙ	24.	ⓕ ⓖ ⓗ ⓙ	38.	ⓕ ⓖ ⓗ ⓙ
11.	ⓐ ⓑ ⓒ ⓓ	25.	ⓐ ⓑ ⓒ ⓓ	39.	ⓐ ⓑ ⓒ ⓓ
12.	ⓕ ⓖ ⓗ ⓙ	26.	ⓕ ⓖ ⓗ ⓙ	40.	ⓕ ⓖ ⓗ ⓙ
13.	ⓐ ⓑ ⓒ ⓓ	27.	ⓐ ⓑ ⓒ ⓓ		
14.	ⓕ ⓖ ⓗ ⓙ	28.	ⓕ ⓖ ⓗ ⓙ		

ACT Science Practice Test 1

1.	(a)	(b)	(c)	(d)
2.	(f)	(g)	(h)	(j)
3.	(a)	(b)	(c)	(d)
4.	(f)	(g)	(h)	(j)
5.	(a)	(b)	(c)	(d)
6.	(f)	(g)	(h)	(j)
7.	(a)	(b)	(c)	(d)
8.	(f)	(g)	(h)	(j)
9.	(a)	(b)	(c)	(d)
10.	(f)	(g)	(h)	(j)
11.	(a)	(b)	(c)	(d)
12.	(f)	(g)	(h)	(j)
13.	(a)	(b)	(c)	(d)
14.	(f)	(g)	(h)	(j)

15.	(a)	(b)	(c)	(d)
16.	(f)	(g)	(h)	(j)
17.	(a)	(b)	(c)	(d)
18.	(f)	(g)	(h)	(j)
19.	(a)	(b)	(c)	(d)
20.	(f)	(g)	(h)	(j)
21.	(a)	(b)	(c)	(d)
22.	(f)	(g)	(h)	(j)
23.	(a)	(b)	(c)	(d)
24.	(f)	(g)	(h)	(j)
25.	(a)	(b)	(c)	(d)
26.	(f)	(g)	(h)	(j)
27.	(a)	(b)	(c)	(d)
28.	(f)	(g)	(h)	(j)

29.	(a)	(b)	(c)	(d)
30.	(f)	(g)	(h)	(j)
31.	(a)	(b)	(c)	(d)
32.	(f)	(g)	(h)	(j)
33.	(a)	(b)	(c)	(d)
34.	(f)	(g)	(h)	(j)
35.	(a)	(b)	(c)	(d)
36.	(f)	(g)	(h)	(j)
37.	(a)	(b)	(c)	(d)
38.	(f)	(g)	(h)	(j)
39.	(a)	(b)	(c)	(d)
40.	(f)	(g)	(h)	(j)

ACT English Practice Test 1

75 Questions—45 Minutes

Read each passage through once before you begin to answer any questions. You will see that certain words or phrases in the following five passages have been underlined and numbered. Following each passage, you will see alternatives for those underlined words or phrases. Choose the one that best expresses the idea of the passage, is the best use of standard English, or is most consistent with the tone and style of the passage. If you find the underlined part to be correct, choose "NO CHANGE." Note that to answer many of the questions you will probably need to read several sentences beyond the question. You may also find questions about a section of the passage or the passage as a whole, rather than about an underlined part.

Passage I—Sigmund Freud

The father and originator of[1] psychoanalysis, Sigmund Freud (1856–1939), is largely responsible for the way we understand ourselves, as creatures, with[2] conflicting "selves" and desires. Freud posited[3] the notion that the mind is teeming with "psychic energy" and that our personality is shaped largely by the interactions of the levels of the mind. Among Freud's most important contributions to modern psychology and the contemporary understanding of the self is his theory of the unconscious.

(1) According to Freud, the mind is much like an iceberg. (2) Most of our minds[4] activities, then, occur beneath the surface, in the unconscious and beyond our knowing. (3) The *conscious* is the part of the mind of which we are aware; it is the tip of the iceberg that is visible above the water. (4) The *unconscious, on the other hand,*[5] is all that is below the surface—the thoughts, feelings, and desires that we are not aware of but that nonetheless affect our behavior.

Freud believed that the unconscious is *deterministic*. That is, our behaviors are caused (determined) by thoughts and impulses deep in our unconscious—of which thoughts and impulses we are not aware.[6] This is related to the phenomenon called "Freudian slip."[7] Unless we psychoanalyze ourselves, we may never be aware of the hidden reasons for our actions. This suggests that the notion of free will might have been[8] an illusion and that our choices are governed by hidden mental processes which we have no control over.[9]

Repression is the act of pushing our conflicts to the unconscious. So that[10] we are no longer aware of them. It is our chief *defense mechanism* (a way to avoid conflict between our true desires and our senses of right and wrong[11]). Freud believed that too much repression can lead to neurosis, a mental disorder resulting in depression or abnormal behavior, sometimes with physical symptoms but with no evidence of disease.

1. **a.** NO CHANGE
   b. father (and originator) of
   c. father, and originator of,
   d. father of

2. **f.** NO CHANGE
   g. ourselves as creatures with
   h. ourselves, being like creatures with
   j. ourselves. As creatures with

3. **a.** NO CHANGE
   b. positioned
   c. deposited
   d. supposed

4. **f.** NO CHANGE
   g. mind
   h. mind's
   j. minds'

5. **a.** NO CHANGE
   b. likewise,
   c. unfortunately,
   d. thereby,

6. **f.** NO CHANGE
   g. we are not aware of which thoughts and impulses.
   h. thoughts and impulses of which we are not aware.
   j. which we are not aware of, these thoughts and impulses.

7. Upon revising this essay, the writer would be wise to
   a. leave this sentence exactly as it is.
   b. delete this sentence from the paragraph.
   c. move this sentence to the end of the paragraph.
   d. use a better phrase than *related to*.

8. **f.** NO CHANGE
   g. would be
   h. has been
   j. is

9. **a.** NO CHANGE
   b. we have no control over.
   c. we can't control.
   d. over which we have no control.

10. **f.** NO CHANGE
   g. unconscious of which
   h. unconscious so that
   j. unconscious, for

11. **a.** NO CHANGE
   b. our sense of right and wrong
   c. our senses of rights and wrongs
   d. our sense of rights and wrongs

12. The most logical sequence of sentences for paragraph 2 is which of the following?
   f. NO CHANGE
   g. 1, 3, 4, 2
   h. 3, 4, 1, 2
   j. 2, 1, 3, 4

13. The author's use of italics is designed to do which of the following?
   a. indicate that a foreign language is being used
   b. call attention to Freud's genius
   c. create a more emotional tone
   d. highlight key terms that are defined in the text

14. Which of the following choices provides the most logical and effective transition from the third paragraph to the fourth paragraph?
   f. Sometimes the impulses for our behavior come from repressed desires.
   g. Another theory of Freud's is *repression*.
   h. Freud also believed in repression.
   j. Neurosis can be caused by repression to the unconscious.

15. The first sentence of the second paragraph contains a
   a. metaphor.
   b. simile.
   c. analogy.
   d. hyperbole.

Passage II—Yoga

One of today's hottest fads is also one of the world's oldest practices: the ancient art of yoga. At first, I thought yoga was just another fitness fad, like step aerobics classes or Tae Bo. But after my first class, I understood why yoga has lasted for thousands of years and why so many people are completely into[16] this practice.

Yoga is different from other fitness activities because it is not only physical. In the correct form,[17] yoga is a practice of unification: an emotional, spiritual, *and* physical exercise.

Although it may seem easy to those who[18] have never practiced, yoga poses require great concentration, and they are[19] surprisingly affective[20] in stretching and strengthening muscles. A simple sitting pose such as *staff pose*, for example, requires you to tighten and lengthen stomach, back, and arm muscles as you stretch you're[21] legs out in front of you and place your hands by your side. More difficult poses, such as *brave warrior*, require you to balance on one leg and hold a pose that strengthens leg, back, and stomach muscles, which is good for you.[22]

While yoga tones and strengthens the body, it also tones and strengthens the mind. Many poses can be only held[23] if you are completely focused on the task, and full benefit of the poses comes only through proper breathing. Concentrated deep breathing during yoga helps you extend more fully into the poses, thereby gaining greater benefit from the stretch. And the steady[24] circulation of breath through your body both calms and energizes.

I am still relatively new to yoga. I have only been practicing for one year. I am addicted to yoga[25] unlike any other physical activity because it is also a spiritual practice. Through yoga, I am able to release tensions that lodge in various parts of my body: the tight shoulders, the cramped legs, the belly that is in knots.[26] The physical release is also a spiritual release: I feel calm after doing yoga, reconnected to my body, reconnected to myself, more[27] at peace with the world. After a series of asanas (poses), I feel the universal life force within.

16. **f.** NO CHANGE
   g. hooked on
   h. devoted to
   j. practitioners of

17. **a.** NO CHANGE
   b. Done correctly,
   c. To do it correctly,
   d. Omit the underlined portion.

18. **f.** NO CHANGE
   g. that
   h. whom
   j. which

19. **a.** NO CHANGE
   b. concentration, and is
   c. concentration, and are
   d. concentration and is

20. **f.** NO CHANGE
   g. affected
   h. effected
   j. effective

21. **a.** NO CHANGE
   b. one's
   c. your
   d. these

22. **f.** NO CHANGE
   g. which benefits you.
   h. which is good for your health.
   j. Omit the underlined portion, and change the comma to a period.

23. a. NO CHANGE
   b. are only holding
   c. can only be holden
   d. can be held only

24. f. NO CHANGE
   g. stretch, the steady
   h. stretch. The steady
   j. stretch, also the steady

25. To improve the sentence structure here by combining sentences, which of the following choices is the most effective option?
   a. I am still relatively new to yoga. Practicing only for one year, I am addicted to yoga . . .
   b. Still relatively new to yoga, I have been practicing for only one year. But I am addicted to yoga . . .
   c. I am still relatively new to yoga—I have been practicing for only one year—but I am addicted to yoga . . .
   d. Although I am relatively new to yoga, I have been practicing for only one year. Still, I am addicted to yoga . . .

26. f. NO CHANGE
   g. knotted belly.
   h. knots within the belly.
   j. aching within the stomach area.

27. a. NO CHANGE
   b. to myself more,
   c. to myself more, and
   d. to myself, and more

28. To add some figurative language to the essay, which of the following images would be most effective and appropriate?
   f. I feel like a million bucks after doing yoga.
   g. Yoga is like a warm blanket.
   h. Yoga is like a drug.
   j. Yoga is a peaceful journey.

29. If the writer were to combine two paragraphs, which two paragraphs would it be most logical to connect?
   a. paragraphs 1 and 2
   b. paragraphs 2 and 3
   c. paragraphs 3 and 4
   d. paragraphs 4 and 5

30. The writer would like readers to do some basic yoga poses after reading this essay. To achieve this goal, the writer should
   f. list the best yoga videos so readers can purchase them.
   g. compare and contrast yoga to another fitness activity, such as aerobics.
   h. tell readers how to get into those basic positions.
   j. describe the benefits of deep-breathing exercises.

Passage III—The Cold War

(1) The Cold War was one of the most interesting and troubling times in American history. (2) Several dramatically important historical events[31] led to the Cold War. (3) First, in 1939, Albert Einstein wrote a letter to President Franklin D. Roosevelt. (4) In that letter, Einstein tells[32] Roosevelt that it was possible to create an atomic weapon, and he asked Roosevelt to fund research and experiment[33] in atomic weapons. (5) Roosevelt agreed, and the government created the Manhattan Project, a massive effort to develop nuclear weapons. (6) This was the first important step toward the

Cold War. (7) Next came the date that will live in history: August 6, 1945. (8) The United States dropped an atomic bomb on <u>a civilian, not military, target, Hiroshima, Japan.</u>[34] (9) An <u>estimate of</u>[35] 150,000 civilians were killed in the attack. (10) President Harry Truman and others claimed at the time that dropping the bomb was necessary to force Japan to surrender <u>to</u>[36] end World War II. (11) Others argue that we used the bomb largely to show the Soviet Union that we were a superior world power. (12) Although the United States and the USSR were officially allies, <u>tension</u>[37] between the two countries were already high. (13) A deep ideological battle between the two countries—one communist, the other capitalist—was already <u>in place; and</u>[38] each country was determined to outdo the other. (14) Two years later, in 1947, President Truman established the Truman Doctrine. (15) This important document <u>renamed</u>[39] American foreign policy. (16) It created a "policy of containment," which framed our foreign policy as a battle between "good" and "evil." (17) This dramatically increased the growing animosity <u>between the two opposing sides.</u>[40] (18) These tensions did not lead to an actual war between the world powers, which might have had disastrous results. (19) Instead, they were the cause of years of <u>political, economic, and diplomatic</u>[41] conflict: the Cold War.

31. a. NO CHANGE
   b. important dramatic historical events
   c. important historical events
   d. dramatically historical events

32. f. NO CHANGE
   g. told
   h. had told
   j. would tell

33. a. NO CHANGE
   b. research
   c. researching and experimentation
   d. research and experiments

34. f. NO CHANGE
   g. Hiroshima, Japan.
   h. Hiroshima, Japan—a civilian, not military, target.
   j. a civilian target.

35. a. NO CHANGE
   b. estimate of around
   c. estimated
   d. estimate was

36. f. NO CHANGE
   g. so to
   h. so
   j. and to

37. a. NO CHANGE
   b. the tension
   c. tensions
   d. a tension

38. f. NO CHANGE
   g. in place and
   h. in place, and
   j. in place. And

39. a. NO CHANGE
   b. redefined
   c. redetermined
   d. reestablished

---

40. f. NO CHANGE
g. amongst the two opposing sides.
h. between the two sides.
j. between the opposing sides.

41. a. NO CHANGE
b. political, economic and diplomatic
c. political, economical, and diplomatical
d. political, economic, and diplomacy

42. The best place to end a first paragraph and begin a new one would be after
f. sentence 5.
g. sentence 6.
h. sentence 7.
j. sentence 8.

43. The best place to end a second paragraph and begin a new one would be after
a. sentence 11.
b. sentence 12.
c. sentence 13.
d. sentence 14.

44. The writer is considering changing the first sentence to "The Cold War dominated American foreign policy in the mid-twentieth century." This change would
f. make no difference.
g. make the opening more vague.
h. make the opening less powerful.
j. make the opening more specific.

45. The writer is considering changing the title of this essay. The best title would be
a. A History of the Cold War.
b. Events of the Cold War.
c. The Road to the Cold War.
d. A Dark Time in American History: The Cold War.

Passage IV—
The Industrial Revolution

(1) In the first century of the Industrial Revolution, the country undergoing the most dramatic change was England. (2) After 1850, the Industrial Revolution spread rapidly[46] throughout Europe. (3) While the pace of change during the Industrial Revolution was indeed very rapid, the Industrial Revolution itself stretched over a rather long period of time—from the middle of the eighteenth century in the 1700s[47] through World War I (1914).

The Industrial Revolution was essentially a rapid change in the method of production of material goods.[49] Products once made by hand were now able to be produced by machine or by chemical processes. The Industrial Revolution transformed Western society, creating an international capitalist economy, urbanization, labor reforms, a system to educate the public,[50] and labor specialization.

Several key discoveries and inventions enabled the Industrial Revolution to take place, included[51] machines and tools like the cotton gin, the radio, the circular saw, the cylindrical press, and steam engine.[52] Cement, dynamite, and aluminum were invented, as were the bleaching and paper-making processes. At the same time,[53] there was a tremendous growth in population and urbanization. In fact, the population growth in England was so dramatic that the countries[54] population doubled between 1750–1820.[55] This meant a great demand for food, clothing, and shelter, demands <u>that became the driving force behind</u>[56] the Industrial Revolution.

Mass production of goods was largely made possible <u>due to</u>[57] the steam engine. The steam engine enabled factories to move from the countryside (where there were bodies of water, their source of power) into cities and towns, which were becoming increasingly crowded.

46. f. NO CHANGE
 g. was quickly spreading
 h. spread with great rapidity
 j. spread fast

47. a. NO CHANGE
 b. from the middle of the century eighteen
 c. from the mid-1700s
 d. beginning in the middle of the 1700s, around 1750,

48. The most logical sequence for paragraph 1 is
 f. NO CHANGE.
 g. 2, 1, 3.
 h. 3, 2, 1.
 j. 3, 1, 2.

49. The writer changed the underlined text to *in how material goods were produced.* The result is a sentence that is
 a. more dramatic.
 b. more concise.
 c. more complex.
 d. more accurate.

50. f. NO CHANGE
 g. a public education system,
 h. systematizing education,
 j. public education,

51. a. NO CHANGE
 b. place. These included
 c. place. Thus including
 d. place, including

52. f. NO CHANGE
 g. the cylindrical press and steam engine.
 h. the cylindrical press and the steam engine.
 j. the cylindrical press, and the steam engine.

53. The writer wants to change this phrasing. Which of the following would be the best choice?
 a. During this same period,
 b. Simultaneously,
 c. Likewise,
 d. Also,

54. f. NO CHANGE
 g. countries'
 h. countrys'
 j. country's

55. a. NO CHANGE
   b. between 1750 to 1820.
   c. from 1750 and 1820.
   d. between 1750 and 1820.

56. f. NO CHANGE
   g. which had become the driving force of
   h. that forced the driving of
   j. that drove the force behind

57. a. NO CHANGE
   b. by
   c. from
   d. in regard to

58. Which of the following alternatives provides the most logical and effective conclusion for paragraph 4?
   f. Today, we are living in an Information Revolution.
   g. In cities and towns, factories found a ready workforce and large consumer base for their products.
   h. Railroads took goods out of the city back to the countryside.
   j. Overcrowding was a major problem to be dealt with in the cities.

59. The writer wishes to add a fifth paragraph. Which of the following topics would best fit the audience and purpose of this essay?
   a. the work conditions in the factories
   b. child labor
   c. the impact of mass production on the economy
   d. the population explosion and its effects

60. For the sake of logic and coherence, the first paragraph should be placed
   f. where it is now.
   g. after paragraph 2.
   h. after paragraph 3.
   j. after paragraph 4.

Passage V—Science Fiction

One of the most famous novels of all <u>time, Mary Shelley's *Frankenstein*, marked</u>[61] not only the high point of a young woman's literary <u>career. But</u>[62] also the beginning of a brand-new genre of <u>literature being science fiction.</u>[63] In her remarkable tale, Shelley explores what might happen if a scientific possibility—the ability to restore life to the dead—were to become a reality. Science fiction explores <u>how what *might* be would affect our world if it really *was*.</u>[64]

What Shelley began, H.G. Wells perfected in dozens of science fiction <u>works including his most famous works:</u>[65] *The Time Machine* and *The War of the Worlds*. While Shelley's Frankenstein created a living creature from the body parts of the dead, Wells's characters traveled through time; created half-animal, half-human creatures; made themselves invisible; and <u>having been attacked by Martians.</u>[66] In all of his novels, <u>Wells; like Shelley,</u>[67] used scientific possibilities to analyze and often criticize his own society. *The War of the Worlds*, for example, is a thinly disguised attack on the British colonialism of his time.

Science fiction flourished in the United States in the 1920s and 1930s with pulp <u>magazines that for the masses churned out science fiction stories.</u>[68] Meanwhile, in Europe, science fiction writers were using science fiction to help bring about political change. Yevgeny Zamyatin's classic novel *We*, for example, <u>is against</u>[69] the Soviet Union's communist agenda.

Today, science fiction writers around the world continue to explore possibilities—possibilities that are fast becoming realities. Much of what science fiction writers only dreamed of a century ago, such as cloning and space travel, <u>have</u>[70] already come to pass. What <u>lies</u>[71] ahead? How will we handle these and other upcoming advances? Let us hope that science fiction writers are wrong, for all too often, characters in science fiction stories, like <u>they're</u>[72] forefather Victor Frankenstein, <u>are unable to handle</u>[73] the responsibility of having so much power over nature.

61. **a.** NO CHANGE
b. time Mary Shelley's *Frankenstein* marked
c. time—Mary Shelley's *Frankenstein*—marked
d. time, Mary Shelley's *Frankenstein* marked

62. **f.** NO CHANGE
g. career; but,
h. career, but
j. career, and

63. **a.** NO CHANGE
b. literature: science fiction.
c. literature, that was, science fiction.
d. literature (science fiction).

64. **f.** NO CHANGE
g. what happens when fiction becomes reality.
h. what happen if fictions became reality.
j. the effects of *what if* becoming reality.

65. **a.** NO CHANGE
b. works. His most famous works were
c. works, including his most famous,
d. works, including his most famous works:

66. **f.** NO CHANGE
g. are attacked by Martians.
h. faced attacks from Martians.
j. being attacked by Martians.

67. **a.** NO CHANGE
b. Wells like Shelley,
c. Wells who was like Shelley
d. Wells, like Shelley,

68. **f.** NO CHANGE
g. magazines that churned out for the masses science fiction stories.
h. magazines, that, churned out science fiction stories, for the masses.
j. magazines that churned out science fiction stories for the masses.

69. The writer wishes to use a much stronger word or phrase to convey this idea. Which of the following choices achieves that purpose and maintains the tone of the essay?
a. criticizes
b. takes to task
c. is a scathing indictment of
d. rips apart

70. **f.** NO CHANGE
g. had
h. has
j. would

71. **a.** NO CHANGE
b. lays
c. lie
d. lay

72. **f.** NO CHANGE
g. there are
h. their
j. whose

73. **a.** NO CHANGE
  b. handling bad
  c. do not handle well
  d. are badly handling

74. Which of the following revisions would most improve paragraph 4?
  f. adding a sentence about the issues today's science fiction writers are addressing
  g. adding a quotation from *Frankenstein*
  h. adding a brief summary of Mary Shelley's life
  j. answering the questions in the paragraph

75. The writer wishes to add a brief summary of the plot of *Frankenstein*. The most logical place for this addition would be
  a. to add it to the end of paragraph 1.
  b. to create a new paragraph between paragraphs 1 and 2.
  c. to add it after the third sentence in paragraph 1.
  d. to create a new paragraph between paragraphs 2 and 3.

ACT Mathematics
Practice Test 1

60 Questions—60 Minutes

For each problem, choose the correct answer. You are allowed to use a calculator on this test for any problems you choose. Unless the problem states otherwise, you should assume that figures are *not* drawn to scale. For this test, all geometric figures lie in a plane, the word *line* refers to a straight line, and the word *average* refers to the arithmetic mean.

1. The expression $a[b - (c - d)]$ is equivalent to
  a. $ab - ac - ad$
  b. $ab + ac - ad$
  c. $ab - c - d$
  d. $ab - ac + ad$
  e. $ab - c + d$

2. To date, a student has four test scores of 81, 87, 91, and 86. What must he receive on his fifth test to achieve an average of 88 for the five tests?
  f. 79
  g. 88
  h. 95
  j. 99
  k. He cannot earn an average of 88.

3. What two distinct integers should be placed in the blank spaces so that the difference between the four integers is the same?
  23, _____, _____, 62
  a. 33, 52
  b. 42, 43
  c. 36, 49
  d. 35, 50
  e. 24, 61

4. Sasha ran $2\frac{1}{3}$ miles on Monday, $3\frac{3}{4}$ miles on Tuesday, and $5\frac{2}{3}$ miles on Wednesday. How many miles in total did she run in those three days?

  f. $10\frac{1}{4}$

  g. $10\frac{6}{10}$

  h. $11\frac{1}{4}$

  j. $11\frac{3}{4}$

  k. $12\frac{3}{4}$

5. What is the value of the expression $h(h + 1)^2$ for $h = 3$?

  a. 24

  b. 48

  c. 64

  d. 84

  e. 144

6. Company X sells 80 markers for $49.60, and Company Y sells 125 of the same markers for $72.50. Which company offers a better price per marker, and how much less is its price?

  f. Company X, 4 cents

  g. Company X, 2 cents

  h. Company Y, 4 cents

  j. Company Y, 58 cents

  k. The costs are the same

7. A rectangular lot is entirely enclosed by a fence. If the lot measures 225 feet long and 165 feet wide, what is the length, in yards, of the fence?

  a. 360

  b. 390

  c. 260

  d. 1,560

  e. 2,340

8. A ladder is 16 feet long and reaches 10 feet up a wall. Approximately how many feet from the bottom of the wall is the base of the ladder?

  f. 5.5

  g. 6

  h. 8.5

  j. 10

  k. 12.5

9. If $7x - 12 = 11x + 24$, then $x =$

  a. −9

  b. −6

  c. −3

  d. 3

  e. 9

10. Mr. Johnson teaches fifth grade at Littleton Elementary School and earns $21,850 for teaching a 190-day school year. He is going on a five-day vacation, and his substitute will be paid $90 per day. How much money will Littleton Elementary School save while Mr. Johnson is away?

  f. $90

  g. $125

  h. $225

  j. $450

  k. $1,250

11. If x is a real number so that $x^3 = 125$, then $2(x^2 + x) =$

  a. 25

  b. 50

  c. 60

  d. 125

  e. 250

12. If a marble is chosen at random from a bag that contains 16 blue marbles, 12 red marbles, 6 green marbles, and 10 white marbles, what is the probability that the marble chosen will NOT be blue?

   f. $\frac{7}{11}$

   g. $\frac{4}{11}$

   h. $\frac{4}{7}$

   j. $\frac{7}{10}$

   k. $\frac{8}{11}$

13. For all values of x, the quantity $(5x + 2)^2 =$

   a. $10x^2 + 4$

   b. $25x^2 + 4$

   c. $25x^2 + 10x + 4$

   d. $10x^2 + 10x + 4$

   e. $25x^2 + 20x + 4$

14. On the number line of all real numbers, what is the midpoint of −12 and 20?

   f. −2

   g. 4

   h. 6

   j. 7

   k. 8

Use the following information to answer questions 15 through 17.

The chart shows the current enrollment in classes at Hawley Middle School.

COURSE	PERIOD	SECTION	# OF STUDENTS
English	1	A	29
	3	B	27
mathematics	2	A	24
	1	B	26
history	1	A	23
	2	B	27
science	3	A	29
	4	B	21
Spanish	5	A	49

15. What is the average number of students taking a class during period 1?

   a. 23

   b. 24

   c. 26

   d. 27

   e. 29

16. During which period do the fewest students take class?

   f. 1

   g. 2

   h. 3

   j. 4

   k. 5

17. The school owns 52 chairs, but 6 are broken. For which period(s) will there not be enough chairs to seat all of the students in classes?

   a. period 1 only

   b. period 4 only

   c. periods 1 and 4

   d. all but period 4

   e. all of the periods

18. The formula for the volume V of a sphere with a radius of r is $V = \frac{4}{3}\pi r^3$. If a spherical ball has a radius of $3\frac{1}{4}$ inches, what is its volume to the nearest cubic inch?

  f. 9
  g. 24
  h. 104
  j. 124
  k. 143

19. Celia has five blouses, four pairs of pants, three scarves, and three hats. If every outfit must include one blouse, one pair of pants, one scarf, and one hat, how many different outfits can Celia create?

  a. 15
  b. 60
  c. 120
  d. 180
  e. 360

20. Wool socks cost $9.60 for a package of three pairs of socks. If you buy three packages, you receive one free pair of wool socks. What would be the average cost of a pair of socks when you buy three packages?

  f. $2.60
  g. $2.80
  h. $2.88
  j. $3.08
  k. $3.20

21. For the system of linear equations shown, which of the following would describe the graph of this system in a standard coordinate plane?

$2y = -4x + 7$
$2y = 4x - 7$

  a. a single line with a positive slope
  b. a single line with a negative slope
  c. two parallel lines with positive slopes
  d. two parallel lines with negative slopes
  e. two distinct intersecting lines

22. Which of the following is a solution to the quadratic equation $x^2 - 24x = 0$?

  f. −36
  g. −24
  h. 2
  j. 6
  k. 24

23. At Mount Pleasant Ski Resort, 300,000 tons of snow are required to cover 1.5 acres of ski slope. How much snow would be required to cover 6.5 acres?

  a. 950,000 tons
  b. 1,050,000 tons
  c. 1,150,000 tons
  d. 1,250,000 tons
  e. 1,300,000 tons

24. In the right triangle $\triangle ABC$ shown, tangent $B =$

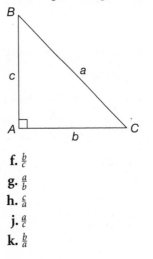

  f. $\frac{b}{c}$
  g. $\frac{a}{b}$
  h. $\frac{c}{a}$
  j. $\frac{a}{c}$
  k. $\frac{b}{a}$

25. A rectangle measures 32 yards by 46 yards. What is the approximate measurement, in feet, of the diagonal of this rectangle?

  a. 38
  b. 56
  c. 74
  d. 168
  e. 204

26. For what values of x will the equation
$(x + a)(x - a) = 0$ be true?

  f. a and x

  g. $-a$ and $-x$

  h. x and 0

  j. $-a$ and a

  k. none of the above

27. On the number line shown, an object moves
from A to B, from B to C, from C to D, and
finally from D to E. What is the total distance
the object moves?

```
   A     E   C        B     D
   |-------|-----|------------|-------|
  -12    -6   -1          7     12
```

  a. 28

  b. 36

  c. 56

  d. 58

  e. 62

28. What number can you add to the numerator
and denominator of $\frac{8}{13}$ to get 6?

  f. -14

  g. -12

  h. 4

  j. 10

  k. 14

29. For what value of x is the equation $\log_x 64 = 3$?

  a. 2

  b. 3

  c. 4

  d. 8

  e. 16

30. In circle C, shown here, a chord 32 inches long
is 10 inches from the center of the circle. What
is the radius of the circle, to the nearest tenth
of an inch?

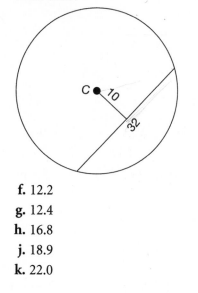

  f. 12.2

  g. 12.4

  h. 16.8

  j. 18.9

  k. 22.0

31. The formula for the length of a spring is given
by the equation $L = \frac{2}{3}F + 0.03$, where F is the
applied force, in newtons. What is the force,
in newtons, if the length of the spring is
0.83 meters?

  a. 0.8

  b. 1.2

  c. 1.4

  d. 1.6

  e. 2.2

32. If $y = x + 2$, then $(x - y)^5 =$

  f. -128

  g. -64

  h. -48

  j. -32

  k. 32

33. A mall has the shape and dimensions, in blocks, indicated in the diagram. There is a statue located halfway in between points E and B. What is the location of the statue relative to point C?

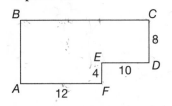

a. 16 blocks west and 4 blocks south
b. 20 blocks west and 6 blocks south
c. 14 blocks west and 8 blocks south
d. 16 blocks west and 6 blocks north
e. 6 blocks east and 16 blocks north

34. A circle C is inscribed in a square as shown. If the area of the square is 256 units square, what is the radius of the circle?

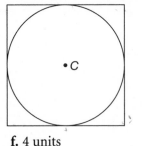

f. 4 units
g. 6 units
h. 8 units
j. 10 units
k. 12 units

35. In the standard coordinate plane, what is the y-coordinate of the point of intersection of the two lines $y = 4x - 6$ and $y = 2x + 2$?

a. 6
b. 10
c. 12
d. 16
e. 24

36. The ratio of three sides of a triangle is 16:19:28. If the length of the short side of a similar triangle is 20, what is the length of the longest side of the similar triangle?

f. 32
g. 33
h. 34
j. 35
k. 36

37. Which of the following inequalities describes the solution set for the inequality $25 - 6x \geq 9$?

a. $x \geq \frac{8}{3}$
b. $x \geq -\frac{8}{3}$
c. $x \leq -\frac{8}{3}$
d. $x \leq \frac{8}{3}$
e. $x \geq \frac{2}{3}$

38. The solution set of $\sqrt{x-1} > 7$ is the set of all real numbers where

f. $x > 6$
g. $x > 8$
h. $x > 50$
j. $x > 51$
k. $x > 52$

39. In the standard coordinate plane, what is the distance between the points $(6, -2)$ and $(-4, 8)$?

a. $\sqrt{18}$
b. $10\sqrt{2}$
c. $10\sqrt{6}$
d. 30
e. $10\sqrt{10}$

40. In the figure, points *A*, *B*, *C*, and *D* are collinear. Angles *A*, *E*, *F*, and *D* are as marked. What is the measure of angle *G*?

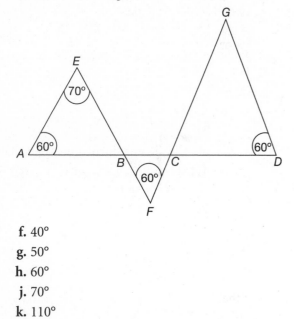

f. 40°
g. 50°
h. 60°
j. 70°
k. 110°

41. Light travels at approximately 186,000 miles per second. At that rate, approximately how many miles will it travel in *3 hours*?
a. 1.6×10^5
b. 1.6×10^8
c. 2.0×10^8
d. 2.0×10^9
e. 2.2×10^9

42. The ratio of the diameters of two circles is 6:10. What is the ratio of their areas?
f. 3:5
g. 3:10
h. 6:10
j. 9:25
k. 9:100

43. Hexagons, as pictured here, have nine diagonals. How many diagonals does the octagon have?

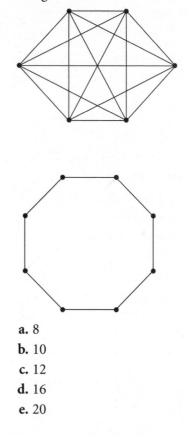

a. 8
b. 10
c. 12
d. 16
e. 20

44. If 80% of a number is 260, what is 116% of the same number?
f. 340
g. 360
h. 376
j. 377
k. 390

45. Of the 504 girls in Radcliffe Day School, $\frac{3}{8}$ are left-handed and $\frac{2}{3}$ of those have brown hair. How many brown-haired, left-handed girls attend Radcliffe Day School?
a. 104
b. 126
c. 146
d. 168
e. 189

46. As shown here, Xs are arranged in a triangular pattern by adding two Xs to each additional row. If n = number of rows, which of the following properly describes the total number of Xs in the triangular pattern for any value of n?

    X
   X X X
  X X X X X
 X X X X X X X
X X X X X X X X X

  f. $n + 2$

  g. $n + 3$

  h. $2n$

  j. $2n - 1$

  k. n^2

47. In the right triangle pictured, $\sin(C) \times \tan(B) =$

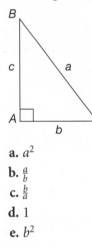

  a. a^2

  b. $\frac{a}{b}$

  c. $\frac{b}{a}$

  d. 1

  e. b^2

48. Alice is about to cover a patch of her backyard with decorative bricks that measure 2 inches by 6 inches. The area she wishes to cover measures 6 feet by 12 feet. What is the minimum number of bricks she must use to cover such an area?

  f. 72

  g. 144

  h. 432

  j. 720

  k. 864

49. If the imaginary number $i^2 = -1$, then the complex number operation of $\frac{1}{i-1} \cdot \frac{i+1}{i+1} =$

  a. $i - 1$

  b. $i + 1$

  c. $\frac{i+1}{2}$

  d. $\frac{i+1}{-2}$

  e. $1 - i$

50. In the standard coordinate plane, a circle is tangent to the y-axis at 5 and tangent to the x-axis at -5. What is the equation of the circle?

  f. $x^2 + y^2 = 5$

  g. $x^2 + y^2 = 25$

  h. $(x + 5)^2 + (y - 5)^2 = 25$

  j. $(x + 5)^2 + (y + 5)^2 = 25$

  k. $(x - 5)^2 + (y + 5)^2 = 25$

51. If the ratio of $x{:}y$ is 4:5, and the ratio of $y{:}z$ is 8:9, what is the ratio of $x{:}z$?

  a. 8:10

  b. 8:14

  c. 12:14

  d. 32:45

  e. 36:40

52. There are 420 people living in a small town. The 190 men have an average age of 42, and the women have an average age of 37. What is the average age, to the nearest year, of the residents of the town?

  f. 37

  g. 38

  h. 39

  j. 40

  k. 41

53. In the graph, the x-axis is intersected by the graph at $\frac{\pi}{2}, \frac{3\pi}{2}, \frac{5\pi}{2}, \frac{7\pi}{2}$, and so on. The curve over any one interval is a repetition of the other intervals. What is the period of the function?

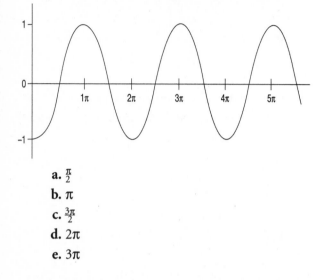

   a. $\frac{\pi}{2}$
   b. π
   c. $\frac{3\pi}{2}$
   d. 2π
   e. 3π

54. Two triangular prisms are similar. The smaller one has a triangular face with an altitude of 10, and the larger one has a triangular face with an altitude of 15. If the volume of the smaller prism is 4,000, what is the volume of the larger prism?
   f. 6,000
   g. 8,500
   h. 10,000
   j. 11,500
   k. 13,500

55. If $(x - 3)$ is a factor of the equation $3x^2 - 11x + n$, what is the value of n?
   a. −6
   b. 6
   c. 10
   d. 12
   e. 24

56. If $f(x) = 2x^2 + 2$, then $f(x + k) =$
   f. $2x^2 + 4kx + 2$
   g. $2x^2 + 2k + 2$
   h. $2x^2 + 2k^2 + 2$
   j. $4x^2 + 2k^2 + 2$
   k. $2x^2 + 4kx + 2k^2 + 2$

57. If $\sin a = -\frac{4}{5}$, and $\pi < a < \frac{3\pi}{2}$, then $\cos a =$
   a. $-\frac{3}{5}$
   b. $\frac{3}{5}$
   c. $\frac{4}{5}$
   d. $-\frac{5}{4}$
   e. There is not enough information to determine the value.

58. Which of the following graphs would be the correct graph of the equation $y = \dfrac{3x^2 + 3x}{x}$?

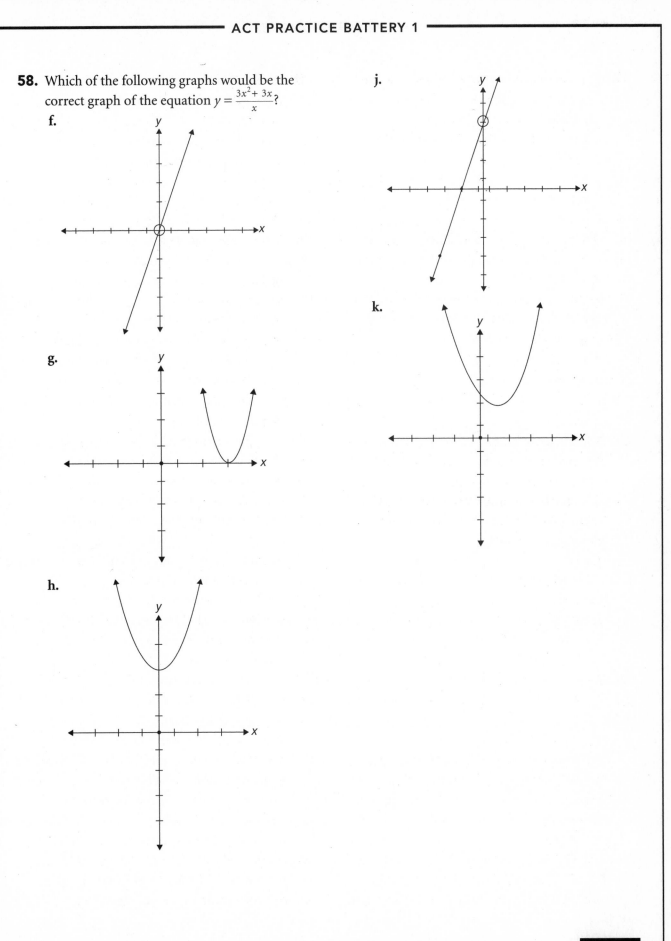

f.

g.

h.

j.

k.

59. Given the pair of equations $A = 6C + 4$ and $B = -3C - 5$, express the value of A in terms of B.

   a. $2B + 6$

   b. $3B - 1$

   c. $-2B + 6$

   d. $2B - 6$

   e. $-2B - 6$

60. A guitar was marked to be sold in a store for $120 and then marked down 15%. A month later it was marked down an additional 5%. If the same guitar was available online for $100, what percent could be saved by buying it at the store after the second markdown?

   f. 0.31%

   g. 0.4%

   h. 3.1%

   j. 4.0%

   k. 20%

ACT Reading Practice Test 1

40 Questions—35 Minutes

In this test you will find four passages, each followed by several questions. Read each passage carefully and then select the best possible answer for each question.

Passage I—Prose Fiction

This passage is taken from Babbitt, *by Sinclair Lewis, 1922.*

1   There was nothing of the giant in the aspect of
2   the man who was beginning to awaken on the
3   sleeping-porch of a Dutch Colonial house in
4   that residential district of Zenith known as Flo-
5   ral Heights.
6   His name was George F. Babbitt. He was
7   forty-six years old now, in April, 1920, and he
8   made nothing in particular, neither butter nor
9   shoes nor poetry, but he was nimble in the call-
10   ing of selling houses for more than people could
11   afford to pay.
12   His large head was pink, his brown hair
13   thin and dry. His face was babyish in slumber,
14   despite his wrinkles and the red spectacle-dents
15   on the slopes of his nose. He was not fat but he
16   was exceedingly well fed; his cheeks were pads,
17   and the unroughened hand which lay helpless
18   upon the khaki-colored blanket was slightly
19   puffy. He seemed prosperous, extremely mar-
20   ried and unromantic; and altogether unroman-
21   tic appeared this sleeping-porch, which looked
22   on one sizable elm, two respectable grass-plots,
23   a cement driveway, and a corrugated iron
24   garage. Yet Babbitt was again dreaming of the
25   fairy child, a dream more romantic than scarlet
26   pagodas by a silver sea.
27   For years the fairy child had come to him.
28   Where others saw but Georgie Babbitt, she dis-
29   cerned gallant youth. She waited for him, in the
30   darkness beyond mysterious groves. When at
31   last he could slip away from the crowded house
32   he darted to her. His wife, his clamoring
33   friends, sought to follow, but he escaped, the
34   girl fleet beside him, and they crouched
35   together on a shadowy hillside. She was so slim,
36   so white, so eager! She cried that he was gay and
37   valiant, that she would wait for him, that they
38   would sail—
39   Rumble and bang of the milk-truck.
40   Babbitt moaned; turned over; struggled
41   back toward his dream. He could see only her
42   face now, beyond misty waters. The furnace-
43   man slammed the basement door. A dog barked
44   in the next yard. As Babbitt sank blissfully into
45   a dim warm tide, the paper-carrier went by
46   whistling, and the rolled-up *Advocate* thumped
47   the front door. Babbitt roused, his stomach
48   constricted with alarm. As he relaxed, he was
49   pierced by the familiar and irritating rattle of
50   someone cranking a Ford: snapah-ah,

51 snap-ah-ah, snap-ah-ah. Himself a pious
52 motorist, Babbitt cranked with the unseen
53 driver, with him waited through taut hours for
54 the roar of the starting engine, with him ago-
55 nized as the roar ceased and again began the
56 infernal patient snap-ah-ah—a round, flat
57 sound, a shivering cold-morning sound, a
58 sound infuriating and inescapable. Not till the
59 rising voice of the motor told him that the Ford
60 was moving was he released from the panting
61 tension. He glanced once at his favorite tree,
62 elm twigs against the gold patina of sky, and
63 fumbled for sleep as for a drug. He who had
64 been a boy very credulous of life was no longer
65 greatly interested in the possible and improba-
66 ble adventures of each new day.
67   He escaped from reality till the alarm-
68 clock rang, at seven-twenty.
69   It was the best of nationally advertised
70 and quantitatively produced alarm-clocks, with
71 all modern attachments, including cathedral
72 chime, intermittent alarm, and a phosphores-
73 cent dial. Babbitt was proud of being awakened
74 by such a rich device. Socially it was almost as
75 creditable as buying expensive cord tires.
76   He sulkily admitted now that there was no
77 more escape, but he lay and detested the grind
78 of the real-estate business, and disliked his fam-
79 ily, and disliked himself for disliking them. The
80 evening before, he had played poker at Vergil
81 Gunch's till midnight, and after such holidays
82 he was irritable before breakfast. It may have
83 been the tremendous home-brewed beer of the
84 Prohibition era and the cigars to which that
85 beer enticed him; it may have been resentment
86 of return from this fine, bold man-world to a
87 restricted region of wives and stenographers,
88 and of suggestions not to smoke so much.
89   From the bedroom beside the sleeping-
90 porch, his wife's detestably cheerful "Time to
91 get up, Georgie boy," and the itchy sound, the

92 brisk and scratchy sound, of combing hairs out
93 of a stiff brush.
94   He grunted; he dragged his thick legs, in
95 faded baby-blue pajamas, from under the khaki
96 blanket; he sat on the edge of the cot, running
97 his fingers through his wild hair, while his
98 plump feet mechanically felt for his slippers. He
99 looked regretfully at the blanket—forever a
100 suggestion to him of freedom and heroism. He
101 had bought it for a camping trip which had
102 never come off. It symbolized gorgeous loafing,
103 gorgeous cursing, virile flannel shirts.

1. What physical attributes of George Babbitt can
be inferred from the passage?
  a. He is overweight.
  b. He is skinny.
  c. He is of average build.
  d. He is very tall.

2. According to the passage, George Babbitt is
  f. a poet.
  g. a shoemaker.
  h. a real estate broker.
  j. unemployed.

3. It can be inferred from the passage that George
Babbitt is
  a. good at his job.
  b. lazy.
  c. a hard worker.
  d. overworked.

4. What can be inferred from the passage about
Babbitt's relationship with his wife?
  f. It is romantic and passionate.
  g. They openly dislike each other.
  h. They have no strong feelings about each
    other.
  j. Babbitt dislikes his wife and feels guilty
    about it.

5. As it is used in line 62, the word *patina* most
nearly means
  a. the pattern of clouds in the sky.
  b. the pattern of the elm tree branches.
  c. the leaves of the tree.
  d. the color of the sky.

6. Which is the first noise to wake Babbitt from
his sleep?
  f. his alarm clock
  g. a milk truck
  h. the paperboy
  j. a car starting

7. The blanket in the last paragraph represents
what to Babbitt?
  a. a manly freedom that he has had to abandon
  b. beauty over practicality
  c. warmth and comfort
  d. the sleep to which he wishes to return

8. Which of the following statements best
explain(s) Babbitt's reluctance to get out
of bed?
  I. He dislikes his job.
  II. He has a hangover.
  III. He has had a fight with his wife.
  f. I and II
  g. I only
  h. II only
  j. I, II, and III

9. The young girl in Babbitt's dream best symbol-
izes what desire?
  a. to return to sleep
  b. to be young and free from his workaday
world
  c. the love he once had for his wife
  d. his desire to move out of the suburbs

10. The sentence *He who had been a boy very credulous of life was no longer greatly interested in the
possible and improbable adventures of each new
day* (lines 63–66) most closely means that
  f. as a child, Babbitt was optimistic about life,
but he now believes it will always be the
same.
  g. Babbitt has never seen the possibilities of
life.
  h. Babbitt has always looked forward to each
new day.
  j. as a boy Babbitt was pessimistic about his
life, but now sees its possibilities.

Passage II—Humanities

*This passage is excerpted from "Leonardo da Vinci"
from* Knights of Art: Stories of the Italian Painters, *by
Amy Steedman, 1907.*

1　On the sunny slopes of Monte Albano, between
2　Florence and Pisa, the little town of Vinci lay
3　high among the rocks that crowned the steep
4　hillside. Here in the year 1452 Leonardo, son of
5　Ser Piero da Vinci, was born. It was in the age
6　when people told fortunes by the stars, and
7　when a baby was born they would eagerly look
8　up and decide whether it was a lucky or
9　unlucky star which shone upon the child.
10　Surely if it had been possible in this way to tell
11　what fortune awaited the little Leonardo, a
12　strange new star must have shone that night,
13　brighter than the others and unlike the rest in
14　the dazzling light of its strength and beauty.
15　　Leonardo was always a strange child. Even
16　his beauty was not like that of other children.
17　He had the most wonderful waving hair, falling
18　in regular ripples, like the waters of a fountain,
19　the color of bright gold, and soft as spun silk.
20　His eyes were blue and clear, with a mysterious
21　light in them, not the warm light of a sunny
22　sky, but rather the blue that glints in the

23 iceberg. They were merry eyes too, when he
24 laughed, but underneath was always that
25 strange cold look. There was a charm about his
26 smile which no one could resist, and he was a
27 favorite with all. Yet people shook their heads
28 sometimes as they looked at him, and they
29 talked in whispers of the old witch who had
30 lent her goat to nourish the little Leonardo
31 when he was a baby. The woman was a dealer in
32 black magic, and who knew but that the child
33 might be a changeling?

34   It was the old grandmother, Mona Lena,
35 who brought Leonardo up and spoilt him not a
36 little. His father, Ser Piero, was a lawyer, and
37 spent most of his time in Florence, but when he
38 returned to the old castle of Vinci, he began to
39 give Leonardo lessons and tried to find out
40 what the boy was fit for. But Leonardo hated
41 those lessons and would not learn, so when he
42 was seven years old he was sent to school.

43   This did not answer any better. The rough
44 play of the boys was not to his liking. When he
45 saw them drag the wings off butterflies, or tor-
46 ture any animal that fell into their hands, his
47 face grew white with pain, and he would take
48 no share in their games. The Latin grammar,
49 too, was a terrible task, while the many things
50 he longed to know no one taught him.

51   So it happened that many a time, instead
52 of going to school, he would slip away and
53 escape up into the hills, as happy as a little wild
54 goat. Here was all the sweet fresh air of heaven,
55 instead of the stuffy schoolroom. Here were no
56 cruel, clumsy boys, but all the wild creatures
57 that he loved. Here he could learn the real
58 things his heart was hungry to know, not
59 merely words which meant nothing and led to
60 nowhere.

61   For hours he would lie perfectly still with
62 his heels in the air and his chin resting in his
63 hands, as he watched a spider weaving its web,
64 breathless with interest to see how the delicate

65 threads were turned in and out. The gaily
66 painted butterflies, the fat buzzing bees, the lit-
67 tle sharp-tongued green lizards, he loved to
68 watch them all, but above everything he loved
69 the birds. Oh, if only he too had wings to dart
70 like the swallows, and swoop and sail and dart
71 again! What was the secret power in their
72 wings? Surely by watching he might learn it.
73 Sometimes it seemed as if his heart would burst
74 with the longing to learn that secret. It was
75 always the hidden reason of things that he
76 desired to know. Much as he loved the flowers
77 he must pull their petals off, one by one, to see
78 how each was joined, to wonder at the dusty
79 pollen, and touch the honey-covered stamens.
80 Then when the sun began to sink he would
81 turn sadly homewards, very hungry, with torn
82 clothes and tired feet, but with a store of sun-
83 shine in his heart.

84   His grandmother shook her head when
85 Leonardo appeared after one of his days of
86 wandering.

87   "I know thou shouldst be whipped for
88 playing truant," she said; "and I should also
89 punish thee for tearing thy clothes."

90   "Ah! But thou wilt not whip me,"
91 answered Leonardo, smiling at her with his
92 curious quiet smile, for he had full confidence
93 in her love.

94   "Well, I love to see thee happy, and I will
95 not punish thee this time," said his grand-
96 mother; "but if these tales reach thy father's ears,
97 he will not be so tender as I am towards thee."

98   And, sure enough, the very next time that
99 a complaint was made from the school, his
100 father happened to be at home, and then the
101 storm burst.

102   "Next time I will flog thee," said Ser Piero
103 sternly, with rising anger at the careless air of
104 the boy. "Meanwhile we will see what a little
105 imprisonment will do towards making thee a
106 better child."

107   Then he took the boy by the shoulders
108   and led him to a little dark cupboard under
109   the stairs, and there shut him up for three
110   whole days.
111   There was no kicking or beating at the
112   locked door. Leonardo sat quietly there in the
113   dark, thinking his own thoughts, and wonder-
114   ing why there seemed so little justice in the
115   world. But soon even that wonder passed away,
116   and as usual when he was alone he began to
117   dream dreams of the time when he should have
118   learned the swallows' secrets and should have
119   wings like theirs.
120   But if there were complaints about Leon-
121   ardo's dislike of the boys and the Latin gram-
122   mar, there would be none about the lessons he
123   chose to learn. Indeed, some of the masters
124   began to dread the boy's eager questions, which
125   were sometimes more than they could answer.
126   Scarcely had he begun the study of arithmetic
127   than he made such rapid progress, and wanted
128   to puzzle out so many problems, that the mas-
129   ters were amazed. His mind seemed always
130   eagerly asking for more light, and was never
131   satisfied.

11. It can reasonably be inferred from the passage
that Leonardo's grandmother did not punish
him because she
   a. knew his father would punish him.
   b. believed it would not do any good.
   c. was afraid of Leonardo's magic powers.
   d. enjoyed seeing him happy.

12. What can you infer about Leonardo's teachers
from the last paragraph of the passage?
   f. They were afraid he would ask questions
      they could not answer.
   g. They thought he was unable to learn.
   h. They thought he had no desire to learn.
   j. They believed he should try to get along
      with the other students.

13. The person or people who was/were most
responsible for raising Leonardo was/were his
   a. father.
   b. mother.
   c. teachers.
   d. grandmother.

14. As he is depicted in the passage, Leonardo as a
boy can be described as
   f. popular among the other children.
   g. insensitive and cruel.
   h. a talented artist.
   j. eager to learn about what interested him.

15. It can be inferred from the passage that
Leonardo
   I. did not mind being alone.
   II. was fascinated by flight.
   III. was popular with the other students.
   a. I and II only
   b. I, II, and III
   c. I only
   d. II only

16. What year was Leonardo first sent to school?
   f. 1452
   g. 1455
   h. 1459
   j. 1461

17. According to the passage, all the following are
true EXCEPT:
   a. Leonardo enjoyed learning Latin grammar.
   b. Leonardo enjoyed learning math.
   c. Leonardo enjoyed studying nature.
   d. Leonardo was curious about the way things
      worked.

18. Which of the following statements best sums up what is meant by lines 76–79 (*Much as he loved the flowers he must pull their petals off, one by one, to see how each was joined, to wonder at the dusty pollen, and touch the honey-covered stamens*)?

   f. Leonardo's desire to learn how things worked was not stronger than his affection for nature.

   g. Leonardo's love of flowers drove him to destroy them.

   h. Leonardo revered all of nature.

   j. Leonardo's curiosity led him to destructive acts.

19. When Leonardo's father punished him, his reaction could be best described as

   a. anger.

   b. resignation.

   c. spite.

   d. sadness.

20. According to the passage, one reason Leonardo skipped school was

   f. he knew his grandmother would not punish him.

   g. the other students taunted him.

   h. Latin grammar bored him.

   j. he had no interest in any school subjects.

Passage III—Social Studies

This passage is adapted from How the Other Half Lives, *by Jacob A. Riis, 1890. The word* tenements *used throughout the passage refers to rental apartments that are generally of substandard quality.*

1   Long ago, it was said that "one half of the world
2   does not know how the other half lives." That
3   was true then. The half that was on top cared
4   little for the struggles, and less for the fate of
5   those who were underneath, so long as it was
6   able to hold them there and keep its own seat.
7   There came a time when the discomfort and
8   crowding below were so great, and the conse-
9   quent upheavals so violent, that it was no lon-
10   ger an easy thing to do, and then the upper half
11   fell to wondering what was the matter. Infor-
12   mation on the subject has been accumulating
13   rapidly since, and the whole world has had its
14   hands full answering for its old ignorance.
15   In New York, the youngest of the world's
16   great cities, that time came later than elsewhere,
17   because the crowding had not been so great.
18   There were those who believed that it would
19   never come; but their hopes were vain. Greed
20   and reckless selfishness delivered similar results
21   here as in the cities of older lands. "When the
22   great riot occurred in 1863," reads the testi-
23   mony of the Secretary of the Prison Association
24   of New York before a legislative committee
25   appointed to investigate causes of the increase
26   of crime in the State twenty-five years ago,
27   "every hiding-place and nursery of crime dis-
28   covered itself by immediate and active partici-
29   pation in the operations of the mob. Those very
30   places and domiciles, and all that are like them,
31   are today nurseries of crime, and of the vices
32   and disorderly courses which lead to crime. By
33   far the largest part—80% at least—of crimes
34   against property and people are perpetrated by
35   individuals who have either lost connection
36   with home life, or never had any, or whose
37   homes had ceased to afford what are regarded
38   as ordinary wholesome influences of home and
39   family. . . . The younger criminals seem to come
40   almost exclusively from the worst tenement
41   house districts, that is, when traced back to the
42   very places where they had their homes in the
43   city here." One thing New York was made sure
44   of at that early stage of the inquiry: the bound-
45   ary line of the Other Half lies through the
46   tenements.
47   It is ten years and over, now, since that
48   line divided New York's population evenly.

49 Today three fourths of New Yorkers live in the
50 tenements, and the nineteenth century drift of
51 the population to the cities is only increasing
52 those numbers. The fifteen thousand tenant
53 houses in the past generation have swelled into
54 thirty-seven thousand, and more than twelve
55 hundred thousand persons call them home.
56 The one way out—rapid transit to the sub-
57 urbs—has brought no relief. We know now
58 that there is no way out; that the "system" that
59 was the evil offspring of public neglect and pri-
60 vate greed is here to stay, forever a center of our
61 civilization. Nothing is left but to make the
62 best of a bad bargain.
63   The story is dark enough, drawn from the
64 plain public records, to send a chill to any
65 heart. If it shall appear that the sufferings and
66 the sins of the "other half," and the evil they
67 breed, are but as a fitting punishment upon the
68 community that gave it no other choice, it will
69 be because that is the truth. The boundary line
70 lies there because, while the forces for good on
71 one side vastly outweigh the bad—not other-
72 wise—in the tenements all the influences make
73 for evil; because they are the hotbeds of the
74 epidemics that carry death to rich and poor
75 alike; the nurseries of poverty and crime that
76 fill our jails and courts; that throw off forty
77 thousand human wrecks to the island asylums
78 and workhouses year by year; that turned out
79 in the last eight years a round half million beg-
80 gars to prey upon our charities; that maintain a
81 standing army of ten thousand panhandlers
82 with all that that implies; because, above all,
83 they touch the family life with deadly moral
84 poison. This is their worst crime, inseparable
85 from the system. That we have to own it, the
86 child of our own wrong, does not excuse it,
87 even though it gives it claim upon our utmost
88 patience and tenderest charity.

21. The main idea of the first paragraph is that
   a. the rich do not care about the poor until their own lives are affected.
   b. the rich know nothing about the lives of the poor.
   c. the rich and the poor lead very different lives.
   d. the poor revolted against the rich.

22. According to the passage, *the other half* refers to
   f. the rich.
   g. criminals.
   h. children.
   j. the poor.

23. According to the Secretary of the Prison Association, the main reason for increased crime was
   a. younger criminals.
   b. a lack of decent housing for the poor.
   c. the wealthy people's indifference to the poor.
   d. a shortage of prisons.

24. At the time the passage was written, how many people lived in tenement housing?
   f. more than 120,000
   g. 37,000
   h. 15,000
   j. more than 1,200,000

25. As it is used in line 30, the word *domiciles* most closely means
   a. dome-shaped.
   b. prisons.
   c. living places.
   d. orphanages.

26. In the third paragraph, the statement *It is ten years and over, now, since that line divided New York's population evenly* (lines 47–48) best means that
  f. tenements are no longer located in one area of the city.
  g. the crimes of the poor affect the rich.
  h. more than half of New York's population lives in poverty.
  j. the poor no longer live only in tenements.

27. According to the author, the only way for the poor to successfully escape poverty is
  a. nothing—there is no escape.
  b. by moving to the suburbs.
  c. through hard work.
  d. through crime.

28. According to the last paragraph, the following statement(s) about tenements is/are true:
  I. They foster illegal activity.
  II. They spread disease to the rich.
  III. Rich and poor alike may find themselves living there.
  f. I only
  g. II only
  h. I and II
  j. I, II, and III

29. According to the author, crime committed by the poor
  a. is not as widespread as the government claims.
  b. is unavoidable, considering their living conditions.
  c. is a problem that should be dealt with harshly.
  d. should be ignored because of their inhumane living conditions.

30. It can be inferred from the passage that the author's opinion of the poor is
  f. sympathetic.
  g. hostile.
  h. indifferent.
  j. objective.

Passage IV—Natural Science

This passage is taken from a U.S. Fish and Wildlife Service pamphlet titled "Migration of Birds," by Frederick C. Lincoln, 1935.

1   The changing picture of bird populations
2   throughout the year intrigues those who are
3   observant and who wish to know the source
4   and destination of these birds. While many spe-
5   cies of fish, mammals, and even insects under-
6   take amazing migratory journeys, birds as a
7   group are the most mobile creatures on Earth.
8   Even humans with their many vehicles of loco-
9   motion do not equal some birds in mobility.
10 No human population moves each year as far as
11 from the Arctic to the Antarctic with subse-
12 quent return, yet the arctic terns do.
13   Birds are adapted in their body structure
14 and physiology to life in the air. Their feathered
15 wings and tails, bones, lungs and air sacs, and
16 their metabolic abilities all contribute to this
17 amazing faculty. These adaptations make it
18 possible for birds to seek out environments
19 most favorable to their needs at different times
20 of the year. This results in the marvelous phe-
21 nomenon we know as migration—the regular,
22 recurrent, seasonal movement of populations
23 from one geographic location to another and
24 back again.
25   Throughout human experience, migra-
26 tory birds have been important as a source of
27 food after a lean winter and as the harbinger of
28 a change in seasons. The arrival of certain spe-
29 cies has been heralded with appropriate

30 ceremonies in many lands. Among the Eskimos
31 and other tribes this phenomenon is the
32 accepted sign of the imminence of spring, of
33 warmer weather, and a reprieve from winter
34 food shortages. The European fur traders in
35 Alaska and Canada offered rewards to the
36 Native American who saw the first flight of
37 geese in the spring, and all joined in jubilant
38 welcome to the newcomers. As North America
39 became more thickly settled, the large flocks of
40 ducks and geese, as well as migratory rails,
41 doves, and woodcock that had been hunted for
42 food became objects of the enthusiastic atten-
43 tion of an increasing army of sportsmen. Most
44 of the nongame species were also found to be
45 valuable as allies of the farmer in his never-
46 ending confrontation against insect pests and
47 weed seeds. And in more recent years, all spe-
48 cies have been of ever-increasing recreational
49 and esthetic value for untold numbers of peo-
50 ple who enjoy watching birds. We soon realized
51 that our migratory bird resource was an inter-
52 national legacy that could not be managed
53 alone by one state or country and that all
54 nations were responsible for its well-being. The
55 need for laws protecting game and nongame
56 birds, as well as the necessity to regulate the
57 hunting of diminishing game species, followed
58 as a natural consequence. In the management
59 of this wildlife resource, it has become obvious
60 that studies must be made of the species' habits,
61 environmental needs, and travels. In the United
62 States, the Department of the Interior recog-
63 nized the value of this resource and is devoted
64 to programs that will ensure sustainability for
65 these populations as they are faced with the
66 impacts of alteration in land use, loss of habitat,
67 and contaminants from our technological soci-
68 ety. Hence bird investigations are made by the
69 U.S. Fish and Wildlife Service, the arm of the
70 Department of Interior charged by Congress

71 under the Migratory Bird Treaty Act with the
72 duty of protecting those avian species that in
73 their yearly journeys pass back and forth
74 between the United States and other countries.
75 In addition, the federal government through
76 the activities of the Biological Resources Divi-
77 sion of the U.S. Geological Survey also pro-
78 motes basic research on migration. Federal
79 agencies cooperate with their counterparts in
80 other countries as well as with state agencies,
81 academic institutions, and nongovernmental
82 groups to gain understanding and for the pro-
83 tection of migratory species through such
84 endeavors as Partners in Flight, a broadly based
85 international cooperative effort in the Western
86 Hemisphere.
87   For almost a century the Fish and Wildlife
88 Service and its predecessor, the Biological Sur-
89 vey, have been collecting data on the important
90 details of bird migration. Scientists have gath-
91 ered information concerning the distribution
92 and seasonal movements of many species
93 throughout the Western Hemisphere, from the
94 Arctic Archipelago south to Tierra del Fuego.
95 Supplementing these investigations is the work
96 of hundreds of United States, Latin American,
97 and Canadian university personnel and volun-
98 teer bird-watchers, who report on the migra-
99 tions and status of birds as observed in their
100 respective localities. This data, stored in field
101 notes, computer files, and scientific journals,
102 constitutes an enormous reservoir of informa-
103 tion pertaining to the distribution and move-
104 ments of North American birds.
105   The purpose of this publication is to sum-
106 marize this data and additional information
107 from other parts of the world to present the
108 more important facts about our current under-
109 standing of the fascinating subject of bird
110 migration. The U.S. Fish and Wildlife Service is
111 grateful to the many people who have

112 contributed their knowledge so that others,
113 whether in biology or ornithology classes,
114 members of conservation organizations, or just
115 individuals interested in the welfare of the
116 birds, may understand and enjoy this precious
117 resource as well as preserve it for generations
118 to come.

31. The migratory path of the arctic tern
   a. varies depending on the year.
   b. is from the Arctic to the Antarctic and back to the Arctic.
   c. is from the Arctic to the Antarctic.
   d. is to the south in the summer and north in the winter.

32. According to the author, the main reason birds migrate is
   f. that their body structure and physiology are best suited for migration.
   g. to find the best climate at different times during the year.
   h. that birds enjoy flying great distances.
   j. that birds are an important source of food in different parts of the world.

33. It can be inferred from the passage that the relationship between the European fur traders and the Native Americans was
   a. friendly.
   b. hostile.
   c. based on commerce.
   d. nonexistent.

34. Which governmental agency is responsible for investigating threats to migratory birds?
   f. the U.S. Fish and Wildlife Service
   g. the Department of the Interior
   h. Congress
   j. the Migratory Bird Act

35. Which best describes the role of the Biological Survey?
   a. the agency is responsible for collecting data on bird migration
   b. the agency, in connection with the U.S. Fish and Wildlife Service, is responsible for collecting data on bird migration
   c. the agency was responsible for collecting data on bird migration before the U.S. Fish and Wildlife Service
   d. the agency is responsible for investigating threats to migratory birds

36. The passage states that all of the following are threats to migratory bird populations EXCEPT
   f. pollution.
   g. hunting.
   h. loss of habitat.
   j. insect pests.

37. As it is used in line 32 of the passage, the word *imminence* most nearly means
   a. importance.
   b. celebration.
   c. close arrival.
   d. warmth.

38. According to the passage, with the increasing population in North America, migratory birds no longer hunted for food were appreciated by all of the following EXCEPT
   f. sportsmen.
   g. bird-watchers.
   h. European fur traders.
   j. farmers.

39. According to the passage, the need for laws to protect migratory birds was brought about by
  a. a realization of their value as something other than a source of food.
  b. the increase in sport hunting.
  c. the devastating effects of pollution.
  d. the creation of the Migratory Bird Act.

40. According to the passage, which group(s) keep(s) data on the migration and status of birds?
  f. university personnel and volunteer bird-watchers
  g. the U.S. Fish and Wildlife Service
  h. the Biological Survey
  j. the U.S. Fish and Wildlife Service along with university personnel and volunteer bird-watchers

ACT Science Practice Test 1

40 Questions—35 Minutes

The passages in this test are followed by several questions. After reading each passage, choose the best answer to each question. You may refer back to the passages as often as necessary. You are *not* permitted to use a calculator on this test.

Passage I—Data Representation

The earth's gravitational force produces a downward acceleration of 9.8 m/s^2 on all objects near the earth's surface. Other forces, including those produced by wind and aerodynamic lift, as well as jet, rocket, internal combustion or other engines may also exert upward or downward forces on these objects. These other forces, acting in combination with gravity, can cause a net force greater than or less than gravity, and, therefore, a net acceleration different from the downward acceleration of 9.8 m/s^2 caused by gravity.

Table 1 and Figure 1 provide information about the vertical velocities measured for three different objects without regard to the horizontal motion of the objects. Each of the objects is operating under the influence of gravity for the entire 45 seconds being studied. They each may also be influenced by other vertical forces for all or part of that period. Where other forces have been applied, they always begin and end at one of the 5-second intervals.

Table 1 indicates the vertical velocities of the three different objects as measured every 5 seconds. Positive velocities indicate motion upward, and negative velocities indicate motion downward.

	0 SECONDS	5 SECONDS	10 SECONDS	15 SECONDS	20 SECONDS	25 SECONDS	30 SECONDS	35 SECONDS	40 SECONDS	45 SECONDS
TABLE 1 VERTICAL VELOCITIES										
object 1	−100.00	−49.00	2.00	53.00	104.00	155.00	204.00	157.00	108.00	59.00
object 2	50.00	1.00	−48.00	−97.00	−96.00	−95.00	−94.00	−93.00	−142.00	−191.00
object 3	490.00	441.00	392.00	343.00	294.00	245.00	196.00	147.00	98.00	49.00

Figure 1 is a graphical representation of the velocity of each object at every point during the 45 seconds under review.

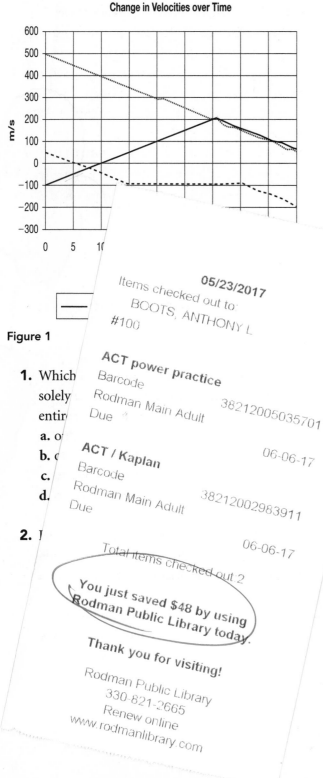

Figure 1

1. Which
solely
entir

  a. o
  b. c
  c.
  d.

2.

3. For second 5 through second 25, which of the objects is/are moving with constant acceleration?
  a. only object 3
  b. objects 1, 2, and 3
  c. objects 2 and 3
  d. objects 1 and 3

4. Which answer best describes the motion of object 1?
  f. It travels downward from second 0 for 9.8 seconds. Then it travels upward with increasing speed until second 30. It continues to move upward at a continually decreasing speed until second 45.
  g. It travels upward at a constant speed from cond 0 to second 30 and then travels ownward at a constant speed until econd 45.
  It travels downward from second 0 for 9.8 seconds. Then it travels upward with increasing speed until second 30. It then continues to move upward with a more gradual increase in speed until second 45.
  j. It travels upward at increasing speed until second 30 and then continues upward at decreasing speed until second 45.

5. From second 15 to second 35 the velocity of object 2 undergoes only very small changes. What is the best explanation for this?
  a. It leveled off and was flying at the same altitude for that time period.
  b. An upward force adequate to cause an acceleration of 0.2 m/s^2 was applied.
  c. An upward force adequate to cause an acceleration of 10 m/s^2 was applied.
  d. The force of gravity was reduced because it was flying over a deep valley.

Passage II—Research Summary

Titration is a method used to measure the concentration level of a given substance in a solution. A solution of known concentration, called the titrant, is slowly added, in measured amounts, to the solution being titrated. The titrant must contain a substance that reacts with the titrated solution, and the reaction must be measurable. Once the two substances have fully reacted, we know the mass of the titrant used and can calculate the mass of the titrated substance.

The reaction of hydrochloric acid (HCl) and sodium hydroxide (NaOH), a strong base, is represented as $HCl + NaOH \rightarrow H_2O + NaCl$.

This experimental series involves three trials. Each uses a sodium hydroxide solution at 0.2 M concentration as the titrant. The solution to be titrated is precisely 20 ml of hydrochloric acid solution at a concentration between 0.1 M and 0.3 M. (A 1.0 M concentration means 1.0 mole/1.0 liters of water.) The resulting products, water and sodium chloride, are acid neutral. When pH 7.0 (acid neutrality) is reached, the reaction is complete.

Table 1 shows the pH values after each addition of 2 ml of the titrant, up to 30 ml, for each of the three trials.

Table 1 pH Level after Each ml of Titrant is Added

ml NaOH	Trial 1	Trial 2	Trial 3	Average
0	2.03	2.06	2.01	2.03
2	2.06	2.10	2.03	2.06
4	2.09	2.14	2.04	2.09
6	2.13	2.18	2.06	2.12
8	2.27	2.52	2.10	2.30
10	2.32	7.03	2.17	3.84
12	2.34	11.26	2.25	5.28
14	2.37	11.34	2.34	5.35
16	2.42	11.42	2.47	5.44
18	2.48	11.50	2.62	5.53
20	6.92	11.57	2.87	7.12
22	11.23	11.61	7.13	9.99
24	11.55	11.64	11.26	11.48
26	11.72	11.67	11.31	11.57
28	11.81	11.70	11.33	11.61
30	11.94	11.72	11.35	11.67

Tables 2, 3, and 4 show a detailed view of what happens to the pH levels in the vicinity of pH 7.0 as titrant is added.

Table 2 Trial 1 pH Levels from 19.25 to 21.00 ml NaOH

ml NaOH	19.25	19.50	19.75	20.00	20.25	20.50	20.75	21.00
pH	3.42	3.87	4.54	6.92	8.20	9.12	10.02	10.73

Table 3 Trial 2 pH Levels from 9.25 to 11.00 ml NaOH

ml NaOH	9.25	9.50	9.75	10.00	10.25	10.50	10.75	11.00
pH	3.10	3.47	4.05	7.03	9.78	10.35	10.74	11.06

Table 4 Trial 3 pH Levels from 21.00 to 22.75 ml NaOH

ml NaOH	21.00	21.25	21.50	21.75	22.00	22.25	22.50	22.75
pH	3.56	4.22	4.72	5.96	7.13	8.30	9.26	10.03

6. Based on the formula for the reaction between hydrochloric acid and sodium hydroxide, how many moles of sodium hydroxide are required to fully react with one mole of hydrochloric acid?

 f. 2

 g. 4

 h. 1

 j. 3

7. The molar mass of HCl is 36.5 grams and the molar mass of NaOH is 40.0 grams. How many grams of HCl must be dissolved in a 20 ml solution to bring it to a concentration of 0.1 M?

 a. 8.00 grams

 b. 0.0730 grams

 c. 0.365 grams

 d. 0.080 grams

8. Based on Tables 2, 3, and 4, what is the best estimate that can be made of how many ml of the NaOH titrant it took to neutralize the HCl solutions used in trials 1, 2, and 3?

 f. 20.00, 10.00, 22.00

 g. 22.00, 10.00, 20.00

 h. 09.99, 21.95, 20.10

 j. 20.10, 09.99, 21.95

9. How many ml of titrant were used in the trials?

 a. enough to neutralize the HCl

 b. at least 30

 c. enough to reach the maximum pH

 d. exactly 30

10. What substances should we expect to discover in the titrated solution at the end of the trials?

 f. NaCl

 g. NaOH

 h. NaOH and NaCl

 j. NaOH, NaCl, and NH_3

11. How should the mass of HCl in the titrated solution be calculated?

 a. $(c \times v) \times 40.0$ g, where c is the concentration of the titrant (0.2 moles/liter) and v is the volume in liters of the titrant used to reach pH 7.0.

 b. $(c \times v) \times 36.5$ g, where c is the concentration of the titrant (0.2 moles/liter) and v is the volume in liters of the titrant used to reach pH 7.0.

 c. It is equal to the number of ml of titrant used.

 d. Heat the neutralized solution until all water is evaporated and weigh the solid crystals that remain.

Passage III—Conflicting Viewpoints

A geneticist and a physiologist each explained what causes the wide variety of different height profiles found among different countries and ethnic groups on the planet.

The geneticist pointed to data such as that represented by Figure 1. Each curve shows the reported distribution of the specified adult population over the spectrum of heights. One represents an estimate of global averages, and the other two are estimates for two countries. He argued that the distinctive height profile of each separate population grouping supported the hypothesis that height is determined by each gene pool.

Distribution of Adult Population by Height

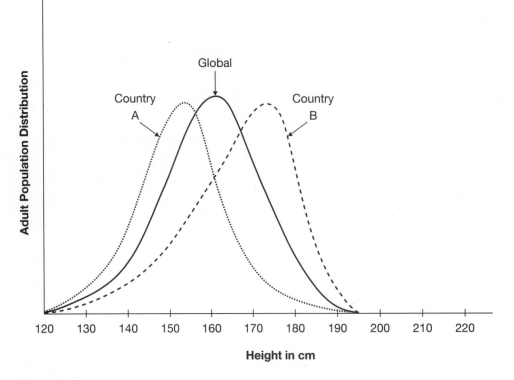

Figure 1

The physiologist said there were significant differences between the global profile and those of the two countries in terms of nutritional and other health-related factors. She also pointed to estimated historical data. Table 1 and the bar chart in Figure 2 present an image of long-term trends in typical height. She argued that if genetics determined the height, no such change would occur.

Table 1

Global	152	151	153	156	156	157	157	159	161	161	160	162	165	168
Country A	150	150	151	151	150	151	152	153	152	151	151	153	156	158
Country B	154	155	156	157	161	164	165	172	173	173	174	177	179	180
Year	1750	1770	1790	1810	1830	1850	1870	1890	1910	1930	1950	1970	1990	2010

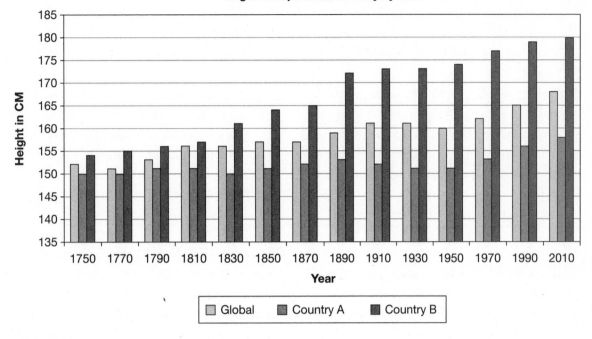

Figure 2

12. Based on Figure 1, what is a typical height in country A?

   f. 180 cm

   g. 168 cm

   h. 153 cm

   j. 70 cm

13. Based on Figure 1, what is the most typical height in country B?

   a. 174 cm

   b. 168 cm

   c. 158 cm

   d. 70 cm

14. What is the best description of the relationship between the shapes of the three curves shown in Figure 1?

   f. There is no significant relationship.

   g. The shapes are identical, but the positions of the curves for countries A and B are shifted to the left and right, respectively, of the global curve.

   h. All three are approximately in the same position, but their shapes are different. The global curve is symmetrical. Country A increases more steeply from shorter heights to its peak, remaining above the global curve, and then decreases more steeply, remaining below the other two curves as it descends to the right. Country B's curve increases gradually from the left, remaining below the other two curves until it approaches its peak; then it descends more steeply to the right but always remains above the other two curves.

   j. They are scientifically identical.

15. Which statement is supported by Table 1 and Figure 2 but not supported by Figure 1?

   a. None. Table 1 and Figure 2 present the same basic data as Figure 1 but in different formats.

   b. For significant time periods, some countries experience changes in typical adult height in approximately the same pattern as others.

   c. When more people move from country to country, genetic diversity produces taller adults.

   d. Some countries have larger typical adult heights than others.

16. Which is the most complete statement about country B supported by Table 1 and Figure 2?

   f. The adults of country B have been above the global typical height since at least 1750, and this difference has increased significantly throughout the period from 1750 to 2010.

   g. Country B's adults started out taller than any other country's, and they've been getting taller at an increasing rate.

   h. Country B must have had difficulties between 1890 and 1910 because the rate of increase in height of its people leveled off in that period.

   j. The height of country B's adults increased even when country A's decreased.

17. Which statement about country A is supported by Table 1 and Figure 2?

   a. The height of country A's adults increased even when country B's decreased.

   b. Country A's adults started out shorter than any other country's, but they've been gaining slowly and consistently.

   c. Country A's adults increased barely half as much in height as country B's between 1750 and 2010.

   d. The adult height in country A became smaller during two periods reported.

18. What hypothesis is supported by a comparison of the three curves in Figure 1?

   f. People in country B are better nourished than those in either the global average or country A.

   g. Country A needs a national fitness program.

   h. The upper and lower limits of adult human height are relatively constant in different countries, but the typical height varies from country to country.

   j. People in crowded areas are smaller than people in rural areas.

Passage IV—Research Summary

NASA is operating the satellite-based Solar Radiation and Climate Experiment (SORCE). Its purpose is to improve our understanding of the nature, including changes in quality and intensity, of solar radiation reaching our planet, by continuously monitoring the intensity of solar radiation by time and by frequency.

Five different instruments are mounted in the satellite to achieve coverage of the desired spectrum range. Table 1 shows the instruments used and the wavelength (λ) range monitored by each. Figure 1 illustrates how they are arranged in the satellite.

TABLE 1 SATELLITE INSTRUMENTATION AND WAVELENGTHS	
DEVICE	**λ RANGE**
Spectral Irradiance Monitor (SIM)	310–2,400
Solar Stellar Irradiance Comparison Experiment (SOLSTICE) A	115–180
Solar Stellar Irradiance Comparison Experiment (SOLSTICE) B	180–310
XUV Photometer System (XPS)	1–27
Total Irradiance Monitor (TIM)	TSI, all

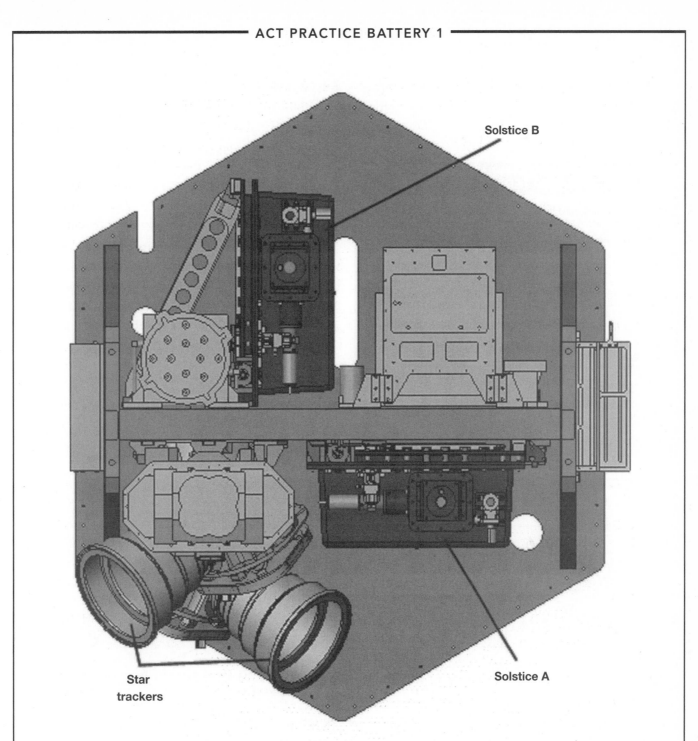

Figure 1

Table 2 names the major categories of electromagnetic radiation and shows the frequency range included in each.

TABLE 2 WAVELENGTHS (λ) IN NANOMETERS OF ELECTROMAGNETIC RADIATION		
TYPE OF RADIATION	FROM λ	TO λ
gamma ray	?	1.E − 03
x-ray	1.E − 03	1.E + 00
ultraviolet	1.E + 00	4.E + 02
visible light	4.E + 02	7.E + 02
infrared	7.E + 02	1.E + 04
microwave	1.E + 04	1.E + 07
radio	1.E + 07	1.E + 12

Experiment 1

The Total Irradiance Monitor (TIM) monitors the total solar irradiance (TSI) over the entire electromagnetic spectrum. Figure 2 shows the average daily TSI, measured in watts/meter^2 (W/m^2) as measured by the TIM for December 20 through 26, 2010.

Experiment 2

The other instruments measure irradiance by wavelength. This measure is called solar spectral irradiance (SSI). Figure 3 shows the SSI for December 24, 2010, in watts/meter^2/nanometer (W/m^2/nm). This is a measure of the intensity of solar irradiance by wavelength.

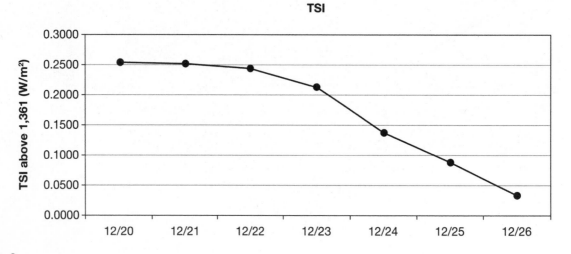

Figure 2

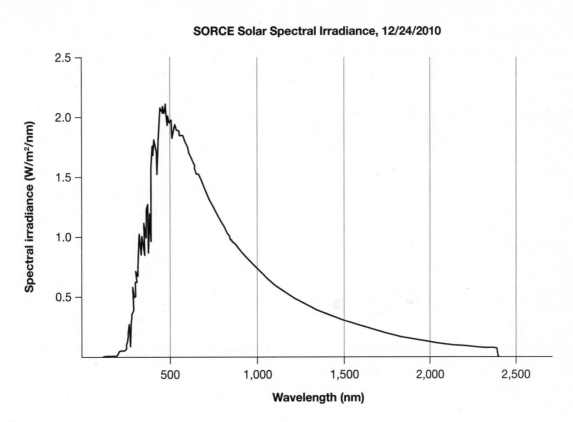

SORCE Solar Spectral Irradiance, 12/24/2010

Figure 3

19. Based on Tables 1 and 2, which types of electromagnetic radiation are measured in the SORCE experiment by instruments other than the TIM?

   a. gamma ray, x-ray, visible light

   b. x-ray, ultraviolet, visible light, infrared

   c. radio, microwave, infrared, ultraviolet

   d. visible

20. According to Table 2 and Figure 3, what is the difference between the lowest and the highest daily average of total solar irradiance (TSI)?

   f. 0.2184 W/m^2

   g. $0.2184 \text{ W/m}^2/\text{nm}$

   h. $1.\text{E} + 10 \text{ W/m}^2$

   j. $2,513.\text{E} - 4 \text{ W/m}^2$

21. Approximately what proportion of the average daily solar irradiance is the difference between the week's highest level and its lowest level?

   a. 1.6000

   b. $\frac{1}{150}$

   c. $\frac{1}{1,000}$

   d. 1.5 E^{-4}

22. Based on Figure 3, which wavelength transmitted the highest level of solar irradiance?

   f. 2,500 nm

   g. 2.0 nm

   h. 460 nm

   j. 460 Hz

23. What best describes the difference between total solar irradiance (TSI) and solar spectral irradiance (SSI)?

   a. TSI is the total amount of power delivered through a given cross-sectional area. SSI is the residual effect of that power after it has passed.

   b. TSI is the total amount of power delivered through a given cross-sectional area. SSI provides a profile of solar irradiance delivered by wavelength range.

   c. TSI is the total solar energy measured. SSI is the profile of solar energy delivered by wavelength range.

   d. TSI is the total solar energy measured in space. SSI is the energy level that strikes the earth.

24. Based on Figure 3 and Table 1, which type of electromagnetic radiation carries the most solar irradiance?

   f. gamma ray

   g. visible light

   h. microwave

   j. infrared

25. Refer again to Figure 3. After visible light, which type of electromagnetic radiation carries the most solar irradiance?

   a. ultraviolet

   b. radio waves

   c. infrared

   d. x-ray

Passage V—Research Summary

Microbe populations, including those of disease-producing bacteria, can change their characteristics over relatively short periods of time. A series of experiments involving pneumococci were conducted to determine whether and how these changes take place. In all three of the experiments described here, measures were taken to protect against contamination from other bacteria throughout the course of the experiments.

Experiment 1

A five-year study was conducted of the prevalence of each type of pneumococcus found in pneumonia victims. Table 1 shows the results. For the purpose of simplification, the pneumococcal types I through VI referred to here do not necessarily correspond either to those used in the original study or to those in current usage.

TABLE 1	TYPES OF PNEUMOCOCCI IN PNEUMONIA CASES				
TIME PERIOD	NUMBER OF CASES	% TYPE I	% TYPE II	% TYPE III	% TYPE IV
04/1920–01/1922	151	30.6	32.6	6.6	30.0
02/1922–10/1924	61	42.6	21.3	3.2	32.7
11/1924–03/1927	67	34.3	7.4	4.4	53.7

Experiment 2

A subsequent study was conducted to determine what happens to strains of pneumococci in a disease victim. It examined changes both to the pneumococci infecting the victim and to those extracted from the victim.

First, samples were taken from a patient who was initially analyzed to be infected only with type I pneumococci. Cultures were grown from these samples in three ways and analyzed. The first was simply to grow bacterial colonies from the sample in petri dishes. The second was to examine what happened when the same bacteria infected others. Mouse A was inoculated with untreated infected material. Then mouse B was inoculated with type I serum, which kills type I bacteria, and with the infected material from the patient. Table 2 reports those results. (Note: each day a different mouse B and mouse A were used.)

TABLE 2	PNEUMOCOCCI TYPES EXTRACTED FROM ONE PNEUMONIA CASES		
		FROM INNOCULATED MOUSE	
DAY EXTRACTED	GROWN ON CULTURE	MOUSE A INNOCULATED WITH UNTREATED SAMPLE	MOUSE B WITH UNTREATED SAMPLE AND TYPE I SERUM
4	type I (3 colonies)	type I	type V
6	type I (7 colonies)	type I	type IV, type VI
8	no culture made	type I, type VI	not tested
12	no culture made	type I	not tested
15	type IV (1 colony)	type IV	not tested
17	type VI (2 colonies)	type IV	not tested
19	no culture made	type II, type VI	not tested
21	no pneumococci colonies	type I	not tested

Experiment 3

The next experiment examined the changes that occurred when bacteria from six different pneumococcal colonies were used to inoculate mice. These colonies were cultured in laboratory conditions to eliminate uncertainties of the previous experiments. All of these colonies were of rough (R) bacteria. Bacteria can be divided into smooth or encapsulated (S) and rough or unencapsulated (R). The smooth, encapsulated bacteria are the most dangerous because they are coated with material that protects them from antigens. The rough, unencapsulated bacteria are usually harmless.

In each case, a mouse was inoculated with R bacteria from the colony. The mice either died after between 2 and 12 days or survived indefinitely. The blood of each deceased mouse was then cultured and tested for pneumococci that were examined to determine whether they were R or S bacteria. Table 3 reports the results.

	TABLE 3 THREE SUCCESSIVE INNOCULATIONS WITH R PNEUMOCOCCI DERIVED FROM SIX DIFFERENT COLONIES						
	INOCULATION 1			INOCULATION 2		INOCULATION 3	
COLONY	DAYS SURVIVED	R, S, 0		DAYS SURVIVED	R, S, 0	DAYS SURVIVED	R, S, 0
1	2	S		2	S	2	S
2	2	S		2	S	2	S
3	2	S		2	S	2	S
4	12	0		survived	0	survived	0
5	4	S		3	S	2	S
6	survived	0		survived	0	survived	0

26. Consider the results reported in Table 2. Which of the following statements about the samples taken directly from the patient and culture is correct and important for the study?
    f. The patient was cured by day 19.
    g. Although the patient started with evidence of only type I infection, that disappeared, to be replaced by first type IV and then type VI infection.
    h. The type I bacteria died of overpopulation after day 6.
    j. Type IV bacteria are the mildest of those involved with this disease.

27. Based on the overall findings reported by Table 2, which of the following answers is most correct?
    a. The mice became infected with whatever bacteria the patient was infected with when the sample was taken.
    b. The appearance of type VI bacteria indicates that the disease has run its course.
    c. Bacteria change by escalating from lower types to higher types.
    d. The type of bacteria changes both in the patient and in the mice inoculated with the patient's infection, without any clear relationship between the two.

28. From the standpoint of understanding how bacterial strains change over time, what is the most interesting thing about the results reported in Table 3?

   f. Any of the mice survived.

   g. All of the bacterial strains, without exception, changed from R to S.

   h. There was only one fatality in the mice inoculated with strains 4 and 6, and that took much longer than the deaths caused by the other strains.

   j. All of the bacterial strains extracted and tested exhibited a change from R to S.

29. Which answer is the most important statement supported by the data reported from the three experiments?

   a. All bacteria are potential killers.

   b. Pneumococcus strains do apparently shift their characteristics significantly over time, and it is possible to learn about the conditions under which this happens.

   c. Mice are more susceptible to disease than humans.

   d. Bacteria undergo random mutations that we cannot predict.

30. Which statement is best supported by the data in Table 2, viewed in conjunction with the other data?

   f. A single type of bacterium infects the victim and then reproduces until it kills the patient or the patient kills it.

   g. The progress of the disease involves changes not only in the intensity but also in the nature of the infection.

   h. The bacterial strain causing the infection will tend to destroy itself.

   j. The bacteria can never be completely eliminated.

Passage VI—Data Representation

Variations in the proportion of the two major isotopes of oxygen, ^{18}O and ^{16}O, in seawater or land-based water, including glacial ice, are believed to be a proxy for changes in temperature. ^{16}O is lighter than ^{18}O, so it evaporates first from seawater. This leaves a higher concentration of ^{18}O in seawater and a lower concentration in the evaporated water, which then falls to Earth as precipitation. If the falling water freezes, glaciers are formed, which trap the low ^{18}O precipitated water. In glacial periods, oceans are richer in ^{18}O, but in interglacial periods the glaciers melt and ^{16}O-rich water flows back into the oceans. For this reason high ^{18}O concentrations in seawater are believed to be an indication of cold climate periods in which glaciers are built up.

The measure of how far above normal the concentration of ^{18}O in a sample is is called $\delta^{18}O$. It is computed as follows:

$$\delta^{18}O = \left[\left(\frac{^{18}O_{sample}}{^{16}O_{sample}} \div \frac{^{18}O_{normal}}{^{16}O_{normal}} \right) - 1 \right] \times 1,000$$

Thus high $\delta^{18}O$ means more ^{18}O and less ^{16}O than normal. Low $\delta^{18}O$ is the reverse.

Figure 1 illustrates the $\delta^{18}O$ cycle from seawater to the atmosphere to glaciers on land and back to seawater.

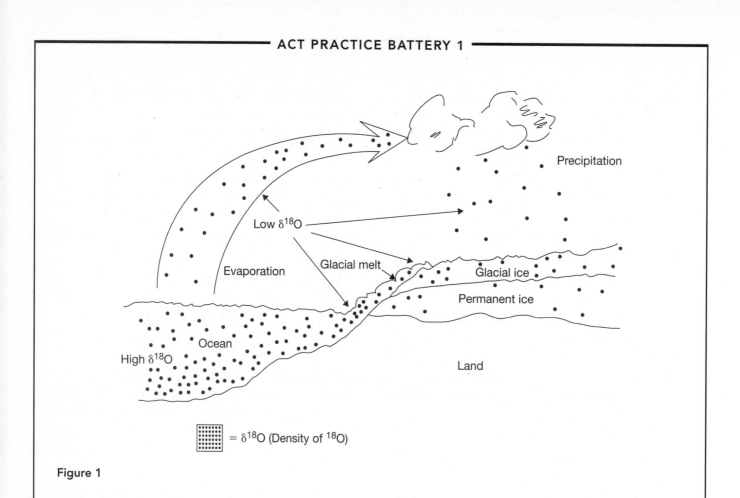

= $\delta^{18}O$ (Density of ^{18}O)

Figure 1

Low $\delta^{18}O$ water evaporates from the ocean, leaving higher $\delta^{18}O$ water behind.

The evaporated water falls as precipitation, forming low $\delta^{18}O$ glaciers.

In interglacial periods, the glaciers melt, and ^{16}O flows back into the ocean, reducing $\delta^{18}O$ there.

Figure 2 is a simplified representation of the changes in seawater $\delta^{18}O$ for the past 2,000,000 years. The high $\delta^{18}O$ periods are when ^{16}O evaporates from the seawater and is frozen into glaciers. The low $\delta^{18}O$ periods are when the glaciers melt and return the ^{16}O to the seawater.

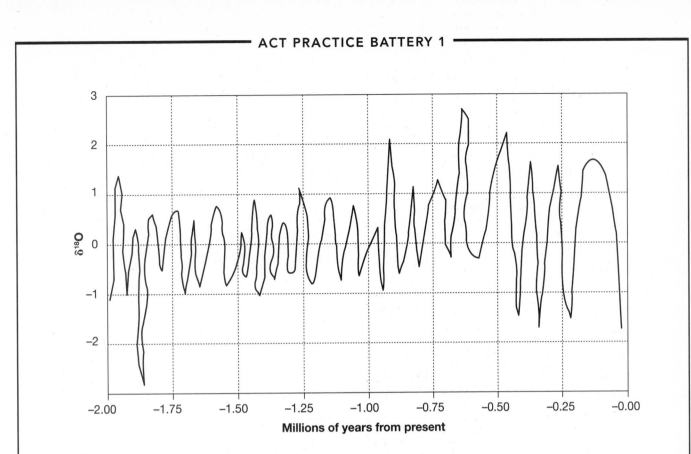

Figure 2

31. Based on Figure 2 and the relationship between $\delta^{18}O$, glaciation, and climate, how long ago was the period with the coldest temperatures and the most glaciation?
 a. 1.85 million years
 b. 0.12 million years
 c. 0.65 million years
 d. Between 1.00 and 1.75 million years

32. Based on Figure 2 and the relationship between $\delta^{18}O$ and the return of melted glaciers to the ocean, how long ago would sea levels have been highest?
 f. 0.65 million years
 g. 0.90 million years
 h. 1.93 million years
 j. 1.85 million years

33. Referring to Figure 2, how many periods of glacial buildup occurred between 0.25 and 0.50 million years ago?
 a. three
 b. two
 c. one
 d. six

34. Based on Figure 2, what is the highest number of glacial melting periods to occur within one 0.25-million-year span?
 f. three
 g. five
 h. two
 j. four

35. During what period shown on Figure 2 were the temperature swings between glacial build-ups and glacial melts consistently the most mild over an extended period of time?

    a. −0.50 to −0.85 million years

    b. −0.90 to −1.75 million years

    c. 0.00 to −0.50 million years

    d. −1.85 to −2.00 million years

Passage VII—Data Representation

Valency is a concept in chemistry that provides rules for determining which chemical elements can combine in what proportions to form compound substances. Protons and neutrons together form the nucleus at the center of an atom. The much lighter electrons whirl around the nucleus in what are called shells, rings, orbits, or energy levels. The left-hand diagram in Figure 1 is a representation of this structure.

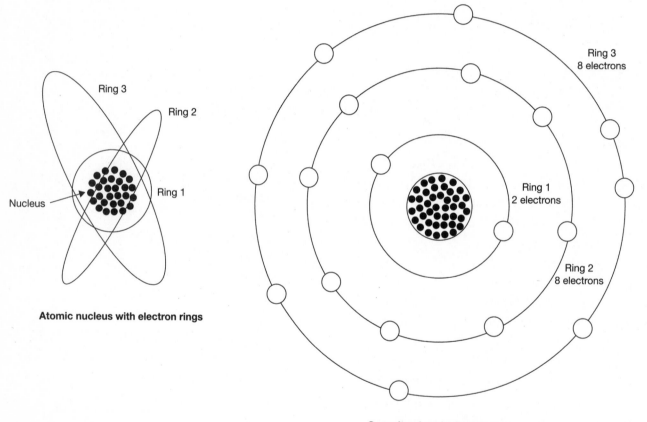

Atomic nucleus with electron rings

Capacity of each electron ring

Figure 1

At right in Figure 1 is a representation of valency. Each electron ring has a normal electron capacity. The first ring's capacity is two electrons. The other rings each have a capacity of eight electrons. Atoms tend to bring their outer rings to capacity through some kind of collaboration or exchange with other atoms. The valency of an atom is the number of surplus or deficit electrons in its outer ring.

Ionic bonding involves a combination of atoms having only one or two electrons in their outer rings with others that need only one or two electrons to complete their outer rings. The first type empty their incomplete outer rings by lending out their outer-ring electrons, and the second type borrow them to complete their outer rings. This is called ionic bonding because the atoms become electrically charged ions. The attraction between the positive ions that give up their electrons and the negative ions that receive them helps to bind the resulting compound.

Figure 2 shows how this works in the case of two common substances, H_2O and $NaCl$, water and salt.

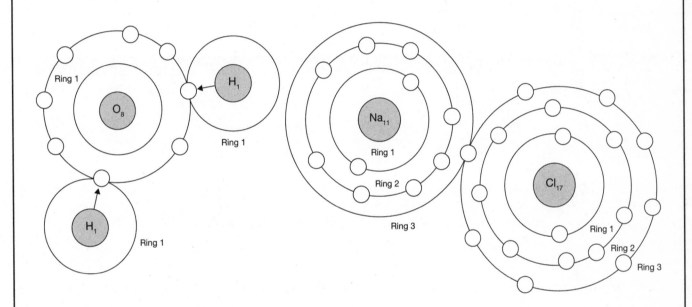

Figure 2

Tables 1 and 2 show how each atom borrows or loans electrons either to complete or to empty its outer ring.

TABLE 1 IONIC BONDING OF WATER (H_2O)					
ELEMENT, ATOMIC NUMBER × NUMBER IN MOLECULE	ELECTRONS IN OUTER RING	ELECTRONS BORROWED	ELECTRONS LENT	ELECTRONS LEFT IN OUTER RING	ELECTRICAL CHARGE
Hydrogen 1 × 2	1 × 2	0	1 × 2	0	+1 × 2
Oxygen 8 × 1	6	2	0	8	−2
				Total charge	0

TABLE 2 IONIC BONDING OF SALT (NaCl)					
ELEMENT, ATOMIC NUMBER × NUMBER IN MOLECULE	ELECTRONS IN OUTER RING	ELECTRONS BORROWED	ELECTRONS LENT	ELECTRONS LEFT IN OUTER RING	ELECTRICAL CHARGE
Sodium 11 × 1	1	0	1	0	+1
Chlorine 17 × 1	7	1	0	8	−1
				Total charge	0

36. According to Tables 1 and 2, what is the resulting charge of each compound?

   f. H_2O is positive and NaCl is negative.

   g. They are both negative.

   h. NaCl is positive and H_2O is neutral.

   j. They are both neutral.

37. Refer to Tables 1 and 2 and Figure 1. When sodium (Na) is stripped of the one electron in its outer shell, what is its electrical charge?

   a. +1

   b. 10

   c. −1

   d. 11

38. Based on Figure 2 and the explanations presented here, how many electron rings does a positive sodium ion have?

   f. one

   g. two

   h. three

   j. none

39. Based on the data presented here about ionic bonding, which element other than sodium would chlorine (Cl) be most likely to form an ionic bond with?

   a. oxygen

   b. itself

   c. Hydrogen and oxygen are equally likely.

   d. hydrogen

40. As shown in Figure 2 and Table 1, hydrogen and sodium each have only one electron in their outer rings. In light of the information presented here, what is the best explanation for why it takes one sodium atom to form a compound with one chlorine atom, but it takes two hydrogen atoms to form a compound with one oxygen atom?

   f. Hydrogen is atomic number 1, and sodium is 11. It takes more hydrogen atoms to balance the weight of oxygen than sodium atoms to balance chlorine.

   g. The electrons of sodium and chlorine total 28, which is an even number. Two hydrogen atoms are required to produce an even number of electrons with oxygen.

   h. Chlorine needs only one electron to complete its outer ring. Oxygen needs two. One sodium atom provides the one electron that chlorine needs, but it takes two hydrogen atoms to provide the two electrons that oxygen needs.

   j. Sodium and chlorine start with the same number of electron rings, but hydrogen has only one ring to oxygen's two.

ACT Writing Practice Test 1

You have 30 minutes to complete this essay. Remember to:

- Address the specific topic and writing task.
- Create a well-organized response.
- Include developed supporting ideas and specific details.
- Use sentence variety and strong word choices.

In an effort to reduce juvenile violence and crime, many towns have chosen to enforce curfews on minors under the age of 18. These curfews make it illegal for any minor to loiter, wander, stroll, or play in public streets, highways, roads, alleys, parks, playgrounds, or other public places between the hours of 10:00 p.m. and 5:00 a.m. Supporters of the curfew believe that it will reduce community problems such as violence, graffiti, and drugs. Those who oppose curfews for minors claim these laws violate the Fourteenth Amendment rights to equal protection and due process for U.S. citizens. They also believe that such curfews stereotype minors by presupposing that citizens under the age of 18 are the only people who commit crimes.

In your essay, take a position on this question. You may write about either of the two points of view given, or you may present a different point of view on the topic. Use specific reasons and examples to support your position.

Answers

ACT English Practice Test 1
Passage I—Sigmund Freud

1. **d.** This is the most concise choice. The other options are all redundant.
2. **g.** The commas here are superfluous. Choice **j** would create a sentence fragment.
3. **a.** The verb *to posit* means to postulate or assume as truth.
4. **h.** The singular possessive form is appropriate for this sentence.
5. **a.** This is the most appropriate transitional phrase for this sentence.
6. **h.** This is the most correct word order.
7. **b.** This sentence is related, but not within the focus of the paragraph. It is best omitted.
8. **j.** The simple present tense is correct here.
9. **d.** This provides a clear alternative and avoids ending the sentence with a preposition.
10. **h.** This corrects the sentence fragment.
11. **b.** This correctly describes a single sense of right and wrong.
12. **g.** This should be clear from the transitions and the simile comparing the mind to an iceberg.
13. **d.** A definition is offered after each italicized term.
14. **f.** This connects the main ideas in each paragraph: the impulses that control behavior and repression.
15. **b.** The presence of the word *like* indicates a similarity, and thus a simile.

Passage II—Yoga

16. **h.** This is the most appropriate and precise word choice.
17. **b.** The introductory phrase is most effective with the verb *to do*, and this is the correct form to use.
18. **f.** The reference is to people, so *who* is correct, and the subject form is also correct, as opposed to *whom*.
19. **a.** *Yoga poses* agrees with *are*, so the sentence is correct as it is.
20. **j.** The poses produce a desired effect, so they are *effective*.
21. **c.** The possessive pronoun is required here. *One's* is incorrect because it creates a shift in pronoun (from *you* to *one*).
22. **j.** This statement is self-evident and should be omitted.
23. **d.** This is the correct word order.
24. **h.** *And* is awkward and unnecessary.
25. **c.** This is the most correct and effective combination of sentences. The other versions misuse transitions.
26. **g.** This choice makes the sentence parallel and is the most concise.
27. **d.** The final member of a list should be preceded by a comma and the word *and*.
28. **j.** This is the most appropriate metaphor. Choice **f** is a cliché. Choice **g** is ineffective; it is unclear what emotion the simile is trying to convey. Without further explanation, choice **h** is an inappropriate comparison.
29. **a.** The second paragraph continues to explain why yoga is different and expresses the main idea of the essay.
30. **h.** This is the best way to achieve the goal of getting readers to do poses. The writer needs to provide some instruction.

Passage III—The Cold War

31. **c.** This is the clearest and most concise answer. *Dramatically* is redundant.
32. **g.** The simple past tense is appropriate here.
33. **d.** The correct interpretation would be that more than one experiment would be needed.
34. **h.** In this case, the modifiers should follow the noun.
35. **c.** This is the proper form of the word.
36. **j.** The goals were for Japan to surrender *and to* end World War II.

37. c. The plural form is necessary in order to agree with *were* later in the sentence.

38. h. This is the proper way to introduce a dependent clause.

39. b. This would be the most accurate usage.

40. j. This best defines the relationship without being redundant.

41. a. The sentence is correct as is, using the appropriate adjectives and separating them properly with commas.

42. g. This logically separates the first important event from the second one.

43. c. This would appropriately introduce the final important event, the Truman Doctrine.

44. j. The mention of foreign policy and the mid-twentieth century would make it more specific.

45. c. While all are related to the subject matter, this best describes the essay, which focuses on the events leading to the Cold War.

Passage IV—The Industrial Revolution

46. f. This is the most correct and concise choice.

47. c. This is the most concise choice. Choices **a** and **d** are redundant; choice **b** has improper word order.

48. j. This is the most logical sequence: first, the sentence giving the overall timeline of the revolution; then, the next two sentences in chronological order.

49. b. This indeed makes the sentence more concise.

50. g. This is the proper parallel structure.

51. d. This is the best choice. Choice **b** is grammatically correct, but **d** combines the sentences for greater sentence variety.

52. j. The list requires commas separating each item, and each item requires an article—*the*—to create the proper parallel structure.

53. a. This is the most accurate description of the events.

54. j. The singular possessive form is correct.

55. d. The proper complement to *between* is *and*, as in *between this and that*.

56. f. This presents the correct word order and conveys the correct idea.

57. b. This is the correct prepositional idiom.

58. g. This ties in the issues in the paragraph: mass production, moving into cities and towns, and large populations. Choice **f** is irrelevant, and choices **h** and **j** are related but off topic.

59. c. All of the topics are related to the Industrial Revolution, but the essay focuses on mass production, so this topic would be the most logical to add.

60. g. Paragraph 2 introduces the Industrial Revolution, and paragraph 1 begins to describe it. The two paragraphs should be reversed.

Passage V—Science Fiction

61. d. This provides the proper separation of the modifying clause from the subject of the sentence.

62. h. This choice corrects the sentence fragment and keeps the *not only . . . but also* construction intact.

63. b. Choice **a** incorrectly uses *being*; choice **c** includes superfluous commas and uses the past tense, though the genre still exists; and choice **d** sets off what is important in the sentence—the name of the new genre—in parentheses, indicating that it is *not* important.

64. g. This provides a clear statement that agrees with the active tense *explores*.

65. c. This avoids reusing the word *works* and provides proper punctuation.

66. h. This agrees with the earlier verbs *traveled*, *created*, and *made*.

67. d. This correctly sets off the transitional phrase with commas.

68. j. This choice presents the correct word order, placing what was churned out immediately after the verb, and then the prepositional phrase after that to show who received those stories.

69. c. This is the most strongly worded choice and is consistent with the tone of the essay.

70. h. The correct form is the present tense and is in agreement with *much*.

71. a. The usage of this form of the verb *to lie* is correct as is.

72. h. The possessive pronoun should be used here.

73. a. This version is correct as it stands. The verb *are* agrees with *characters*, and the word order is appropriate.

74. f. This is relevant and would show the current direction of the genre. It is appropriate because the paragraph is about looking ahead to the future of science fiction and humankind. The quotation from *Frankenstein* might or might not be relevant; a summary of Shelley's life would be out of place in this paragraph; and the author is unable to answer the questions in the paragraph—he or she can only make an educated guess.

75. b. The introduction is too general to include a focus on the plot of *Frankenstein*, and because this novel marked the beginning of science fiction, it is entitled to its own paragraph. It would be out of chronological order to place it anywhere after that.

ACT Mathematics Practice Test 1

1. d. First distribute the negative sign outside the parentheses, which changes the d to a positive value. Then distribute the a to all three terms.

2. h. To average 88 for five tests, one would need an aggregate score of 440. The first four tests total 345, meaning that a 95 would be necessary on the final test.

3. c. The separation between 23 and 62 is 39, and adding two numbers in between will create three gaps, so each gap must be a space of 13.

4. j. There is no need to find a common denominator; simply add the distances from Monday and Wednesday (exactly 8), and then add Tuesday's distance to that total.

5. b. The proper order of operations is to add the values inside the parentheses, square that value, and then multiply it by 3.

6. h. Simple division shows that Company X sells its pens for 62 cents each, and Company Y sells them for 58 cents each (4 cents less).

7. c. The perimeter of a rectangle is found by adding two widths and two lengths. Divide by 3 to convert length to yards.

8. k. Use the Pythagorean theorem to find the missing value, in this case the short leg of the triangle.

9. a. Use basic algebra and first subtract $7x$ from both sides, then subtract 24 from both sides.

10. g. Simple division shows that Mr. Johnson earns $115 per day, or $25 more than his substitute, which will be $125 saved over a five-day period.

11. c. First solve for x, which must equal 5, and then plug it into the equation. Following proper order of operations, first square 5, then add it to 5, and then multiply the sum by 2.

12. f. Probability is found by dividing the desired outcome by all possible outcomes. In this case, the desired outcome is "not blue," which has 28 possibilities, and the total number of outcomes (marbles) is 44. Then reduce the fraction.

13. e. Proper technique for squaring the expression—first times first, outside times outside, inside times inside, and last times last (FOIL)—yields the correct answer.

14. g. The two values are separated by 32, which means the midpoint must be 16 from each one.

15. c. The chart indicates there are three period 1 classes, with enrollments of 23, 26, and 29, and thus an average of 26.

16. j. Period 4 has only one class, with an enrollment of 21.

17. d. Period 1 has 78 students, period 2 has 51 students, period 3 has 56 students, and period 5 has 49 students. Only period 4 has fewer than 46 students.

18. k. First plug in the value for the radius, then cube that value, and then multiply by both π (3.14) and $\frac{4}{3}$.

19. d. To find the number of combinations created by a series of options, in this case types of clothing, multiply the numbers. So the options for Celia are $5 \times 4 \times 3 \times 3$, or 180.

20. h. The total cost of the three packages would be $28.80, and the total number of pairs of socks would be $9 + 1$, or 10. Then use simple division to find the cost per pair of socks.

21. e. The two equations have different slopes, −2 and 2, and therefore are two distinct lines that intersect in one point.

22. k. By factoring out an x, you get $x(x - 24) = 0$, and plugging 24 in for x yields an answer of 0.

23. e. Set up a proportion of $\frac{300,000}{1.5} = \frac{x}{6.5}$, cross multiply, and solve for x.

24. f. The tangent of an angle is found by dividing the opposite side by the adjacent side.

25. d. Using the Pythagorean theorem, the diagonal is the square root of $32^2 + 46^2$, or 56 yards. Multiply by 3 to convert to feet.

26. j. Set each of the two factors, $(x + a)$ and $(x - a)$, equal to 0, and solve for x.

27. d. Find the difference between the coordinates in each of the moves, and add the four differences together.

28. f. Adding −14 to both the top and the bottom of the fraction creates a new fraction of $\frac{-6}{-1}$, or +6.

29. c. $\log_x 64 = 3$ means $x^3 = 64$, so $x = 4$.

30. j. The distance from the center meets the chord at a right angle at its midpoint. You then use the Pythagorean theorem to solve for the radius, which is 18.86, or 18.9 to the nearest tenth.

31. b. Simply plug 0.83 in for L, and then solve for F by first subtracting 0.03 from both sides and then dividing both sides by $\frac{2}{3}$.

32. j. Replace y in the second equation with $(x + 2)$, and then subtract that quantity from x. The result is −2, which is then raised to the fifth power.

33. a. The distance between E and B (east to west) along $\overline{BC}$ is 12, so half of that is 6. Add that to the distance between E and C (west to east) along $\overline{ED}$, which is 10, and the statue is 16 west of C. The distance between B and E (north to south) along $\overline{BA}$ is 8. Half of that is 4, so the statue is 4 south of C.

34. h. If the area of the square is 256, then the length of one side is the square root of 256, or 16, and the radius of the circle is half of the length of the side of the square.

35. b. By setting the two equations equal to each other and solving for x, you find $x = 4$. Then plug that value in for x in either equation and solve for y.

36. j. Set up a proportion, where $\frac{16}{20} = \frac{28}{x}$. Cross multiply, so $16x = 20 \times 28$, and divide both sides by 16.

37. d. Using basic algebra to solve, subtract 25 from both sides, divide both sides by −6, and reverse the inequality sign when dividing by a negative number.

38. h. Since the square root of 49 is 7, the value in the square root sign must be greater than 49, and x must be greater than 50.

39. b. Using the distance formula, find the square of the difference in the y coordinates (-2 minus 8, or -10, which squared is 100) and the square of the difference of the x coordinates (6 minus -4, or 10, which squared is 100), and add them (200). Then take the square root of 200.

40. g. Since the angles of a triangle add up to 180°, $\angle ABE$ must equal 50°. Therefore, by vertical angles, $\angle CBF$ is also 50°. Repeat this process to solve for $\angle BCF$ and $\angle DCG$, and then for $\angle G$.

41. c. To solve, multiply 186,000 by 60 to find the distance per minute, then by 180 to find the distance in 3 hours. Convert the answer to scientific notation.

42. j. If the ratio of the diameter of the two circles is 6:10, then the radius is 3:5. The formula for the area of a circle is πr^2, so the ratio of the areas is $9\pi:25\pi$, or 9:25.

43. e. Working systematically, connect each vertex to every other, not including the sides of the octagon.

44. j. To start, let $0.80x = 260$. Then multiply the solution by 116%, or 1.16, to find the answer.

45. b. Multiply 504 times $\frac{3}{8}$ (0.375), or divide 504 by 8 and then multiply that answer by 3. Then take this answer and multiply by $\frac{2}{3}$, or divide it by 3 and then multiply by 2.

46. k. Try each answer. The first row contains one x, the first two rows contain four x's, the first three rows contain nine x's, the first four rows contain 16 x's, so the rule is that n rows contain n^2 x's.

47. c. $\sin(C) = \frac{\text{opp}}{\text{hyp}}$, or $\frac{c}{a}$, and $\tan(B) = \frac{\text{opp}}{\text{adj}}$, or $\frac{b}{c}$. Then multiply $\frac{c}{a}$ times $\frac{b}{c}$.

48. k. First, convert the dimensions of space to be covered to inches, and then find the area (10,368 inches²). Then find the area of each brick (12 inches²), and divide into the total area. Check to confirm that the bricks will fit evenly into the space, which they will, since both of the dimensions (in inches) are divisible by both 2 and 6.

49. d. Multiply the numerator times the numerator and the denominator times the denominator. If you properly FOIL the denominator, the answer is $\frac{i+1}{i^2-1}$. Then convert i^2 to -1.

50. h. Since the circle is tangent to the indicated points, its center must be at $(-5,5)$, and it must have a radius of 5. These are the values (h,k) and r in the equation of a circle. Then plug these values into the equation for a circle, which is $(x-h)^2 + (y-k)^2 = r^2$.

51. d. Convert the y values to a common value of 40 by multiplying the first ratio by 8 and the second ratio by 5. The x value becomes 32, and the z value becomes 45.

52. h. An average is found by dividing the total amount (in this case, years) by the total number (in this case, people). Multiply the number of men by their average age, the number of women (found by subtracting 190 from 420) by their average age, add these two values together, and divide by 420.

53. d. The period is found by measuring the distance the graph takes to complete one full curve from $y = -1$ to $y = -1$. This full curve takes place over a distance of 2π.

54. k. The linear relationship of the corresponding parts of the similar prisms is 10:15, or 2:3. Therefore, the cubic relationship of the prisms must be $(2:3)^3$, or 8:27. Set up a proportion of $8:27 = 4,000:x$, and solve.

55. **b.** If $(x - 3)$ is a factor of $3x^2 - 11x + n$, then $(3x - a)$ must be a factor as well, where $(-3)(-a) = n$, and $(-3)(3) + (-a)(1) = -11$. Solve for a in the second equation, and $a = -2$, and then plug that value into the first equation to solve for n.

56. **k.** Plug $(x + k)$ into the function $2x^2 + 2$ in place of x, then square $(x + k)$, distribute the 2, and then add 2.

57. **a.** Sin is equal to $\frac{\text{opp}}{\text{hyp}}$ or $\frac{y}{\text{hyp}}$; therefore the y-value is -4, and the hypotenuse is 5. This indicates a 3–4–5 right triangle, so the missing side is 3. Since the angle must be less than $\frac{3\pi}{2}$, it must be located in the third quadrant of a standard (x,y) coordinate plane, and x must therefore be -3. Cos is $\frac{\text{adj}}{\text{hyp}}$, or $\frac{x}{\text{hyp}}$.

58. **j.** While this seems too complicated to be a linear graph, it is. Factor out an x in the numerator, and you are left with $3x + 3$; the numerator and denominator x's cancel out. However, the graph is undefined at $x = 0$, so there is a hole in the graph at that value.

59. **e.** First, use algebra to solve for C in terms of A in the first equation. Then replace C in the second equation with the value found in the first equation. Now, again use basic algebra to solve for A in the second equation.

60. **h.** First, find 15% of $120 and subtract that from $120, leaving $102. Next, subtract 5% of $102 from $102, leaving $96.90. Now find the difference between this number and $100, and determine what percent of $100 it is.

ACT Reading Practice Test 1
Passage I—Prose Fiction

1. **c.** The best way to handle this question is to go through the possible answers and eliminate the incorrect ones. The first line states that there *was nothing of the giant* in Babbitt, which eliminates choice **d**, because he was not tall. Lines 15–16 say *He was not fat*, but he was *well fed*, which eliminates his being overweight (choice **a**) or skinny (choice **b**).

2. **h.** The passage lists a number of occupations that Babbitt does not perform, but line 10 says what he does do: sell houses.

3. **a.** The reader knows that, on this particular day, Babbitt is having a difficult time getting out of bed. Does this mean he is lazy? It could, but later we learn that the poker game he went to the night before may have something to do with his prolonged slumber. We are never given any indication that Babbitt works hard at his job, but lines 9–11 say *he was nimble in the calling of selling houses for more than people could afford to pay*; in other words, he was good at his job, but did not necessarily work hard at it.

4. **j.** This question asks that you infer something about the relationship that Babbitt has with his wife by paying attention to how they interact. We know that they do not openly dislike each other because Babbitt's wife tries to wake him by cheerfully calling him *Georgie boy* (lines 90–91). But in the same lines Babbitt refers to this cheerfulness as detestable to him, so we know his feelings are not romantic and passionate, but that Babbitt has strong feelings about his wife (thus eliminating choices **f** and **h** as possible answers). Lines 78–79 come the closest to stating Babbitt's feeling toward his wife (and family), saying that he disliked them and disliked himself for feeling that way.

5. d. The biggest clue that the meaning of *patina* is color is the fact that the word *gold* immediately precedes it.

6. g. There are many things that wake Babbitt from his sleep, but the first one can be found on line 39. We know that the noise of the milk truck wakes him because the next line is *Babbitt moaned; turned over; struggled back toward his dream.* All the other options may have woken Babbitt, but choice **g** is the first and therefore correct.

7. a. It is perfectly clear that Babbitt wishes to return to sleep, but this fact has nothing to do with his blanket. His blanket may indeed offer him warmth and comfort, but the passage does not say as much, and we know that Babbitt bought this blanket for a camping trip he never took.

8. f. When the alarm goes off, what keeps Babbitt in bed is stated in lines 77–78: He *detested the grind of the real-estate business.* This makes it clear that Babbitt dislikes his job. Although the next line refers to his dislike of his family, we cannot assume that he has had a fight with his wife (she seems cheerful enough when she calls him *Georgie boy* to wake him). We also learn in the lines immediately following that he went to a poker game where he drank beer and smoked cigars, so he may have a hangover.

9. b. Lines 28–29 give the best clues as to the meaning of Babbitt's dream. The fairy sees Babbitt as nobody else sees: a *gallant youth,* or young. He also escapes from his wife and friends who attempt to follow him in this dream (he is free).

10. f. This question asks you to find a more succinct way of stating lines 63–66, which basically say that, as a boy, Babbitt was more interested in life. Even if you do not know what the word *credulous* means here, you can still assume that it is something different from the way he is now from the way the sentence is phrased. We know that now he is not interested in life, or *each new day.*

Passage II—Humanities

11. d. Although it is true that Leonardo's father would punish him if he caught Leonardo skipping school (choice **a**), this is not what the question asked. You also know from the text that Leonardo continued to skip school (choice **b**), but whether his grandmother knew this would happen is irrelevant. The reason that his grandmother did not punish him can be found in line 94, where she says that she loves to see him happy.

12. f. Because the question refers only to the last paragraph, any opinions that Leonardo's teachers may have elsewhere in the text do not apply. It is true that Leonardo did not get along with the other students (choice **j**), but nowhere does it say that his teachers had any opinion on this. This is a basic inference question in that the last paragraph states that some of Leonardo's teachers dreaded his questions because they *were sometimes more than they could answer* (line 125). From this statement, you can infer that they were afraid they would not have the knowledge to answer his questions and therefore afraid he might ask questions they could not answer.

13. d. The text mentions many people as having something to do with raising Leonardo, but lines 34–35 state *It was the old grandmother, Mona Lena, who brought Leonardo up.*

14. j. Although you may already know that Leonardo da Vinci was a talented artist, this is not mentioned in the text, which means that choice **h** is incorrect. Lines 52–54 show that Leonardo spent the time he skipped school studying nature, which was what interested him.

15. a. When Leonardo was punished for skipping school (lines 104–106), his father locked him in the cupboard, and instead of protesting, he soon found himself lost in his own thoughts. This is how the reader knows that he did not mind being alone; therefore statement I is true. Lines 68–72 show that Leonardo was fascinated by birds and the *secret power in their wings*, which makes statement II correct. Lines 43–44 describe Leonardo as not enjoying the company of other boys, from which one can reasonably infer he was not popular, which makes statement III incorrect.

16. h. The only date mentioned specifically in the passage is 1452, which was the year of Leonardo's birth. Lines 41–42 state he was seven years old when he was sent to school, which would make the year 1459.

17. a. This question asks you to distill a lot of information about Leonardo as a boy and find the one fact that is incorrect. In lines 48–49, it says that Leonardo found Latin grammar *a terrible task*, which makes choice **a** correct.

18. j. The lines referred to in the question describe an aspect of Leonardo's personality, but the question asks you to sum up exactly what that aspect is. The line says *he loved the flowers*, but he still pulled off their petals because he wanted to understand *how each was joined*. Therefore, his desire to learn how things worked led him to destructive acts.

19. b. Lines 111–119 describe Leonardo's reaction to his punishment. Specifically, it says that he did not kick the door (was not angry), and that he only briefly felt it was unfair to be punished. The best way to describe his reaction was that he accepted it and occupied himself with his own thoughts, or resigned himself to his punishment.

20. h. We know that many of the answers in this question are, in fact, true statements, but they do not answer the question. He may have known that his grandmother would not punish him, but nowhere does it say this had anything to do with his motivation to skip school. The answer can be found in lines 48–49, which state that Latin grammar *was a terrible task* and continues to state that he therefore skipped school.

Passage III—Social Studies

21. a. The first part of the paragraph explains how the rich were unaware of the plight of the poor and therefore did not care: *"one half of the world does not know how the other half lives." That was true then* (lines 1–3). But the paragraph goes on to say that it was only when conditions became so bad that it became *no longer an easy thing* for the rich to ignore the poor (lines 9–10). Although choices **b**, **c**, and **d** may be correct statements, they do not summarize the main idea of the whole paragraph.

22. j. The meaning of this phrase can be found throughout the passage, but because the passage is from *How the Other Half Lives* and it is about the conditions of the poor, one can reasonably assume it refers to the poor.

23. b. For this question it is important to sift through a lot of details to get to the main point of the statement, which is that a majority of crimes are committed by those *whose homes had ceased to afford what are regarded as ordinary wholesome influences of home and family* (lines 36–39). In other words, without good housing, there can be a lack of good family values, which in turn leads to increased crime.

24. j. There are a lot of numbers mentioned in the passage, but the number specifically attributed to the number of people living in tenement housing can be found in lines 54–55, more than *twelve hundred thousand persons call them home*, or 1,200,000.

25. c. Because the secretary's statement refers to the living environment of the poor, it can be assumed that the word *domiciles* can be defined as living places.

26. h. The word *line* refers to the sentence immediately preceding the one in the question: *the boundary line of the Other Half lies through the tenements* (lines 44–46). It is important to find and understand this reference before you can make sense of the question. Here the line refers to those living in tenements. Therefore, if the line no longer divides the population evenly, more than half live in poverty.

27. a. The only reference in the entire passage to an escape from poverty can be found in lines 56–57, *The one way out—rapid transit to the suburbs—has brought no relief*. But because it *has brought no relief* and the statement immediately following reads *we know now that there is no way out*, you can infer that the author believes there is no way to escape poverty.

28. h. The statement in lines 75–76, *the nurseries of poverty and crime that fill our jails and courts* make statement I true, and immediately prior to that statement it says the tenements *are the hotbeds of the epidemics that carry death to rich and poor alike* (lines 73–75), making statement II true. There is no reference to rich living in tenements in the passage; therefore, statement III is incorrect.

29. b. The easiest way to answer this type of question, which really refers to the entire passage, is to eliminate answers you know are wrong. The author makes no statement that crime is overreported, nor does he say how criminals should be punished, or whether they should be punished at all; therefore, choices **a**, **c**, and **d** are incorrect. Throughout the passage, crime is blamed on life in the tenements.

30. f. The first clue that the author is not being objective is that he uses words like *greed and reckless selfishness* (lines 19–20). And because the author says that poverty is inescapable in lines 57–58 (*We know now that there is no way out*), one can only conclude that his opinion is sympathetic.

Passage IV—Natural Science

31. b. Lines 11–12 state that every year the arctic tern migrates *from the Arctic to the Antarctic with subsequent return.*

32. g. Although the body structure of birds is well suited to migration, it is not the reason they migrate. Lines 17–20 state that this makes *it possible for birds to seek out environments most favorable to their needs at different times of the year.*

33. a. Lines 37–38 state that when the first migrating geese were spotted, the fur traders and Native Americans *all joined in jubilant welcome to the newcomers*. Therefore, it can be inferred that their relationship was a friendly one.

34. f. There are many groups mentioned in association with the migrating birds, but lines 68–69 (*bird investigations are made by the U.S. Fish and Wildlife Service*) is where you will find the answer to this question.

35. c. Lines 87–90 explain that the role of the Biological Survey was to collect data on migrating birds before the Fish and Wildlife Service was established.

36. j. Lines 43–47 state that birds ate the insects that were troublesome to farmers; therefore, the insects were not threats to the birds.

37. c. The preceding lines explain how the arrival of the birds signaled a change in season and the start of celebrations; therefore, even if you do not know the meaning of the word, you can assume that the *imminence of spring* means that spring was soon to arrive.

38. h. Although the European fur traders appreciated the migrating birds, they did so because the birds indicated the arrival of spring. Fur traders were also around before the increasing population of North America referred to in lines 38–39.

39. a. Immediately preceding the statement that *We soon realized that our migratory bird resource was an international legacy* (lines 50–52) is a list of reasons people appreciated the migrating birds, and it does not include their being a source of food.

40. j. If you read only the beginning of the next to last paragraph, you might think the answer is choice **g**, but if you continue reading, you learn that many others help the Fish and Wildlife Service.

ACT Science Practice Test 1
Passage I—Data Representation

1. d. The force of gravity produces an acceleration of -9.8 m/s^2. This means that the velocity must change by -49 m/s every 5 seconds because $5 \times -9.8 = -49$. Object 3 begins with an upward velocity of 490 m/s but is reduced by exactly 49 m/s during every 5-second interval shown. None of the other objects consistently experiences a change in velocity of -49 m/s every 5 seconds. Object 1 has a positive change of 51 m/s in the first 5 seconds. Object 2 operates under the influence of gravity alone for 15 seconds but then between seconds 15 and 20 has a positive change in velocity of 1 m/s.

2. g. For at least part of the period shown, objects 1, 2, and 3 experience a change in velocity of -49 m/s every 5 seconds, which is the magnitude of change gravity causes. For object 1, this occurs between seconds 35 and 45. For object 2 this occurs from second 0 to second 15 and also from second 35 to second 45. Object 3 experiences a reduction of 49 m/s in velocity every 5 seconds from second 0 to second 45.

3. d. Constant acceleration means that the change in velocity for the period specified from second 5 to second 25 must always be the same. This is true for object 1 and object 3. Object 1 has an upward (positive) change in velocity of 51 m/s every 5 seconds for the period being looked at. Object 3 has been shown to be operating only under the influence of gravity, producing a change in velocity of -49 m/s every 5 seconds for the entire period, including the one asked about here. Object 2 has a constant change of -49 m/s only for second 5 to second 15. It then changes to $+1$ m/s for second 15 to 35, so the change is not constant for the entire period specified.

4. f. In Table 1, downward velocity is represented by negative numbers, and upward velocity is represented by positive numbers. Therefore, everything below the zero line in Figure 1 represents downward motion, and everything above represents upward motion, regardless of which direction the line on the graph is headed. When the graph line crosses 0, this indicates that the direction of the object changes at that point.

A positive change in the direction of the line on the graph indicates a positive change in velocity. If the line is below zero, this means that the object moves downward but at decreasing speed. If the line is moving upward above zero, this means the object is moving upward at an increasing speed.

Only answer choices **f** and **g** state that the object is traveling downward at second 0. This is correct because the graph line begins at –100. Figure 1 indicates that the object reaches zero velocity at approximately 10 seconds. Changing from negative to positive velocity means it changes direction from downward to upward. Table 1 indicates that that point is a bit before second 10 since it is already traveling upward at 2 m/s by second 10. We can calculate that the change in direction occurs at 9.8 seconds. Answer choice **f** correctly states that the object's speed decreases after second 30 as indicated by the downward slope in Figure 1 and the decreasing numbers in Table 1. Answer choice **c**, which is correct until that point, incorrectly states that the object's speed continues to increase.

5. c. For the period from second 15 to second 35, object 2 has a positive change in velocity of 1 m/s every 5 seconds. An upward force slightly greater than the force of gravity is required to produce this small upward acceleration. Answer choice **c**, which points to a counterforce capable of producing a 10 m/s^2 upward acceleration against gravity's –9.8 m/s^2, is the only one that could be even approximately correct, so it is the *best* answer. To calculate the answer precisely, first divide the results reported for each 5 seconds by 5 to convert them to 1-second-interval results. This shows that instead of the 9.8 m/s^2 downward acceleration due to gravity, object 2 experienced +0.2 m/s^2 upward acceleration due to the unknown force. Add 0.2 m/s^2 to 9.8 m/s^2 to calculate the correct acceleration level, which is 10 m/s^2.

Answer choice **a** is incorrect because object 2 has not leveled off. Its *velocity* has nearly leveled off, but it is still falling at nearly 100 m/s. Answer choice **d** is incorrect because the changes in gravitational force due to even the most extreme terrain changes are far too small to produce the result described.

Passage II—Research Summary

6. h. The reaction involves one molecule of each substance. Since a mole of any substance has the same number of particles as a mole of any other substance, this reaction requires the same number of moles of each.

7. b. Multiply 0.1, the desired concentration in moles per liter, by 36.5, the mole mass of HCl, by 0.02 liters of solution.

8. j. The tables show only the pH levels for every 0.25 ml of titrant added. pH 7.0 does not occur at any of those precise points. Answer choice **j** is based on estimating the actual titrant volume at the point pH 7.0 is reached. Answer choice **f** is less accurate than choice **j** because it gives the volume of the titrant only to the closest 0.25 ml shown on the table. Answer choices **g** and **h** give the results in the wrong order.

9. a. The table shows that at least 30 ml were added in each trial. We do not know if the trial ended at that point.

10. h. NaCl is a product of the reaction. The NaOH titrant continued to be added after the reaction was complete, so NaOH will also be present. Answer choice **j** is incorrect because this reaction does not produce NH_3, and there is no indication of NH_3 being present or being introduced into the solution.

11. b. Multiplying the concentration of the titrant, given in moles/liter (M), by the number of liters used ($c \times v$) gives us the number of moles of NaOH in the titrant that were used in the reaction. This is also the number of moles of HCl used, because one molecule of HCl reacts with one molecule of NaOH. The mass of HCl is determined by multiplying the number of moles by the mole mass, which is 36.5 grams. The final calculation is 0.2 moles/liter $\times$ v liters $\times$ 36.5 grams/mole.

Passage III—Conflicting Viewpoints

12. h. The highest concentration, indicated by the highest point of the distribution curve, is at about 153 cm for country A.

13. a. The highest concentration, indicated by the highest point of the distribution curve, is at about 174 cm for country B.

14. h. Answer choice **h** provides the most complete description of the similarities and differences. Answer choice **f** ignores the clear similarities between the curves, and choice **j** ignores the differences. Answer choice **g** misidentifies the difference in shape as a difference in position.

15. b. Table 1 and Figure 2 accurately describe the time comparison shown, which consists of data absent from Figure 1. Answer choice **a** is incorrect because Figure 1 presents no data on change over time. Answer choice **c** is not supported by Figure 2. Answer choice **d** is incorrect because it is also supported by Figure 1.

16. f. It reports what the chart indicates. Answer choice **g** is correct for most of the period shown but not for its entirety. For the period 1970 to 2010, country B's height increase is less than both the global increase and country A's increase.

17. d. From 1810 and 1830 and again from 1890 to 1930, country A's typical adult height was reduced. Answer choice **a** is incorrect because there was no point shown at which country B's adult height decreased. Answer choice **b** is incorrect because country A's overall progress in height has been interrupted by periods of decline. Answer choice **c** is incorrect because country A's adult height actually increased less than one-third as much as country B's.

18. h. The right and left extremes of the curve, where the population distribution approaches zero, is nearly identical in each of the curves. Answer choices **f**, **g**, and **j** are not supported by the data given.

Passage IV—Research Summary

19. b. Translated from scientific notation to standard notation, Table 2 looks like this:

TABLE 2 WAVELENGTHS (λ) IN NANOMETERS OF ELECTROMAGNETIC RADIATION		
TYPE OF RADIATION	**FROM λ**	**TO λ**
gamma ray	?	0.001
x-ray	0.001	1.000
ultraviolet	1.000	400.000
visible light	400.000	700.000
infrared	700.000	10,000.000
microwave	10,000.000	10,000,000.000
radio	10,000,000.000	1,000,000,000,000.000

The SIM covers part of the ultraviolet, visible light, and infrared spectrums. SOLSTICE A and B each cover part of the ultraviolet range. XPS begins at 1 nm, which is the upper end of the x-ray range, and extends into the ultraviolet range.

20. f. The highest level is 1,361.2513 W/m², and the lowest is 1,361.0329 W/m². The difference is 0.2184 W/m². Answer choice **g** is in the wrong units, and answer choices **h** and **j** are not even approximately correct.

21. d. The proportion is approximately 2E − 1 divided by 1.6E + 3. That would have to be approximately $(\frac{2}{1.6}) \times 10^{-4}$. Answer choice **d** is the only answer that approximates that.

22. h. The wavelength in nanometers (nm) is shown on the x-axis, and the level of solar irradiance is shown on the y-axis. The highest point is approximately 2.1 W/m²/nm (watts/meter²/nanometers). This occurs at a wavelength somewhat less than 500 nm.

23. b. TSI is measured in watts/meter², which is a measure of power. SSI is a measure of the same power separated into different wavelength ranges. The definition of SSI given in answer choice **a** has no definite meaning. Answer choices **c** and **d** refer to solar energy, but TSI and SSI are magnitudes of power, not energy.

24. g. The largest area under the SSI curve occurs between approximately 400 and 700 nm, which is the visible light range.

25. c. According to Figure 3, almost all of the irradiance is delivered in the visible light, infrared, and ultraviolet spectra. The magnitude of irradiance delivered by the other types does not even appear clearly on the graph. The ultraviolet irradiance is defined by the small sliver of area under the curve between 0 and 400 nm. The infrared area from 700 to 2,500 nm is significantly larger.

Passage V—Research Summary

26. g. Answer choice **g** presents evidence of exactly what is being looked for: a change in the nature of the bacterial population. Answer choice **f** is not correct because we do not know why no culture was made on day 19. Answer choices **h** and **j** are conjectures for which there is no strong evidence presented in the table.

27. d. Answer choice **d** indicates a fact relevant to the purpose of the study. The cultures taken directly from the patient showed first type I, then type IV without type I, and then type VI without either type I or type IV. Type I dominated the results of the inoculated mouse A, but it did not appear in the day 15 or 17 samples. It then reappeared on day 19, along with type VI, but reappeared alone on day 21 even though the culture from the patient grew no colonies. Answer choice **a** is not correct. On days 4 and 6, mouse B was infected with types V and VI pneumococci, without any evidence that these were in the sample from the patient. On day 8 mouse A was infected with type VI, which did not appear in the patient until day 17. Answer choice **b** is not correct because that day's sample infected mouse A with both type I and type VI, and we are not even sure this patient, let alone most patients, was cured at the point of type VI's appearance. Answer choice **c** draws a conclusion based on how the bacterial types were numbered, rather than on the observed operation of the bacteria.

28. j. The consistency of this result is a strong indicator that the colonies do change their characteristics in a systematic way. Answer choices **f** and **h** indicate only that some strains are more virulent than others, but that is to be expected. Answer choice **g** incorrectly claims that all of the samples changed, but the surviving mice were not tested.

29. b. The data here do not provide a solid theory concerning the cause of the changes observed, but there are clear patterns in the differences between the behavior of strains in culture, in the inoculated mice, and under the influence of type I serum that point to the possibility of expanding understanding of the phenomena. Answer choices **a** and **c** are not supported by the data. Answer choice **d** is inaccurate. There are indications of nonrandom ordering, particularly in experiment 3.

30. g. It is important to be able to look at the data presented and draw conclusions from what seems to make sense based on other inputs. The idea that one stable form of bacteria is at work from the beginning to the end of this course of illness is refuted. Answer choice **f** is refuted by the data. Answer choice **h** is not supported. The original type I strain seems to have been weakened or transformed to others, but there is no evidence that it destroyed itself. There is also nothing to support answer choice **j**.

Passage VI—Data Representation

31. c. Always make sure you understand what each direction on the chart, table, or graph means. In this case, high $\delta^{18}O$ means cold climate and glaciation. The highest $\delta^{18}O$ level shown is about 2.5, which occurred at about −0.65 million years.

32. j. High sea levels occur when glaciers melt, filling the oceans with low $\delta^{18}O$ water. The lowest $\delta^{18}O$ level shown is about 2.8, which occurred at about −1.85 million years. Answer choice **h** is incorrect. The peak at 1.93 million years ago would indicate low seas, rich in $\delta^{18}O$.

33. a. Periods of glacial buildup are marked by peaks in $\delta^{18}O$. There were three between -0.25 and -0.50 million years.

34. j. Glacial melts dilute the high $\delta^{18}O$ seawater with ^{16}O-rich glacial water, and are marked by low $\delta^{18}O$ seawater. Between -1.25 and -1.50 million years there are four $\delta^{18}O$ troughs.

35. b. Temperature swing is indicated by the difference between the highest and lowest $\delta^{18}O$ levels. From -0.90 to -1.75 million years, $\delta^{18}O$ rose to 1 and no higher and then dropped to -1 and no lower, almost like clockwork. That is a range of only 2 between high and low. For the rest of the span of time shown, the $\delta^{18}O$ high levels were generally above 1 and as high as 2.7. The lows were as low as -2.7.

Passage VII—Data Representation

36. j. The tables show that the total charge for each substance is zero. Due to their electrical charge, ions tend to move away from like-charged ions and toward oppositely charged ions to form electrically neutral compounds.

37. a. Electrons are negatively charged, so removing one produces a charge of $+1$.

38. g. Sodium has an atomic number 11, and, therefore, neutral sodium has 11 electrons. The first ring has two and the second has eight. That leaves one electron to form the third ring. That electron is given up when sodium is ionized, leaving the first two rings.

39. d. Chlorine needs just one electron to complete its outer ring of eight, and hydrogen is able to donate it. Ionic bonds are formed between atoms needing electrons to fill a nearly complete outer ring (positive valence) and those needing to get rid of atoms in a nearly empty outer ring (negative valence). It might seem that an atom like chlorine could just as easily get rid of all seven of its outer ring electrons as acquire one, but that kind of reaction is very rare.

40. h. The key in ionic bonding is not the number of atoms combined, but the number of electrons required or available to produce complete outer electron rings. Chlorine needs only one and sodium has one extra to provide. Oxygen needs two, but hydrogen only has one per atom to provide. That is why water has two hydrogen atoms to donate electrons and salt has only one sodium atom.

ACT Writing Practice Test 1
Sample "Score 6" Essay

Imagine your parents or grandparents as teenagers: Do you think they were running around vandalizing movie theaters and ripping off ice cream parlors? Decades ago, our parents and grandparents enjoyed parties and late-night diner runs as much as we do today. They were not out to scandalize their communities; they simply wanted to enjoy life. Yet now, these same freedom-loving people want to suppress our freedom by enforcing a law that would prevent any teen from attending parties or working late to earn a little extra money. A curfew for minors under the age of 18 not only will have little effect on crime rates, but also will wrongly restrict the social life and employability of many teens.

According to supporters of this legislation, enforcing a curfew on children under the age of 18 would "reduce community problems such as violence, graffiti, and drugs." There are many problems with this statement. For instance, violence does not take place in a community only at night. The events at Columbine High School in 1999 proved that violence can take place in broad daylight, and that the root of this violence can sometimes begin at home. While graffiti is ugly and destructive, it is not done only in "alleys, parks, or playgrounds." There are scribblings and drawings on many of the desks and textbooks in my school, yet they were done in the daylight and are just as destructive. Similarly, drugs are a problem in every community and do not discriminate against any type of student or time of day. It is unfortunate but true that a student can sell drugs just as easily in school as he or she can in a park at midnight. What this law is doing is not eliminating these problems, but simply shifting them to different public places during different times of the day.

One argument of those opposed to this legislation is that "curfews stereotype minors by presupposing that citizens under the age of 18 are the only people who commit crimes." This is true. While many community problems can be attributed to minors,

the same problems can also be attributed to adults. This fact is supported by the large number of men and women over the age of 18 in our prison system. The community may save money by keeping a few young vandals or drug dealers out of juvenile prison, but they will certainly continue to pay for those mature men and women who have chosen to support themselves by selling drugs to minors in the first place. It should also be noted that while a curfew may keep minors under the age of 18 from loitering and causing destruction, there is a group of young adults between the ages of 18 and 21 that cannot legally drink alcohol but still do. The curfew will do nothing to stop the destruction of property or even lives that may result from this action.

A curfew like this would only restrict the positive outlets many teenagers have, such as healthy interaction with their peers and work. Many teens have long days filled with school and after-school activities such as sports or clubs, chores, and homework. Most of my friends do not even have a free moment until about 9:00 or 10:00 p.m. It is then that many teens go out and see a movie or visit with friends. This curfew would all but prevent most teens from being able to socialize with other teens in person. Teenagers would be relegated to online and phone friendships. Another problem with this curfew is that it would prevent many teens from having a job, which many teens need. Many jobs for teenagers are at fast-food restaurants where the late-night shifts are the only ones teens are able to get because they are in school all day long. This curfew would make it very difficult for teens to obtain jobs and earn money for college. Social interaction and work are both healthy experiences that make teens into good, productive community members. This curfew would prevent that.

Obviously, by encouraging this legislation, the supporters of this curfew feel they are protecting their rights as well as those of the community. The minors of previous generations have grown up to be mature and responsible citizens with legitimate concerns about youth and community. While there may be more evils lurking in society than in decades past, these people must realize that putting a time limit on problems cannot solve them. Perhaps instead of trying to contain them, their time would be better spent finding the root of the crime, violence, and drug problems that are rampant in our society today. By working these troubles out instead of locking them in, it is possible that both adults and minors may work together to make our community a better place.

Critique

This essay shows an excellent and insightful understanding of the prompt. It clearly addresses the prompt. The student creates a clear and creative opening and closing, and the point of the essay is clear: the student disagrees with the curfew. The student maintains the focus of the paper by using well-developed paragraphs, as in paragraph 2, where the student states that *There are many problems with this statement* and gives several examples of these problems (*violence does not take place in a community only at night; drugs are a problem in every community and do not discriminate against any type of student or time of day*). The student uses counterarguments in paragraphs 2 and 3 to logically refute the opposition's opinion. The student uses transitions to smoothly join the paragraphs and examples together (*According to supporters, A curfew like this, Obviously*). The details and examples in the body paragraphs show that the student has carefully planned the argument. In addition to good content and organization, the essay uses strong vocabulary (*scandalize, lurking*). The sentences are varied and interesting, and there are few, if any, grammatical errors.

Sample "Score 5" Essay

To try to reduce juvenile violence and crime, many towns have chosen to enforce curfews on minors under the age of 18. People who support these curfews believe they would lower community problems such as violence, graffiti, and drugs. People who oppose curfews for minors claim that these curfews stereotype minors by assuming that citizens under the age of 18 are the only people who commit crimes. I actually think a curfew would be a good idea. A curfew in our community would make the community a safer, cleaner place and would help build stronger families.

Many teens get into a lot of trouble late at night. They are out late hanging around doing very little that is constructive. Teens who are out past 10:00 p.m. are more likely to drink alcohol, experiment with drugs, and commit crimes such as vandalism and robbery. It's too hard for teens to resist peer pressure when it's late and they are sleep-deprived. A curfew would ensure that most teens are safely in there homes late at night. This way the teens themselves are safer from peer-pressure and other community members are safe from teens who might do terrible things while sleep-deprived or under the influence of drugs and alcohol. It's true that not every crime is committed by a teenager, but if we can eliminate some crime with this curfew, it allows the police to concentrate on other people committing crimes. Either way, crime is reduced and the community us safer.

You may notice that teens are not the neatest people in the world. Most teens rooms are a disaster area. Teens who are permitted to wander aimlessly around the neighborhood tend to create a mess. Even if they are not drinking alcohol, teens gathering in a park or parking lot will tend to leave cans, food wrappers, and sometimes cigarette butts all over the place. Some teens deliberately cause a mess by overturning garbage cans, spray painting on buildings and fences, or breaking windows. Of course, most teens are going to wait until the cover of night to do this, so having a curfew would eliminate these problems. Finally, having a curfew would help build stronger families. Many teens go out and stay out all night long. They never interact with their parents or siblings. They think a night at home will be boring. But a curfew like this would force teens to stay home with their families. At first it may seem like torture, but if parents take advantage of it and create a warm, loving, fun home environment, teens will enjoy staying home and families will become stronger.

Without the curfew, it's too difficult for parents to force their teens to stay at home; it becomes a source of arguments. If there were a curfew, the parents could "blame" it on the law. That way it doesn't feel so much like the parents are harassing the teenager. I think a curfew is a good idea. As a teenager myself I see the trouble teens get into late at night. I have a good time when I stay home with my family and I'd like to see other teens have this experience too.

Critique

This essay shows a good understanding of the prompt and shows some insight into the complexities of this issue. It has a clear thesis statement. The essay contains specific examples to support the thesis, showing how teenagers get into trouble late at night, and contains a counterargument in paragraph 2. Overall, the essay is generally well organized; it uses clear logic with good transitions between ideas. The essay shows good command of written English with attempts at varying sentence structure and attempts at sophisticated vocabulary use that may not be as successful as the model score 6.

Sample "Score 4" Essay

Curfews for minors are a bad idea. Curfews make it illegal for minors to be out in public between the hours of 10 PM and 5 AM. These curfews are a bad idea for several reasons. If a minor is out after 10 PM, it does not mean that this minor is comiting a crime. People over the age of 18 commit crimes too. Sometimes it is necessary for a minor to be out after 10 PM for work and or friends. Also, just because a minor is out after 10 PM doesn't mean he's a bad kid. He shouldn't get in trouble for not really doing anything bad.

The people who want to create a curfew think that it'll create less crime in the community. It might do that with some kids, sure, but it won't stop crime all together. If a kid knows he has to be in by 10 PM he might decide not to write graffiti on the walls or hang out and do drugs, but that doesn't mean that other people won't. Old people commit crimes too. Also, a kid can do drugs after school at a friends house. He doesn't have to do it at night. He can draw or write on the sides of buildings before 10 PM too. In the wintertime, it is dark outside at 7 PM. Kids will do the same things, they will just do them earlier in the day.

Sometimes, too, a minor needs to be out after 10 PM. For example a kid might have a job that doesn't get out until 10 PM and than the kid needs to drive home. If he gets caught driving, he could get in trouble. Or what if he is at a friends house and they are just having a fun time or doing there

homework, not doing anything wrong or anything, but just hanging out. If he forgets what time it is and he leaves a little too late he could get in trouble. That is not fair if he is a good kid.

This brings me to my last point. If a minor gets in trouble for staying out after the curfew it could ruin his reputation. He might be a good student who wants to get a scholership to college. He can't get a scholership with a police record. He was probably out late studying anyway if he's a smart kid. Maybe the people who create these curfews could make some guidelines to follow so that kids could stay out later if there is a special event or for work or studying. That would make it easier to follow and good kids wouldn't get in trouble. In conclusion, I think that curfews are a bad idea. They don't change anything and don't make kids stop doing inapropriate things.

Critique

This essay is an adequate response. In the opening, the student states the main idea of the essay: *Curfews for minors are a bad idea.* The student then briefly outlines the content of the essay. The student continues the focus throughout the essay, staying with the position of disagreeing with the curfew legislation, and develops the essay by attempting to give three distinct reasons. However, paragraphs 3 and 4 are quite similar and possibly could have been discussed in one paragraph. The student does attempt transitions between both sentences and paragraphs (*Sometimes, too; For example; This brings me to my last point*). Although this helps the organization of the essay, it does little to add to the development of the paragraphs, which is weak. Paragraph 2 gives several details to support the student's opinion that curfews do not lessen crime in a community (*Old people commit crimes too; a kid can do drugs after school; Kids will do the same things, they will just do them earlier in the day*). However, paragraph 4 lacks solid details or examples to support the student's idea that a curfew could ruin a minor's reputation. There is only one sketchy detail (*He can't get a scholarship with a police record*). This uneven development hinders the effectiveness of the essay.

The student uses basic vocabulary and sentences, and makes several spelling and grammatical errors (*scholership, just having a fun time or doing there homework, at a friends house*), but they do not interfere with the meaning of the essay.

Sample "Score 3" Essay

I'm getting very tired of adults not trusting teenagers. This curfew idea just adds to the problem. It's a terrible idea.

People who want this curfew think that all teenagers are out to vandelize and cause trouble. That's not true. Some teens are trouble-makers but most aren't. Most teens are good kids. They want to go out at night to have fun, not cause trouble. If we had a curfew teens would probably not be able to have much fun. They would have to go in their houses so early that they wouldn't be able to really do anything.

The curfew might keep the bad teens from doing bad things but it punnishes the good teens at the same time and that's not fair. The curfew would make it pratically immpossible for teens to have jobs and that also wouldn't be fair. Teens can't really get a job at McDonalds if they can't work passed 10:00pm.

The whole problem is that adults don't trust teens and they should. Most teens are fine. Maybe only teens that have been bad should have the curfew instead of everyone.

Critique

This essay shows developing skill. The writer shows a clear understanding of the assignment and takes a clear stand on the issue. The essay lacks adequate development, however. The ideas are very general and somewhat repetitive: *Some teens are trouble-makers but most aren't. Most teens are good kids. They want to go out at night to have fun, not cause trouble.* The essay has an adequate organization but lacks strong transitions between ideas. The essay shows some control of written language but makes some obvious spelling errors (*vandelize, punnishes*) and lacks sophistication.

Sample "Score 2" Essay

A curfew is when there is a time limit on when you can go out. Sometimes a curfew can be good or bad.

Its bad to have a curfew when you want to do something fun like go to a movie or out with friends. But a curfew could be good if it keeps you out of trouble, like if your drinking or something then youd have to stop because of the curfew. People think teens do bad things when their out late at night and sometimes their right, but ususally teens are just hanging out and that's not that bad.

I think a curfew might be a good idea in bad arreas of town, but I wouldn't want to have a curfew even though I don't do bad things.

Critique

This essay shows a weak understanding of the prompt. The writer does not take a clear stand on the issue and offers no counterarguments. There are no transitions between ideas, and the ideas themselves are vague and confusing. It's difficult to tell whether the writer is for or against the curfew. The essay contains a number of grammatical and spelling errors that show a poor grasp of written language.

Sample "Score 1" Essay

I dont think that kids are crimanales. My mom lets me stay out late and im not a crimanale. I dont do drugs.

sometimes policeman chais 14 yearolds down the street on tv butt I dont see that in my town becawse they dont. besids, 14 yearolds get privleges. it says so in that adendmint.

if you play your stero loud at night you might comit a crim because it is a minor but the police shud not chais you becawse of privleges.

no one shud inforce laws on kids who are not crimanales.

Critique

This essay shows little or no understanding of the prompt. The student confused much of the information. For example, the student confused the Fourteenth Amendment with 14-year-olds. The random and inappropriate details (*sometimes policeman chais 14 yearolds down the street*) weaken the attempt made by the student to establish the main idea stated in paragraph 1. The student writes about very few, if any, outside details. The student also makes severe grammatical errors that take away from the meaning of the essay and make it quite difficult to read (*crimanales, adendmint*).

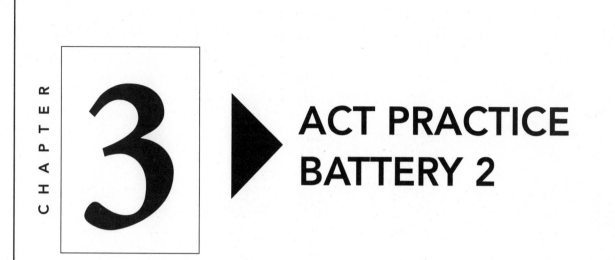

3 ▶ ACT PRACTICE BATTERY 2

This is the second of four complete practice ACTs in this book. In this chapter you'll find full English, Mathematics, Reading, Science, and Writing tests. Complete answers are at the end of the chapter, and instructions on how to score these practice tests are in Chapter 6. Good luck!

ACT English Practice Test 2

1.	ⓐ	ⓑ	ⓒ	ⓓ	26.	ⓕ	ⓖ	ⓗ	ⓙ	51.	ⓐ	ⓑ	ⓒ	ⓓ
2.	ⓕ	ⓖ	ⓗ	ⓙ	27.	ⓐ	ⓑ	ⓒ	ⓓ	52.	ⓕ	ⓖ	ⓗ	ⓙ
3.	ⓐ	ⓑ	ⓒ	ⓓ	28.	ⓕ	ⓖ	ⓗ	ⓙ	53.	ⓐ	ⓑ	ⓒ	ⓓ
4.	ⓕ	ⓖ	ⓗ	ⓙ	29.	ⓐ	ⓑ	ⓒ	ⓓ	54.	ⓕ	ⓖ	ⓗ	ⓙ
5.	ⓐ	ⓑ	ⓒ	ⓓ	30.	ⓕ	ⓖ	ⓗ	ⓙ	55.	ⓐ	ⓑ	ⓒ	ⓓ
6.	ⓕ	ⓖ	ⓗ	ⓙ	31.	ⓐ	ⓑ	ⓒ	ⓓ	56.	ⓕ	ⓖ	ⓗ	ⓙ
7.	ⓐ	ⓑ	ⓒ	ⓓ	32.	ⓕ	ⓖ	ⓗ	ⓙ	57.	ⓐ	ⓑ	ⓒ	ⓓ
8.	ⓕ	ⓖ	ⓗ	ⓙ	33.	ⓐ	ⓑ	ⓒ	ⓓ	58.	ⓕ	ⓖ	ⓗ	ⓙ
9.	ⓐ	ⓑ	ⓒ	ⓓ	34.	ⓕ	ⓖ	ⓗ	ⓙ	59.	ⓐ	ⓑ	ⓒ	ⓓ
10.	ⓕ	ⓖ	ⓗ	ⓙ	35.	ⓐ	ⓑ	ⓒ	ⓓ	60.	ⓕ	ⓖ	ⓗ	ⓙ
11.	ⓐ	ⓑ	ⓒ	ⓓ	36.	ⓕ	ⓖ	ⓗ	ⓙ	61.	ⓐ	ⓑ	ⓒ	ⓓ
12.	ⓕ	ⓖ	ⓗ	ⓙ	37.	ⓐ	ⓑ	ⓒ	ⓓ	62.	ⓕ	ⓖ	ⓗ	ⓙ
13.	ⓐ	ⓑ	ⓒ	ⓓ	38.	ⓕ	ⓖ	ⓗ	ⓙ	63.	ⓐ	ⓑ	ⓒ	ⓓ
14.	ⓕ	ⓖ	ⓗ	ⓙ	39.	ⓐ	ⓑ	ⓒ	ⓓ	64.	ⓕ	ⓖ	ⓗ	ⓙ
15.	ⓐ	ⓑ	ⓒ	ⓓ	40.	ⓕ	ⓖ	ⓗ	ⓙ	65.	ⓐ	ⓑ	ⓒ	ⓓ
16.	ⓕ	ⓖ	ⓗ	ⓙ	41.	ⓐ	ⓑ	ⓒ	ⓓ	66.	ⓕ	ⓖ	ⓗ	ⓙ
17.	ⓐ	ⓑ	ⓒ	ⓓ	42.	ⓕ	ⓖ	ⓗ	ⓙ	67.	ⓐ	ⓑ	ⓒ	ⓓ
18.	ⓕ	ⓖ	ⓗ	ⓙ	43.	ⓐ	ⓑ	ⓒ	ⓓ	68.	ⓕ	ⓖ	ⓗ	ⓙ
19.	ⓐ	ⓑ	ⓒ	ⓓ	44.	ⓕ	ⓖ	ⓗ	ⓙ	69.	ⓐ	ⓑ	ⓒ	ⓓ
20.	ⓕ	ⓖ	ⓗ	ⓙ	45.	ⓐ	ⓑ	ⓒ	ⓓ	70.	ⓕ	ⓖ	ⓗ	ⓙ
21.	ⓐ	ⓑ	ⓒ	ⓓ	46.	ⓕ	ⓖ	ⓗ	ⓙ	71.	ⓐ	ⓑ	ⓒ	ⓓ
22.	ⓕ	ⓖ	ⓗ	ⓙ	47.	ⓐ	ⓑ	ⓒ	ⓓ	72.	ⓕ	ⓖ	ⓗ	ⓙ
23.	ⓐ	ⓑ	ⓒ	ⓓ	48.	ⓕ	ⓖ	ⓗ	ⓙ	73.	ⓐ	ⓑ	ⓒ	ⓓ
24.	ⓕ	ⓖ	ⓗ	ⓙ	49.	ⓐ	ⓑ	ⓒ	ⓓ	74.	ⓕ	ⓖ	ⓗ	ⓙ
25.	ⓐ	ⓑ	ⓒ	ⓓ	50.	ⓕ	ⓖ	ⓗ	ⓙ	75.	ⓐ	ⓑ	ⓒ	ⓓ

ACT Mathematics Practice Test 2

1. a b c d e	21. a b c d e	41. a b c d e
2. f g h j k	22. f g h j k	42. f g h j k
3. a b c d e	23. a b c d e	43. a b c d e
4. f g h j k	24. f g h j k	44. f g h j k
5. a b c d e	25. a b c d e	45. a b c d e
6. f g h j k	26. f g h j k	46. f g h j k
7. a b c d e	27. a b c d e	47. a b c d e
8. f g h j k	28. f g h j k	48. f g h j k
9. a b c d e	29. a b c d e	49. a b c d e
10. f g h j k	30. f g h j k	50. f g h j k
11. a b c d e	31. a b c d e	51. a b c d e
12. f g h j k	32. f g h j k	52. f g h j k
13. a b c d e	33. a b c d e	53. a b c d e
14. f g h j k	34. f g h j k	54. f g h j k
15. a b c d e	35. a b c d e	55. a b c d e
16. f g h j k	36. f g h j k	56. f g h j k
17. a b c d e	37. a b c d e	57. a b c d e
18. f g h j k	38. f g h j k	58. f g h j k
19. a b c d e	39. a b c d e	59. a b c d e
20. f g h j k	40. f g h j k	60. f g h j k

ACT Reading Practice Test 2

1. a b c d	15. a b c d	29. a b c d
2. f g h j	16. f g h j	30. f g h j
3. a b c d	17. a b c d	31. a b c d
4. f g h j	18. f g h j	32. f g h j
5. a b c d	19. a b c d	33. a b c d
6. f g h j	20. f g h j	34. f g h j
7. a b c d	21. a b c d	35. a b c d
8. f g h j	22. f g h j	36. f g h j
9. a b c d	23. a b c d	37. a b c d
10. f g h j	24. f g h j	38. f g h j
11. a b c d	25. a b c d	39. a b c d
12. f g h j	26. f g h j	40. f g h j
13. a b c d	27. a b c d	
14. f g h j	28. f g h j	

ACT Science Practice Test 2

1.	a	b	c	d
2.	f	g	h	j
3.	a	b	c	d
4.	f	g	h	j
5.	a	b	c	d
6.	f	g	h	j
7.	a	b	c	d
8.	f	g	h	j
9.	a	b	c	d
10.	f	g	h	j
11.	a	b	c	d
12.	f	g	h	j
13.	a	b	c	d
14.	f	g	h	j

15.	a	b	c	d
16.	f	g	h	j
17.	a	b	c	d
18.	f	g	h	j
19.	a	b	c	d
20.	f	g	h	j
21.	a	b	c	d
22.	f	g	h	j
23.	a	b	c	d
24.	f	g	h	j
25.	a	b	c	d
26.	f	g	h	j
27.	a	b	c	d
28.	f	g	h	j

29.	a	b	c	d
30.	f	g	h	j
31.	a	b	c	d
32.	f	g	h	j
33.	a	b	c	d
34.	f	g	h	j
35.	a	b	c	d
36.	f	g	h	j
37.	a	b	c	d
38.	f	g	h	j
39.	a	b	c	d
40.	f	g	h	j

ACT English Practice Test 2

75 Questions—45 Minutes

Read each passage through once before you begin to answer any questions. You will see that certain words or phrases in the following five passages have been underlined and numbered. Following each passage, you will see alternatives for those underlined words or phrases. Choose the one that best expresses the idea of the passage, is the best use of standard English, or is most consistent with the tone and style of the passage. If you find the underlined part to be correct, choose "NO CHANGE." Note that to answer many of the questions you will probably need to read several sentences beyond the question. You may also find questions about a section of the passage or the passage as a whole, rather than about an underlined part.

Passage I—Wilma Rudolph

Wilma Rudolph was born a premature child in 1940, in Clarksville, <u>Tennessee. Weighing</u>[1] only four and a half pounds. Wilma's mother did her best to care for her daughter, but the Rudolphs were very poor, and the local hospital would not care for Wilma. During her childhood, Wilma contracted measles, mumps, scarlet fever, chicken pox, pneumonia, and, later, polio, a crippling disease that at that time had no cure. At <u>the age of four, doctors told her</u>[2] she would never walk again.

But Wilma's mother refused to give up. She found an African American medical college 50 miles away that would give Wilma the care <u>she needs.</u>[3] Although it was difficult to make the trip, Wilma's mother took Wilma to the college twice a week. After two years of treatment, Wilma could walk with a brace. With her family's help, Wilma was able to walk <u>by age 12 normally without the aid of a crutch or brace.</u>[4]

But simply walking wasn't enough for <u>Wilma, who wanted to be</u>[5] an athlete. She decided to play basketball, and <u>for three years she practiced</u>[6] with the team but didn't play in a single game. Then, in her sophomore year of high school, Wilma became a starting guard. <u>For scoring she broke the state records</u>[7] and led her team to the state championship. At the age of 16, she traveled to Melbourne, Australia, to run track events in the 1956 Olympics. She earned a bronze medal as part of a relay team.

(1) <u>After the high school from which she graduated,</u>[8] Wilma was awarded a full scholarship to Tennessee State University, and her track career went into high gear. (2) Before <u>she had earned</u>[9] her degree in education, she took a year off from her studies to compete all over the world. (3) In 1960, Wilma's career as a runner reached its apex. (4) She set a world record in the 200-meter race at the Olympic <u>trials,</u>[10] in Rome, she won the 100-meter race and the 200-meter race, and ran the anchor leg on the winning 4 × 100-meter relay team. (5) Wilma was proudest of a different kind of victory, <u>in conclusion.</u>[11] (6) When she returned from her triumphs in Rome, she insisted that the homecoming parade held in her honor not be a segregated event. (7) This parade was the first racially integrated event ever held in Clarksville. (8) Wilma continued to participate in protests until Clarksville's segregation laws were finally <u>changed.</u>[12]

1. **a.** NO CHANGE
   b. Tennessee. She weighed
   c. Tennessee, who weighed
   d. Tennessee, when born weighing

2. f. NO CHANGE
   g. age four, doctors told her
   h. age four, she was told by doctors that
   j. four, she by doctors was told that

3. a. NO CHANGE
   b. she needed
   c. needed by Wilma
   d. Omit the underlined portion.

4. f. NO CHANGE
   g. by age 12 without the aid of a crutch or brace normally.
   h. normally without the aid of a crutch or brace by age 12.
   j. normally by age 12 without the aid of a crutch or brace.

5. a. NO CHANGE
   b. Wilma, wanting to be
   c. Wilma who wanted to be
   d. Wilma; who wanted to be

6. f. NO CHANGE
   g. for three years, she practiced
   h. for three years, practiced
   j. practiced years

7. a. NO CHANGE
   b. She for scoring broke the state records
   c. She broke the state records for scoring
   d. She breaks the state records of scoring

8. f. NO CHANGE
   g. After graduating from high school,
   h. Since high school graduation,
   j. Omit the underlined portion.

9. a. NO CHANGE
   b. she would have earned
   c. Wilma had earned
   d. she earned

10. f. NO CHANGE
   g. trials. Then;
   h. trials—then—
   j. trials; then,

11. a. NO CHANGE
   b. however
   c. as a result
   d. therefore

12. f. NO CHANGE
   g. made illegal.
   h. struck down.
   j. removed.

13. While revising, the writer realizes the passage needs an introduction to convey the main idea of the essay. Which of the following sentences should he or she use as the first sentence to best achieve that purpose?
   a. No one would have guessed that Wilma Rudolph, a sick child, would someday become an Olympic track star.
   b. Wilma Rudolph owes a great deal to her family, who helped her survive several severe illnesses.
   c. Wilma Rudolph was a famous Olympic athlete who had a lot of health problems as a child.
   d. Wilma Rudolph suffered from diseases that few children contract today.

14. The writer wishes to add the following sentence to highlight how impressive Rudolph's achievements are: "She was the first American woman ever to win three gold medals at a single Olympics." The most logical place to insert this sentence would be

   f. after the new introductory sentence.
   g. at the end of paragraph 3.
   h. after sentence 4 in paragraph 4.
   j. at the beginning of paragraph 5.

15. The writer would like to separate the final paragraph into two paragraphs. The appropriate place to do so would be before

   a. sentence 4.
   b. sentence 5.
   c. sentence 6.
   d. sentence 7.

Passage II—Bicycles

(1) Today, bicycles are so common that it's hard to believe they haven't always been around. (2) But 200 years ago, <u>bicycles weren't even existing,</u>[16] and the first bicycle, invented in Germany in 1818, was nothing like our bicycles today—it was made of wood and didn't even have pedals. (3) Since then, however, numerous innovations and improvements in design <u>make</u>[17] the bicycle one of the most popular means of recreation and transportation around the world.

(4) In 1839, Kirkpatrick <u>Macmillan a Scottish blacksmith</u>[18] dramatically improved upon the original bicycle design. (5) Macmillan's machine had tires with iron rims to keep them from getting worn down. (6) He also used foot-operated cranks similar to pedals so his bicycle <u>could be ridden at a quick pace.</u>[19] (7) It <u>hadn't looked</u>[20] much like a modern bicycle, though, because its back wheel was substantially larger than its front wheel. (8) In 1861, the French Michaux brothers took the <u>evolution of the bicycle</u>[21] a step further by inventing an improved crank mechanism.

(9) Ten years later, James Starley, an English inventor, revolutionized bicycle design. (10) <u>He, made</u>[22] the front wheel many times larger than the back wheel, <u>putting a gear on</u>[23] the pedals to make the bicycle more efficient, and lightened the wheels by using wire spokes. (11) While much lighter and less tiring to ride, <u>most people found that</u>[24] the bicycle was still clumsy, extremely top-heavy, and ridden mostly for entertainment.

(12) It wasn't until 1874 that the first truly modern bicycle appeared on the scene. (13) <u>Today there built,</u>[25] used, and enjoyed all over the world. (14) <u>H.J. Lawson, invented by another Englishman,</u>[26] the "safety bicycle" would look familiar to today's cyclists. (15) This bicycle had equal-sized wheels, which made it less prone to toppling over. (16) Lawson also attached a chain to the pedals to drive the rear wheel. (17) With these improvements, the bicycle became extremely popular and useful for <u>easy transport.</u>[27]

16. **f.** NO CHANGE
   g. there was no such thing as a bicycle,
   h. bicycles were uninvented,
   j. whoever heard of a bicycle,

17. **a.** NO CHANGE
   b. made
   c. were made to
   d. have made

18. **f.** NO CHANGE
   g. Macmillan was a Scottish blacksmith
   h. Macmillan, a Scottish blacksmith,
   j. Macmillan, he was a Scottish blacksmith,

19. **a.** NO CHANGE
   b. could be rode quickly.
   c. could have been ridden fast.
   d. could ride at a quick pace.

20. **f.** NO CHANGE
   g. looked not
   h. didn't look
   j. wasn't looking

21. **a.** NO CHANGE
   b. evolvement of the bicycle
   c. evolution in the bicycle
   d. evolving bicycle

22. **f.** NO CHANGE
   g. He made
   h. He had made
   j. He; made

23. **a.** NO CHANGE
   b. putted a gear on
   c. put a gear in
   d. put a gear on

24. **f.** NO CHANGE
   g. people found that
   h. most people found
   j. Omit the underlined portion.

25. **a.** NO CHANGE
   b. Today there are built
   c. Today, they are built
   d. Today they, are built

26. **f.** NO CHANGE
   g. H.J. Lawson invented by another Englishman
   h. Invented by another Englishman, H.J. Lawson,
   j. Another Englishman inventor, H.J. Lawson,

27. **a.** NO CHANGE
   b. being easily transported.
   c. easy transporting.
   d. easy transportation.

28. If the writer were trying to convince readers to buy a bicycle, he would
   f. change nothing.
   g. add a paragraph describing the health and environmental benefits of riding a bike.
   h. add a paragraph comparing the cost and quality of today's best-selling bicycles.
   j. add a paragraph about the Tour de France and other bicycle races.

29. Which of the following sequences makes paragraph 4 most logical?
   a. NO CHANGE
   b. 12, 14, 15, 16, 17, 13
   c. 12, 17, 14, 15, 16, 13
   d. 12, 13, 14, 16, 17, 15

30. The most appropriate title for this passage would be
   f. The Evolution of the Bicycle.
   g. Who Invented the Bicycle?
   h. The Bicycle: A Popular Phenomenon.
   j. How Bicycles are Built.

Passage III—The Gateway Arch

The skyline of St. Louis, Missouri, is fairly unremarkable, with one huge exception, the[31] Gateway Arch that stands on the banks of the Mississippi. Part of the Jefferson National Expansion Memorial, the arch is a really cool monument[32] built to honor St. Louis's role as the gateway to the West.

Construction on the 630-foot-high structure, began in 1961,[33] and was completed four years later in 1965. The monument includes an underground visitor center that explores westward expansion through galleries and a theater. Two passenger tram takes visitors[34] to the observation room and the Museum of Westward Expansion at the top.

(1) In 1947, a group of interested citizens known as the Jefferson National Expansion Memorial Association held a nationwide competition to select a design for a new monument that would celebrate[35] the growth of the United States. (2) Other U.S. monuments are spires, statues, or imposed buildings,[36] but the winner of this contest was a plan for a completely unique structure. (3) The man that[37] submitted the winning design, Eero Saarinen, later went on to become[38] a famous architect. (4) In designing the arch, Saarinen wanted to "create a monument which would have lasting significance and would be a landmark of our time." (5) Saarinen helped create the international image of the United States with many of its[39] designs. (6) He also designed the General Motors Technical Center in Detroit, Michigan, and the TWA Terminal at New York's John F. Kennedy Airport.

The Gateway Arch is a masterpiece of engineering, a monument even taller than the Great Pyramids in Egypt, and on its own way,[40] at least as majestic. The arch is an inverted catenary curve, the same shape that a heavy chain will form if suspended between two points.

Covered from top to bottom with a sleek stainless steel coating,[41] sunlight often reflects off of the arch in dazzling bursts.[42] In a beautiful display of symmetry, the height of the arch is the same as the distance between the legs at ground level.

31. a. NO CHANGE
   b. exception: the
   c. exception; the
   d. exception. The

32. f. NO CHANGE
   g. a structure that inspires amazement
   h. an amazing structure
   j. Omit the underlined portion.

33. a. NO CHANGE
   b. , begun in 1961,
   c. had begun in 1961
   d. began in 1961

34. f. NO CHANGE
   g. trams takes visitors
   h. trams take visitors
   j. trams takes visitor

35. a. NO CHANGE
   b. should celebrate
   c. did celebrate
   d. would have celebrated

36. f. NO CHANGE
   g. imposing buildings,
   h. buildings that imposed,
   j. buildings that are imposed,

37. a. NO CHANGE
  b. which
  c. who
  d. whom

38. f. NO CHANGE
  g. later went on to became
  h. went on to became
  j. later became

39. a. NO CHANGE
  b. his
  c. their
  d. our

40. f. NO CHANGE
  g. and, in its own way,
  h. and—in its own way;
  j. and in it's own way

41. a. NO CHANGE
  b. Covered with sleek stainless steel all over its body,
  c. Covered with a skin made of steel that is stainless,
  d. Covered with a sleek skin of stainless steel,

42. f. NO CHANGE
  g. sunlight off the arch often reflects in dazzling bursts.
  h. the arch often reflects dazzling bursts of sunlight.
  j. sunlight often reflects in dazzling bursts off the arch.

43. What is the most logical sequence of paragraphs for this essay?
  a. 1, 2, 3, 4
  b. 1, 3, 2, 4
  c. 4, 1, 3, 2
  d. 1, 2, 4, 3

44. The writer is considering omitting sentences 5 and 6 in paragraph 3. Those sentences should be
  f. deleted because they are not pertinent.
  g. deleted because they are poorly written.
  h. kept because they add interesting details about the subject matter.
  j. kept because they supplement the information on the arch with information on its creator.

45. The writer has been asked to write a short essay describing in detail a national monument and what the monument honors. Would this essay fulfill that assignment?
  a. Yes, because it focuses on the design of the arch.
  b. Yes, because the writer describes the arch and tells why it was commissioned.
  c. No, because the writer does not tell us enough about the designer of the arch and what he was trying to accomplish.
  d. No, because the writer does not tell us enough about St. Louis's role as a gateway to westward expansion.

Passage IV—Annie Smith Peck

<u>Since a hundred years,</u>[46] the highest mountains in South America have lured climbers from all over the world. But until 1908, Peru's Mount Huascaran <u>was resisting</u>[47] the efforts of all those who attempted to reach its summit. One mountaineer, Annie Smith Peck, vowed to overcome the obstacles and be the first to the top of Mt. Huascaran. In order to succeed, she would have to organize <u>expeditions—deal with reluctant companions—survive bad weather, and</u>[48] climb steep cliffs of ice and rock.

Peck was born in the United States in 1850. Although she didn't start mountain climbing until she was in her <u>thirties, it</u>[49] soon became clear that she had found her life's work. A natural mountaineer, Peck was soon setting records on expeditions <u>on North America and Europe.</u>[50] She traveled to Bolivia in 1903 and found Mount Huascaran, which had yet to be surmounted, <u>a challenge she simply could not resist.</u>[51]

(1) Peck mounted four expeditions and made five attempts before she finally conquered Mount Huascaran. (2) During free periods <u>amongst</u>[52] those expeditions, Peck returned to the United States to raise money. (3) She received help from many scientific organizations, including the Museum of Natural History. (4) The museum had also supported Admiral Peary on his trip to the North Pole. (5) Still, Peck struggled at least as much to raise money as she did <u>climbing</u>[53] her beloved mountains.

In 1908, Peck scraped together the funds for yet another expedition to Mount Huascaran. This time, she hired two Swiss guides <u>to assist</u>[54] her with the climb. On their first trip up the mountain's slopes, one of the guides became ill, and the entire team was forced to turn back <u>even though they were very close to the top.</u>[55] Being so close to success was very frustrating for Peck, who could not even prove how close they had come because she had accidentally brought the wrong kind of film and was unable to photograph the climb.

The team rested for a few days, the guide recovered, and on August 28, they set off again. The climb was extremely difficult. Steps had to be <u>cut</u>[56] one by one into the steep ice; snow bridges and crevasses had to be carefully crossed. The weather was so cold that everyone suffered from frostbite. When Peck and her two guides were just a short distance from the top, they stopped to determine the exact height of the mountain. At that moment, one of the guides took advantage of Peck's distraction and climbed the few remaining feet to the summit so that he was the first to reach the peak. <u>What a jerk!</u>[57] Although Peck was understandably <u>angry, she</u>[58] focused on the triumph of achieving her goal: standing at last on the top of Mount Huascaran.

46. **f.** NO CHANGE
   g. Through the passing of a hundred years,
   h. For over a hundred years,
   j. In the time of the last century,

47. **a.** NO CHANGE
   b. had been resisted
   c. had resisted
   d. were resisting

48. **f.** NO CHANGE
   g. expeditions, deal with reluctant companions, survive bad weather, and
   h. expeditions; deal with reluctant, companions; survive bad weather; and
   j. expeditions: deal with reluctant companions, survive bad weather, and

49. **a.** NO CHANGE
    b. thirty's, it
    c. thirties. It
    d. thirties, thus it

50. **f.** NO CHANGE
    g. on two continents, North America and Europe.
    h. in North America and Europe.
    j. in two continents, North America and Europe.

51. **a.** NO CHANGE
    b. an irresistible challenge.
    c. and just had to climb it.
    d. the one mountain she just had to climb to the top of.

52. **f.** NO CHANGE
    g. during
    h. amidst
    j. between

53. **a.** NO CHANGE
    b. climbed
    c. proving she climbed
    d. to climb

54. **f.** NO CHANGE
    g. assisting
    h. would assist
    j. who had assisted

55. **a.** NO CHANGE
    b. even though close to the top.
    c. even though it was close to the top.
    d. even though they were close.

56. **f.** NO CHANGE
    g. hacked
    h. put
    j. done

57. **a.** NO CHANGE
    b. What, a jerk!
    c. He was such a jerk.
    d. Omit the underlined passage.

58. **f.** NO CHANGE
    g. angry; she
    h. angry—she
    j. angry. She

59. In revising paragraph 3, the writer would be wise to
    a. switch sentences 2 and 3.
    b. eliminate sentence 4.
    c. combine sentences 3 and 4.
    d. explain why Peck's previous attempts to climb Mount Huarascan had failed.

60. The writer wishes to add to the final sentence. The best choice would be
    f. what an achievement for a woman.
    g. , quite an achievement.
    h. finally, after much effort.
    j. wow!

Passage V—Batman

Pow. Bam. Zap![61] Batman triumphs again, foiling evildoers like the Joker, Penguin, and Catwoman to save the citizens of Gotham City. This superhero created in 1939 and known worldwide, continues[62] to be one of the most popular comic strip characters ever created.

    Batman was the brainchild of comic book artist Bob Kane. Who was[63] just 22 years old when he was asked to create a new superhero for DC Comics. Superman was a phenomenal success, and DC Comics wanted another comic book character to appeal to its readers fascinations with superheros.[64] Kane's idea for Batman reportedly came from Leonardo da Vinci's famous sketch of a man flying with batlike wings[65] and the masked heroes of the Shadow and Zorro series.

(1) The masked hero soon moved from comic books to its own newspaper strip, and in 1943, *Batman* episodes were aired on the radio. (2) Kane's Batman was a big success[66] right from the start. (3) The series was wildly popular and the syndicated show[67] still airs today on channels such as the Cartoon Network and Nickelodeon. (4) In 1966, live-action *Batman* shows hit the TV screen, giving the ABC network the ratings boost it badly needed.

Why was Batman so popular? The answer may lay[68] in the background Kane gave his character. Batman is really Bruce Wayne, a millionaire who witnessed the murder of his parents as a child. He vows to avenge their deaths and the bringing of criminals[69] to justice. He does not have any supernatural powers. Instead, he devotes[70] his life to training his body and mind to fight crime and uses his wealth to develop high-tech tools and weapons, like his famous Batmobile, to aid him in his quest. Thus[71] Kane created a superhero who is just as human as the rest of us, one who[72] suffered and has dedicated himself to righting wrongs. In Batman, Kane gave us an image of our own superhero potential.

61. **a.** NO CHANGE
  b. Pow, bam, zap!
  c. Pow-bam-zap!
  d. *Pow! Bam! Zap!*

62. **f.** NO CHANGE
  g. superhero, created in 1939, and known worldwide continues
  h. superhero, created in 1939 and known worldwide, continues
  j. superhero; created in 1939, and know worldwide continues

63. **a.** NO CHANGE
  b. Kane; who was
  c. Kane, who was
  d. Kane, being

64. **f.** NO CHANGE
  g. its readers' fascinations with superheros.
  h. its reader's fascinations with superheros.
  j. it's readers fascinations with superheros.

65. **a.** NO CHANGE
  b. with bat, like wings
  c. with bat like wings
  d. with wings that are like a bat's

66. **f.** NO CHANGE
  g. was a really successful character whom everyone liked a lot
  h. was liked a lot by a lot of people
  j. was an overwhelming success

67. **a.** NO CHANGE
  b. wildly popular and syndicated. The show
  c. wildly popular, and the syndicated show
  d. wildly popular. And the syndicated show

68. **f.** NO CHANGE
  g. lie
  h. have lain
  j. be lying

69. **a.** NO CHANGE
   b. bring criminals to justice
   c. criminals being brought to justice
   d. finding justice to bring to criminals

70. **f.** NO CHANGE
   g. has devoted
   h. did devote
   j. devoted

71. **a.** NO CHANGE
   b. Accordingly,
   c. For instance,
   d. Furthermore,

72. **f.** NO CHANGE
   g. one who has
   h. which
   j. Omit the underlined portion.

73. The writer introduces the passage with the words *Pow*, *Bam*, and *Zap* in order to
   a. set a lighthearted, silly tone for the essay.
   b. demonstrate the effect of onomatopoeia and exclamation points.
   c. establish a connection to the topic of a comic book hero.
   d. show that in Batman comic books, there was typically a lot of fighting.

74. What is the proper order for the sentences in paragraph 3?
   f. 1, 2, 3, 4
   g. 1, 2, 4, 3
   h. 2, 1, 4, 3
   j. 2, 1, 3, 4

75. The author wishes to add the following sentence in order to show why people like Batman and to provide readers with more information about the plot of a typical *Batman* episode: "People loved seeing Batman rush in and save the day whenever a villain threatened Gotham City." In order to accomplish this goal, it would be most logical and appropriate to place this sentence
   a. at the end of paragraph 2.
   b. after the second sentence in paragraph 3 (as written).
   c. after the first sentence in paragraph 3 (as written).
   d. at the end of paragraph 3.

ACT Mathematics Practice Test 2

60 Questions—60 Minutes

For each problem, choose the correct answer. You are allowed to use a calculator on this test for any problems you choose. Unless the problem states otherwise, you should assume that figures are *not* drawn to scale. For this test, all geometric figures lie in a plane, the word *line* refers to a straight line, and the word *average* refers to the arithmetic mean.

1. How is five hundred twelve and sixteen thousandths written in decimal form?
   a. 512.016
   b. 512.16
   c. 512,160
   d. 51.216
   e. 512.0016

2. Simplify $|3 - 11| + 4 \times 2^3$.
   f. 24
   g. 40
   h. 96
   j. 520
   k. 32

3. The ratio of boys to girls in a kindergarten class is 4 to 5. If there are 18 students in the class, how many are boys?
   a. 9
   b. 8
   c. 10
   d. 7
   e. 12

4. What is the median of 0.024, 0.008, 0.1, 0.024, 0.095, and 0.3?
   f. 0.119
   g. 0.095
   h. 0.0595
   j. 0.024
   k. 0.092

5. Which of the following is NOT the graph of a function?

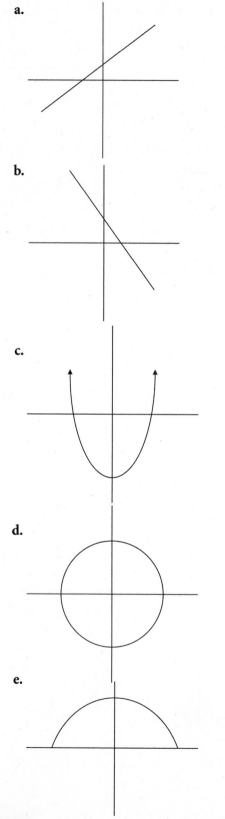

a.

b.

c.

d.

e.

6. What is the value of x^5 for $x = -3$?

  f. −243

  g. −15

  h. 15

  j. 125

  k. 243

7. What is the next number in the following pattern?

    0, 3, 8, 15, 24, . . .

  a. 33

  b. 35

  c. 36

  d. 37

  e. 41

8. What is the prime factorization of 84?

  f. 42×2

  g. $7 \times 2 \times 3$

  h. $2^2 \times 3 \times 7$

  j. $2^2 \times 6 \times 7$

  k. $2^3 \times 7$

9. Find the slope of the line $7x = 3y - 9$.

  a. 3

  b. −9

  c. $\frac{7}{3}$

  d. −3

  e. $\frac{3}{7}$

10. The perimeter of a rectangle is 20 cm. If the width is 4 cm, find the length of the rectangle.

   f. 5 cm

   g. 6 cm

   h. 12 cm

   j. 15 cm

   k. 24 cm

11. Find the area of the following figure.

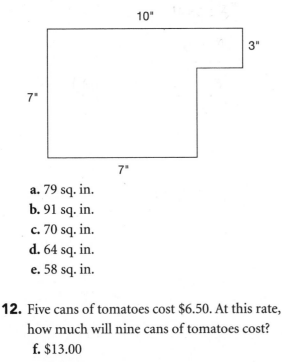

   a. 79 sq. in.

   b. 91 sq. in.

   c. 70 sq. in.

   d. 64 sq. in.

   e. 58 sq. in.

12. Five cans of tomatoes cost $6.50. At this rate, how much will nine cans of tomatoes cost?

   f. $13.00

   g. $11.70

   h. $1.30

   j. $11.90

   k. $12.40

13. For all $x \neq 0$, $\frac{2}{3x} + \frac{1}{5} =$

   a. $\dfrac{2}{15x}$

   b. $\dfrac{10 + 3x}{15 + x}$

   c. $\dfrac{3}{3x + 15}$

   d. $\dfrac{10 + 3x}{15x}$

   e. $\dfrac{1}{5x}$

14. Which inequality best represents the following graph?

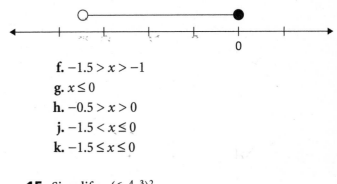

   f. $-1.5 > x > -1$

   g. $x \leq 0$

   h. $-0.5 > x > 0$

   j. $-1.5 < x \leq 0$

   k. $-1.5 \leq x \leq 0$

15. Simplify $-(6x^4y^3)^2$.

   a. $-36x^6y^5$

   b. $36x^2y$

   c. $-36x^8y^6$

   d. $36x^8y^4$

   e. $-36xy$

16. If $2x + 3y = 55$ and $4x = y + 47$, find $x - y$.

   f. 5

   g. 12

   h. 16

   j. 24

   k. 28

17. Simplify $\sqrt[3]{16x^5y^4}$.

   a. $2xy\sqrt[3]{2x^2y}$

   b. $8x^2y$

   c. $8xy\sqrt[3]{2}$

   d. $2xy\sqrt[3]{xy}$

   e. $4x^2y^2$

18. The formula to convert Celsius to Fahrenheit is $F = \frac{5}{9}C + 32$, where F is degrees Fahrenheit, and C is degrees Celsius. What Fahrenheit temperature is equivalent to 63°C?

  f. 32°

  g. 47°

  h. 67°

  j. 83°

  k. 95°

19. What are the solutions to the equation $x^2 + 8x + 15 = 0$?

  a. {8,15}

  b. {0}

  c. {−5,−3}

  d. no solution

  e. {2,4}

20. If $5k = 9m − 18$, then $m =$

  f. $5k + 18$

  g. $\frac{5k + 18}{9}$

  h. $−9 + 5k$

  j. $\frac{5k + 9}{9}$

  k. $9k + 18$

21. What are the solutions of the equation $5x − 7 = 5(x + 2)$?

  a. {2}

  b. {7}

  c. all positive numbers

  d. all real numbers

  e. empty set

22. Simplify $\frac{4x^2 + 11x − 3}{x + 3}$ for all $x \neq −3$.

  f. $3x^2 + 11$

  g. $2x + 1$

  h. $4x^2 + 12x$

  j. $4x^2 + 10x − 6$

  k. $4x − 1$

23. If $x = \begin{pmatrix} 3 & 4 \\ 5 & 6 \end{pmatrix}$ and $y = \begin{pmatrix} −2 & 4 \\ −1 & 0 \end{pmatrix}$, find $x − y$.

  a. $\begin{pmatrix} 5 & 0 \\ 6 & 6 \end{pmatrix}$

  b. $\begin{pmatrix} −5 & 0 \\ −6 & −6 \end{pmatrix}$

  c. $\begin{pmatrix} 1 & 8 \\ 4 & 6 \end{pmatrix}$

  d. $\begin{pmatrix} 4 & 1 \\ 2 & 8 \end{pmatrix}$

  e. $\begin{pmatrix} 6 & 1 \\ 2 & 5 \end{pmatrix}$

24. If $\log_3 x = 2$, then $x =$

  f. 6

  g. 9

  h. $\frac{2}{3}$

  j. 4

  k. $\frac{1}{2}$

25. The vertices of a triangle are $A(−1,3)$, $B(3,0)$, and $C(−2,−1)$. Find the length of side AC.

  a. $\sqrt{15}$

  b. $\sqrt{17}$

  c. 19

  d. 17

  e. $3\sqrt{6}$

26. Which of the following equations has a graph that has a y-intercept of 4 and is parallel to $3y - 9x = 24$?

  f. $-12x + 4y = 16$

  g. $9x - 3y = -15$

  h. $2y = 4x + 8$

  j. $7y = 14x + 7$

  k. $3x - 9y = 14$

27. The best approximation of $\sqrt{37} \times \sqrt{125}$ is

  a. 52

  b. 4,600

  c. 150

  d. 66

  e. 138

28. If a coin is flipped and a number cube is rolled, what is the probability of getting tails and 3?

  f. $\frac{1}{2}$

  g. $\frac{1}{12}$

  h. $\frac{1}{6}$

  j. $\frac{1}{4}$

  k. $\frac{1}{8}$

29. What is $\frac{1}{2}$% of 90?

  a. 45

  b. 0.045

  c. 4.5

  d. 0.45

  e. 450

30. Mike has 12 bags of shredded cheese for making pizzas. If he uses $\frac{3}{4}$ of a bag of cheese for each pizza, how many pizzas can he make?

  f. 9

  g. 12

  h. 36

  j. 24

  k. 16

31. Greene ran the 100-meter dash in 9.79 seconds. What was his speed in km/h (rounded to the nearest km)?

  a. 31 km/h

  b. 37 km/h

  c. 1 km/h

  d. 10 km/h

  e. 25 km/h

32. Larry has 4 pairs of pants, 6 pairs of socks, and 10 shirts in his dresser. How many days could Larry go without wearing the same combination of 1 pair of pants, 1 pair of socks, and 1 shirt?

  f. 20

  g. 24

  h. 44

  j. 152

  k. 240

33. What is the product of 5×10^{-4} and 6×10^8?

    a. 11×10^4

    b. 3×10^4

    c. 1.1×10^5

    d. 3×10^5

    e. 5.6×10^{-4}

34. What is the sine of angle B in the triangle?

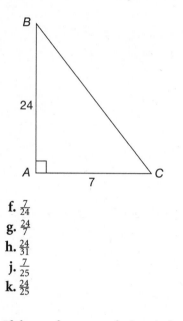

    f. $\frac{7}{24}$

    g. $\frac{24}{7}$

    h. $\frac{24}{31}$

    j. $\frac{7}{25}$

    k. $\frac{24}{25}$

35. If the surface area of a box is found by taking the sum of the areas of each of the faces of the box, what is the surface area of a box with dimensions 6 in. by 8 in. by 10 in.?

    a. 376 sq. in.

    b. 138 sq. in.

    c. 346 sq. in.

    d. 480 sq. in

    e. 938 sq. in.

36. Find the area of the shaded region.

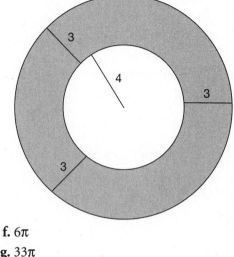

    f. 6π

    g. 33π

    h. 49π

    j. 72π

    k. 121π

37. The area of square $WXYZ$ is 100 sq. cm. Find the length of diagonal WY in cm.

    a. $10\sqrt{2}$ cm

    b. 15 cm

    c. 20 cm

    d. $20\sqrt{2}$ cm

    e. $10\sqrt{5}$ cm

38. Which of the following could be the value of x when y is equal to 15 for the equation $y = 4x^2 - 1$?

    f. -4

    g. -2

    h. 0

    j. $\sqrt{5}$

    k. 3

39. At Roosevelt High, Kristen won the election for class president with 60% of the vote. Of that 60%, 75% were female. If 540 students voted, how many female students voted for Kristen?

   a. 195

   b. 405

   c. 324

   d. 227

   e. 243

40. If $\cos\theta = \frac{12}{13}$ and $\tan\theta = \frac{5}{12}$, then $\sin\theta =$

   f. $\frac{5}{13}$

   g. $\frac{13}{12}$

   h. $\frac{1}{13}$

   j. $\frac{13}{5}$

   k. $\frac{12}{5}$

41. The formula for the volume of a rectangular solid is $V = lwh$. If each dimension is tripled, how many times the original volume will the new volume be?

   a. 3

   b. 9

   c. 12

   d. 27

   e. 81

42. In a right triangle, the two non-right angles measure $7x$ and $8x$. What is the measure of the smaller angle?

   f. 15°

   g. 60°

   h. 30°

   j. 48°

   k. 42°

43. The length of a rectangle is twice the width. If the perimeter of the rectangle is 72 feet, what is the length of the rectangle?

   a. 6 ft.

   b. 12 ft.

   c. 24 ft.

   d. 36 ft.

   e. 48 ft.

44. The area of a triangle is 80 sq. in. Find the height if the base is 5 in. more than the height.

   f. $\frac{1 + \sqrt{629}}{2}$

   g. $\frac{-9 \pm \sqrt{5}}{2}$

   h. $4 \pm \sqrt{85}$

   j. $5 - \sqrt{665}$

   k. $\frac{-5 + \sqrt{665}}{2}$

45. Three of the vertices of a square are $(-2,3)$, $(5,3)$, and $(-2,-4)$. What is the length of a side of the square?

   a. 5

   b. 4

   c. 3

   d. 7

   e. 8

46. Which of the following lines is perpendicular to $y = 3x + 1$?

   f. $6x + 5 = 2y$

   g. $4 + y = 3x$

   h. $-9y = -3 + 2x$

   j. $2x + y = 4$

   k. $3y + x = 5$

47. What is the midpoint of line *XY* if *X*(−4,−2) and *Y*(3,8)?

　a. (−7,6)

　b. (−0.5,3)

　c. (−1,6)

　d. (−7,−10)

　e. (2,−1.5)

48. Simplify $(\frac{1}{2}x^2)^{-3}$

　f. $6x^6$

　g. $8x^6$

　h. $\frac{1}{6x^6}$

　j. $\frac{8}{x^6}$

　k. $\frac{1}{8x^3}$

49. Line *l* is parallel to line *m*. Find the measure of angle *x*.

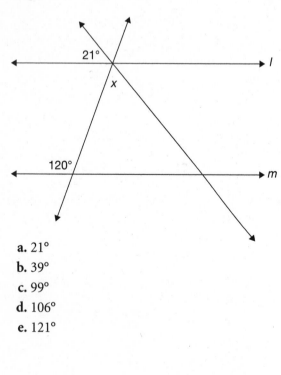

　a. 21°

　b. 39°

　c. 99°

　d. 106°

　e. 121°

50. Find the radius of the circle with center (4,−2) that is tangent to the *y*-axis.

　f. 2

　g. 6

　h. 1

　j. 4

　k. 10

51. Find the area, in square units, of the circle shown by the equation $(x − 5)^2 + (y − 2)^2 = 36$.

　a. 4π

　b. 6π

　c. 25π

　d. 36π

　e. 48π

52. $m\angle ABC = 120°$ and $m\angle CDE = 110°$. Find the measure of $\angle C$.

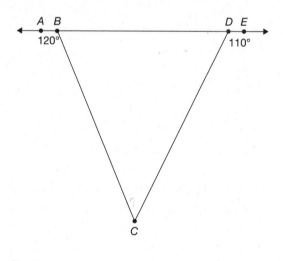

　f. 70°

　g. 50°

　h. 60°

　j. 150°

　k. 40°

53. What is the minimum value of 9 cos x?

   a. −9
   b. −2
   c. 0
   d. 2
   e. 9

54. The Abrams put a cement walkway around their rectangular pool. The pool's dimensions are 12 ft. by 24 ft., and the width of the walkway is 5 ft. in all places. The area of the walkway is

   f. 205 sq. ft.
   g. 288 sq. ft.
   h. 460 sq. ft.
   j. 493 sq. ft.
   k. 748 sq. ft.

55. Triangle XYZ is an equilateral triangle. $\overline{YW}$ is an altitude of the triangle. If $\overline{YX}$ is 10 in., what is the length of the altitude?

   a. 5 in.
   b. $5\sqrt{3}$ in.
   c. 10 in.
   d. $10\sqrt{3}$ in.
   e. $5\sqrt{2}$ in.

56. Find the value of cos A if angle A is acute and sin $A = \frac{7}{10}$

   f. $\frac{3}{10}$
   g. $\frac{1}{10}$
   h. $\frac{7}{\sqrt{51}}$
   j. $\frac{51}{10}$
   k. $\frac{\sqrt{51}}{10}$

57. Find the value of x.

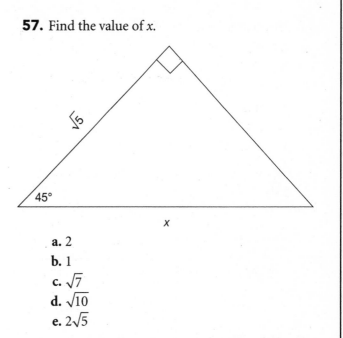

   a. 2
   b. 1
   c. $\sqrt{7}$
   d. $\sqrt{10}$
   e. $2\sqrt{5}$

58. Which equation corresponds to the graph?

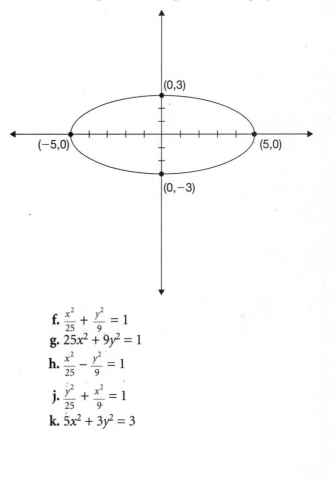

   f. $\frac{x^2}{25} + \frac{y^2}{9} = 1$
   g. $25x^2 + 9y^2 = 1$
   h. $\frac{x^2}{25} - \frac{y^2}{9} = 1$
   j. $\frac{y^2}{25} + \frac{x^2}{9} = 1$
   k. $5x^2 + 3y^2 = 3$

59. What is the inequality that corresponds to the graph?

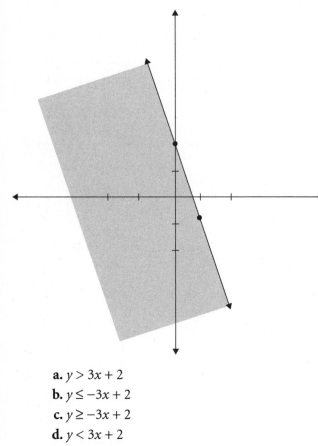

   a. $y > 3x + 2$
   b. $y \leq -3x + 2$
   c. $y \geq -3x + 2$
   d. $y < 3x + 2$
   e. $y < -3x + 2$

60. What is the domain of the function $f(x) = \frac{4x - 5}{x^2 + 3x - 4}$?
   f. $\{\bar{x} \mid x \neq 0\}$
   g. $\emptyset$
   h. all real numbers
   j. $\{x \mid x \neq 3\}$
   k. $\{x \mid x \neq -4 \text{ and } x \neq 1\}$

ACT Reading Practice Test 2

40 Questions—35 Minutes

In this test you will find four passages, each followed by several questions. Read each passage carefully and then select the best possible answer for each question.

Passage I—Humanities

This passage is taken from the personal memoirs of Ulysses S. Grant, 1885–1886.

1   The Cause of the Great War of the Rebellion
2   against the United States will have to be attrib-
3   uted to slavery. For some years before the war
4   began it was a trite saying among some politi-
5   cians that "A state half slave and half free can-
6   not exist." All must become slave or all free, or
7   the state will go down. I took no part myself in
8   any such view of the case at the time, but since
9   the war is over reviewing the whole question, I
10 have come to the conclusion that the saying is
11 quite true.
12   Slavery was an institution that required
13 unusual guarantees for its security wherever it
14 existed; and in a country like ours where the
15 larger portion of it was free territory inhabited
16 by an intelligent and well-to-do population, the
17 people would naturally have but little sympathy
18 with demands upon them for its protection.
19 Hence the people of the South were dependent
20 upon keeping control of the general govern-
21 ment to secure the perpetuation of their favor-
22 ite restitution. They were enabled to maintain
23 this control long after the States where slavery
24 existed had ceased to have the controlling
25 power, through the assistance they received
26 from odd men here and there throughout the
27 Northern States. They saw their power waning,
28 and this led them to encroach upon the prerog-
29 atives and independence of the Northern States

30 by enacting such laws as the Fugitive Slave Law.
31 By this law every Northern man was obliged,
32 when properly summoned, to turn out and
33 help apprehend the runaway slave of a South-
34 ern man. Northern marshals became slave-
35 catchers, and Northern courts had to
36 contribute to the support and protection of the
37 institution.
38   This was a degradation which the North
39 would not permit any longer than until they
40 could get the power to expunge such laws from
41 the statute books. Prior to the time of these
42 encroachments the great majority of the people
43 of the North had no particular quarrel with
44 slavery, so long as they were not forced to have
45 it themselves. But they were not willing to play
46 the role of police for the South in the protec-
47 tion of this particular institution. In the early
48 days of the country, before we had railroads,
49 telegraphs, and steamboats—in a word, rapid
50 transit of any sort—the States were each almost
51 a separate nationality. At that time the subject
52 of slavery caused but little or no disturbance to
53 the public mind. But the country grew, rapid
54 transit was established, and trade and com-
55 merce between the States got to be so much
56 greater than before, that the power of the
57 National government became more felt and
58 recognized and, therefore, had to be enlisted in
59 the cause of this institution.
60   It is probably well that we had the war
61 when we did. We are better off now than we
62 would have been without it, and have made
63 more rapid progress than we otherwise should
64 have made. The civilized nations of Europe
65 have been stimulated into unusual activity, so
66 that commerce, trade, travel, and thorough
67 acquaintance among people of different nation-
68 alities, has become common; whereas, before, it
69 was but the few who had ever had the privilege
70 of going beyond the limits of their own country
71 or who knew anything about other people.

72 Then, too, our republican institutions were
73 regarded as experiments up to the breaking out
74 of the rebellion, and monarchical Europe gen-
75 erally believed that our republic was a rope of
76 sand that would part the moment the slightest
77 strain was brought upon it. Now it has shown
78 itself capable of dealing with one of the greatest
79 wars that was ever made, and our people have
80 proven themselves to be the most formidable in
81 war of any nationality.
82   But this war was a fearful lesson, and
83 should teach us the necessity of avoiding wars
84 in the future. The conduct of some of the Euro-
85 pean states during our troubles shows the lack
86 of conscience of communities where the
87 responsibility does not come upon a single
88 individual. Seeing a nation that extended from
89 ocean to ocean, embracing the better part of a
90 continent, growing as we were growing in pop-
91 ulation, wealth and intelligence, the European
92 nations thought it would be well to give us a
93 check. We might, possibly, after a while,
94 threaten their peace, or, at least, the perpetuity
95 of their institutions. Hence, England was con-
96 stantly finding fault with the administration at
97 Washington because we were not able to keep
98 up an effective blockade. She also joined, at
99 first, with France and Spain in setting up an
100 Austrian prince upon the throne in Mexico,
101 totally disregarding any rights or claims that
102 Mexico had of being treated as an independent
103 power. It is true they trumped up grievances as
104 a pretext, but they were only pretexts which can
105 always be found when wanted.

1. According to the passage, which of the following statement(s) is/are true?
   I. The North was always against slavery.
   II. The North was indifferent toward slavery as long as they were not forced to support it.
   III. The North always supported slavery.
   a. I only
   b. II only
   c. II and III
   d. III only

2. According to the passage, which factors contributed to the North's rejection of slavery?
   I. the introduction of rapid transit
   II. the legal obligations to support slavery
   III. its moral obligation to defend what is right
   f. I and II
   g. II only
   h. III only
   j. II and III

3. One of the main points the author makes in the first paragraph is that
   a. slavery must be abolished.
   b. the entire country must either be for or against slavery.
   c. the North and the South can never live in peace.
   d. slavery was an accepted practice.

4. According to the second paragraph, what were the effects of the Fugitive Slave Law?
   f. It freed the slaves.
   g. It angered the South.
   h. It forced the North to enforce laws it did not necessarily believe were right.
   j. It forced the North to fight the South.

5. As it is used in line 40, the word *expunge* most closely means
   a. enact.
   b. hold one against his will.
   c. be powerless.
   d. remove.

6. According to the passage, the South enacted the Fugitive Slave Law because
   f. it had too many runaway slaves.
   g. slavery was important to the livelihood of the North.
   h. the South was afraid that slavery would be abolished.
   j. it needed help from the North in keeping slavery alive.

7. According to the next to last paragraph, one of the things that changed after the war was that
   a. slavery was abolished.
   b. Europeans were exposed to different cultures.
   c. runaway slaves were captured without the help of the North.
   d. the North and the South united.

8. According to the last paragraph, the author believes that the European countries felt
   f. threatened by our unified strength.
   g. slavery was wrong.
   h. they owed us money.
   j. betrayed by the United States.

9. The phrase *rope of sand* in lines 75–76 most nearly means something that is
   a. weakly connected.
   b. shackled.
   c. broken in two.
   d. tightly bound.

10. The author believes that war

   f. should be avoided at all costs.

   g. is the best way to end disputes.

   h. can have beneficial results but should be avoided.

   j. is morally wrong.

Passage II—Natural Sciences
Asthma

1 No longer is asthma considered a condition
2 with isolated, acute episodes of bronchospasm.
3 Rather, asthma is now understood to be a
4 chronic inflammatory disorder of the air-
5 ways—that is, inflammation makes the airways
6 chronically sensitive. When these hyperrespon-
7 sive airways are irritated, airflow is limited, and
8 attacks of coughing, wheezing, chest tightness,
9 and breathing difficulty occur.
10   Asthma involves complex interactions
11 among inflammatory cells, mediators, and the
12 cells and tissues in the airways. The interactions
13 result in airflow limitation from acute broncho-
14 constriction, swelling of the airway wall,
15 increased mucus secretion, and airway remod-
16 eling. The inflammation also causes an increase
17 in airway responsiveness. During an asthma
18 attack, the patient attempts to compensate by
19 breathing at a higher lung volume in order to
20 keep the air flowing through the constricted
21 airways, and the greater the airway limitation,
22 the higher the lung volume must be to keep air-
23 ways open. The morphologic changes that
24 occur in asthma include bronchial infiltration
25 by inflammatory cells. Key effector cells in the
26 inflammatory response are the mast cells, T
27 lymphocytes, and eosinophils. Mast cells and
28 eosinophils are also significant participants in
29 allergic responses, hence the similarities
30 between allergic reactions and asthma attacks.
31 Other changes include mucus plugging of the
32 airways, interstitial edema, and microvascular
33 leakage. Destruction of bronchial epithelium

34 and thickening of the subbasement membrane
35 are also characteristic. In addition, there may be
36 hypertrophy and hyperplasia of airway smooth
37 muscle, increase in goblet cell number, and
38 enlargement of submucous glands.
39   Although causes of the initial tendency
40 toward inflammation in the airways of patients
41 with asthma are not yet certain, to date the
42 strongest identified risk factor is atopy. This
43 inherited familial tendency to have allergic
44 reactions includes increased sensitivity to aller-
45 gens that are risk factors for developing asthma.
46 Some of these allergens include domestic dust
47 mites, animals with fur, cockroaches, pollens,
48 and molds. Additionally, asthma may be trig-
49 gered by viral respiratory infections, especially
50 in children. By avoiding these allergens and
51 triggers, a person with asthma lowers his or her
52 risk of irritating sensitive airways. A few avoid-
53 ance techniques include: keeping the home
54 clean and well ventilated, using an air condi-
55 tioner in the summer months when pollen and
56 mold counts are high, and getting an annual
57 influenza vaccination. Of course, asthma suffer-
58 ers should avoid tobacco smoke altogether.
59 Cigar, cigarette, or pipe smoke is a trigger
60 whether the patient smokes or inhales the
61 smoke from others. Smoke increases the risk of
62 allergic sensitization in children, increases the
63 severity of symptoms, and may be fatal in chil-
64 dren who already have asthma. Many of the risk
65 factors for developing asthma may also provoke
66 asthma attacks, and people with asthma may
67 have one or more triggers, which vary from
68 individual to individual. The risk can be further
69 reduced by taking medications that decrease
70 airway inflammation. Most exacerbations can
71 be prevented by the combination of avoiding
72 triggers and taking anti-inflammatory medica-
73 tions. An exception is physical activity, which is
74 a common trigger of exacerbations in asthma
75 patients. However, asthma patients should not

76 necessarily avoid all physical exertion, because
77 some types of activity have been proven to
78 reduce symptoms. Rather, they should work in
79 conjunction with a doctor to design a proper
80 training regimen, which includes the use of
81 medication.
82   In order to diagnose asthma, a healthcare
83 professional must appreciate the underlying
84 disorder that leads to asthma symptoms and
85 understand how to recognize the condition
86 through information gathered from the
87 patient's history, physical examination, mea-
88 surements of lung function, and allergic status.
89 Because asthma symptoms vary throughout the
90 day, the respiratory system may appear normal
91 during physical examination. Clinical signs are
92 more likely to be present when a patient is
93 experiencing symptoms; however, the absence
94 of symptoms upon examination does not
95 exclude the diagnosis of asthma.

11. According to the passage, what is the name for
the familial inclination to have hypersensitivity
to certain allergens?
  a. interstitial edema
  b. hyperplasia
  c. hypertrophy
  d. atopy

12. Why does a person suffering from an asthma
attack attempt to inhale more air?
  f. to prevent the loss of consciousness
  g. to keep air flowing through shrunken air
passageways
  h. to prevent hyperplasia
  j. to compensate for weakened mast cells, T
lymphocytes, and eosinophils

13. The passage suggests that, in the past, asthma
was regarded as which of the following?
  a. a result of the overuse of tobacco products
  b. a hysterical condition
  c. mysterious, unrelated attacks affecting the
lungs
  d. a chronic condition

14. Which of the following would be the best
replacement for the word *exacerbations* in lines
70 and 74 of this passage?
  f. allergies
  g. attacks
  h. triggers
  j. allergens

15. The passage mentions all of the following
bodily changes during an asthma attack except
  a. severe cramping in the chest.
  b. heavy breathing.
  c. airways blocked by fluids.
  d. constricted airways.

16. Although it is surprising, which of the following triggers is mentioned in the passage as possibly reducing the symptoms of asthma in some
patients?
  f. using a fan instead of an air conditioner in
summer months
  g. exposure to secondhand cigarette smoke
  h. the love of a family pet
  j. performing physical exercise

17. Why might a patient with asthma have an apparently normal respiratory system during an examination by a doctor?
- **a.** Asthma symptoms come and go throughout the day.
- **b.** Severe asthma occurs only after strenuous physical exertion.
- **c.** Doctors' offices are smoke free and very clean.
- **d.** The pollen and mold count may be low that day.

18. Who might be the most logical audience for this passage?
- **f.** researchers studying the respiratory system
- **g.** healthcare professionals
- **h.** a mother whose child has been diagnosed with asthma
- **j.** an antismoking activist

19. What is the reason given in this passage for why passive smoke should be avoided by children?
- **a.** A smoke-filled room is a breeding ground for viral respiratory infections.
- **b.** Smoke can stunt an asthmatic child's growth.
- **c.** Smoke can heighten the intensity of asthma symptoms.
- **d.** Breathing smoke can lead to a fatal asthma attack.

20. What is the main point of the final paragraph?
- **f.** Do not trust a doctor who says you do not have asthma.
- **g.** Diagnosing asthma can be a tricky and complicated process.
- **h.** It is impossible to accurately diagnose asthma.
- **j.** Since asthma is difficult to diagnose, do not bother going to the doctor.

Passage III—Prose Fiction

This passage was adapted from "The Necklace," by Guy de Maupassant.

She was one of those pretty, charming women who are born, as if by an error of Fate, into a petty official's family. She had no dowry, no hopes, nor the slightest chance of being loved and married by a rich man—so she slipped into marriage with a minor civil servant.

Unable to afford jewels, she dressed simply: But she was wretched, for women have neither caste nor breeding—in them beauty, grace, and charm replace pride of birth. Innate refinement, instinctive elegance, and wit give them their place on the only scale that counts, and these make humble girls the peers of the grandest ladies.

She suffered, feeling that every luxury should rightly have been hers. The poverty of her rooms—the shabby walls, the worn furniture, the ugly upholstery caused her pain. All these things that another woman of her class would not even have noticed, made her angry. The very sight of the little Breton girl who cleaned for her awoke rueful thoughts and the wildest dreams in her mind. She dreamt of rooms with Oriental hangings, lighted by tall, bronze torches, and with two huge footmen in knee breeches made drowsy by the heat from the stove, asleep in the wide armchairs. She dreamt of great drawing rooms upholstered in old silks, with fragile little tables holding priceless knickknacks, and of enchanting little sitting rooms designed for tea-time chats with famous, sought-after men whose attentions all women longed for.

She sat down to dinner at her round table with its three-day-old cloth, and watched her husband lift the lid of the soup tureen and delightedly exclaim: "Ah, a good homemade beef stew! There's nothing better!" She visualized elegant dinners with gleaming silver and gorgeous china. She yearned for wall hangings peopled with knights and ladies and exotic birds in a fairy forest. She dreamt of eating the pink flesh of trout or the wings of grouse. She had no proper wardrobe, no jewels, nothing. And those were the only things that she loved—she felt she was made for them. She would have so loved to charm, to be envied, to be admired and sought after.

She had a rich friend, an old school friend whom she refused to visit, because she suffered so keenly when she returned home. She would weep whole days, with grief, regret, despair, and misery.

21. Which word best describes the actual living conditions of the couple in the selection?
   a. destitute
   b. poor
   c. comfortable
   d. wealthy

22. Which line best demonstrates the couple's true economic standing?
   f. "She had no dowry, no hopes, nor the slightest chance of being loved and married by a rich man."
   g. "The poverty of her rooms—the shabby walls, the worn furniture, the ugly upholstery caused her pain."
   h. "She sat down to dinner at her round table with its three-day-old cloth, and watched her husband lift the lid of the soup tureen."
   j. "The very sight of the little Breton girl who cleaned for her awoke rueful thoughts and the wildest dreams in her mind."

23. According to the selection, what can be stated about the marriage of this woman?
   a. She married but was ashamed of the insignificant position her husband held.
   b. She married on the rebound after a wealthy suitor had abandoned her.
   c. She married for love without realizing the consequences to her social standing.
   d. She never loved her husband.

24. The inclusion of *Oriental hangings* and *tea-time chats* in the description of the woman's imagined home likely indicates that she
   f. is fascinated with things from the Orient.
   g. is herself of Oriental heritage.
   h. associates those things with the wealth she desires.
   j. would be happy if only she had those two things.

25. What can be inferred about the values of both husband and wife?
   a. They share the same values.
   b. The husband values family and simple comforts of home, whereas his wife views these comforts as cause for her anguish.
   c. The husband has ceased to enjoy the simple things and only strives to quench his wife's insatiable desire for luxury.
   d. The husband believes that a wholesome meal can solve all problems, while his wife believes it is the presentation of the meal that counts.

26. The woman can best be described as
   f. serene.
   g. pensive.
   h. morose.
   j. manic.

27. The main idea of the passage is
  a. to have the reader feel great sympathy for the wife.
  b. to have the reader feel great sympathy for the husband.
  c. to show the class distinctions that were so obvious during the setting of the story.
  d. to show the reader how selfish and self-centered the wife is.

28. What part of speech does de Maupassant employ to weave the rich images he presents through the wife's descriptions?
  f. adjectives
  g. adverbs
  h. nouns
  j. verbs

29. The passage implies that the woman does not contact her old friend because
  a. she dislikes how the woman has changed.
  b. she envies the woman's wealth.
  c. she does not know how to contact her.
  d. she does not like the woman's home.

30. The narrator's point of view is that of
  f. a friend of the woman.
  g. a disinterested observer.
  h. an omniscient observer.
  j. a biased storyteller.

Passage IV—Social Sciences
The Great Depression

The worst and longest economic crisis in the modern industrial world, the Great Depression in the United States had devastating consequences for American society. At its lowest depth (1932–1933), more than 16 million people were unemployed, more than 5,000 banks had closed, and over 85,000 businesses had failed. Millions of Americans lost their jobs, their savings, and even their homes. The homeless built shacks for temporary shelter—these emerging shantytowns were nicknamed Hoovervilles, a bitter homage to President Herbert Hoover, who refused to give government assistance to the jobless. The effects of the Depression—severe unemployment rates and a sharp drop in the production and sales of goods—could also be felt abroad, where many European nations still struggled to recover from World War I.

Although the stock market crash of 1929 marked the onset of the Depression, it was not the *cause* of it: deep, underlying fissures already existed in the economy of the Roaring Twenties. For example, the tariff and war-debt policies after World War I contributed to the instability of the banking system. American banks made loans to European countries following World War I. However, the United States kept high tariffs on goods imported from other nations. These policies worked against one another. If other countries could not sell goods in the United States, they could not make enough money to pay back their loans or to buy American goods.

Moreover, while the United States seemed to be enjoying a prosperous period in the 1920s, the wealth was not evenly distributed. Businesses made gains in productivity, but only one segment of the population—the wealthy—reaped large profits. Workers received only a small share of the wealth they helped produce. At the same time, Americans spent more than they earned. Advertising encouraged Americans to buy cars, radios, and household appliances instead of saving or purchasing only what they could afford. Easy credit policies allowed consumers to borrow money and accumulate debt. Investors also wildly speculated on the stock market, often borrowing money on credit to buy shares of a company. Stocks increased beyond their worth, but investors were willing to pay inflated prices because they believed stocks would continue to rise. This bubble burst in the fall of 1929, when investors lost confidence that stock prices would keep rising. As investors sold off stocks, the market spiraled downward. The stock market crash affected the economy in the same way that a stressful event can affect the human body, lowering its resistance to infection.

The ensuing Depression led to the election of President Franklin D. Roosevelt in 1932. Roosevelt introduced relief measures that would revive the economy and bring needed relief to Americans suffering the effects of the Depression. In his first 100 days in office, Roosevelt and Congress passed major legislation that saved banks from closing and regained public confidence. These measures, called the New Deal, included the Agricultural Adjustment Act, which paid farmers to slow their production in order to stabilize food prices; the Federal Deposit Insurance Corporation, which insured bank deposits if banks failed; and the Securities and Exchange Commission, which regulated the stock market. Although the New Deal offered relief, it did not end the Depression. The economy sagged until the nation entered World War II. However, the New Deal changed the relationship between government and American citizens, by expanding the role of the central government in regulating the economy and creating social assistance programs.

31. The author's main point about the Great Depression is that
   a. government policies had nothing to do with it.
   b. the government immediately stepped in with assistance for the jobless and homeless.
   c. underlying problems in the economy preceded it.
   d. the New Deal policies introduced by Franklin D. Roosevelt ended it.

32. This passage is best described as
   f. an account of the causes and effects of a major event.
   g. a statement supporting the value of federal social policies.
   h. a condemnation of outdated beliefs.
   j. a polite response to controversial issues.

33. The author cites the emergence of Hoovervilles in paragraph 1 as an example of
   a. federally sponsored housing programs.
   b. the resilience of Americans who lost their jobs, savings, and homes.
   c. the government's unwillingness to assist citizens in desperate circumstances.
   d. the effectiveness of the Hoover administration in dealing with the crisis.

34. All of the following are cited as causes of the depression EXCEPT
   f. overspending by consumers.
   g. rampant inflation.
   h. post–World War I European debt.
   j. investor overspeculation in the stock market.

35. The term *policies*, as it is used in paragraph 2, most nearly means
   a. theories.
   b. practices.
   c. laws.
   d. examples.

36. The passage suggests that the 1920s was a decade that extolled the value of
   f. thrift.
   g. prudence.
   h. balance.
   j. extravagance.

37. The example of the human body as a metaphor for the economy, which is found at the end of paragraph 3, suggests that

   a. a stressful event like the stock market crash of 1929 probably made a lot of people sick.

   b. the crash weakened the economy's ability to withstand other pressures.

   c. the crash was an untreatable disease.

   d. a single event caused the collapse of the economy.

38. It can be inferred from the passage that over-production by farmers

   f. stabilizes food prices.

   g. causes food to go to waste.

   h. destabilizes food prices.

   j. helps the economy in general.

39. The content in the last paragraph of the passage would most likely support which of the following statements?

   a. The New Deal policies were not radical enough in challenging capitalism.

   b. The economic policies of the New Deal brought about a complete business recovery.

   c. The Agricultural Adjustment Act paid farmers to produce surpluses.

   d. The federal government became more involved in caring for needy members of society.

40. Which of the following would logically have been a result of the New Deal as it is described in this passage?

   f. renewed faith in the stock market

   g. more frequent elections

   h. a welfare system

   j. higher taxes

ACT Science Practice Test 2

40 Questions—35 Minutes

The passages in this test are followed by several questions. After reading each passage, choose the best answer to each question. You may refer back to the passages as often as necessary. You are *not* permitted to use a calculator on this test.

Passage I—Data Representation

Sound is transmitted through the air in wave patterns. The human ear can hear sound waves between about 15 and 20,000 cycles per second (cps). Most music and other common sounds occur in the range of 32 to 4,096 Hz. High-frequency, short-wavelength sound waves are heard as high pitched and low-frequency, long-wavelength sound waves are heard as low pitched.

Like other wave phenomena, sounds have a quality of harmonic dissonance or consonance. We experience these two types of sound mixtures as being different to our senses, but they also have important physical properties quite apart from human feelings about them. All materials vibrate to some extent. Both natural and artificial dissonances and consonances in both natural and artificial structures are very important phenomena.

Figure 1 is an image of five different sound wave patterns that demonstrate the principle of dissonance and consonance. Tones *a*, *b*, and *d* are each single tones. Tones *c* and *e* are formed by sounding *a* with *b* and sounding *a* with *d*.

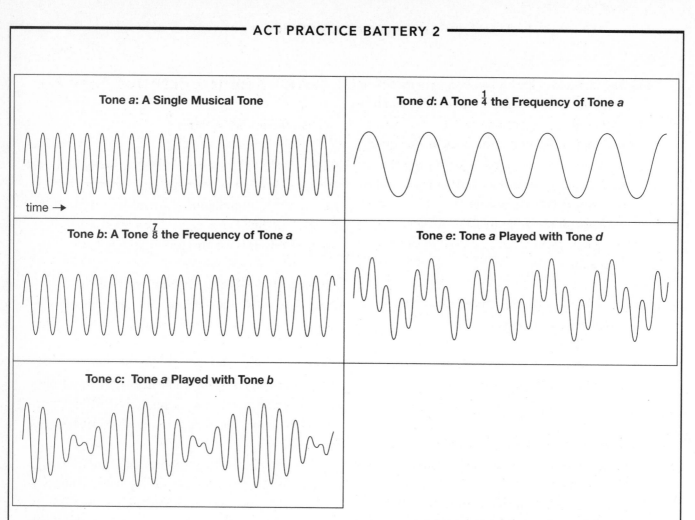

Tone a: A Single Musical Tone

time →

Tone b: A Tone $\frac{7}{8}$ the Frequency of Tone a

Tone c: Tone a Played with Tone b

Tone d: A Tone $\frac{1}{4}$ the Frequency of Tone a

Tone e: Tone a Played with Tone d

Figure 1

The frequencies of *a* and *b* are not divisible by each other or by any small multiple of each other, and they combine to form a bumpy combined tone, sound *c*. Sound *d* is one-quarter the frequency of *a*. Sound *e* is a combination of *a* and *d*. This is a highly consonant combination of tones. Other simple ratios of frequencies such as 2:3, 3:4, and 4:5 also form consonances.

The amplitude of each sound is the air pressure produced by the wave. Its fluctuations are indicated by the peaks and valleys of the graph lines. Although sound is generally not highly destructive, sounds can reach amplitudes that not only can damage sensitive hearing organs but can bring bridges and other structures crashing down.

1. Dissonances made by combining two tones close to each other in frequency produce what are called beats. The beats are alternating loud and soft percussive sounds created from two sounds of relatively constant volume. The number of beats produced each second equals the difference between the frequencies in cycles per second of the two tones. Assuming that tone *a*'s frequency is 8 cps, what is the clearest evidence of beats in Figure 1?
   a. Tone *d* has a regular pattern of rising and falling amplitude.
   b. Tone *c*'s amplitude has a high point and a low point every eighth cycle of sound *a*.
   c. Tone *e* has an obvious beat every fourth cycle.
   d. Tone *c* and *e* each have beats but at different frequencies because the tones that compose them have different frequencies.

2. The musical interval called an octave occurs between two tones whose sounds seem to blend into each other's because the higher-pitched one has precisely twice the frequency of the other. Each successively higher octave is twice the frequency of the next lower one. Are any of the tones shown in Figure 1 in an octave relationship with another tone?

   f. No.

   g. Yes; 7 × 8 is 56, so the third octave above tone *b* will be seven octaves above tone *a*.

   h. Yes; tone *e* is two octaves above tone *a*.

   j. Yes; tone *a* is two octaves above tone *e*.

3. When two tones are played together, the absolute values of their amplitudes are added together when they both have the same sign. One is subtracted from the other when they have different signs. The single tones *a*, *b*, and *d* each vary in amplitude from +1 to −1. What is the maximum absolute amplitude that can be reached by the mixed tones? *Note:* These graphs are not necessarily all drawn to the same vertical scale.

   a. 2 for both *c* and *e*

   b. 2 for *e*. Tone *c* cannot be determined because its two frequencies are not equally divisible.

   c. 2 for *e* and $1\frac{7}{8}$ for *c*

   d. There is no maximum. The amplitude keeps building as the sound continues.

4. Throughout history, humans have known that some materials will dampen the transmission of sound and others will enhance it. Effective soundproofing by using sound insulation has always required bulky materials. However, high-speed, modern sound-sensing and production devices have made it possible to cancel out sound with devices weighing only a few grams. This is based on the principle of sound interference: vibrations in opposite directions cancel each other out. Examine Figure 1 in light of this and explain how this is possible.

   f. Consonant sounds blend together, so a soft consonance will dampen a loud one.

   g. Dissonances interfere with each other. If a sufficient array of dissonant sounds is played against a tone, it will drown it out.

   h. Positive and negative vibrations tend to cancel each other out. Noise-canceling devices depend on detecting noise and then creating a noise with a pattern of vibration exactly opposite the one to be canceled.

   j. Sound levels are relative. Bursts of very loud tones that last only a few thousandths of a second are not noticed by a listener, but they dull the ability to hear softer noise.

5. All structures have resonant characteristics. This means they will vibrate at certain frequencies. Musical instruments, including the various elements composing human vocal capabilities, are designed to maximize their resonant capabilities. Based on Figure 1, the discussion in question 3, and elsewhere, which of the following are reasons why engineers are careful to avoid strongly resonant structures?

   a. It is preferable that engineering structures be quiet.

   b. Consistent vibrations can gradually fatigue materials and lead to early structural failure.

   c. The magnitudes of consonant sound waves add up. Disturbances, including sounds consonant with the resonant frequency of a structure, can cause a rapid increase in the energy of a structure's vibration and lead to catastrophic failure.

   d. all of the above

Passage II—Conflicting Viewpoints

The paradoxical nature of the speed of light and all electromagnetic radiation is one of the great historical issues of science. Figure 1 illustrates the problem. A scientist with a powerful searchlight and a radar speed gun is standing on the side of a perfectly straight highway in Kansas. The searchlight and the speed gun are both pointed straight along the highway. A sports car drives by and the scientist measures its speed at 120 km/hr. Then a maglev train whizzes by on the central median at 480 km/hr. From the maglev, a passenger with a radar gun confirms that the train is moving away from the scientist at 480 km/hr and away from the sports car at 360 km/hr. The passenger in the sports car measures the speed of the receding scientist at 120 km/hr and the speed of the maglev, receding in the opposite direction, at 360 km/hr.

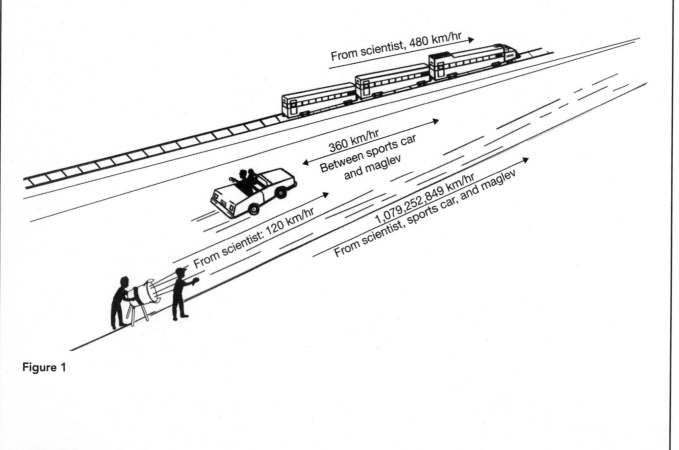

Figure 1

The scientist and the passengers in the maglev and the sports car also have equipment to measure the speed of the searchlight beam traveling along the highway. All three measure the beam's speed at 1,079,252,849 km/hr. Table 1 shows the results of all of the speed measurements. What are called material objects all have speeds relative to each other, but electromagnetic radiation has the same speed relative to all. Two young scientists attempt to explain this.

SPEED MEASURED FROM THIS OBJECT	SEARCH-LIGHT	SPORTS CAR	MAGLEV	LIGHT BEAM
Searchlight	0	120	480	1,079,252,849
Sports car	120	0	360	1,079,252,849
Maglev	480	360	0	1,079,252,849

TABLE 1 — TO THIS OBJECT IN KM/HR

Explanation 1

Al proposes that time stretches out for objects moving relative to each other. This is called time dilation. He suggests that there could be identical clocks on the maglev, in the sports car, and with the scientist, which the scientist could read. If a second measured on the sports car took longer than the scientist's second, and if one on the maglev took even longer, then light, traveling past all three, would be measured at the same speed as it moved past all three, even though the speeds of each differ relative to the others.

Al's hypothesis and his method for calculating the exact quantity of time dilation from the speed of separation of two objects is illustrated in Figure 2. The clock consists of two mirrors parallel to each other, a beam of light that bounces back and forth between them, and a device that measures how long each round trip of the light takes. When the clock is stationary relative to the observer, the distance the light travels is 2 × the perpendicular distance between the mirrors (2ls). When the clock is moving, the observer sees the light moving along a zigzag path because the mirrors keep moving forward as the light bounces back and forth (2lm). The zigzag path is longer than the vertical path, so the clock appears to have longer seconds. An observer traveling with the clock, however, will see only the vertical up-and-down motion, and the seconds of the clock will be just like any other clock that appears stationary.

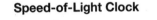

Speed-of-Light Clock

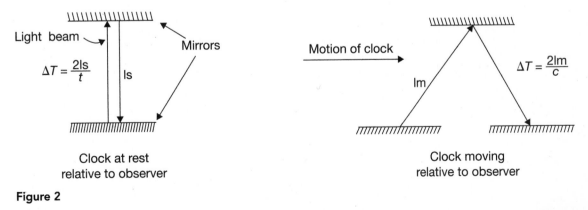

Figure 2

The formula derived from this model for the factor of difference in time is $T = 1 \div \sqrt{1 - \dfrac{v^2}{c^2}}$.

T is the ratio of increase in time on the apparently moving clock compared to the apparently stationary one. The speed at which the clocks are moving away from each other is v, and c is the speed of light.

Explanation 2

Al's friend, Alby, explains that the phenomenon could also be accounted for if the length of an object moving away from another contracted relative to its length when stationary. If the length of an object contracts as it approaches the speed of light, the speed of light will appear to remain the same relative to it.

This theory of relativistic length is illustrated in Figure 3. The length of each object contracts in the direction it is moving away from the other, as the speed of separation increases. At low speeds, such as those we see, this contraction is not even measurable with highly precise instrumentation. As the speed of light is reached, the lengths of the objects shrink to zero.

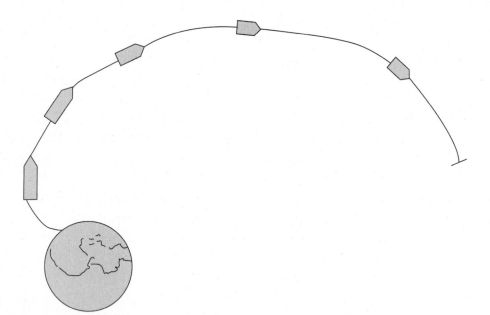

Figure 3 Relativistic Length Contraction as a Space Probe Reaches the Speed of Light

6. Look at the formula for time dilation provided by Al. According to this formula, what will be the factor of time dilation between two objects moving away from each other at the speed of light?

   f. infinite or undefined

   g. zero

   h. one

   j. the square root of −1

7. Look at Figure 2, Table 1, and Al's theory of time dilation. Which of these answers best describes the phenomenon of time dilation relative to an observer A and an observer B, moving away from each other at a large fraction of the speed of light?

   a. B's time slows down as observed from A, and A's time speeds up as observed from B.

   b. A's time is unchanged, but B's time slows down.

   c. B's time slows down as observed from A, and A's time slows down as observed from B.

   d. B's time speeds up as observed from A, and A's time speeds up as observed from B.

8. Look again at Al's time dilation formula. Which answer best describes time dilation as the velocity of separation goes from 0 to the speed of light?

   f. Time dilation is inversely proportional to the velocity of separation.

   g. Time dilation is proportional to the velocity of separation.

   h. Time dilation is proportional to the inverse square of the velocity of separation.

   j. Time dilation is inversely proportional to the square root of 1 minus the square of the velocity of separation divided by the speed of light.

9. Redshift occurs in the radiation emitted from far distant astronomical bodies moving rapidly away from our solar system. Electromagnetic patterns emitted by these bodies are shifted from their usual place in the spectrum toward the red, low-frequency end of the spectrum. Which statement about this phenomenon is consistent with the theory of time dilation presented here?

   a. Interstellar matter filters out higher-frequency emissions. This allows the lower ones to reach Earth.

   b. Redshift is associated with lower frequencies, which means the wave cycles of the electromagnetic radiation reaching us from these objects are slower than those from nearby objects emitting the same type of radiation. This is consistent with time dilation theory.

   c. Redshift is unrelated to time dilation.

   d. Redshift tends to disprove time dilation. If time slowed down on distant bodies moving away from us, then higher, not lower, frequencies would reach us.

10. Examine Al's formula again. If two objects are stationary relative to each other, what will the time dilation factor be?

   f. infinite or undefined

   g. zero

   h. inversely proportional to the square of their distance from each other

   j. 1

11. Consider Al's and Alby's hypotheses together. It is generally accepted among scientists that both time dilation and relativistic length contraction occur. In view of what has been presented here, describe what this would mean for an object as it reaches the speed of light.

  a. Nothing. These changes are perceived by a distantly receding observer, but from the standpoint of the moving object, the speed cannot be detected.

  b. Time would virtually stop and length would be contracted to nearly zero.

  c. Whatever happened to the object speeding away would also happen to the observer.

  d. Answers **a**, **b**, and **c** are each consistent with the theory presented here.

12. Consider Figure 2 and Al's time dilation formula, which is derived from it. How would the formula or its results be different if the objects were moving toward each other?

  f. The formula would remain the same, but the velocity of separation would be negative instead of positive, so time would speed up for each object relative to the other.

  g. The formula would be changed from $T = 1 \div \sqrt{1 - \frac{v^2}{c^2}}$ to $T = 1 \div \sqrt{1 + \frac{v^2}{c^2}}$. This would then show that time would speed up for each object relative to the other.

  h. According to the formula, it makes no difference whether the velocity between the objects is negative or positive because $v^2 = (-v)^2$. This is consistent with the rationale given for the formula because, whether the objects are moving toward each other or away from each other, the same zigzag motion will be observed in each from the other.

  j. none of the above

Passage III—Research Summary

Matthew Meselson and Franklin Stahl conducted an experimental series to demonstrate the mechanism for DNA replication. It had been known that the complex double strands of DNA molecules perpetuate their genetic structure by replicating themselves, but it was not known how this was done. Three hypotheses, as illustrated in Figure 1, were current.

Replication Hypotheses

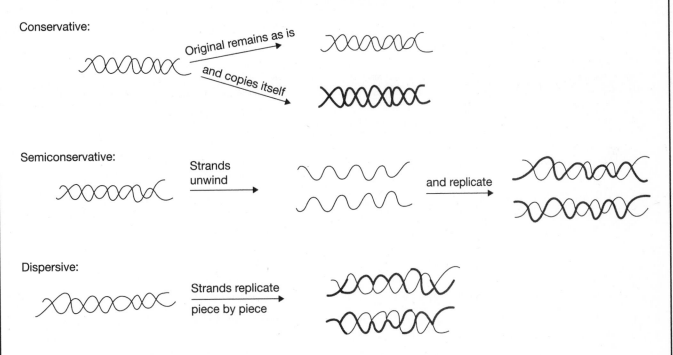

Figure 1

1. *Conservative:* The entire double helix remains intact as it replicates itself from available material.

2. *Semiconservative:* The two DNA strands unravel and each then creates a new second strand for itself out of new materials.

3. *Dispersive:* The original DNA strand breaks into pieces and replicates itself piece by piece. Each piece replicates itself from new material. The next piece of old DNA attaches itself to the new DNA and replicates a new piece, which gets attached to the end of the last old piece, until an entire DNA molecule is replicated.

Experiment 1

Two batches of *E. coli* bacteria are cultured using only ammonia as the source for nitrogen. One batch uses only ^{14}N and the other only ^{15}N. After several replication cycles, the DNA from both batches is mixed in equal proportions and then centrifuged. As intended, the DNA separates into two distinct areas, heavy and light. Their location in the centrifuged test tube is noted.

Experiment 2

E. coli bacteria are cultured in a medium rich in ^{15}N, which is heavier than the normal nitrogen isotope, ^{14}N. After enough time passes to develop a significant proportion of the DNA to be composed using only ^{15}N, the mixture is centrifuged to separate out the heavy DNA.

Experiment 3

The heavy DNA is introduced into a ^{14}N medium and allowed to replicate. All new DNA elements will be composed only of ^{14}N. Based on the known *E. coli* rate of reproduction and other observations, it is determined when the DNA in the culture has been fully replicated. At the completion of each full replication, a sample is taken and centrifuged to determine the ratio of different weights of DNA.

Table 1 is a simplified report of the results. It shows that quantities of heavy, light, and intermediate (having a weight close to midway between heavy and light) DNA are found. No DNA of other weights is found. Replication 0 is the composition when the first heavy DNA culture is introduced. Replications 1, 2, and 3 are the subsequent generations of replication.

TABLE 1 DNA REPLICATION TRIALS				
REPLICATION	% HEAVY	% INTERMEDIATE	% LIGHT	% OTHER
0	100	0	0	0
1	0	100	0	0
2	0	50	50	0
3	0	25	75	0

13. What is the most reasonable explanation of the purpose of experiment 1?
    a. To prove that *E. coli* bacteria do not change the nitrogen from one isotope to another.
    b. To make sure the *E. coli* bacteria is not contagious.
    c. To demonstrate that the centrifuge apparatus successfully separates out the DNA by weight, and to be able to recognize which weight is which.
    d. To prove that the DNA is always half heavy and half light.

14. After one replication cycle, what would be the expected proportion of DNA weights if the conservative replication model were followed?
    f. Half the DNA would be heavy and half would be light because the conservative model preserves the original DNA, which is all heavy, and produces new DNA using the nitrogen in the medium, which is all light.
    g. There would be random distribution between heavy and light because natural reproduction is random.
    h. All the DNA would be light because all new DNA produced would have to be light.
    j. All the DNA would be heavy because it is all produced by heavy DNA.

15. If there were random weights of DNA between heavy and light, which replication hypothesis would be correct?
  a. None of them would be correct.
  b. Any of them would be correct because over time the different weights will gradually mix and average out.
  c. The dispersive method would be correct because under the conservative method the original heavy DNA would remain heavy, and all new DNA would be light. Under the semiconservative method all DNA would have either two heavy strands, two light strands, or one of each.
  d. The dispersive method or the semiconservative method would be correct because each of them mixes light with heavy DNA.

16. Based on the results of replication 1 reported in Table 1 only, which replication methods were ruled out and which remained as possibly correct, pending additional trials?
  f. None were ruled out.
  g. The conservative and dispersive methods were ruled out—the conservative because the original heavy DNA was eliminated, and the dispersive because it results in a random distribution of weights.
  h. The dispersive method was ruled out because the results were not random.
  j. The conservative method was ruled out because the original heavy DNA is no longer there. The other two remain possible because they both involve replicating new DNA half out of the old DNA and half out of the new light nitrogen.

17. At which replication trial was it proven which replication method is really used?
  a. Replication 2. Replication 1 ruled out the conservative method. With the semiconservative method, each DNA molecule would have one strand of heavy and one of light after replication 1. Each of these strands would then create a second strand for itself using light nitrogen. The result would be 50% intermediate and 50% light as shown in Table 1 for replication 2. The dispersive method would have produced a more random mixture of weights.
  b. It is still not clear.
  c. Replication 3. Replication 2 made it look like the semiconservative method, but replication 3 provided the extra insurance needed.
  d. Replication 1. Only the semiconservative method could produce all intermediate-weight DNA.

18. What is likely to happen during succeeding replication cycles?
  f. The heavy DNA would die off and disappear.
  g. A point of balance would be reached and maintained between light and intermediate DNA.
  h. There is no way to predict.
  j. Each replication cycle would halve the percentage of intermediate DNA and increase the amount of light DNA by a corresponding amount.

Passage IV—Research Summary

A series of experiments conducted at the close of the nineteenth and the dawn of the twentieth century concluded that electricity consists of particles, rather than a continuous fluid; accurately determined the quantity of a single unit of electrical charge; and accurately determined the mass of an electron.

Previously, electrical charge had been thought to be a continuous fluid, and the proton, thousands of times larger than the newly discovered electron, had been considered the smallest building block of matter.

Experiment 1

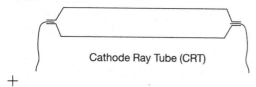

Cathode Ray Tube (CRT)

+   −

Figure 1

Figure 1 illustrates a simple cathode ray tube (CRT). Applying an electrical voltage to these partially evacuated tubes creates a visible brilliant ray and causes the interior and the glass surface of the tube to shimmer and glow with light. Applying a magnetic field causes the ray to change directions. In the experiments, the rays responded to magnetic fields as a negatively charged substance would be expected to do, but with two differences: the calculated ratio of mass to charge was thousands of times smaller than what had been calculated for positively charged matter, and, unlike positively charged matter, the rays did not respond to electrical fields.

Experiment 2

It was discovered that if the strength of the vacuum in a CRT is increased sufficiently, the cathode ray does respond to electrical as well as magnetic fields. The measured magnitudes involved suggest that cathode rays are composed of negatively charged matter whose ratio of mass to charge is a tiny fraction of the mass of previously known positively charged particles.

Experiment 3

Next, the properties of the hypothesized discovered particles were determined. Figure 2 illustrates the apparatus used. It has two chambers. A mist of oil is sprayed into the top chamber, and is examined and measured with the aid of a microscope in the lower chamber. There are two steps:

1. A fine spray of electrically charged oil falls from the upper chamber through the lower. When a droplet stops accelerating downward, the gravitational force acting on it is balanced by the viscosity and flotation force of the air. From the known density of the oil and viscosity of the air, its mass and the magnitude of the forces keeping it in balance are computed.

2. A known voltage of electricity is applied to the plates in the lower chamber. The size of the electrical charge on the oil droplet is computed from the strength of the electrical field required to stop the downward motion of the known mass of oil.

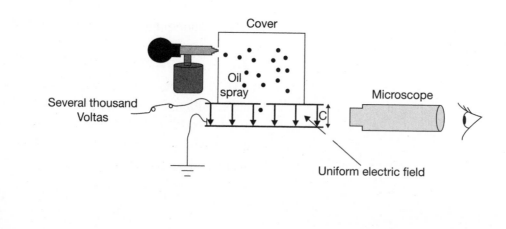

Figure 2

The charge, in coulombs (C), was calculated for many oil droplets. Table 1 illustrates the nature of the results obtained.

TABLE 1 CHARGE ON OIL DROPLETS IN COULOMB × 10^{-21}, ORDERED FROM LOWEST TO HIGHEST	
DROPLET #	CHARGE
1	477
2	795
3	1,113
4	1,272
5	1,431
6	1,590
7	2,067
8	2,226
9	2,385
10	2,544
11	2,703
12	3,021
13	3,339
14	3,498
15	3,657
16	3,816
17	4,134
18	4,452
19	4,611
20	4,929
21	5,088
22	5,406
23	5,724
24	5,883
25	6,042
26	6,201
27	6,678
28	6,837
29	6,996
30	7,155
31	7,314
32	7,632
33	7,950
34	8,109
35	8,268
36	8,427
37	8,745
38	9,063
39	9,222
40	9,540

19. Results in a pattern such as that in Table 1 support the idea that electrical charges are carried by particles, each carrying the same charge. What feature of the results indicates this?

  a. They proceed in order from lower numbers to higher numbers.

  b. The lowest number reported is 477 and the highest equals 20 × 477.

  c. All of the results are equally divisible by 159.

  d. Number 20's charge is slightly more than one half of number 40's, so the rate of increase declines.

20. After experiment 3 determined that negatively charged substances are all composed of specific quantities of single particles, each of which carries the same charge, which of these statements explains how the mass of each particle can be calculated?

   f. The mass of each oil droplet was calculated. Dividing that by the number of charged particles will give the mass per particle.

   g. The report on experiment 1 states that the ratio of mass to electrical charge (m/e) was already known. Multiplying that ratio by the electrical charge (e) of each particle gives the mass.

   h. The mass of a hydrogen atom, consisting of one proton and one electron, is known. Dividing that by 2 gives you the mass of one electron.

   j. Add up all of the electrical charge values in Table 1 and divide by 40.

21. Look again at the accounts of experiment 1 and experiment 2. How did experiment 2 correct the findings of experiment 1?

   a. In experiment 2, the CRTs do not glow because the vacuum is too strong.

   b. In experiment 2, it was discovered that the cathode rays are negatively charged.

   c. In experiment 2, it was discovered that cathode rays respond to magnetic fields.

   d. The results of experiment 1 seemed to show that cathode rays were not influenced by electrical fields, but experiment 2 demonstrated that if the tubes had a strong enough vacuum, the rays did respond.

22. In experiment 3, why are the oil droplets permitted to float down through the lower chamber before the electrical field is activated?

   f. To establish the mass and the magnitude of the nonelectrical forces acting on the droplet.

   g. To conserve electricity.

   h. To build up momentum against which the electrical forces will work.

   j. To verify that the droplets are actually negatively charged.

23. Consider the state of understanding as of experiment 1 and the conclusions of experiment 3. What was demonstrated by the experiment 3 results reported in Table 1 that was not shown by experiment 1?

   a. Negatively charged substances have a very small mass.

   b. Both negatively and positively charged substances respond to magnetic fields.

   c. Both negatively and positively charged substances respond to electrical fields.

   d. Negative charge exists only in units of 1.59×10^{-19} C, and the mass for each unit of charge is thousands of times smaller than previously known particles.

24. One of the scientists involved in this work claims that the newly discovered minuscule particles are the building blocks out of which all larger particles are formed. What aspects of the experimental results support that conclusion?

   f. Larger particles cannot combine to produce smaller ones.

   g. The new particles respond to both electrical and magnetic fields.

   h. Two negatives make a positive, but two positives do not make a negative.

   j. There is no support in the data for that theory.

Passage V—Data Representation

The conical pendulum is a pendulum that is anchored at some height and swings around in a circle rather than swinging back and forth like a standard pendulum. Its chain traces out a cone as the bob circles below the anchor, as shown in Figure 1.

Conical Pendulum

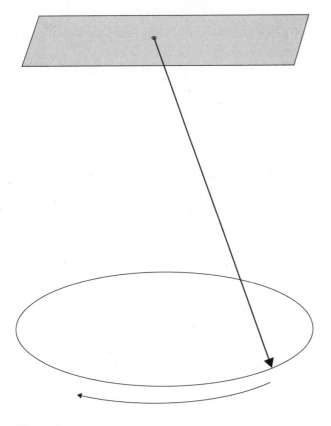

Figure 1

The forces acting on a conical pendulum with constant angular velocity are gravity, g, and the tension on the chain, T. The chain tension has a vertical component that counteracts gravity and a horizontal component, known as the centripetal force, that pulls the pendulum bob toward the center of the circle, forcing it to follow a circular path. These forces are diagrammed in Figure 2.

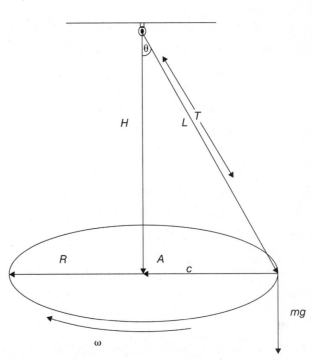

Legend

θ	angle the chain makes with the vertical
L	length of the chain
T	tension on the chain
H	vertical height from the orbit of the pendulum to the anchor
F_C, A_C	centripetal force, centripetal acceleration
R	radius of the pendulum's path
ω	angular velocity of the pendulum bob
m	mass of the pendulum bob
g	force of gravity on the pendulum bob

Figure 2

Vector analysis of these forces using the trigonometric relations $R = \sin(\theta)L$ and $H = \cos(\theta)L$ indicates that

$$T^2 = F_C^{\,2} + g^2$$
$$F_C = T\sin(\theta) = \frac{mV^2}{R}$$
$$g = T\cos(\theta)$$

where V = tangential velocity. If the mass of the chain is negligible compared to the mass of the pendulum bob, the relationships between velocity, radius, and chain length are always the same, regardless of mass.

Here are formulas for acceleration and velocity that ignore mass:

$$A_T^2 = A_C^2 + A_g^2$$
$$A_C = A_T \sin(\theta) = \frac{V^2}{R}$$
$$A_g = A_T \cos(\theta)$$
$$V = \sqrt{\tan\Theta R A_g}$$

where A = acceleration and the subscripts T, C, and g are the acceleration due to tension on the chain, centripetal force, and gravity, respectively. V is the tangential velocity, and R is the radius.

Physically, this means that the pendulum bob is moving with a certain velocity. The force that keeps it from following a straight-line path or falling due to gravity is the tension of the chain (T). T pulls the pendulum bob up to counteract gravity and toward the center of the circle to alter its straight-line path. The relationship between the vertical and horizontal forces of T is that as the chain becomes more horizontal the centripetal force increases in comparison to gravity. This can happen only if the velocity increases, as shown in the formulas. A tetherball apparatus functions like a conical pendulum. As the ball moves faster, it also rises higher. When it slows down, it descends.

Table 1 and Figure 3 show how the velocity, radius, and height change as the angle from the vertical (θ) of a pendulum 20 meters in length changes from 0° to 89°.

TABLE 1			
θ	V	R	H
0	0.000	0.000	20.000
5	1.223	1.743	19.924
10	2.450	3.473	19.696
15	3.687	5.176	19.319
20	4.940	6.840	18.794
25	6.215	8.452	18.126
30	7.522	10.000	17.321
35	8.872	11.472	16.383
40	10.282	12.856	15.321
45	11.773	14.142	14.142
50	13.377	15.321	12.856
55	15.142	16.383	11.472
60	17.146	17.321	10.000
65	19.518	18.126	8.452
70	22.495	18.794	6.840
75	26.581	19.319	5.176
80	33.086	19.696	3.473
85	47.242	19.924	1.743
89	105.958	19.997	0.349

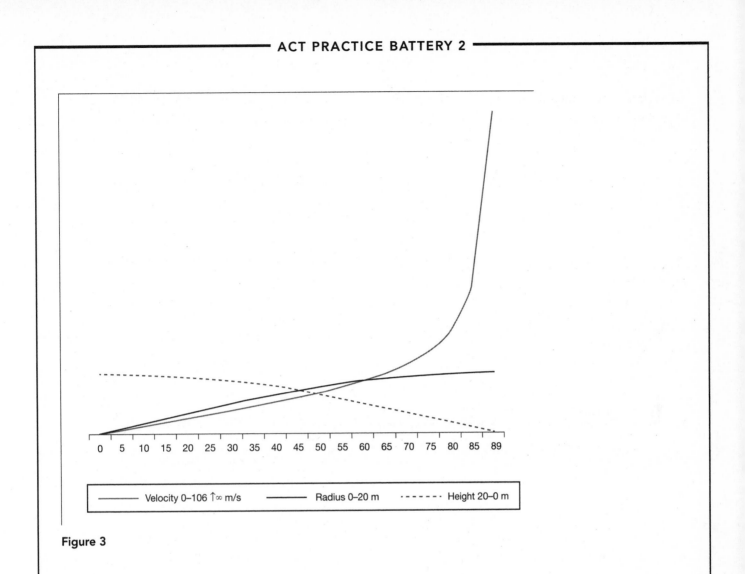

Figure 3

25. Looking at Figures 2 and 3 and Table 1, which figure best illustrates the position of the pendulum bob and chain as θ goes from 0° to 89°?

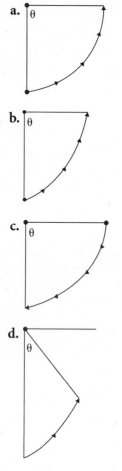

a.

b.

c.

d.

26. According to Table 1, what is the relationship between the radius and height at 45°?

  f. The radius = πH.

  g. The radius = ½ the height.

  h. They are equal.

  j. The height is 1.7321 × the radius.

27. The graphs for radius and height in Figure 3 appear to be the same shape except that one is flipped around a vertical line at 45°. Based on Table 1 and your understanding of how these values are generated, are they the same shape? Why or why not?

  a. Yes, they are because they both end with the pendulum bob at the end of a 20 m chain.

  b. No, they are not because the height decreases as the radius increases.

  c. Yes, they are because they cross at 45°.

  d. Yes they are because the radius = 20 m × sin(θ) and the height = 20 m × cos(θ).

28. Look at the explanation of the forces affecting the pendulum bob, especially the description for velocity V, the graph line given in Figure 3, and the formula for V. Which statement best describes what must happen to V as the pendulum approaches 90° from the vertical?

  f. It increases.

  g. It decreases to nothing.

  h. It increases at a rapidly accelerating rate.

  j. Answer **h** is correct, but no matter how fast the velocity becomes, the pendulum bob can never be perfectly horizontal because if it were there would be no vertical component of the tension force acting against gravity.

29. Consider the formula for centripetal force, $F_C = \frac{mV}{R}$. What happens to the magnitude of the force required to keep the pendulum on its circular path when the angle from the vertical approaches 90°?

    a. It decreases to zero because the height H of the pendulum, which is proportional to the gravitational force, decreases to zero.

    b. It will be at its minimum point because the radius R is at its maximum.

    c. It will accelerate at an accelerating rate with no limit because V, which is the main factor in the formula, is accelerating toward infinity.

    d. It remains the same because H is being changed, not V or R.

Passage VI—Research Summary

Carbon 14 dating is a widely used method for determining the age of formerly living objects. The earth's atmosphere and living things, which derive their carbon directly or indirectly from the atmosphere, all have virtually the same proportions of the carbon isotopes. These are: ^{12}C, 98.89%; ^{13}C, 1.11%; and ^{14}C, 1×10^{-10}%. That means one-trillionth of the carbon in most substances is ^{14}C.

The reason ^{14}C is useful as a measure of age is that it is radioactive. It decays at a rate of half of the atoms in a sample every 5,732 years. When a ^{14}C atom changes to ^{14}N, it emits a beta particle. The beta particles can be counted to measure how many ^{14}C atoms exist in a sample being tested. Living organisms regulate their own composition and are constantly refreshing the compounds out of which they are composed. As long as they are alive, their carbon isotope concentration remains one atom of ^{14}C per trillion atoms of carbon. When they die, the ^{14}C begins decaying according to the formula $T = -5,732 \times \log_2(N/N_o)$, where T is the time since the organism died, 5,732 is the half-life of ^{14}C, N is the number of ^{14}C atoms now in the sample, and N_o is the original number.

Figure 1 shows the expected ratio N/N_o for organic remains that began decaying over the past 60 centuries.

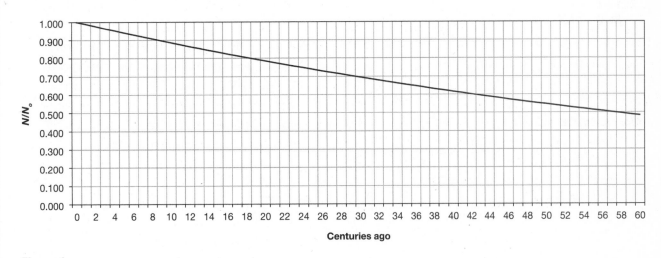

Figure 1

Study 1

In the 1940s, Willard F. Libby and others proposed using carbon 14 dating as a means of determining the age of wood, organic remains, and other materials that could be expected to have had the standard one in a trillion ^{14}C atoms when they died. They conducted a series of experiments on samples taken from artifacts whose age was known from historical records. The results confirmed the usefulness of the method.

Study 2

An expedition to an abandoned campfire site in the Pacific collected a number of artifacts found there. They were sent to a carbon-dating lab, and the beta radiation emissions from samples of the carbon in each artifact were tested to determine the amount of ^{14}C remaining. Table 1 shows the N/N_o (^{14}C now present/original ^{14}C level) ratio for a number of artifacts found at an abandoned campfire site in the Pacific.

TABLE 1	
ARTIFACT	N/N_o
wooden bowl	0.987
bone fragment 1	0.931
bone fragment 2	0.928
ivory fragment	0.927
fur	0.999
spear shank	0.500

30. Based on the description of carbon 14 dating in this passage, why are the N/N_o numbers in Table 1 evidence about the age of the artifacts?
   f. Living organisms all have the same ratio of carbon 14 to total carbon. After they die the carbon 14 decays and the ratio declines. The ratio of carbon 14 remaining to the original amount tells us when the organism began decaying.
   g. Living organisms all contain carbon. When they die, the carbon combines with oxygen and forms carbon monoxide and carbon dioxide gas. This gas is dissipated in the atmosphere.
   h. The carbon becomes radioactive after the organism dies. The more radioactive it is, the longer ago it died.
   j. Carbon is the basis of all organic compounds.

31. Which of the artifacts is the oldest?
   a. fur
   b. bone fragment 2
   c. spear shank
   d. wooden bowl

32. Figure 1 does not give a precise indication of the relationship between years of decay and expected N/N_o values. Is other information presented that can give a more precise dating for one of the artifacts listed in Table 1? Which artifact is it, and how old is it?
   f. No, Figure 1 is the only information available.
   g. The age of the wooden bowl can be estimated at 10 years.
   h. The spear shank is 5,732 years old.
   j. Bone fragment 2 is just a little bit more than 1,800 years old.

33. This table gives a more detailed view of what happens to the N/N_o ratio for items that have been decaying between 580 and 650 years. Compare Table 1 to this table. Which of the following statements is correct?

YEARS AGO	N/N_O
580	0.932
590	0.931
600	0.930
610	0.929
620	0.928
630	0.927
640	0.926
650	0.924

a. The bone fragments and the ivory fragment might have been from the same animal.

b. The ivory fragment and bone fragment 2 might have begun decaying at the same time, but bone fragment 1 died a decade or more later.

c. First bone fragment 1 died, followed by bone fragment 2, and then the ivory.

d. The N/N_o ratio declines by 0.001 every ten years.

34. Figure 2 shows a condensed view of the calculated N/N_o values going back 75,000 years in the past. Which statements are supported by this chart and what this passage has reported about the process of radioactive decay?

f. After about 21,000 years the concentration of ^{14}C drops below one atom of carbon out of 10 trillion.

g. After 50,000 years the concentration of ^{14}C is so diffuse that carbon dating is not at all reliable.

h. More than half of the original ^{14}C has decayed after 6,000 years.

j. all of the above

35. Based on the description of study 1, when carbon 14 dating determines the age of an organic object, what is the event in the history of that object at which the aging began?

a. Its birth for mammals or the equivalent for other animals and plants.

b. When it was formed into the object found. For instance, when a branch was cut from a tree and made into a spear.

c. When its cells died and began decaying.

d. When its carbon molecules were formed.

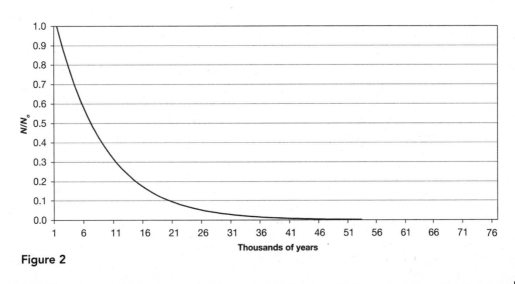

Figure 2

Passage VII—Data Representation

Magnetotactic bacteria (MTB) are bacteria that swim around carrying crystals of magnetic minerals, including magnetite (Fe_3O_4) and greigite (Fe_3S_4) inside their cell walls. These metallic crystals are called magnetosomes. Most organisms contain only trace amounts of iron (Fe), but MTBs have concentrations in the range of 3%. This is high enough so that they are affected by magnetic fields. Many MTB species characteristically swim either parallel to or perpendicular to the earth's magnetic field lines. Since their discovery they have been widely studied as possibly the original source of existing iron ore deposits, as a possible means for concentrating iron now dispersed throughout the earth's lakes and oceans, and for other reasons.

TABLE 1		
Sample	Environment	mg of MTB
M1	Dark brown surface soil	685.5
M2	Dark brown surface soil	1,348.5
M3	Yellow surface soil	90.5
M4	Brown surface soil	500.0
M5	Brown surface soil	328.0
M6	Brown surface soil	162.5
M7	Brown surface soil	416.0
M8	Brown surface soil	1,430.0
M9	Brown surface soil	1,270.0
M10	Brown surface soil	4,139.0
M11	Dark brown surface soil	405.0
M12	Black surface soil	305.5
M13	Dark brown surface soil	1,135.5
M14	Dark brown surface soil	1,542.5
M15	Black surface soil	348.0
M16	Black surface soil	1,086.5
M17	Copper-green surface soil	1,776.0
P1	Black primary iron ore	870.0
P2	Black primary iron ore	2,235.0
P3	Black primary iron ore	658.0
P4	Black primary iron ore	253.5
T1	Brown surface soil	329.0
T2	Brown iron ore	380.5
T3	Brown surface soil/clastic ore	523.5
T4	Brown surface soil/clastic ore	514.0
T5	Brown clastic iron ore	279.0
T6	Gray surface soil	1,213.5
T7	Gray surface soil	482.5
T8	Brown surface soil	60.0

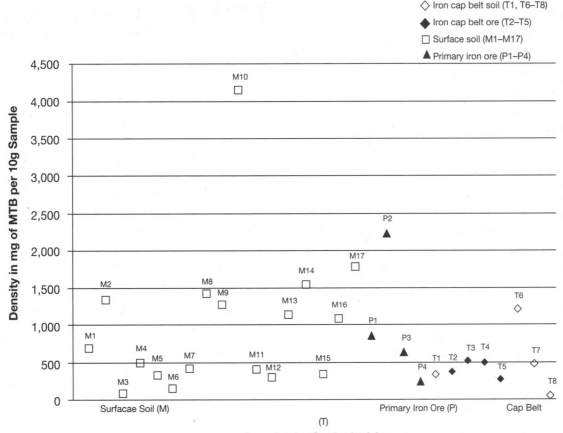

Figure 1

Table 1 and the scatter plot in Figure 1 report on characteristics of MTB populations in a Chinese iron mine region. The purpose of the study was to obtain data on the difference that various environments made on the density of the MTBs' magnetosomes. Samples were taken from 29 different areas as described in Table 1. These are divided into three broad regions: the primary iron ore area (samples P1 to P4); the iron cap belt, which is a secondary concentration of iron ore (samples T1 to T8); and the surface soil (samples M1 to M17). All of the primary ore samples are taken from iron ore. All of the surface soil samples are taken from soil. Both soil and iron ore samples were taken from the cap belt. On the scatter plot all of the soil samples are marked with outlined symbols and the ore samples with solid symbols. The density measure for each sample is the mass in mg of MTBs found in a standard 10 g sample.

Table 2 shows the average MTB density for each of the four types of samples.

TABLE 2	
SAMPLE TYPE	mg OF MTB
Primary ore	1,004.1
Surface soil	998.2
Soil from iron cap	521.3
Ore from iron cap	424.3

36. Look at Table 2 and characterize the sample types from the standpoint of MTB density.

   f. As expected, the primary ore samples are the richest in MTBs, followed by the iron cap ore, then the iron cap soil and the surface soil, in that order.

   g. The primary ore and surface soil samples are approximately twice as rich in MTBs as the iron cap samples.

   h. The surface soil samples appear to be almost as rich as the primary oil samples, but that is because there were many more samples taken.

   j. There is no particular distinction between MTB densities in the different sample types. The primary ore is the highest, but the iron cap ore is the lowest. The two soil categories are in between.

37. Based on Figure 1, characterize the top five soil samples in MTB density.

   a. They are the four primary ore samples plus one iron cap ore sample.

   b. They are all surface soil samples.

   c. All but one of them are surface soil samples. The number 2 sample is primary ore and it is approximately half as dense as the leading soil sample.

   d. Four are surface soil samples and one is iron cap soil.

38. Which statement is most strongly supported by the data presented in Table 1, Table 2, and Figure 1?

   f. Environmental concerns are not relevant to the density of MTBs.

   g. MTB density depends on the density of iron in the environment.

   h. Darker soil has more MTBs than lighter soil.

   j. Environment seems to play a role, but it is not based strictly on density of iron.

39. Some experimenters hypothesize that the MTB richness of the surface soil samples may be because the surface soil is richer in moisture and other nutrients than the ore or iron cap soil samples. If that hypothesis is demonstrated, which of these statements would that support?

   a. MTBs do not require rich iron ore deposits as a source of iron.

   b. If MTBs are well nourished they can travel longer distances to find the iron ore they feed on.

   c. MTBs can convert other minerals into iron.

   d. none of the above

40. Look at Table 1. Which of the four types of samples (surface soil, primary ore, iron cap ore, and iron cap soil) has the largest range in density?

   f. primary ore

   g. iron cap ore

   h. iron cap soil

   j. surface soil

ACT Writing Practice Test 2

You have 30 minutes to complete this essay. Remember to:

- Address the specific topic and writing task.
- Create a well-organized response.
- Include developed supporting ideas and specific details.
- Use sentence variety and strong word choices.

A student activist group on your school campus is protesting the use of animals for dissection in science classes. The group claims that animals have the basic rights of life and happiness and that purposely destroying them for use in classes is cruel. Many of the science students disagree, stating that animals are useful in educating people about important medical and health issues and that eliminating their use in the classes would severely harm students' education.

In your essay, take a position on this question. You may write about either of the two points of view given, or you may present a different point of view on the topic. Use specific reasons and examples to support your position.

Answers

ACT English Practice Test 2
Passage I—Wilma Rudolph

1. **b.** This answer corrects the sentence fragment.

2. **h.** This properly places the subject pronoun *she* immediately after the comma and is the clearest.

3. **b.** This choice makes the sentence consistent in tense and is more concise than answer choice **c**.

4. **h.** This properly sequences the modifiers—*normally* after walk, *without the aid of a crutch or brace* after *normally*, and *by age 12* last.

5. **a.** This is correct as it stands. The *who* clause is nonessential and should be set off by a comma.

6. **f.** The sentence is correct as it is, and is more informative than choice **j**.

7. **c.** This is the correct word order.

8. **g.** This is the most correct and concise version. The transition here should not be omitted, as it makes the passage of time easier to follow.

9. **d.** The simple past tense is most appropriate here.

10. **j.** Choice **f** is a run-on, choice **g** incorrectly uses a semicolon, and choice **h** incorrectly uses dashes.

11. **b.** *However* is the most appropriate transition here.

12. **h.** This answer offers the most precise and vivid word choice.

13. **a.** This choice best conveys the main idea of the passage. Choice **b** focuses only on Rudolph's family; choice **c** understates the physical handicaps she overcame; and choice **d** does not mention her athletic accomplishments.

14. **h.** The most logical place is after the sentence that lists the three gold medals that Rudolph won.

15. **b.** This logically separates her accomplishments in track and field from her accomplishments in fighting segregation.

Passage II—Bicycles

16. **g.** This answer has the most appropriate and correct usage and word choice.

17. **d.** The present perfect tense—*have made*—is correct.

18. **h.** The phrase *a Scottish blacksmith* is relevant but nonessential information and needs to be set off by commas.

19. **a.** This is correct as is.

20. **h.** The verb needs to be in the simple past tense.

21. **a.** This is correct as is.

22. **g.** There should not be a comma between the subject and the verb.

23. **d.** This choice gives the sentence parallel structure.

24. **j.** The subject—*the bicycle*—must immediately follow the comma.

25. **c.** A comma should go after an introductory word or phrase, and *they are* correctly replaces *there*.

26. **h.** This choice presents the correct word order.

27. **d.** The noun form *transportation* is correct.

28. **g.** This choice gives readers reasons to buy a bicycle for themselves.

29. **b.** This is the most logical sequence. The sentence about Lawson and naming the safety bicycle correctly comes before the details of the safety bicycle. Sentence 13 is the best conclusion for the paragraph.

30. **f.** While all the answer choices are relevant to the passage, choice **f** most accurately captures the central theme.

Passage III—The Gateway Arch

31. b. The colon is the most correct punctuation mark here. Colons introduce explanations.

32. h. This answer has the most appropriate and concise word choice. It could be omitted without ruining the sentence (choice **j**), but it would take out an idea central to the essay: that the monument is amazing.

33. d. There are no commas needed here.

34. h. *Take* agrees with *trams*, or *they take visitors*.

35. a. This is the correct helping verb and tense.

36. g. *Imposing* should be a modifier, and using the participial form is the most concise.

37. c. Use *who* when referring to people as the subject of a sentence.

38. j. This is the most concise and effective version.

39. b. *His* agrees with *Saarinen*.

40. g. This is the proper phrasing.

41. d. This is the most concise and effective version.

42. h. The subject, *the arch*, must immediately follow the comma.

43. b. This is the most logical choice. The first paragraph introduces the topic and main idea; the third paragraph then describes the background of the arch and establishes a chronological order; the second paragraph continues the chronology; and the fourth paragraph returns to the idea of the arch's remarkable design, as established in the introduction.

44. f. Saarinen's other work is not pertinent to the St. Louis Arch.

45. d. The passage discusses the design of the monument but does not describe how the city and monument honor St. Louis's role as a gateway to westward expansion. It simply mentions this fact.

Passage IV—Annie Smith Peck

46. h. This is the most accurate and concise choice.

47. c. In this instance, the past perfect is the appropriate tense.

48. g. Separate items in a list with commas, unless one or more items already has a comma (then use a semicolon).

49. a. This is correct as it stands. Choice **c** would create a sentence fragment.

50. h. The correct preposition is *in*, and the word *continents* would be redundant.

51. b. This is the most concise and appropriate version.

52. j. This is the proper usage.

53. d. Using the infinitive gives the sentence parallel structure.

54. f. This is correct as it stands.

55. c. *Team* is a collective singular, so *it was* is the appropriate choice.

56. g. *Hacked* is the most precise and vivid word choice.

57. d. This sentence should be omitted; it does not fit the tone and style of the essay.

58. f. This is correct as it stands. Choice **j** would create a sentence fragment.

59. b. Sentence 4 is off topic and should be eliminated to maintain the focus of the paragraph.

60. g. This is best in tone and phrasing. Choice **f** introduces a new idea, which is not appropriate in a conclusion.

Passage V—Batman

61. d. Each exclamation should be followed by an exclamation point.

62. h. The phrase *created in 1939 and known worldwide* is relevant but not essential information and should be set off by commas.

63. c. The phrase beginning *who was just 22 years old* must be connected to an independent clause; it is not a complete sentence. A period here makes the phrase a fragment. Semicolons can only go between two independent clauses (two complete thoughts).

64. g. The correct form is the plural possessive.

65. a. *Bat* and *like* work together to form one modifier, so *batlike* is correct. This is also the most concise choice.

66. j. *Overwhelming* is a more powerful and precise word than *big*. This version is also more concise than versions **g** and **h**.

67. c. A comma should precede the coordinating conjunction *and* when it separates two independent clauses.

68. g. In the present tense, *lay* is a transitive verb meaning "to place something," and it requires an object; in this case, the correct word is *lie*, used here to mean "be located."

69. b. This version gives the sentence parallel structure and is the most logical word order.

70. f. The sentence has consistent verb tense (all verbs in the present tense).

71. a. This is the most appropriate transition.

72. g. This version gives the sentence parallel structure and consistent verb tense.

73. c. The introduction uses a comic book convention to make a connection between topic and structure. The tone is lighthearted, but not silly. The introduction does demonstrate the effect of onomatopoeia and exclamation points, but it has a more meaningful purpose. It is not intended to show that there is a lot of fighting in a typical Batman comic book, as this is not a theme of the essay.

74. h. This is the most logical sequence, in both topic and chronology of events.

75. b. This is a logical place to insert the sentence, since it provides a reason the show was successful and should follow the general statement that Batman was a success.

ACT Mathematics Practice Test 2

1. a. The word *and* indicates a decimal point. Therefore, the decimal point should go after 512 and before 16 thousandths. The number 16 must end in the thousandths place, which is three digits to the right of the decimal.

2. g. The correct order of operations must be used to simplify the expression. You may remember this as PEMDAS: parentheses, exponents, multiplication, division, addition, subtraction.

3. b. The problem can also be worked with the equation $4x + 5x = 18$, where x equals each unit when there are 4 units of boys and 5 units of girls.

4. h. To find the median, place the numbers in order from least to greatest and find the middle number. Because there are an even number of numbers, there are two middle numbers (0.024 and 0.095). Take the average of these two middle numbers.

5. d. Use the vertical line test to see if each graph is a function. A graph is *not* a function if any vertical line drawn goes through the graph more than once (if there is more than one y value for any x value).

6. f. $-3 \times -3 \times -3 \times -3 \times -3 = -243$.

7. b. Consecutive odd integers starting with 3 are being added to find the next number. Therefore, 11 must be added to 24 to find the next number. The answer is 35.

8. h. First, you can eliminate choices **f** and **j** because they contain numbers that are not prime. Next, use a factor tree to determine the prime factorization. The prime factorization of 84 is $2 \times 2 \times 3 \times 7$, which can be written in exponential notation as $2^2 \times 3 \times 7$.

9. c. To easily see the slope, change the equation into the form $y = mx + b$. The equation is then $y = \frac{7}{3}x + 9$, where m is the slope.

10. g. The perimeter is twice the width plus twice the length: $P = 2w + 2l$. Insert 20 for P and 4 for w, then solve for l.

11. e. Find the lengths of the unlabeled sides by comparing them to the given sides. Find the area of each of the regions and add together to find the total area: $30 + 28 = 58$ sq. in.

12. g. Find the cost for one can (unit rate) by dividing the cost of five cans by 5: $6.50 ÷ 5 = $1.30 per can. Multiply the cost per can by 9 cans: $1.30 × 9 = $11.70. Nine cans cost $11.70.

13. d. Find a common denominator ($15x$). Multiply the numerator and denominator of the first fraction by 5 and of the second fraction by $3x$; then add the two numerators and place them over the common denominator.

14. j. The endpoints are on −1.5 and 0, and the solution set includes 0 but does not include −1.5, as indicated by the open circle.

15. c. First, raise everything in the parentheses to the second power; then apply the negative.

16. f. Use substitution to solve for x and y. First, solve the second equation for y. Next, substitute the value for y into the first equation and solve for x. Finally, subtract y from x.

17. a. Notice that you are taking the *cube* root, *not* the *square* root. Break up the expression under the radical into perfect cubes.

18. h. Substitute the value 63° for C, and solve for F.

19. c. The equation is quadratic. Because it is factorable, solve the equation using factoring: $(x + 5)(x + 3) = 0$. Set each of the factors equal to zero and solve for x: $x + 5 = 0$, $x + 3 = 0$, so $x = -5$ and $x = -3$.

20. g. Solve the equation for m using inverse operations.

21. e. By distributing and then using inverse operations, you get the equation $-7 = 10$, so there are no values for x that make the equation true.

22. k. Factor the numerator into $(4x - 1)(x + 3)$. Cancel out the $(x + 3)$ in numerator and denominator, and $4x - 1$ remains.

23. a. Subtract the numbers in y from the corresponding numbers in x.

24. g. $\text{Log}_3 x = 2$ is equivalent to $3^2 = x$. Therefore, $x = 9$.

25. b. Use the Pythagorean theorem to solve. To use the Pythagorean theorem (which is what the distance formula is derived from), draw the segment on a coordinate plane and create a right triangle where AC is the hypotenuse. The legs of the right triangle are 1 and 4, so the hypotenuse is the square root of $1^2 + 4^2$, or the square root of 17.

26. f. Because the line is parallel to $3y - 9x = 24$, they must have the same slope. Put the equation into $y = mx + b$ form to see the slope is 3 and the y-intercept is 4, so you are looking for the line $y = 3x + 4$. You must put the answer choices in $y = mx + b$ form to compare them to this equation.

27. d. The answer choices are spread out enough that a quick bit of figuring establishes the useful range. Use the square roots that are near the answer. For 37, use 6; for 125, use 11. These will quickly lead to 66 as the correct choice.

28. g. Find the probability of each event and multiply the answers to find the probability of both events occurring. The probability of getting tails is $\frac{1}{2}$, and the probability of rolling a 3 is $\frac{1}{6}$.

29. d. Multiply the decimal equivalent of $\frac{1}{2}$%, or 0.005, by 90.

30. k. Set up a proportion of $\frac{0.75}{1} = \frac{12}{x}$, cross multiply, and solve for x.

31. b. Convert the given rate of meters per second to kilometers per hour. First, multiply $\frac{100}{9.79}$ by $\frac{1}{1,000}$ to change meters to kilometers. Next, multiply that product by $\frac{60}{1}$ to change seconds to minutes. Finally, multiply that product by $\frac{60}{1}$ to changes minutes to hours.

32. k. To find the number of combinations available, multiply the number of choices for each element, or $4 \times 6 \times 10$, which is 240.

33. d. Multiply the 5 by 6 to get 30. Then multiply the powers of 10 to get 10^4, or 10,000. $30 \times 10,000 = 300,000$. Now convert to scientific notation.

34. j. sin = opposite/hypotenuse, so you must find the hypotenuse. To do so, use the Pythagorean theorem (or simply recognize the Pythagorean triple). The hypotenuse is 25, so sin $B = \frac{7}{25}$.

35. a. There are three pairs of sides. The two sides that measure 6×8 each have an area of 48. The two sides that measure 6×10 each have an area of 60. The two sides that measure 8×10 each have an area of 80. Simply multiply and add.

36. g. The radius of the large circle is 7 (add the inner radius plus the extra 3 from the ring); therefore the area of the large circle is 49π. Subtract the area of the inner circle, which is 16π.

37. a. Take the square root of the area to find the length of one side, 10. When the diagonal is drawn, it creates a right triangle with legs of 10 cm each and the diagonal is the hypotenuse. Use the Pythagorean theorem to find the diagonal.

38. g. Substitute 15 for y in the equation and solve for x.

39. e. Find the number of students (male and female) who voted for Kristen by multiplying 540 by 0.60, the decimal equivalent of 60%. Multiply that product by 0.75, the decimal equivalent of 75%.

40. f. cos is adjacent/hypotenuse, and tan is opposite/adjacent. If cos θ is $\frac{12}{13}$, then the hypotenuse is 13. The side opposite θ is 5, so sin $\theta = \frac{\text{opposite}}{\text{hypotenuse}} = \frac{5}{13}$.

41. d. The original formula was $V = lwh$. If each dimension is tripled, the length is $3l$, the width is $3w$, and the height is $3h$. When these values are substituted into the equation, the equation becomes $V = (3l)(3w)(3h)$, or $V = 27lwh$. Thus the new rectangular solid has a volume 27 times the original volume.

42. k. The sum of the measures of the angles in a triangle is 180°. In a right triangle, the right angle is 90°, so another 90° is split between the remaining two angles. Thus $7x + 8x = 90$, and $x = 6$. The value of x is 6, but the question asks for the measure of the smaller angle, which is $7x$, or 42.

43. c. Call the width w and the length $2w$. The perimeter is then $P = w + w + 2w + 2w$; $72 = 6w$; $12 = w$. The width is 12. Because the length is twice the width, the length is 24.

44. k. Call the height h and the base $h + 5$. The area of a triangle is $\frac{1}{2}$(base × height). Substitute h and $h + 5$ for the base and height, and set the area equal to 80. The equation is $\frac{1}{2}h^2 + \frac{5}{2}h = 80$, which is a quadratic equation. Multiply both sides by 2, and subtract 160 from both sides to get $h^2 + 5h - 160 = 0$. Since the equation cannot be factored, use the quadratic formula to solve, and eliminate the negative answer since distance cannot be negative.

45. d. There is no need to use the distance formula if you recognize that the y-coordinate of the first two points is the same (3). This means that the difference in the x-coordinates, which is 7, must be the length of one side of the square.

46. k. The slope of the given equation is 3. The slope of a line perpendicular to the line is the negative reciprocal of 3, or $-\frac{1}{3}$. Arrange each answer choice into the $y = mx + b$ format to find the slope of each choice quickly. Only choice **k** has the proper slope.

47. b. To find the midpoint, use the midpoint formula, which in effect means find the averages of the two x-coordinates and the two y-coordinates.

48. j. Apply the exponent to both $\frac{1}{2}$ and x^2. Because the exponent is negative, take the reciprocal of the fraction and the variable, then raise both 2 and $\frac{1}{x^2}$ to the third power and combine.

49. c. Recall that all triangles have three angles that total 180°. Next, using the two angle measures given, find the two bottom angles of the triangle. The bottom left angle is supplementary (adds to 180°) with 120°; therefore, it is 60°. The bottom right angle is a corresponding angle to the 21° angle and, therefore, is 21°. The three angles in the triangle must add to 180°, so x is 99°.

50. j. Keep in mind that a tangent line will have only one point in common with the circle. Draw the graph of the circle on the coordinate plane to see that the radius must be 4.

51. d. The equation of a circle is in the form $(x - h)^2 + (y - k)^2 = r^2$, where r is the radius. Because the given equation is already in this form, you can find that $r^2 = 36$, or $r = 6$. Use the formula $A = \pi r^2$ to find the area of the circle.

52. g. Find the measures of angles DBC and BDC by using the supplements given (remember that supplementary angles add to 180°). So angle $DBC = 60°$ and angle $BDC = 70°$. The three angles of a triangle must add to 180°. Therefore, angle $BCD = 50°$.

53. a. The cosine graph goes from –1 to 1, meaning the cosine of an angle is between –1 and 1, inclusive, and the minimal value for $\cos x$ is –1. Now multiply by 9 to solve.

54. h. The walkway is 10 ft. longer and 10 ft. wider than the pool (*not* 5 ft.) because 5 ft. is added on *each* side of the pool. To find the area of the walkway, find the area of the large rectangle (walkway and pool combined), and subtract the area of the pool.

55. b. Equilateral triangle XYZ has all 60° angles. Because YW is an altitude, it forms a right angle and bisects the angle at Y. Thus, triangle XYW is a 30–60–90 triangle. The hypotenuse YX is 10 in., and the shortest side XW is half of that, 5 in. The side opposite the 60° angle is $\sqrt{3}$ times the short side.

56. k. Use the identity $\sin^2 A + \cos^2 A = 1$, so $\frac{49}{100} + \cos^2 A = 1$. Now solve by subtracting $\frac{49}{100}$ from both sides, then taking the square root of both sides.

57. d. The triangle given is a 45–45–90 triangle, so the sides are in the ratio $1{:}1{:}\sqrt{2}$. Use a proportion to find x, where $\frac{\sqrt{2}}{1} = \frac{x}{\sqrt{5}}$.

58. f. An ellipse is defined by an equation such as $\frac{x^2}{a^2} + \frac{y^2}{b^2} = 1$, where $+a$ and $-a$ are the x-intercepts, and $+b$ and $-b$ are the y-intercepts. Only choice **f** yields the correct intercepts of $+5$ and -5 for x, $+3$ and -3 for y.

59. b. Notice that the y-intercept is 2 and the slope is -3. Thus the equation must be $y = -3x + 2$. Answer choices **b** and **c** are possibilities. The shading determines which is correct. Substitute $(0,0)$ for x and y. Because the shading includes the point $(0,0)$, find the equation that is satisfied by the point $(0,0)$.

60. k. The only constraint on this function is that the denominator must not be zero. To find which values will yield a denominator of zero, set the denominator equal to zero and solve. $x^2 + 3x - 4 = 0$, so factoring shows $(x + 4)(x - 1) = 0$. Now set each factor equal to zero and solve. $x + 4 = 0$ and $x - 1 = 0$, so $x = -4$ and $x = 1$. These are the values that x *cannot* be, and the domain is written as $\{x \mid x \neq -4 \text{ and } x \neq 1\}$.

ACT Reading Practice Test 2
Passage I—Humanities

1. b. We know that statement I is untrue because lines 42–44 state *the people of the North had no particular quarrel with slavery.* Immediately following, the same lines also disprove statement III.

2. f. The third paragraph establishes the argument that rapid transit was a factor, as was the North's unwillingness to legally support slavery. Although some Northerners would agree with statement III, nowhere in the passage is this stated.

3. b. The author agrees with the statement in lines 5–6: *A state half slave and half free cannot exist,* which essentially means the entire country must be for or against slavery.

4. h. The passage says that because of the Fugitive Slave Law, Northerners were required to chase down runaway slaves. Later in the passage, it says that the North was *not willing to play the role of police for the South* (lines 45–46); therefore, the best answer is that it forced the North to enforce laws it did not believe were right.

5. d. Because it is clear that the North did not approve of the Fugitive Slave Law, the power it would be seeking would be to remove such laws from the books.

6. j. The answer to this question is found in lines 27–30; simply put, *They saw their power waning, and this led them to encroach upon the prerogatives and independence of the Northern States by enacting such laws as the Fugitive Slave Law.*

7. b. Be careful not to use any outside knowledge of the Civil War; in this case, choices **a** and **d** are, in fact, correct but are not discussed in the paragraph.

8. f. The author describes the United States as expanding in size, wealth, and population, and claims Europeans might think the United States would threaten their peace. Another way of saying this is that they are threatened by our unified strength.

9. a. Grant says Europeans believed that it *would part the moment the slightest strain was brought upon it* (lines 76–77), meaning that the only appropriate answer choice is **a.**

10. h. The final paragraph notes the *necessity of avoiding wars* (line 83), which makes choices **g** and **j** incorrect. The opening line of the fourth paragraph notes that *we are better off* after having the war, which makes **h** the best choice.

Passage II—Natural Sciences

11. d. Many asthma sufferers have an inherited tendency to have allergies, referred to as *atopy* in line 42.

12. g. The second paragraph explains that during an attack the person afflicted with asthma will attempt to compensate for constricted airways by breathing a greater volume of air.

13. c. The passage begins with the words *No longer,* indicating that in the past asthma was considered an anomalous inflammation of the bronchi, whereas it is now considered a chronic condition of the lungs.

14. g. While *exacerbation* usually means *an increase in severity,* in this passage *exacerbations* is interchangeable with *attacks.*

15. a. Cramping is not mentioned in the passage, whereas the other three symptoms are mentioned in the second paragraph.

16. j. The third paragraph discusses triggers, and only select physical activity is touted as a possible symptom reducer.

17. a. The final paragraph notes that symptoms come and go throughout the day, making the results of a physical examination inconclusive (lines 89–91).

18. g. All the individuals listed would find the passage in some way useful; however, a health-care professional would find the broad overview of the effects of asthma, combined with the trigger avoidance and diagnosis information, most relevant.

19. d. The middle of the third paragraph (lines 61–64) indicates that secondhand smoke puts children at risk of becoming asthmatic and may be fatal to asthmatic children.

20. g. The paragraph notes a number of factors that must be considered in the diagnosis, as well as the fact that symptoms come and go, thus making diagnosing asthma difficult.

Passage III—Prose Fiction

21. c. The husband had a civil servant's job and received a steady salary, the wife had a servant who cleaned for her, and the couple lived in a dwelling that had several rooms. This implies that they lived comfortably.

22. j. This question relates to the previous one. Choice **f** does not deal with the couple's economic standing, but only the wife's before she was married. Choice **g** is tempting, but the poverty of her rooms is more in her eyes than in reality. Choice **h** deals with a tablecloth that could have been washed by the maid or the wife, and the situation would have been remedied.

23. a. The wife's thoughts in the first paragraph indicate that she wished she had married a rich man. Instead, *she slipped into marriage with a minor civil servant.*

24. h. The specific items mentioned—Oriental hangings, bronze torches, or priceless knickknacks—indicate an overall desire for the finer things in life.

25. b. The husband's delight with the homemade stew only seems to send his wife into another bout of daydreams to escape her middle-class prison.

26. h. The final sentence includes the words *grief, regret, despair,* and *misery,* all of which would make someone morose. The other choices do not apply.

27. d. This is reinforced at the end of the fourth paragraph: the wife admits she loves only rich things, believes she was made for them, and focuses all her desires on being *admired and sought after,* thinking only of herself at all times.

28. f. Adjectives (words that describe nouns) are what truly add dimension to the descriptions of the home and the daydreams of the wife. *Innate, instinctive, grandest, gleaming, gorgeous,* and *pink* are some of the adjectives that enrich the nouns of the wife's dreams. *Shabby, worn, ugly,* and *homemade* are adjectives that add to the undesirable view she has of her present situation. None of the other choices adds such richness to the passage.

29. b. The reasonable inference is that her friend's wealth only makes her feel worse about her own perceived meager existence.

30. h. The narrator's insights into the woman's state of mind, and recounting of events inside the home, indicate an all-knowing, or omniscient, perspective.

Passage IV—Social Sciences

31. c. As stated in the second paragraph, *deep, underlying fissures* that *already existed in the economy* led to the Great Depression.

32. f. The passage is primarily an account that describes the causative factors—for example, tariff and war-debt policies, disproportionate wealth, and the accumulation of debt—that led to the Depression, and the Depression's impact on Americans—business failures, bank closings, homelessness, and federal relief programs.

33. c. Paragraph 1 states that shantytowns were called Hoovervilles because citizens blamed their plight on the Hoover administration's refusal to offer assistance.

34. g. The passage makes no mention of inflation as a cause of the Depression.

35. b. Although *policies* can refer to regulations (laws, choice **c**), or guiding principles (theories, choice **a**), in this context, *policies* refers to the courses of action (practices, choice **b**) taken by a government or business.

36. j. The passage describes the decade as one in which spending dominated over prudent measures like saving (paragraph 3). The wild stock market speculation, also described in that paragraph, is another example of extravagance.

37. b. The analogy depicts the stock market crash of 1929 as a weakening agent to the economy (the way a stressful event may weaken the body's resistance to illness).

38. h. Paragraph 4 states that the New Deal incentivized farmers to slow their production in order to stabilize prices; it can be inferred that unchecked production could destabilize prices.

39. d. This paragraph clearly states that the New Deal expanded the role of the central government in regulating the economy and creating social assistance programs. Choice **a** requires an opinion about the New Deal measures, which the author does not offer.

40. h. The final sentence of the passage indicates that one of the New Deal's accomplishments was creating social assistance programs; welfare would be one such program.

ACT Science Practice Test 2
Passage I—Data Representation

1. b. From the discussion of dissonance, including the content of the question, you know that beats occur in close, but not mutually divisible, frequencies and that the number of beats per second equals the difference in cps between the two tones. Tone *a* is 8 cps, so *b* is 7 cps. The difference is 1, so there should be one beat for every eight vibrations of tone *a*. You can count the bumps and find that both the largest and the smallest amplitude occur once every eight cycles.

Answer choice **c** is wrong for two reasons. If a combination of *a* and *d* produced beats, they would be one every six cycles because that is the difference between 8 and 2. Second, the wave in *e* actually remains in a very small amplitude range but floats up and down, as if sound wave *a* is riding on the back of sound wave *d*.

2. j. Higher frequencies mean higher pitches. Tone *a* is 8 cps and *d* is one-fourth that, which is 2 cps. One octave up from 2 cps is 4 cps. Another octave up is 8 cps. Answer choice **h** has the direction in pitch wrong. Answer choice **g** is totally confused.

3. a. The tones that compose *c* and *e*, respectively, have a maximum amplitude of 1. They can never do more than add their maxima together, so the maximum for each is no more than 2.

4. h. Noise-canceling devices depend on the principle that positive and negative wave motion cancel each other out. If any sound wave pattern, such as the ones shown here, is flipped over and played against itself, the sum of the two waves will be zero.

5. d. Laypersons are very familiar with the problem of noisy buildings, but a number of spectacular collapses over the past century have made it mandatory that buildings be designed without any strong resonance potential.

Passage II—Conflicting Viewpoints

6. f. If the velocity of separation, *v*, equals the speed of light, *c*, then *T* would equal $1 \div \sqrt{1 - \frac{1^2}{1^2}}$, which $= 1 \div \sqrt{1-1}$ or $1 \div 0$.

7. c. The rules of time dilation as given apply to how an observer reads a clock that is moving away. A and B are both moving away from each other and both observing each other. Therefore, each will measure the other's clock as slowing down. No distinction is made in the question between observer A and observer B. Therefore, answer choices **a** and **b** cannot be correct, because they say the two react differently. Answer choice **d** incorrectly states that observed time speeds up, but the time dilation theory says it slows down.

8. j. Answer choices **f** through **h** are relatively simple statements of proportionality. The formula for time dilation is more complex, as stated in answer choice **j**.

9. b. The question asks for an answer based on what is presented on the test, and no evidence is presented here of the light filter effect described in answer choice **a**. There is no support for answer choice **c**. Answer choice **d** is incorrect because higher frequencies mean more cycles per second. If time on the emitting object is slower than time here, its emissions would have fewer cycles per *our* seconds than similar radiation originating here.

10. j. According to the formula, the time dilation factor will be $1 \div \sqrt{1 - \frac{0}{c^2}}$. That is $\frac{1}{\sqrt{1}}$ or $\frac{1}{1}$, which is 1, which means there would be no time dilation in that case.

11. d. All three are consistent with the explanation of time dilation and relativistic length contraction presented here.

12. h. It seems intuitive that if time slows down for the objects relative to each other when they move apart, it should speed up when they move together, but answers must be based on the material presented. The formula and the model illustrated by Figure 2 produce the same results whether the objects are moving toward or away from each other.

Passage III—Research Summary

13. c. This is a control experiment to make sure the apparatus functions as intended. Answer choices **a** and **b** involve well-understood issues that have nothing to do with the purpose of the experiment. Answer choice **d** is incorrect because the control experiment demonstrated only that what was put in came out. It demonstrated nothing about what *always* happens to DNA.

14. f. Answer choice **g** is not correct because the experiment is designed to make sure all of the original DNA is heavy and all of the nitrogen newly incorporated into DNA is light. Answer choice **h** ignores the fact that the old heavy DNA is still in the culture. Answer choice **j** is incorrect because it makes an assumption contrary to the stated purpose of the experiment and contrary to the way chemical combination works. It falsely assumes that in the process of replication DNA can convert light nitrogen to heavy nitrogen.

15. c. In the conservative method, whole DNA molecules are replicated, so the original heavy molecules would remain, and all new ones would be light. There would be no other weights represented. In the semiconservative method, each of the two DNA strands is preserved and forms a second strand using only light nitrogen. The dispersive method, in which the strands are broken up and replicated in pieces, is the only one in which uneven mixtures of heavy and light can exist.

16. j. If the conservative method were used, the only possible result is half heavy and half light DNA. In subsequent trials, the dispersive method could produce various weights, as different-sized pieces of the strands are broken up and replicated, but the first trial would, like the semiconservative method, produce half heavy, half light DNA.

17. a. Answer choice **c** is incorrect because once a principle is definitively proven, no extra insurance is required. Answer choice **d** is incorrect for the reasons given in answer choice **a**.

18. j. Using the semiconservative method, which is what the experiment proves nature does, every replication cycle means that each strand produces a new DNA strand out of itself plus one created using only light nitrogen. The existing light nitrogen DNA will produce new light nitrogen DNA. The existing intermediate DNA will produce half intermediate and half light nitrogen DNA. Hence each cycle will halve the percentage of intermediate DNA. Answer choice **f** ignores the fact that the square of a negative number is positive. Answer choice **g** changes the formula from what is presented by the question without presenting any scientific reason for doing this.

Passage IV—Research Summary

19. c. The fact that all of the charges are multiples of the same number, rather than having a continuous or random change in value, suggests that 159 is the charge on a single particle and that all of the other charges equal the number of particles × 159. Answer choice **a** simply states what the passage said was the order in which the table was arranged. Answer choice **b** points to a clue that there are even multiples in the result, but it does not correctly identify the fact that all of the numbers are even multiples of a least factor. Answer choice **d** is not significant, because this is a random sampling of oil droplets.

20. g. Knowing the ratio of mass to charge means that you can calculate either mass or charge from the other as stated. Once the charge per particle was known, calculating the mass was easy. Answer choice **f** would give the mass of oil, not the mass of an electron. Answer choice **h** is incorrect because it assumes the weight of an electron equals the weight of a proton, even though the second sentence of the passage states that it does not. Answer choice **j** would give the average charge, but the question is asking about the mass.

21. d. Answer choice **a** draws conclusions not presented in the report of the experiment. Answer choices **b** and **c** refer to things already known through experiment 1.

22. f. Answer choices **g**, **h**, and **j** refer to issues not mentioned in the description.

23. d. Answer choices **a** and **b** were known already by experiment 1. Answer choice **c** was known by experiment 2. The importance of experiment 3 is the combination of proving that the charge exists only in discrete units and proving how minuscule the mass of these units is. That combination is not established before experiment 3.

24. j. Answer choices **f** and **g** are true but do not prove the theory. Answer choice **h** is a statement of arithmetic usage but is not a physical principle.

Passage V—Data Representation

25. a. It shows the pendulum hanging vertically, which is what 0° from the vertical is, and then swinging up to a nearly horizontal position, which is what 89° from the vertical is. Illustration **b** swings in the right direction, but the pendulum chain shrinks out as it goes. Illustration **c** swings from 89° to 0°. Illustration **d** swings only halfway, and it stretches as it goes.

26. h. They are both 14.142 m. This makes sense because at 45° the height and radius form an isosceles right triangle with the pendulum chain.

27. d. The sin and cosine are the most important trigonometric functions used in mathematical physics. They follow the same pattern but are always 90° out of synch with each other. Answer choice **a** is not true, as they are both measured from the center of the circle, not from the pendulum bob. Answer choice **b** makes a true statement in support of the incorrect answer. Answer choice **c** is a true statement in support of the correct answer, but the fact that they cross at the midway point does not demonstrate that they are the same shape.

28. j. This is confirmed by the formula for velocity, $V = \sqrt{\tan(\theta)RA_g}$. The tangent function is the opposite leg of a right triangle divided by the adjacent leg. At 90° the adjacent leg shrinks to zero and the opposite leg increases infinitely, so the tangent function always zooms up to infinity at 90°.

29. c. This follows from the discussion of question 28. Answer choice **b** has a conceptual error. It is true that when the pendulum is functioning, $\frac{H}{R}$ equals the force of gravity divided by the centripetal force. However, it is the forces of gravity and velocity that control the centripetal force, not the centripetal force that controls the force of gravity. That proportionality means that as H approaches zero, the centripetal force will have to increase toward the infinite.

Passage VI—Research Summary

30. f. Answer choice **g** is plausible based on general knowledge of biology and chemistry, but it is not what was discussed in the passage. Answer choice **h** confuses material included in the passage. Answer choice **j** is accurate, with some exceptions, and the passage makes it clear that carbon 14 dating depends on this fact, but the fact does not explain how carbon 14 dating works.

31. c. The ratio decreases as the artifact ages. The spear shank with an N/N_o ratio of 0.500 is the oldest artifact.

32. h. The passage says that the half-life of carbon 14 is 5,732 years. The N/N_o ratio of the spear shank is 0.500, which means that half of the original carbon 14 is gone.

33. b. Bone fragment 2 and the ivory fragment are in adjoining decades and could have begun dying at the same time, but bone fragment 1 is at least a decade away. Answer choice **a** is wrong as to timing, but even if the timing were correct, there is no information given to indicate these artifacts might be from the same animal. Answer choice **c** gives the wrong order. Higher numbers in the years ago column indicate earlier years than smaller numbers. Answer choice **d** seems to be correct for most of this small table, but the rate of radioactive decay is logarithmic, not constant.

34. j. N/N_o is the ratio of the remaining carbon 14 concentration to the original concentration. The original concentration is one part in 1 trillion, so when the graph crosses the 0.1 line, it is one in 10 trillion. Figure 1 makes answer choice **g**'s statement about the difficulties in using the method beyond 50,000 years clear. Answer choice **h** cannot be precisely determined from this long-range graph, but the passage states that the half-life of carbon 14 is 5,732 years. On questions with an "all of the above" choice, if two of the three answers are definitely correct, "all of the above" is a safe choice even if the third answer is uncertain. Of course, if the third answer is definitely wrong, reconsider whether the other two are correct.

35. c. The description of study 1 and other references throughout the passage make it clear that the carbon 14 method is based on the idea that carbon 14 concentrations remain at their original level within living organisms and begin decaying when the organisms die. Answer choice **a** is the common definition of age applied to living organisms. Answer choice **b** may or may not be correct for the particular instance it presents, but it does not apply in all cases.

Passage VII—Data Representation

36. g. Answer choice **f** is based on a preconceived idea of what the ordering should be, but it is not supported by the data. Answer choice **h** attempts to explain away the unexpected result, but the data are an average of the samples, not a total. Answer choice **j** dismisses the findings as uninteresting rather than reporting on them.

37. c. Reading the scatter plot from the top down makes this very clear.

38. j. The similarity between the densities of the two types of samples from the iron cap, and the clustering of the soil samples in two narrow ranges indicates an environmental dependence, but there are not enough data on which to state its precise nature. The data tend to refute answer choice **g** because iron ores are richer in iron than soil is, yet the soil seems to have more MTBs. Answer choice **h** is not at all supported, because the relationship between color characterizations and MTB density is quite random.

39. a. The data from the soil samples make it clear that the bacteria can take in iron in relatively iron-poor environments as well as from iron ore. No evidence is provided to support answer choice **b**. Given the limited conditions in which nuclear transformations occur, choice **c** would be highly unlikely.

40. j. Sample M3 has only 90.5 mg of MTBs, but sample M10 is the highest in the study, with 4,139.0 mg. The range in the primary ore samples is less than 2,000 mg, in iron cap soil it is about 1,100 mg, and in iron cap ore it is about 100 mg.

ACT Writing Practice Test 2

Sample "Score 6" Essay

Picture your beloved pet—a dog, cat, bird, or hamster—being killed, then shipped to one of thousands of schools to be dissected by students, many of whom are just taking the course for credit and who have no real interest in learning about health or biology. Now picture an unknown animal. Does the fact that the animal wasn't someone's pet make it any different? Your pet has emotions; it shows love, loyalty, fear, and pain. Obviously, these attributes are not unique to animals that are pets. All animals have these feelings. That is why using any animal for dissection is cruel, a violation of the animal's rights, and completely unnecessary.

The use of animals for dissection in schools is cruel. No matter how "humanely" the animals are put to death, they are still losing their lives. Some of them lose their lives quite young—before they even have a chance to live. Some schools use piglets as dissection animals in classes. Beyond that, some of these animals are specifically bred for dissection purposes. They live their lives in cages basically only being provided the bare necessities until they are put to sleep. Not only does this make their death cruel; it makes their lives cruel as well.

Animals have rights. Just like humans, animals have the right to live their lives and pursue happiness. Many animals enjoy their lives. You can tell when an animal is happy. Whether it be a dog that runs and plays and wags its tail, a cat that contentedly curls up on your lap, a horse that prances in the field, or a bird that sings—all animals show their enjoyment of life. We have no right to take that life away just because we are bigger or stronger or have more power than they do. This is the worst form of bullying. Opponents to this idea cite survival of the fittest or the biblical tradition of having dominion over the earth to support the use of animals in this way. However, simply because humans have advanced technological knowledge does not necessarily mean that the human species is morally or emotionally better than other animals. Therefore, we should not simply use animals for our purposes.

Finally, the use of animals for dissection in school classes is completely unnecessary. Because we as humans have advanced knowledge of technology, we should use it. It is now entirely possible to re-create the internal and external images of animals (and humans) via computer technology. Rather than continuing to take the lives of innocent animals, students should use the information already gained and catalogued in computer programs to study science issues. Not only does this save the lives of animals, but it is probably safer for students because now they do not have to be concerned with contracting a disease while dissecting an infected animal.

We have been destroying animals for our own selfish purposes long enough. It's time to use the brains we were given (or have developed) to make the world a better place for all its inhabitants, not just humans.

Critique

This essay shows an excellent and insightful understanding of the prompt. The student takes a clear stand on the issue and uses specific details and examples (explaining how animals enjoy their lives) to support the thesis. The student provides a counterargument in paragraph 3: *However, simply because humans have advanced technological knowledge does not necessarily mean that the human species is morally or emotionally better than other animals.* In the fourth paragraph, the student provides a strong argument combined with a solution to the problem (using computer-generated images). The essay is well organized with good use of transitions. It shows a strong command of written language and contains virtually no grammatical errors while showing sophisticated vocabulary and varied sentence structure.

Sample "Score 5" Essay

What's more important—animals or humans? The students on campus who are crying out against the use of animals for dissection in science classes obviously think animals are more important. This is a nice sentiment, but what will those same students say when someone in their family contracts an illness and a trial drug to cure the illness needs to be tested on an animal? Then they might have a different story. I believe that we should continue to use animals in science classes.

First of all, using animals for dissection is not cruel. People believe that animals feel the same way about death as humans do. I disagree. Maybe animals show emotion or maybe we just think they show emotions. Animal behaviorists have a difficult time figuring out how much emotion animals have as opposed to how much we just perceive. Either way, animals just do not have the higher thinking power to worry about death the way we do. As long as they are put to death humanely, I don't think the animals even understand that they are dying. They just feel very sleepy.

Another argument these student activists have is that the animals are bred for dissection and don't have fulfilling lives. Again, I don't think animals have the higher order of thinking to worry about whether or not their lives have been fulfilled. Because it would be dangerous to use a diseased animal in a class dissection, the animals we dissect are healthy and usually adult. So they have lived their lives, and they have been well-cared for or they wouldn't be healthy. And the bottom line again is, I don't think the animals even know any better.

Finally, it is necessary to use animals for dissection in science classes. Students learn a great deal by studying real organs and tissues. Some of these students will eventually go on to become doctors or researchers who will eventually save people's lives. I think the sacrifice of a frog, rat, or pig is well worth that. I don't think reading or looking at pictures in a book has the same educational value or will spark the same passion in students to advance their scientific education and careers.

Ultimately, there are more important things in the world to protest than whether or not a rat or a frog winds up on a dissection table. Students should put their energies into more worthwhile causes—causes that will help humankind, the way animal dissection ultimately does.

Critique

This essay shows a good understanding of the prompt and offers some specific arguments to support the idea that animals should be used for dissection. The indirect thesis statement is a bit weak, but it clearly states the writer's point of view. The essay uses logical arguments and contains counterarguments in paragraphs 2 and 3. The essay shows a good command of

written language but lacks the style and sophistication of a model score 6 essay.

Sample "Score 4" Essay

I have been brought up to believe that all life is precious and that the life of an animal is not to be taken unless it's for a very good reason. I love all animals and I am very upset about the animal dissections that occur in science classes. I think this is cruel both for the animals and for the students.

Dissecting an animal is cruel for the animal itself. Even though the animals are already dead when they are dissected, I still think the whole process is cruel. The poor animals that are used in science class are bred just for dissection purposes. It's like they don't even have a real life. As soon as they're big and old enough, they are killed and shipped to schools for dissection. Even the dissection is cruel. Sure the animal is dead, but now instead of being able to just rest in peace, the poor thing is cut up and all its parts are taken out. Think about your favorite pet. Would you like it if your cat or dog died and then someone came in and started cutting it all apart?

The whole process of dissection is also cruel for students. Some students actually get sick from the smell and from having to handle the insides of an animal. I've been in classes where students had to stop dissecting because they felt faint and nauseated. Emotionally, it is hard on some students to have to deal with death. They see something that was once alive, and it is now dead. It reminds them of pets or even people who have died. This can be very upsetting to some students.

There are also other students like me who simply become upset when they think about how these animals died for no reason. Some students may even have moral or religious ideas that state that killing a living thing is wrong. The school should not force these students to go against their beliefs by making them handle a dead animal.

School should be an enjoyable place for students to learn. Cutting up animals makes school an uncomfortable place and a place that brings up a lot of bad feelings in some students. School should be a place where values are supported, especially the value of life.

Critique

This essay shows a good understanding of the assignment. The thesis statement is clear and fairly well supported in the body of the essay with details and examples, although some ideas in paragraphs 3 and 4 are a bit repetitive. The essay contains a weak attempt at a counterargument in paragraph 2: *Even though the animals are already dead when they are dissected, I still think the whole process is cruel.* The arguments against dissection of animals are logical. This essay is well organized overall, with each body paragraph developing an idea to support the thesis that dissection is cruel for animals and students. The essay shows an adequate command of written language but lacks sophistication in vocabulary use and sentence structure.

Sample "Score 3" Essay

There are some students in this school who refuse to dissect animals. They say they feel sorry for the animals. I think they are wrong. Dissecting animals is part of what we have to do for our grade, and the animals are allready dead so they don't know what's going on.

Dissecting animals gives us the chance to see some really cool things. Seeing stuff in a book is not the same as seeing it in real life. Its important for students to have experiances like this in life. We will learn and remember stuff better if we see it and do it for ourselves. Learning about pigs or frogs will help us learn more about ourselves and how our body works.

Another thing is that the animals are dead allready, so we don't have to kill them. They do it in a humane way, which means the animals do not feel anything, they just die. Once their dead, they don't feel anything, so cutting them up is not a problem. Plus, its not like were just going to hack them to pieces. We are going to carefully cut and remove some of the organs. You could think of it as the animals are doing a good thing in their life by helping us learn.

I don't feel sorry for the animals. That's part of what their there for, to help students learn. I think dissecting them is fine and students should'nt worry so much about the animals.

Critique

This essay shows an adequate understanding of the assignment. The thesis statement is a bit weak: *Dissecting animals is part of what we have to do for our grade, and the animals are allready dead so they don't know what's going on.* However, the rest of the essay supports it adequately with some logical arguments. The essay would have been stronger with better organization and better development using specific examples. The essay is a bit repetitive in paragraphs 1 and 3. It contains a weak counterargument in paragraph 3: *Plus, its not like were just going to hack them to pieces. We are going to carefully cut and remove some of the organs.* The essay shows some command of written language but contains some simplistic sentences with simple vocabulary (*Seeing stuff in a book is not the same as seeing it in real life, Another thing is that*) and some awkward sentences (*That's part of what their there for, to help students learn*). There are some spelling, grammar, and punctuation errors, but they do not make the composition very difficult to read or understand.

Sample "Score 2" Essay

Some people think dissecting animals in class is wrong, others don't care. I don't like to dissect animals but I don't think it's really wrong either. Animals can be pets or they can be like lab rats. You wouldn't want to dissect a pet, but its ok to dissect a lab rat. A pet gives you love and companionship. You would be upset if it died. A lab rat is just a thing in a cage. Its purpose is bassically to get dissected. As long as the animal was ment to be dissected I don't have a problem with it. But I wouldn't want to see Fifi on my lab table.

Critique

This essay shows a very weak understanding of the prompt. The writer does not take a clear stand on the issue, as shown in the weak thesis statement. The essay drifts a bit off track by focusing on the differences between pets and lab animals. It is undeveloped

and shows a weak command of written language, as evidenced by grammatical and spelling errors.

Sample "Score 1" Essay

I do not want to dissect animals in sience class. I think it is grose and mean. Animals are living things with a life too and we wouldn't want to be cut up so why should we do it to them.

If I have to cut a frog or a pig I will probally get sick. I will have to leave class and not come back until its done. I think frogs and pigs are cute and I will get very sad to have to cut it up. We did a worm once and I even fealt bad about that. Also the smell. It is grose and makes me sick.

Please don't let us have to dissect animals. We can just look at a picture and that's it.

Critique

This essay shows a poor understanding of the assignment. The writer makes it clear that he or she does not want to dissect an animal but does not give logical arguments against animal dissection as a school policy. There is no clear thesis statement; therefore, the body paragraph does not really support a particular belief. It simply explains what will happen if the writer has to dissect an animal. The essay is not developed enough to show an overall organizational pattern, and the paragraphs themselves lack strong organization. For example, paragraph 2 deals with several different topics at once, without developing any one of them. The language used shows a weak command of written language with simplistic sentence structure and simple vocabulary. There are spelling, grammar, and punctuation errors that sometimes make the composition difficult to read and understand.

4 ▶ ACT PRACTICE BATTERY 3

This is the third of four complete practice ACT tests in this book. In this chapter you'll find full English, Mathematics, Reading, Science, and Writing tests. Complete answers are at the end of the chapter, and instructions on how to score these practice tests are in Chapter 6. Good luck!

ACT English Practice Test 3

1.	ⓐ	ⓑ	ⓒ	ⓓ	26.	ⓕ	ⓖ	ⓗ	ⓙ	51.	ⓐ ⓑ ⓒ ⓓ
2.	ⓕ	ⓖ	ⓗ	ⓙ	27.	ⓐ	ⓑ	ⓒ	ⓓ	52.	ⓕ ⓖ ⓗ ⓙ
3.	ⓐ	ⓑ	ⓒ	ⓓ	28.	ⓕ	ⓖ	ⓗ	ⓙ	53.	ⓐ ⓑ ⓒ ⓓ
4.	ⓕ	ⓖ	ⓗ	ⓙ	29.	ⓐ	ⓑ	ⓒ	ⓓ	54.	ⓕ ⓖ ⓗ ⓙ
5.	ⓐ	ⓑ	ⓒ	ⓓ	30.	ⓕ	ⓖ	ⓗ	ⓙ	55.	ⓐ ⓑ ⓒ ⓓ
6.	ⓕ	ⓖ	ⓗ	ⓙ	31.	ⓐ	ⓑ	ⓒ	ⓓ	56.	ⓕ ⓖ ⓗ ⓙ
7.	ⓐ	ⓑ	ⓒ	ⓓ	32.	ⓕ	ⓖ	ⓗ	ⓙ	57.	ⓐ ⓑ ⓒ ⓓ
8.	ⓕ	ⓖ	ⓗ	ⓙ	33.	ⓐ	ⓑ	ⓒ	ⓓ	58.	ⓕ ⓖ ⓗ ⓙ
9.	ⓐ	ⓑ	ⓒ	ⓓ	34.	ⓕ	ⓖ	ⓗ	ⓙ	59.	ⓐ ⓑ ⓒ ⓓ
10.	ⓕ	ⓖ	ⓗ	ⓙ	35.	ⓐ	ⓑ	ⓒ	ⓓ	60.	ⓕ ⓖ ⓗ ⓙ
11.	ⓐ	ⓑ	ⓒ	ⓓ	36.	ⓕ	ⓖ	ⓗ	ⓙ	61.	ⓐ ⓑ ⓒ ⓓ
12.	ⓕ	ⓖ	ⓗ	ⓙ	37.	ⓐ	ⓑ	ⓒ	ⓓ	62.	ⓕ ⓖ ⓗ ⓙ
13.	ⓐ	ⓑ	ⓒ	ⓓ	38.	ⓕ	ⓖ	ⓗ	ⓙ	63.	ⓐ ⓑ ⓒ ⓓ
14.	ⓕ	ⓖ	ⓗ	ⓙ	39.	ⓐ	ⓑ	ⓒ	ⓓ	64.	ⓕ ⓖ ⓗ ⓙ
15.	ⓐ	ⓑ	ⓒ	ⓓ	40.	ⓕ	ⓖ	ⓗ	ⓙ	65.	ⓐ ⓑ ⓒ ⓓ
16.	ⓕ	ⓖ	ⓗ	ⓙ	41.	ⓐ	ⓑ	ⓒ	ⓓ	66.	ⓕ ⓖ ⓗ ⓙ
17.	ⓐ	ⓑ	ⓒ	ⓓ	42.	ⓕ	ⓖ	ⓗ	ⓙ	67.	ⓐ ⓑ ⓒ ⓓ
18.	ⓕ	ⓖ	ⓗ	ⓙ	43.	ⓐ	ⓑ	ⓒ	ⓓ	68.	ⓕ ⓖ ⓗ ⓙ
19.	ⓐ	ⓑ	ⓒ	ⓓ	44.	ⓕ	ⓖ	ⓗ	ⓙ	69.	ⓐ ⓑ ⓒ ⓓ
20.	ⓕ	ⓖ	ⓗ	ⓙ	45.	ⓐ	ⓑ	ⓒ	ⓓ	70.	ⓕ ⓖ ⓗ ⓙ
21.	ⓐ	ⓑ	ⓒ	ⓓ	46.	ⓕ	ⓖ	ⓗ	ⓙ	71.	ⓐ ⓑ ⓒ ⓓ
22.	ⓕ	ⓖ	ⓗ	ⓙ	47.	ⓐ	ⓑ	ⓒ	ⓓ	72.	ⓕ ⓖ ⓗ ⓙ
23.	ⓐ	ⓑ	ⓒ	ⓓ	48.	ⓕ	ⓖ	ⓗ	ⓙ	73.	ⓐ ⓑ ⓒ ⓓ
24.	ⓕ	ⓖ	ⓗ	ⓙ	49.	ⓐ	ⓑ	ⓒ	ⓓ	74.	ⓕ ⓖ ⓗ ⓙ
25.	ⓐ	ⓑ	ⓒ	ⓓ	50.	ⓕ	ⓖ	ⓗ	ⓙ	75.	ⓐ ⓑ ⓒ ⓓ

ACT Mathematics Practice Test 3

1. (a) (b) (c) (d) (e)
2. (f) (g) (h) (j) (k)
3. (a) (b) (c) (d) (e)
4. (f) (g) (h) (j) (k)
5. (a) (b) (c) (d) (e)
6. (f) (g) (h) (j) (k)
7. (a) (b) (c) (d) (e)
8. (f) (g) (h) (j) (k)
9. (a) (b) (c) (d) (e)
10. (f) (g) (h) (j) (k)
11. (a) (b) (c) (d) (e)
12. (f) (g) (h) (j) (k)
13. (a) (b) (c) (d) (e)
14. (f) (g) (h) (j) (k)
15. (a) (b) (c) (d) (e)
16. (f) (g) (h) (j) (k)
17. (a) (b) (c) (d) (e)
18. (f) (g) (h) (j) (k)
19. (a) (b) (c) (d) (e)
20. (f) (g) (h) (j) (k)

21. (a) (b) (c) (d) (e)
22. (f) (g) (h) (j) (k)
23. (a) (b) (c) (d) (e)
24. (f) (g) (h) (j) (k)
25. (a) (b) (c) (d) (e)
26. (f) (g) (h) (j) (k)
27. (a) (b) (c) (d) (e)
28. (f) (g) (h) (j) (k)
29. (a) (b) (c) (d) (e)
30. (f) (g) (h) (j) (k)
31. (a) (b) (c) (d) (e)
32. (f) (g) (h) (j) (k)
33. (a) (b) (c) (d) (e)
34. (f) (g) (h) (j) (k)
35. (a) (b) (c) (d) (e)
36. (f) (g) (h) (j) (k)
37. (a) (b) (c) (d) (e)
38. (f) (g) (h) (j) (k)
39. (a) (b) (c) (d) (e)
40. (f) (g) (h) (j) (k)

41. (a) (b) (c) (d) (e)
42. (f) (g) (h) (j) (k)
43. (a) (b) (c) (d) (e)
44. (f) (g) (h) (j) (k)
45. (a) (b) (c) (d) (e)
46. (f) (g) (h) (j) (k)
47. (a) (b) (c) (d) (e)
48. (f) (g) (h) (j) (k)
49. (a) (b) (c) (d) (e)
50. (f) (g) (h) (j) (k)
51. (a) (b) (c) (d) (e)
52. (f) (g) (h) (j) (k)
53. (a) (b) (c) (d) (e)
54. (f) (g) (h) (j) (k)
55. (a) (b) (c) (d) (e)
56. (f) (g) (h) (j) (k)
57. (a) (b) (c) (d) (e)
58. (f) (g) (h) (j) (k)
59. (a) (b) (c) (d) (e)
60. (f) (g) (h) (j) (k)

ACT Reading Practice Test 3

1. (a) (b) (c) (d)
2. (f) (g) (h) (j)
3. (a) (b) (c) (d)
4. (f) (g) (h) (j)
5. (a) (b) (c) (d)
6. (f) (g) (h) (j)
7. (a) (b) (c) (d)
8. (f) (g) (h) (j)
9. (a) (b) (c) (d)
10. (f) (g) (h) (j)
11. (a) (b) (c) (d)
12. (f) (g) (h) (j)
13. (a) (b) (c) (d)
14. (f) (g) (h) (j)

15. (a) (b) (c) (d)
16. (f) (g) (h) (j)
17. (a) (b) (c) (d)
18. (f) (g) (h) (j)
19. (a) (b) (c) (d)
20. (f) (g) (h) (j)
21. (a) (b) (c) (d)
22. (f) (g) (h) (j)
23. (a) (b) (c) (d)
24. (f) (g) (h) (j)
25. (a) (b) (c) (d)
26. (f) (g) (h) (j)
27. (a) (b) (c) (d)
28. (f) (g) (h) (j)

29. (a) (b) (c) (d)
30. (f) (g) (h) (j)
31. (a) (b) (c) (d)
32. (f) (g) (h) (j)
33. (a) (b) (c) (d)
34. (f) (g) (h) (j)
35. (a) (b) (c) (d)
36. (f) (g) (h) (j)
37. (a) (b) (c) (d)
38. (f) (g) (h) (j)
39. (a) (b) (c) (d)
40. (f) (g) (h) (j)

ACT Science Practice Test 3

1.	ⓐ	ⓑ	ⓒ	ⓓ	15.	ⓐ	ⓑ	ⓒ	ⓓ	29.	ⓐ	ⓑ	ⓒ	ⓓ
2.	ⓕ	ⓖ	ⓗ	ⓙ	16.	ⓕ	ⓖ	ⓗ	ⓙ	30.	ⓕ	ⓖ	ⓗ	ⓙ
3.	ⓐ	ⓑ	ⓒ	ⓓ	17.	ⓐ	ⓑ	ⓒ	ⓓ	31.	ⓐ	ⓑ	ⓒ	ⓓ
4.	ⓕ	ⓖ	ⓗ	ⓙ	18.	ⓕ	ⓖ	ⓗ	ⓙ	32.	ⓕ	ⓖ	ⓗ	ⓙ
5.	ⓐ	ⓑ	ⓒ	ⓓ	19.	ⓐ	ⓑ	ⓒ	ⓓ	33.	ⓐ	ⓑ	ⓒ	ⓓ
6.	ⓕ	ⓖ	ⓗ	ⓙ	20.	ⓕ	ⓖ	ⓗ	ⓙ	34.	ⓕ	ⓖ	ⓗ	ⓙ
7.	ⓐ	ⓑ	ⓒ	ⓓ	21.	ⓐ	ⓑ	ⓒ	ⓓ	35.	ⓐ	ⓑ	ⓒ	ⓓ
8.	ⓕ	ⓖ	ⓗ	ⓙ	22.	ⓕ	ⓖ	ⓗ	ⓙ	36.	ⓕ	ⓖ	ⓗ	ⓙ
9.	ⓐ	ⓑ	ⓒ	ⓓ	23.	ⓐ	ⓑ	ⓒ	ⓓ	37.	ⓐ	ⓑ	ⓒ	ⓓ
10.	ⓕ	ⓖ	ⓗ	ⓙ	24.	ⓕ	ⓖ	ⓗ	ⓙ	38.	ⓕ	ⓖ	ⓗ	ⓙ
11.	ⓐ	ⓑ	ⓒ	ⓓ	25.	ⓐ	ⓑ	ⓒ	ⓓ	39.	ⓐ	ⓑ	ⓒ	ⓓ
12.	ⓕ	ⓖ	ⓗ	ⓙ	26.	ⓕ	ⓖ	ⓗ	ⓙ	40.	ⓕ	ⓖ	ⓗ	ⓙ
13.	ⓐ	ⓑ	ⓒ	ⓓ	27.	ⓐ	ⓑ	ⓒ	ⓓ					
14.	ⓕ	ⓖ	ⓗ	ⓙ	28.	ⓕ	ⓖ	ⓗ	ⓙ					

ACT English Practice Test 3

75 Questions—45 Minutes

Read each passage through once before you begin to answer any questions. You will see that certain words or phrases in the following five passages have been underlined and numbered. Following each passage, you will see alternatives for those underlined words or phrases. Choose the one that best expresses the idea of the passage, is the best use of standard English, or is most consistent with the tone and style of the passage. If you find the underlined part to be correct, choose "NO CHANGE." Note that to answer many of the questions you will probably need to read several sentences beyond the question. You may also find questions about a section of the passage or the passage as a whole, rather than about an underlined part.

Passage I—The Weekly Visit

The requisite visit happened <u>most typically</u>[1] on sunny Saturdays, when my child spirits were at their highest and could be most diminished by the cramped interior of her house. My mother, accustomed to the <u>bright spacious farmhouse</u>[2] that was once Grandma's, seemed no less susceptible to the gloom. She would set her jaw as Grandma described the many ailments attendant on age and would check her watch—an hour <u>is</u>[3] the minimum she expected herself to withstand. Her barely contained <u>impatience, and</u>[4] my grandmother's crippling age radiated out around me. We were the women of the Carlson clan, each throbbing with agitation, like <u>eccentric,</u>[5] blinking circles on a radar screen.

(1) I would sit at the <u>white, red, metal table</u>[6] with the pull-out leaves and built-in silverware drawer, cracking almonds. (2) I <u>would be lifting</u>[7] the lid carefully and try to set it down on the metal table quietly, and then attempt to crack the nuts without scattering the shell crumbs. (3) This was the one good thing at Grandma's house, the almonds, which she kept in a green Depression glass bowl. (4) It was not good to draw attention to myself at <u>Grandma Carlson's house.</u>[8] Sounding angry, she would call to me in her croupy drawl. When I failed to understand her, she would reach out to me with her palsied, slick, wrinkled hand and shout, <u>"Here"!</u>[9] She would be offering some of her horehound candy, which tasted like a cross between butterscotch and bitter sticks.

There was this lamentable air in the dim house with its itchy mohair furniture and its dark colors, an awareness—Grandma's—<u>underlaying</u>[10] the mentholatum, that her age scared her grandkids. <u>I would during the dutiful visit yearn</u>[11] to get outside into the yard, where Grandma had transplanted a few flowers when she moved from the farm. But even the yard, <u>with its overgrown hedges and rusted metal lawn chairs,</u>[12] seemed dreary. When I came back inside, light and air would burst in with me. <u>Grandma, her hair up in a gray bun, would rock a little and smile.</u>[13] I would lean then against my mother's chair, <u>Grandmas' fond eyes</u>[14] peering at me, and whisper out of the corner of my mouth, "Mom, can we go?"

1. **a.** NO CHANGE
   b. most usually
   c. typically
   d. most typical

2. **f.** NO CHANGE
   g. bright-spacious farmhouse
   h. bright, and spacious farmhouse
   j. bright, spacious farmhouse

3. a. NO CHANGE
b. would be
c. being
d. were

4. f. NO CHANGE
g. impatience. And
h. impatience; and
j. impatience and

5. a. NO CHANGE
b. concentric,
c. egocentric,
d. centric,

6. f. NO CHANGE
g. white, red and metal
h. white and red metal
j. white, and red, metal

7. a. NO CHANGE
b. was lifting
c. lifted
d. would lift

8. f. NO CHANGE
g. Grandma Carlsons house.
h. Grandma Carlson house.
j. Grandma's Carlson house.

9. a. NO CHANGE
b. "Here."
c. "here"!
d. "Here!"

10. f. NO CHANGE
g. laying under
h. underlying
j. lying under

11. a. NO CHANGE
b. During the dutiful visit, I would yearn
c. I during the dutiful visit would yearn
d. I would, during the dutiful visit yearn

12. The writer is considering deleting the underlined portion. Should this be kept or deleted?
f. It should be kept, because the sentence would not be grammatically correct without it.
g. It should be kept, because the images enhance the description of the yard.
h. It should be deleted, because the description is off the topic of family.
j. It should be deleted, because the grammar is incorrect.

13. Which of the following alternatives to the underlined portion would NOT be acceptable?
a. Grandma would, her hair up in a gray bun, rock a little and smile.
b. With her gray hair up in a bun, grandma would rock a little and smile.
c. Grandma, her hair up in a gray bun, would smile and rock a little.
d. Grandma—her hair up in a gray bun— would rock a little and smile.

14. f. NO CHANGE
g. Grandmas's fond eyes
h. Grandma's fond eyes
j. Grandmas fond eyes

15. The most appropriate order for the first four sentences of the second paragraph would be
a. 1, 2, 3, 4
b. 2, 1, 3, 4
c. 1, 2, 4, 3
d. 1, 3, 2, 4

Passage II—My Childhood

I grew up in a large <u>family, as being</u>[16] the oldest of six siblings, and I have many wonderful memories from my childhood. I am very close to most of my siblings and I treasure my relationships with them. But when I <u>have had</u>[17] my own family someday, it won't be as big as the one I grew up in. As much as my large family was full of love, and as much as I learned about sharing, giving, and patience, I think having too many kids strains the parents and the oldest child, <u>both in terms of emotion and money.</u>[18]

(1) When I think back on my early years with my family, I remember playing with my siblings and grandparents. (2) <u>However, I</u>[19] don't remember spending a whole lot of time with my mother and father. (3) They were always around, but they were always busy. (4) My mother was always cooking, cleaning, nursing, changing a diaper, shopping, or <u>had to take</u>[20] someone to baseball practice, and my father was always working. (5) He needed overtime whenever he could get <u>it; and weekends</u>[21] were always full of projects around the house. (6) Money was also a constant worry for my family. (7) With so many children, our budget was always tight. (8) Back-to-school shopping was always a stressful <u>time as we</u>[22] all wanted the latest fashions, but we could only get a few things. My younger siblings lived in hand-me-downs. We shopped at bargain stores and often got clothes that we didn't really like <u>simply because they were on sale and cheap.</u>[23] Our house always needed repairs, and there was never enough money to keep up.

<u>And yet another</u>[24] problem with large families is that the older siblings always end up <u>being a babysitter.</u>[25] Like it or not (and most of the time I didn't like it), I had to watch my younger brothers and sisters. At age six, I could change a diaper like a pro. I was getting my brothers and sisters dressed, giving them breakfast, <u>and helped them get ready for bed.</u>[26] I don't want to give the impression that I didn't have a happy childhood; I most definitely did. I was loved as much as my parents could love me, and I <u>have had</u>[27] wonderful fun with my brothers and sisters. But I always wanted a little more time with Mom and Dad, and I often resented having so much responsibility. I wished my mom wasn't always so tired and my dad didn't have to work so much. Because I want to be there more for my kids, <u>because I want</u>[28] them to be kids throughout their childhood, I plan to have a much smaller family.

16. f. NO CHANGE
  g. family, was
  h. family, I was
  j. family as

17. a. NO CHANGE
  b. will have
  c. had
  d. have

18. f. NO CHANGE
  g. in terms of both emotion and money.
  h. both emotionally and financially.
  j. both in emotion and money.

19. a. NO CHANGE
  b. However I
  c. But,
  d. I however

20. f. NO CHANGE
  g. needed to
  h. had to bring
  j. taking

21. a. NO CHANGE
  b. it, and weekends
  c. it, weekends
  d. it and weekends

22. f. NO CHANGE
  g. time; we
  h. time: we
  j. time. As we

23. a. NO CHANGE
  b. simply because they were on sale, and cheap.
  c. simply for they were on sale and cheap.
  d. simply, because they were on sale and cheap.

24. f. NO CHANGE
  g. And, yet another
  h. Yet, another
  j. Another

25. a. NO CHANGE
  b. a babysitter.
  c. being babysitters.
  d. as a babysitter.

26. f. NO CHANGE
  g. and I helped them get ready for bed.
  h. and helping them get ready for bed.
  j. helped them get ready for bed.

27. a. NO CHANGE
  b. would have
  c. was having
  d. had

28. f. NO CHANGE
  g. and because I want
  h. I want
  j. and for

29. The writer wishes to separate the second paragraph into two paragraphs. The best place to do so would be between
  a. sentences 4 and 5.
  b. sentences 5 and 6.
  c. sentences 6 and 7.
  d. sentences 7 and 8.

30. The writer wishes to change the title of this passage to "Family." This change
  f. should not be made. The passage contains more of the writer's thoughts about childhood than about family.
  g. should not be made. The title is unimportant.
  h. should be made. The passage contains more of the writer's thoughts about family than about childhood.
  j. should be made. The title should not be longer than one word.

Passage III—The Internet Revolution

In today's world, when a question needs to be answered, information needs to be located, or <u>people contacted,</u>[31] the first place people turn to is often the Internet. The Internet has supplanted the traditional <u>encyclopedia. As</u>[32] well as a number of other sources of service and information. We can make reservations, plan vacations, play <u>interaction</u>[33] games, learn a language, listen to music or radio programs, read the newspaper, and find out about a medical condition, without coming face-to-face with another person. There's no <u>limits</u>[34] to the subject matter you can research on the Internet.

The Internet allows you to remain at <u>your computer and shop no matter</u>[35] what you wish to purchase. If you are looking for a bargain or an unusual item, you can go to a popular auction site and either sell or buy. But if you do wish to speak directly to a person, there are chat rooms. On practically any given topic, <u>groups of people converse with each other.</u>[36] They may be giving opinions about a perfect travel itinerary, a book, or even a political party. <u>But perhaps</u>[37] the widest use of the Internet involves directly writing to someone <u>in</u>[38] sending e-mail messages to friends and associates. It is possible to communicate instantly with anyone, anywhere, as long as there is an Internet connection. <u>Added to</u>[39] verbal messages, digital pictures may be transmitted on the Internet.

(1) Unfortunately, there <u>are individuals who misuse the opportunity</u>[40] possible on the Internet. (2) They are less than honest, disguise their identity, bilk people in financial scams, and entice <u>them into giving them</u>[41] personal information. (3) They steal people's identities and use their credit and good names to make purchases, apply for loans, and steal assets. (4) Of course, the Internet providers hope to make money, and there is usually a monthly fee for the hookup. (5) To increase <u>the</u>[42] profits, the providers sell advertising, which may pop up on the <u>subscriber's screens</u>[43] and require the user to stop and respond, either positively or negatively, to the ads. (6) This can be quite a nuisance at times. (7) When you consider that you can hear a concert, read a book, visit a museum and view its contents, visit the websites of numerous individuals and organizations, play a game with one or more people, and pay your bills, you will realize that the uses of the Internet <u>is</u>[44] too vast for a short list. (8) Most would agree that much has been added to people's lives by connecting them to the Internet, and that we probably cannot anticipate what new purposes will be explored in the future.

31. a. NO CHANGE
  b. people needs contacting,
  c. people need to be contacted,
  d. are people who need contacting,

32. f. NO CHANGE
  g. encyclopedia; as
  h. encyclopedia, as
  j. encyclopedia. Also as

33. a. NO CHANGE
  b. interacting
  c. with interaction
  d. interactive

34. f. NO CHANGE
  g. limitations
  h. limiting
  j. limit

35. a. NO CHANGE
  b. your computer, and shop no matter
  c. your computer and shop, no matter
  d. your computer, and shop, no matter

36. f. NO CHANGE
  g. groups of people converse amongst each other.
  h. groups of people converse.
  j. groups of people can converse with each other.

37. a. NO CHANGE
  b. Perhaps
  c. And perhaps
  d. Or perhaps

38. f. NO CHANGE
  g. and
  h. by
  j. with

39. a. NO CHANGE
    b. As well
    c. Also
    d. In addition to

40. f. NO CHANGE
    g. is an individual who misuses the opportunity
    h. are individuals who misuse the opportunity's
    j. are individuals who misuse the opportunities

41. a. NO CHANGE
    b. them into giving others
    c. others into giving them
    d. others into giving others

42. f. NO CHANGE
    g. those
    h. their
    j. one's

43. a. NO CHANGE
    b. subscriber screen
    c. subscriber's screen
    d. subscribers' screen

44. f. NO CHANGE
    g. was
    h. are
    j. were

45. The writer wants to create a distinct concluding paragraph. He should
    a. write and attach an additional paragraph discussing the future of the Internet.
    b. begin the conclusion with sentence 5 of the current final paragraph.
    c. begin the conclusion with sentence 6 of the current final paragraph.
    d. begin the conclusion with sentence 7 of the current final paragraph.

Passage IV—The Letter

As many of you knew, but some do not,[46] an extraordinary charity has existed for the last nine years. The Scotty W. Memorial Fund was created by Scotty's extended family and spearheaded by his brother, Rob, to honor the memory of Scotty, who died when the World Trade Center towers were attacked on 9/11. The fund has achieved some extraordinary things, including creating a college scholarship in Scotty's name in perpetuity,[47] and donating hundreds of thousands of dollars to the Kane Cancer Research Center. The fund's sponsors[48] hold a variety of fund-raising events year-round, and the centerpiece of these events is the Play Ball Weekend, held annually in Woodstock, New York, on the anniversary of 9/11. It is about this event that we contact[49] you.

First, let me mention that we were, and will be,[50] extremely hesitant to send this note, for a number of reasons. Many people are not big fans of impersonal, group mailings when they receive them, and we initially cringed at the idea of sending one. We were also exceptionally[51] hesitant to solicit donations by e-mail. At any rate for any number of reasons,[52] fund-raising for our event this year has been more difficult than usual, and we are trying to explore all possible fund-raising means. Please accept our apologies if anyone feels the least bit offended or <u>feel</u>[53] this to be inappropriate.

Back to the event, which will take place <u>Saturday, September 11, in Woodstock New York.</u>[54] If you have a moment to go to the Scotty IX website, perhaps you can get <u>a sense</u>[55] of the event. In short, it is a joyous, loving, wonderful weekend—quite remarkable, given the horrific nature of its roots. People travel from all around the country to attend. The premise is an <u>athletic (although as we all get older it becomes increasingly less athletic) competition</u>[56] between teams of four people; the purpose is to remember and honor Scotty's life, to remember to celebrate life itself, and to raise money for great causes. <u>Simplier put,</u>[57] it's our favorite weekend of the year.

Any size donation would be wonderful and <u>deeply appreciative.</u>[58] For every $100 donated you will receive one raffle ticket, with prizes ranging from flat screen TVs to $10,000 cash. Event hats and T-shirts are provided to all donors. These are difficult financial times for many, and you may understandably not be in a position to make a donation. We also understand that many of you already donate to other important charities. If you would, however, care to make a donation, <u>you would be becoming</u>[59] part of a growing group who support our efforts. You would become part of the extended Scotty W. family. In any case, thanks for taking the time to read this, and <u>please except in advance</u>[60] our gratitude for any donation you make.

46. **f.** NO CHANGE
g. As many of you know, but some did not,
h. As many of you know, but some do not,
j. As many of you knew, but some also do not,

47. **a.** NO CHANGE
b. a college scholarship in perpetuity in Scotty's name,
c. a perpetual college scholarship in Scotty's name,
d. a college perpetuity scholarship in Scotty's name,

48. **f.** NO CHANGE
g. fund's sponsor
h. funds sponsor
j. fund sponsors

49. **a.** NO CHANGE
b. would contact
c. are contacting
d. would be contacting

50. **f.** NO CHANGE
g. are,
h. would be,
j. are going to be

51. **a.** NO CHANGE
b. expectedly
c. acceptionally
d. especially

52. **f.** NO CHANGE
g. At any rate for many number of reasons
h. At any rate, and for many reasons,
j. At any rate, any number of reasons

53. **a.** NO CHANGE
b. feels
c. is feeling
d. would feel

54. **f.** NO CHANGE
  g. Saturday September 11, in Woodstock, New York.
  h. Saturday, September 11, in Woodstock, New York.
  j. Saturday, September 11 in Woodstock, New York.

55. **a.** NO CHANGE
  b. a sensibility
  c. sensed
  d. sense

56. **f.** NO CHANGE
  g. athletically—year-by-year, increasingly less athletic, as we all get older—competition
  h. athletic, year-by-year, increasingly less athletic as we all get older, competition
  j. athletic, year-by-year as we all get older, increasingly less athletic , competition

57. **a.** NO CHANGE
  b. Quite simplier put,
  c. More simply put
  d. Simply put,

58. **f.** NO CHANGE
  g. deeply appreciated.
  h. we would be deeply appreciative.
  j. would be deeply appreciated.

59. **a.** NO CHANGE
  b. you would join
  c. you would become
  d. you could be becoming

60. **f.** NO CHANGE
  g. please in advance except
  h. please accept in advance
  j. please except, in advance,

Passage V—The Salmon Run

Perhaps one of the most fascinating <u>tales about how animals'</u>[61] breed is the story of the annual salmon run, when mature salmon travel from saltwater to freshwater in order to breed. It is hard not to marvel at the fact that <u>these fish travelling</u>[62] hundreds of miles, back to where their lives began, to spawn. Folklore claims that in order to spawn the fish return to the *exact* spot where they were born, and recent tracking studies have shown this <u>to be true; but</u>[63] the nature of how this memory works has long been debated. Some travel as many as 900 miles to lay their eggs, which are also known as <u>roes.</u>[64] While only a small percentage of the eggs the salmon lay ever survive to adulthood, the trip they make to lay these eggs <u>remain</u>[65] remarkable.

The life cycle of the salmon <u>are</u>[66] fairly simple to understand. After finding their way into the salt water as baby fish, salmon spend <u>from between one to five years in the ocean.</u>[67] When it is time for them to breed, they start their journey back to their original breeding grounds, which is where they deposit their roe. The fish face <u>many numerous dangers</u>[68] and obstacles as they go. Swimming upstream against the current and going past rapids are two <u>obstacles, but</u>[69] some salmon even jump up waterfalls, which shows how intense their instinct is. One type, the Snake River salmon, climbs 7,000 feet to their spawning grounds above the Pacific Ocean—all to return home and continue the cycle of life, a process that's imperative <u>giving</u>[70] the Snake River salmon's classification as an endangered species. In addition to the perils of the water, the salmon <u>must also overcome another</u>[71] obstacle, fishermen who are anxious to catch these tasty fish. When they do make it back to their original breeding grounds, they lay thousands of eggs.

Salmon has a long history as a <u>sustain-ance</u>[72] for human beings. Salmon was an important food to many early American Indians—although their superstitions <u>prevented</u>[73] certain tribe members from handling or eating the fish, because they did not want to anger its spirit and cause it <u>leaving</u>[74] their waters forever. Salmon are considered a healthy food because of the large amount of omega-3 fatty acids and vitamin D they contain. While in general the number of salmon <u>has been declined</u>[75] in recent years,especially the North Atlantic varieties, they are still abundant in Alaska and Canada. There are many reasons for the decline, including illness and overfishing. Government agencies hope that new fishing restrictions will be effective in stopping the decline.

61. **a.** NO CHANGE
   b. tails about how animals'
   c. tales about how animal's
   d. tales about how animals

62. **f.** NO CHANGE
   g. these fish traveled
   h. these fish travel
   j. these fish could be traveling

63. **a.** NO CHANGE
   b. to be true:
   c. true,
   d. to be true, but

64. **f.** NO CHANGE
   g. rose
   h. roe
   j. rows

65. **a.** NO CHANGE
   b. remains
   c. remained
   d. is remaining

66. **f.** NO CHANGE
   g. were
   h. was
   j. is

67. **a.** NO CHANGE
   b. between one and five years in the ocean.
   c. from between one and five years in the ocean.
   d. from one and five years in the ocean.

68. **f.** NO CHANGE
   g. many and numerous dangers
   h. numerous dangers
   j. many, numerous dangers

69. **a.** NO CHANGE
   b. of them
   c. of them, however
   d. of them;

70. **f.** NO CHANGE
   g. while giving
   h. given
   j. getting

71. **a.** NO CHANGE
   b. must yet overcome another
   c. must, however, overcome another
   d. must, as well, overcome another

72. **f.** NO CHANGE
   g. sustaining food
   h. sustenance
   j. sustained food

73. **a.** NO CHANGE
   b. prevent
   c. would prevent
   d. were preventing

74. **f.** NO CHANGE
   g. to leave
   h. to have left
   j. for leaving

75. **a.** NO CHANGE
   b. has been in decline
   c. was declining
   d. was in decline

ACT Mathematics Practice Test 3

60 Questions—60 Minutes

For each problem, choose the correct answer. You are allowed to use a calculator on this test for any problems you choose. Unless the problem states otherwise, you should assume that figures are *not* drawn to scale. For this test, all geometric figures lie in a plane, the word *line* refers to a straight line, and the word *average* refers to the arithmetic mean.

1. If a student got 95% of the questions on a 60-question test correct, how many questions did the student complete correctly?
   a. 57
   b. 38
   c. 46
   d. 53
   e. 95

2. What is the smallest possible product for two positive integers whose sum is 26?
   f. 15
   g. 25
   h. 26
   j. 144
   k. 154

3. What is the value of x in the equation $-2x + 1 = 4(x + 3)$?
   a. $-\frac{11}{6}$
   b. $-\frac{6}{11}$
   c. $\frac{2}{3}$
   d. $\frac{6}{11}$
   e. $\frac{11}{6}$

4. What is the *y*-intercept of the line
$4y + 2x = 12$?

  f. −6

  g. −2

  h. 3

  j. 6

  k. 12

5. The height of the parallelogram is 4.5 cm and the area is 36 square cm. Find the length of side *QR* in centimeters.

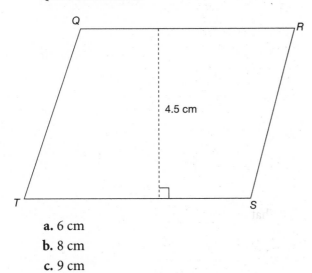

  a. 6 cm

  b. 8 cm

  c. 9 cm

  d. 15.75 cm

  e. 31.5 cm

6. Joey gave away half of his baseball card collection and sold two-thirds of what remained. What fraction of his original collection does he still have?

  f. $\frac{1}{2}$

  g. $\frac{1}{3}$

  h. $\frac{1}{4}$

  j. $\frac{1}{5}$

  k. $\frac{1}{6}$

7. Simplify $\sqrt{40}$.

  a. $2\sqrt{2}$

  b. $4\sqrt{2}$

  c. $2\sqrt{4}$

  d. $2\sqrt{10}$

  e. $4\sqrt{10}$

8. What is the simplified form of $-(3x + 5)^2$?

  f. $9x^2 + 30x + 25$

  g. $-9x^2 - 25$

  h. $9x^2 + 25$

  j. $-9x^2 - 30x - 25$

  k. $-39x^2 - 25$

9. Find the measure of angle *RST* in the triangle.

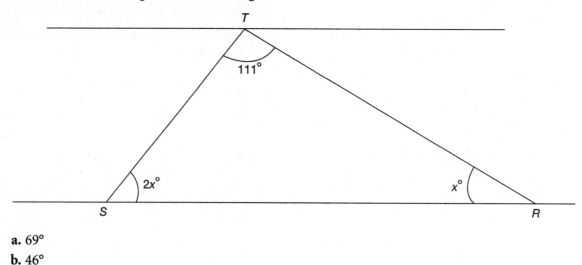

a. 69°

b. 46°

c. 61°

d. 45°

e. 23°

10. The area of a trapezoid is $\frac{1}{2}h(b1 + b2)$, where *h* is the altitude and *b*1 and *b*2 are the parallel bases. The two parallel bases of a trapezoid are 3 cm and 5 cm, and the area of the trapezoid is 28 square cm. Find the altitude of the trapezoid.

f. 1.9 cm

g. 7 cm

h. 9 cm

j. 14 cm

k. 19 cm

11. If $9m - 3 = -318$, then $14m =$

a. −584

b. −504

c. −490

d. −329

e. −28

12. What is the solution set of the following equation?

$$|x + 7| - 8 = 14$$

f. {−14,14}

g. {−22,22}

h. {15}

j. {−8,8}

k. {−29,15}

13. Which point lies on the same line as (2,−3) and (6,1)?

a. (5,−6)

b. (2,3)

c. (−1,8)

d. (7,2)

e. (4,0)

14. In the figure, $MN = 5$ in. and $PM = 13$ in. Find the area of triangle MNP.

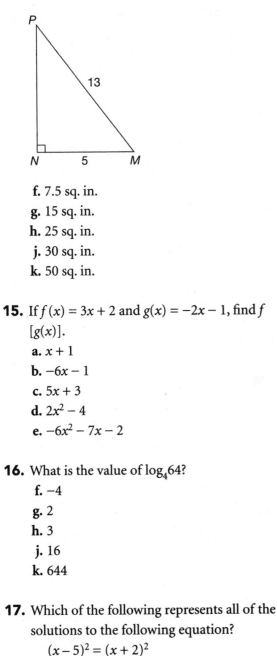

   f. 7.5 sq. in.

   g. 15 sq. in.

   h. 25 sq. in.

   j. 30 sq. in.

   k. 50 sq. in.

15. If $f(x) = 3x + 2$ and $g(x) = -2x - 1$, find $f[g(x)]$.

   a. $x + 1$

   b. $-6x - 1$

   c. $5x + 3$

   d. $2x^2 - 4$

   e. $-6x^2 - 7x - 2$

16. What is the value of $\log_4 64$?

   f. -4

   g. 2

   h. 3

   j. 16

   k. 644

17. Which of the following represents all of the solutions to the following equation?

$$(x - 5)^2 = (x + 2)^2$$

   a. 5 and -2

   b. -5 and 2

   c. -1.5

   d. 1.5

   e. 3.5

18. A circular lamp has a base with a circumference of 16π inches. When placed on a table, approximately how much of the table does it cover, in square inches?

   f. 50

   g. 125

   h. 200

   j. 225

   k. 250

19. Which of the following is the slope of a line parallel to the line $y = -2.5x + 8$?

   a. $-\frac{5}{2}$

   b. $-\frac{2}{5}$

   c. $\frac{2}{5}$

   d. $\frac{5}{2}$

   e. No such line exists.

20. In the right triangle shown, the perimeter is $30 + 10\sqrt{3}$. What is the value of x?

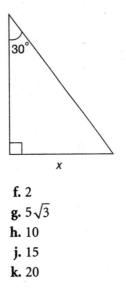

   f. 2

   g. $5\sqrt{3}$

   h. 10

   j. 15

   k. 20

21. The fixed costs of publishing a certain magazine are $800 per week. The variable costs are $0.50 per copy. Which of the following expresses the total cost of publishing m magazines for w weeks?

 a. $\$800w - \$0.50m$

 b. $\dfrac{\$800}{w} + \dfrac{\$0.50}{m}$

 c. $(\$800 + \$0.50)(mw)$

 d. $\dfrac{\$800w}{\$0.50m}$

 e. $\$800w + \$0.50m$

22. Cube X has an edge length of 15 inches. Cube Y has an edge length that is $\frac{1}{5}$ as long. What is the volume of cube Y in cubic inches?

 f. 9

 g. 27

 h. 81

 j. 125

 k. 243

23. In a three-dimensional space (X, Y, Z), the figure created by all points that are 10 units from the y-axis is:

 a. a line

 b. two parallel lines

 c. a circle

 d. a sphere

 e. a cylinder

24. Due to inflation, an automobile that used to sell for $32,000 in 2002 now sells for $40,000. What percent of the original price is the new price?

 f. 20%

 g. 25%

 h. 108%

 j. 120%

 k. 125%

25. A map is drawn so that 1.2 inches represents 200 miles. About how many miles are represented by 1.4 inches?

 a. 210

 b. 233

 c. 254

 d. 261

 e. 275

26. The number 0.009 is 100 times larger than

 f. 0.0000009

 g. 0.000009

 h. 0.00009

 j. 0.0009

 k. 0.09

27. Which of the following is equivalent to $(\frac{1}{4} - \frac{1}{5}) \div (\frac{1}{4} + \frac{1}{5})$?

 a. $-\frac{1}{9}$

 b. $-\frac{1}{7}$

 c. $\frac{1}{9}$

 d. $\frac{1}{7}$

 e. 1

28. The polygon pictured was originally a rectangle. What is the perimeter of this polygon?

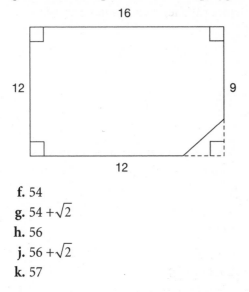

16

12

9

12

  f. 54
  g. 54 + $\sqrt{2}$
  h. 56
  j. 56 + $\sqrt{2}$
  k. 57

29. Points *X* and *Y* lie on segment *WZ* as shown. Segment *WZ* is 42 units long, segment *WY* is 25 units long, and segment *XZ* is 23 units long. How many units long is segment *XY*?

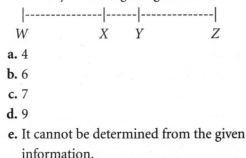

  a. 4
  b. 6
  c. 7
  d. 9
  e. It cannot be determined from the given information.

30. While renovating his yard, John removed an estimated 7,000 cubic feet of dirt in order to put in a pool. If this dirt were spread evenly over his neighbor's adjoining yard, measuring 36 by 48 feet, how deep, in feet, would the dirt be?
  f. less than 1
  g. between 1 and 2
  h. between 2 and 3
  j. between 3 and 4
  k. greater than 4

31. When a group of students sits in rows of six chairs, the last row has one empty chair. When this same group sits in rows with seven chairs, there is once again one empty chair. What is the least number of students in this group?
  a. 23
  b. 41
  c. 62
  d. 83
  e. 125

32. The ratio of the side lengths of a triangle is exactly 15:14:12. The longest side of a second, similar triangle is 10 feet long. What is the length of the shortest side of the second triangle, to the nearest tenth of a foot?
  f. 7.2
  g. 8
  h. 8.4
  j. 9
  k. 9.2

33. A circle in the standard (x,y) coordinate plane has the center $(12,-5)$ and a radius of 4 units. Which of the following is the equation of the circle?

a. $(x-12)^2 + (y-5)^2 = 4$
b. $(x+12)^2 - (y+5)^2 = 4$
c. $(x-12)^2 + (y-5)^2 = 8$
d. $(x+12)^2 + (y-5)^2 = 16$
e. $(x-12)^2 + (y+5)^2 = 16$

34. The hypotenuse of right triangle XYZ shown is 16 inches long. The sine of angle X is $\frac{3}{5}$. About how many inches long is side YZ?

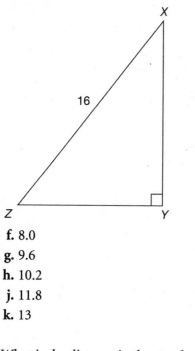

f. 8.0
g. 9.6
h. 10.2
j. 11.8
k. 13

35. What is the distance in the standard (x,y) coordinate plane between the points $(1,0)$ and $(5,5)$?

a. $\sqrt{28}$
b. $\sqrt{41}$
c. 6
d. 8
e. 16

36. If x and y are positive integers, and the greatest common factor of xy^3 and x^2y^2 is 27, then which of the following could equal y?

f. 3
g. 6
h. 9
j. 18
k. 27

37. Evan can run 3.5 miles in $2x$ minutes. At that rate, how long will it take him to run 17.5 miles?

a. $16x$ minutes
b. $14x$ minutes
c. $12x$ minutes
d. $10x$ minutes
e. $8x$ minutes

38. What is the slope of any line parallel to the x-axis in the (x,y) coordinate plane?

f. -1
g. 0
h. 1
j. undefined
k. It cannot be determined from the given information.

39. Which of the following expressions will result in an even integer for any integer x?

a. $2x^2 + 9$
b. $3x^3 + 5$
c. $5x^2 + 4$
d. $6x^4 + 6$
e. $x^6 - 3$

40. A certain rectangle is four times as long as it is wide. If both the length and the width are tripled, how many times larger is the perimeter of the new rectangle compared to the perimeter of the original rectangle?

   f. 3

   g. 6

   h. 9

   j. 12

   k. 15

41. The product of two integers is between 145 and 159. Which of the following cannot be one of the integers?

   a. 9

   b. 11

   c. 12

   d. 15

   e. 16

42. In the figure shown, *ABCD* is a trapezoid. Line *CE* is an extension of line *DC*. What is the measure of angle *ACB*?

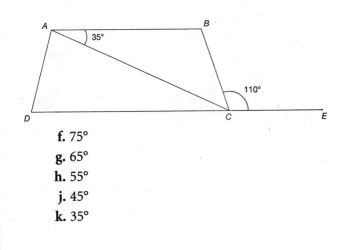

   f. 75°

   g. 65°

   h. 55°

   j. 45°

   k. 35°

43. The average of nine consecutive numbers is 23. What is the sum of the least and greatest of the nine integers?

   a. 41

   b. 44

   c. 46

   d. 47

   e. 49

44. In the pentagon shown, one angle is 52° as marked. What is the total measure of the other four interior angles?

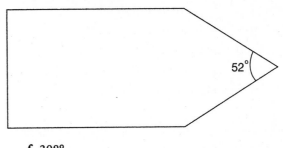

   f. 308°

   g. 398°

   h. 448°

   j. 488°

   k. 548°

45. What is the value of $\log_4 256$?

   a. 3

   b. 4

   c. 6

   d. 8

   e. 12

46. Which of the following is the solution set to the inequality $x - 7 < x - 9$?

   f. the empty set

   g. the set containing all nonnegative real numbers

   h. the set containing all negative real numbers

   j. the set containing only zero

   k. the set containing all real numbers

47. What fraction lies exactly halfway in between $\frac{2}{3}$ and $\frac{3}{4}$?

   a. $\frac{5}{7}$

   b. $\frac{7}{10}$

   c. $\frac{11}{15}$

   d. $\frac{15}{23}$

   e. $\frac{17}{24}$

48. When updating his business account, Ezra incorrectly enters an expense of $22.50 as income. The balance of his account now indicates

   f. $45.00 more than it should.

   g. $22.50 more than it should.

   h. the correct amount.

   j. $22.50 less than it should.

   k. $45.00 less than it should.

49. If $x^2 - 36b^2 = 9xb$, what are the two solutions for x in terms of b?

   a. $-12b$ or $3b$

   b. $-9b$ or $4b$

   c. $12b$ or $-3b$

   d. $12b$ or $3b$

   e. $9b$ or $4b$

50. For all values of x where $\sin x$, $\cos x$, and $\tan x$ exist, the value of $(\cos x)/(\tan x)(\sin x) =$

   f. $\tan^2 x$

   g. $\frac{\cos^2 x}{\sin^2 x}$

   h. 1

   j. $\sin^2 x$

   k. $\sec^2 x$

51. An integer is to be chosen at random from the numbers 10 to 99, inclusive. What is the probability that the number chosen will have a 0 in it?

   a. $\frac{9}{89}$

   b. $\frac{10}{89}$

   c. $\frac{9}{100}$

   d. $\frac{1}{10}$

   e. $\frac{11}{100}$

52. A 16-centimeter-by-18-centimeter rectangle is inscribed in a circle, as shown. What is the area of the circle, to the nearest square centimeter?

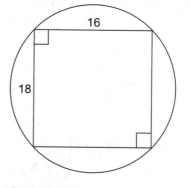

   f. 24π sq. cm

   g. 48π sq. cm

   h. 81π sq. cm

   j. 121π sq. cm

   k. 145π sq. cm

53. If $\log_a x = q$ and $\log_a y = r$, then $\log_a(xy)^2 =$

   a. qr

   b. $2qr$

   c. $4qr$

   d. $q + r$

   e. $2(q + r)$

54. The average of a set of six integers is 35. Adding a seventh integer to the set increases the average to 41. What is the seventh integer?

  f. 67

  g. 77

  h. 107

  j. 210

  k. 287

55. If $f(x) = x^2 + 3$, then $f(x + y) =$

  a. $x^2 + 2xy + y^2 + 3$

  b. $x^2 + 3 + y$

  c. $x^2 + 2xy + 3$

  d. $x^2 + 2xy + y^2$

  e. $x^2 + y^2$

56. A total of x men went on a fishing trip. Each of y boats that were used could carry f fishermen. If all boats but one were filled, and that boat had five open seats, which of the following equations correctly describes this situation?

  f. $yf + 5 = x$

  g. $yf - 5 = x$

  h. $y + f + 5 = x$

  j. $yx = f + 5$

  k. $yx = f - 5$

57. What is the smallest possible positive value of x where $y = \sin 2x$ reaches its maximum?

  a. 4π

  b. 2π

  c. π

  d. $\frac{\pi}{2}$

  e. $\frac{\pi}{4}$

58. In the figure shown, A and B lie on the circle C, which has a radius of 15. If angle ABC is 120°, what is the area of sector ABC?

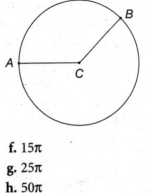

  f. 15π

  g. 25π

  h. 50π

  j. 75π

  k. 90π

59. A bag contains only pennies, nickels, and dimes. The probability of randomly selecting a penny is $\frac{1}{8}$. The probability of randomly selecting a nickel is $\frac{2}{7}$. Which of the following could be the total number of coins in the bag?

  a. 78

  b. 87

  c. 96

  d. 112

  e. It cannot be determined from the information provided.

60. The ratio of red chips to blue chips in a barrel is 4:3. There are 91 chips in the barrel. How many red chips must be added to create a 5:3 ratio?

  f. 8

  g. 12

  h. 13

  j. 19

  k. 24

ACT Reading Practice Test 3

40 Questions—35 Minutes

In this test you will find four passages, each followed by several questions. Read each passage carefully and then select the best possible answer for each question.

Passage I—Humanities

In 1804 President Thomas Jefferson sent army officers Meriwether Lewis and William Clark on an expedition to explore the territory of the Louisiana Purchase and beyond and to look for a waterway that would connect the Atlantic and Pacific oceans. This passage describes the collision of cultures that occurred between Native Americans and the representatives of the U.S. government.

1   When Thomas Jefferson sent Lewis and Clark
2   into the West, he patterned their mission on the
3   methods of Enlightenment science: to observe,
4   collect, document, and classify. Such strategies
5   were already in place for the epic voyages made
6   by explorers like Cook and Vancouver. Like
7   their contemporaries, Lewis and Clark were
8   more than representatives of European ratio-
9   nalism. They also represented a rising American
10   empire, one built on aggressive territorial
11   expansion and commercial gain.
12   But there was another view of the West:
13   that of the native inhabitants of the land. Their
14   understandings of landscapes, peoples, and
15   resources formed both a contrast and a counter-
16   point to those of Jefferson's travelers. One of
17   Lewis and Clark's missions was to open diplo-
18   matic relations between the United States and
19   the Native American nations of the West. As Jef-
20   ferson told Lewis, "It will now be proper you
21   should inform those through whose country you
22   will pass . . . that henceforth we become their
23   fathers and friends." When Euro-Americans and
24   Native Americans met, they used ancient diplo-
25   matic protocols that included formal language,
26   ceremonial gifts, and displays of military power.
27   But behind these symbols and rituals there were
28   often very different ways of understanding
29   power and authority. Such differences some-
30   times made communication across the cultural
31   divide difficult and open to confusion and
32   misunderstanding.
33   An important organizing principle in
34   Euro-American society was hierarchy. Both sol-
35   diers and civilians had complex gradations of
36   rank to define who gave orders and who
37   obeyed. While kinship was important in the
38   Euro-American world, it was even more funda-
39   mental in tribal societies. Everyone's power and
40   place depended on a complex network of real
41   and symbolic relationships. When the two groups
42   met—whether for trade or for diplomacy—
43   each tried to reshape the other in the group's
44   own image. Lewis and Clark sought to impose
45   their own notions of hierarchy on Native
46   Americans by "making chiefs" with medals,
47   printed certificates, and gifts. Native people
49   tried to impose the obligations of kinship on
40   the visitors by means of adoption ceremonies,
50   shared names, and ritual gifts.
51   The American republic began to issue
52   peace medals during the first Washington
53   administration, continuing a tradition estab-
54   lished by the European nations. Lewis and
55   Clark brought at least 89 medals in five sizes in
56   order to designate five "ranks" of chief. In the
57   eyes of Americans, Native Americans who
58   accepted such medals were also acknowledging
59   American sovereignty as "children" of a new
60   "great father." And in a moment of imperial
61   bravado, Lewis hung a peace medal around the
62   neck of a Piegan Blackfeet warrior killed by the
63   expedition in late July 1806. As Lewis later
64   explained, he used a peace medal as a way to let
65   the Blackfeet know "who we were."

66   In tribal society, kinship was like a legal
67 system—people depended on relatives to pro-
68 tect them from crime, war, and misfortune.
69 People with no kin were outside of society and
70 its rules. To adopt Lewis and Clark into tribal
71 society, the Plains Indians used a pipe cere-
72 mony. The ritual of smoking and sharing the
73 pipe was at the heart of much Native American
74 diplomacy. With the pipe the captains accepted
75 sacred obligations to share wealth, aid in war,
76 and revenge injustice. At the end of the cere-
77 mony, the pipe was presented to them so they
78 would never forget their obligations.
79   Gift giving was an essential part of diplo-
80 macy. To Native Americans, gifts proved the
82 giver's sincerity and honored the tribe. To Lewis
82 and Clark, some gifts advertised the technologi-
83 cal superiority and others encouraged the
84 Native Americans to adopt an agrarian lifestyle.
85 Like salesmen handing out free samples, Lewis
86 and Clark packed bales of manufactured goods
87 to open diplomatic relations with Native Amer-
89 ican tribes. Jefferson advised Lewis to give out
90 corn mills to introduce the Native Americans to
91 mechanized agriculture as part of his plan to
92 "civilize and instruct" them. Clark believed the
93 mills were "verry Thankfully recived," but by
94 the next year the Mandan had demolished
95 theirs to use the metal for weapons.

1. The goals of the Lewis and Clark expedition
include all of the following purposes EXCEPT
to
  a. expand scientific knowledge.
  b. strengthen American claims to western
    territory.
  c. overcome Native American resistance with
    military force.
  d. introduce native inhabitants to the ways of
    Euro-American culture.

2. According to the passage, the U.S. government
primarily viewed its role in relation to Native
Americans as one of
  f. creator.
  g. master.
  h. admirer.
  j. collaborator.

3. The word *protocols* as it is used in line 25 most
nearly means
  a. beliefs.
  b. tenets.
  c. codes.
  d. tactics.

4. According to the passage, the distribution of
peace medals exemplifies
  f. a cultural bridge connecting the Euro-
    Americans with Native American tribes.
  g. the explorers' respect for Native American
    sovereignty.
  h. the acknowledgment of the power and
    authority of Native American chiefs.
  j. the imposition of societal hierarchy on
    Native Americans.

5. The description of Lewis's actions in lines
60–63 is used to
  a. depict the expedition in a patriotic light.
  b. contradict commonly held views of
    imperialism.
  c. make an ironic statement about the meaning
    of the peace medals.
  d. provide a balanced report of two opposing
    points of view.

6. The description of the pipe ceremony in lines 72–78 is used to illustrate
  f. the naïveté of the Plains Native Americans.
  g. cultural confusion.
  h. the superiority of the native inhabitants.
  j. how Plains Native Americans honored low-ranking members of society.

7. In line 70, *adopt* most nearly means
  a. advocate.
  b. nurture.
  c. foster.
  d. practice.

8. The author uses the image of *salesmen handing out free samples* (lines 85–88) in order to
  f. depict Lewis and Clark as entrepreneurs.
  g. suggest that Lewis and Clark hoped to personally profit from their travels.
  h. imply that everyone likes to get something for free.
  j. show the promotional intent behind the explorers' gift giving.

9. The passage is developed primarily through
  a. the contrast of different abstract principles.
  b. quotations from one specific text.
  c. the analysis of one extended example.
  d. first-person narratives.

10. The author's primary purpose in the passage is to
  f. describe Lewis and Clark's expedition into the West.
  g. show the clashing views of the Native American nations versus those of the new American republic.
  h. explore the tribal system of kinship.
  j. make an argument supporting Jefferson's quest for scientific knowledge.

Passage II—Prose Fiction

In this excerpt from Charlotte Brontë's novel Jane Eyre, *the narrator decides to leave Lowood, the boarding school where she has lived for eight years.*

1 Miss Temple, through all changes, had thus far
2 continued superintendent of the seminary; to
3 her instruction I owed the best part of my
4 acquirements; her friendship and society had
5 been my continual solace: she had stood me in
6 the stead of mother, governess, and, latterly,
7 companion. At this period she married, removed
8 with her husband (a clergyman, an excellent
9 man, almost worthy of such a wife) to a distant
10 county, and consequently was lost to me.
11   From the day she left I was no longer the
12 same: with her was gone every settled feeling,
13 every association that had made Lowood in
14 some degree a home to me. I had imbibed from
15 her something of her nature and much of her
16 habits: more harmonious thoughts: what
17 seemed better-regulated feelings had become
18 inmates of my mind. I had given in allegiance
19 to duty and order; I was quiet; I believed I was
20 content: to the eyes of others, usually even to
21 my own, I appeared a disciplined and subdued
22 character.
23   But destiny, in the shape of the Rev. Mr.
24 Nasmyth, came between me and Miss Temple: I
25 saw her in her traveling dress step into a post-
26 chaise, shortly after the marriage ceremony; I
27 watched the chaise mount the hill and disap-
28 pear beyond its brow; and then retired to my
29 own room, and there spent in solitude the
30 greatest part of the half-holiday granted in
31 honor of the occasion.
32   I walked about the chamber most of the
33 time. I imagined myself only to be regretting
34 my loss, and thinking how to repair it; but
35 when my reflections concluded, and I looked
36 up and found that the afternoon was gone, and
37 evening far advanced, another discovery

38 dawned on me, namely, that in the interval I
39 had undergone a transforming process; that my
40 mind had put off all it had borrowed of Miss
41 Temple—or rather that she had taken with her
42 the serene atmosphere I had been breathing in
43 her vicinity—and that now I was left in my nat-
44 ural element, and beginning to feel the stirring
45 of old emotions. It did not seem as if a prop
46 were withdrawn, but rather as if a motive were
47 gone; it was not the power to be tranquil which
49 had failed me, but the reason for tranquility
40 was no more. My world had for some years
50 been in Lowood: my experience had been of its
51 rules and systems; now I remembered that the
52 real world was wide, and that a varied field of
53 hopes and fears, of sensations and excitements,
54 awaited those who had courage to go forth into
55 its expanse, to seek real knowledge of life
56 amidst its perils.
57   I went to my window, opened it, and
58 looked out. There were the two wings of the
59 building; there was the garden; there were the
60 skirts of Lowood; there was the hilly horizon.
61 My eye passed all other objects to rest on those
62 most remote, the blue peaks: it was those I
63 longed to surmount; all within their boundary
64 of rock and heath seemed prison ground, exile
65 limits. I traced the white road winding round
66 the base of one mountain, and vanishing in a
67 gorge between two: how I longed to follow it
68 further! I recalled the time when I had traveled
69 that very road in a coach; I remembered
70 descending that hill at twilight: an age seemed
71 to have elapsed since the day which brought me
72 first to Lowood, and I had never quitted it
73 since. My vacations had all been spent at
74 school: Mrs. Reed had never sent for me to
75 Gateshead; neither she nor any of her family
76 had ever been to visit me. I had had no com-
77 munication by letter or message with the outer
78 world: school-rules, school-duties, school-
79 habits and notions, and voices, and faces, and

80 phrases, and costumes, and preferences, and
81 antipathies: such was what I knew of existence.
82   And now I felt that it was not enough: I
83 tired of the routine of eight years in one after-
84 noon. I desired liberty; for liberty I gasped; for
85 liberty I uttered a prayer; it seemed scattered on
86 the wind then faintly blowing. I abandoned it
87 and framed a humbler supplication; for change,
88 stimulus: that petition, too, seemed swept off
89 into vague space: "Then," I cried, half desperate,
90 "grant me at least a new servitude!"

11. Miss Temple was the narrator's
    I. teacher.
    II. friend.
    III. mother.
  a. I only
  b. II only
  c. III only
  d. I and II

12. The word *appeared*, as used in the sentence, *I believed I was content: to the eyes of others, usually even to my own, I appeared a disciplined and subdued character* (lines 19–22), implies that
  f. the narrator often dressed in prim and conservative clothing.
  g. this appearance did not reflect her deeper feelings.
  h. the narrator was only concerned with appearance.
  j. the reader cannot draw an inference from this statement.

13. While Miss Temple was at Lowood, the narrator
  a. was calm and content.
  b. was often alone.
  c. had frequent disciplinary problems.
  d. longed to leave Lowood.

14. The word *inmates* in line 18 means
  f. patients.
  g. prisoners.
  h. residents.
  j. convalescents.

15. Mrs. Reed (line 74) is most likely
  a. the narrator's mother.
  b. the headmistress of Lowood.
  c. the narrator's former guardian.
  d. the narrator's friend.

16. It can be inferred from the passage that life at Lowood was
  f. very unconventional and modern.
  g. very structured and isolated.
  h. harsh and demeaning.
  j. liberal and carefree.

17. After Miss Temple's wedding, the narrator
  a. realizes she wants to experience the world.
  b. decides that she must get married.
  c. realizes she can never leave Lowood.
  d. determines to follow Miss Temple.

18. The passage suggests that the narrator
  f. was sent to Lowood by mistake.
  g. is entirely dependent upon Miss Temple.
  h. has run away from Lowood before.
  j. is naturally curious and rebellious.

19. In lines 86–90, the narrator reduces her supplication to simply a *new servitude* because she
  a. doesn't believe in prayer.
  b. is not in a free country.
  c. has been offered a position as a servant.
  d. knows so little of the real world.

20. As used in the final sentence, the word *petition* means
  f. piece of paper.
  g. prayer.
  h. question.
  j. possibility.

Passage III—Social Sciences

This passage describes the public's growing interest in alternative medicine practices in twenty-first-century United States.

1 Once people wore garlic around their necks to
2 ward off disease. Today, most Americans would
3 scoff at the idea of wearing a necklace of garlic
4 cloves to enhance their well-being. However,
5 you might find a number of Americans willing
6 to ingest capsules of pulverized garlic or other
7 herbal supplements in the name of health.
8 　　Complementary and alternative medicine
9 (CAM), which includes a range of practices
10 outside of conventional medicine such as herbs,
11 homeopathy, massage, yoga, and acupuncture,
12 holds increasing appeal for Americans. In fact,
13 according to one estimate, 42% of Americans
14 have used alternative therapies. A Harvard
15 Medical School survey found that young adults
16 (at the time of the study, those born between
17 1965 and 1979) are the most likely to use alter-
18 native treatments, whereas people born before
19 1945 are the least likely to use these therapies.
20 Nonetheless, in all age groups, the use of
21 unconventional healthcare practices has
22 steadily increased since the 1950s, and the trend
23 is likely to continue.
24 　　CAM has become a big business as Ameri-
25 cans dip into their wallets to pay for alternative
26 treatments. A 1997 American Medical Associa-
27 tion study estimated that the public spent $21.2
28 billion for alternative medicine therapies in that
29 year, more than half of which were out-of-
30 pocket expenditures, meaning they were not

31 covered by health insurance. Indeed, Americans
32 made more out-of-pocket expenditures for
33 alternative services than they did for out-of-
34 pocket payments for hospital stays in 1997. In
35 addition, the number of total visits to alterna-
36 tive medicine providers (about 629 million)
37 exceeded the tally of visits to primary care phy-
38 sicians (386 million) in that year.
39 However, the public has not abandoned
40 conventional medicine for alternative health-
41 care. Most Americans seek out alternative ther-
42 apies as a complement to their conventional
43 healthcare, whereas only a small percentage of
44 Americans rely primarily on alternative care.
45 Why have so many patients turned to alterna-
46 tive therapies? Frustrated by the time con-
47 straints of managed care and alienated by
49 conventional medicine's focus on technology,
40 some feel that a holistic approach to healthcare
50 better reflects their beliefs and values. Others
51 seek therapies that will relieve symptoms asso-
52 ciated with chronic disease, symptoms that
53 mainstream medicine cannot treat.
54 Some alternative therapies have crossed
55 the line into mainstream medicine as scientific
56 investigation has confirmed their safety and
57 efficacy. For example, today physicians may
58 prescribe acupuncture for pain management or
59 to control the nausea associated with chemo-
60 therapy. Most U.S. medical schools teach
61 courses in alternative therapies, and many
62 health insurance companies offer some alterna-
63 tive medicine benefits. Yet, despite their gaining
64 acceptance, the majority of alternative therapies
65 have not been researched in controlled studies.
66 New research efforts aim at testing alternative
67 methods and providing the public with infor-
68 mation about which are safe and effective and
69 which are a waste of money, or possibly
70 dangerous.
71 So what about those who swear by the
72 health benefits of the so-called smelly rose,
73 garlic? Observational studies that track disease
74 incidence in different populations suggest that
75 garlic use in the diet may act as a cancer-fighting
76 agent, particularly for prostate and stomach
77 cancer. However, these findings have not been
78 confirmed in clinical studies. And yes, reported
79 side effects include garlic odor.

21. The author's primary purpose in the passage is
to
   a. confirm the safety and effectiveness of
   alternative medicine approaches.
   b. convey the excitement of crossing new
   medical frontiers.
   c. describe the recent increase in the use of
   alternative therapies.
   d. explore the variety of practices that fall into
   the category of alternative medicine.

22. The author describes wearing garlic (lines 1–2)
as an example of
   f. an arcane practice considered odd and
   superstitious today.
   g. the ludicrous nature of complementary and
   alternative medicine.
   h. a scientifically tested medical practice.
   j. a safe and reliable means to prevent some
   forms of cancer.

23. The word *conventional* as it is used in line 10
most nearly means
   a. appropriate.
   b. established.
   c. formal.
   d. moralistic.

24. The author most likely uses the Harvard survey results (lines 14–19) to imply that
   f. as people age they always become more conservative.
   g. people born before 1945 view alternative therapies with disdain.
   h. the survey did not question baby boomers (those born between 1945 and 1965) on the topic.
   j. many young adults are open-minded to alternative therapies.

25. The statistic comparing total visits to alternative medicine practitioners with those to primary care physicians (lines 34–38) is used to illustrate the
   a. popularity of alternative medicine.
   b. public's distrust of conventional healthcare.
   c. affordability of alternative therapies.
   d. ineffectiveness of most primary care physicians.

26. In line 42, *complement* most nearly means
   f. tribute.
   g. commendation.
   h. substitute.
   j. addition.

27. The information in lines 46–53 indicates that Americans believe that conventional healthcare
   a. offers the best relief from the effects of chronic diseases.
   b. should not use technology in treating illness.
   c. combines caring for the body with caring for the spirit.
   d. falls short of their expectations in some aspects.

28. The author suggests that *cross[ing] the line into mainstream medicine* (lines 54–57) involves
   f. performing stringently controlled research on alternative therapies.
   g. accepting the spiritual dimension of preventing and treating illness.
   h. approving any treatments that a patient is interested in trying.
   j. notifying your physician about herbs or alternative therapies you are using.

29. In lines 73–79, the author refers to garlic use again in order to
   a. cite an example of the fraudulent claims of herbal supplements.
   b. suggest that claims about some herbs may be legitimate.
   c. mock people who take garlic capsules.
   d. offer a reason why some Americans are drawn to alternative health methods.

30. Which of the following best describes the approach of the passage?
   f. matter-of-fact narration
   g. sarcastic criticism
   h. playful reporting
   j. impassioned argument

Passage IV—Natural Sciences

The following passage describes the composition and nature of ivory.

Ivory skin, Ivory Soap, Ivory Snow—we hear *ivory* used all the time to describe something fair, white, and pure. But where does ivory come from, and what exactly is it? Is it natural or man-made? Is it a modifier, meaning something pure and white, or is it a specialized and discrete substance?

Historically, the word *ivory* has been applied to the tusks of elephants. However, the chemical structure of the teeth and tusks of mammals is the same regardless of the species of origin, and the trade in certain teeth and tusks other than elephant is well established and widespread. Therefore, ivory can correctly be used to describe any mammalian tooth or tusk of commercial interest that is large enough to be carved or scrimshawed. Teeth and tusks have the same origins. Teeth are specialized structures adapted for food mastication. Tusks, which are extremely large teeth projecting beyond the lips, have evolved from ordinary teeth and give certain species an evolutionary advantage that goes beyond chewing and breaking down food into digestible pieces. Furthermore, the tusk can be used to actually secure food through hunting, killing, and then breaking up large chunks of food into manageable bits.

The teeth of most mammals consist of a root as well as the tusk proper. Teeth and tusks have the same physical structures: a pulp cavity, dentine, cementum, and enamel. The innermost area is the pulp cavity. The pulp cavity is an empty space within the tooth that conforms to the shape of the pulp. Odontoblastic cells line the pulp cavity and are responsible for the production of dentine. Dentine, which is the main component of carved ivory objects, forms a layer of consistent thickness around the pulp cavity and comprises the bulk of the tooth and tusk. Dentine is a mineralized connective tissue with an organic matrix of collagenous proteins. The inorganic component of dentine consists of dahllite. Dentine contains a microscopic structure called dentinal tubules, which are micro-canals that radiate outward through the dentine from the pulp cavity to the exterior cementum border.

These canals have different configurations in different ivories, and their diameters range between 0.8 and 2.2 microns. Their length is dictated by the radius of the tusk. The three-dimensional configuration of the dentinal tubules is under genetic control and is therefore a characteristic unique to the order of the mammal.

Exterior to the dentine lies the cementum layer. Cementum forms a layer surrounding the dentine of tooth and tusk roots. Its main function is to adhere the tooth and tusk root to the mandibular and maxillary jawbones. Incremental lines are commonly seen in cementum.

Enamel, the hardest animal tissue, covers the surface of the tooth or tusk that receives the most wear, such as the tip or crown. Ameloblasts are responsible for the formation of enamel and are lost after the enamel process is complete. Enamel exhibits a prismatic structure with prisms that run perpendicular to the crown or tip. Enamel prism patterns can have both taxonomic and evolutionary significance.

Tooth and tusk ivory can be carved into an almost infinite variety of shapes and objects. Examples of carved ivory objects are netsukes, jewelry, flatware handles, furniture inlays, and piano keys. Additionally, warthog tusks, as well as teeth from sperm whales, killer whales, and hippopotamuses can also be scrimshawed or superficially carved, thus retaining their original shapes as morphologically recognizable objects. The identification of ivory and ivory

81 substitutes is based on the physical and chemi-
82 cal class characteristics of these materials. A
83 common approach to identification is to use
84 the macroscopic and microscopic physical
85 characteristics of ivory in combination with a
86 simple chemical test using ultraviolet light.

31. In line 7, what does the term *discrete* most
nearly mean?
  a. tactful
  b. distinct
  c. careful
  d. prudent

32. Which of the following titles is most appropriate for this passage?
  f. Ivory: An Endangered Species
  g. Elephants, Ivory, and Widespread Hunting
  in Africa
  h. Ivory: Is It Organic or Inorganic?
  j. Uncovering the Truth about Natural Ivory

33. The word *scrimshawed* in line 17 and line 77
most nearly means
  a. floated.
  b. waxed.
  c. carved.
  d. sunk.

34. Which of the following choices is NOT part of
the physical structure of teeth?
  f. pulp cavity
  g. dentine
  h. cementum
  j. tusk

35. As used in line 19, what is the best synonym for
mastication?
  a. digestion
  b. tasting
  c. biting
  d. chewing

36. Which sentence best describes *dentinal tubules*?
  f. Dentinal tubules are a layer surrounding the
  dentine of tooth and tusk roots.
  g. Dentinal tubules are micro-canals that
  radiate outward through the dentine from
  the pulp cavity to the exterior cementum
  border.
  h. Dentinal tubules cover the surface of the
  tooth or tusk that receives the most wear,
  such as the tip or crown.
  j. Dentinal tubules are extremely large teeth
  projecting beyond the lips that have evolved
  from ordinary teeth and give certain species
  an evolutionary advantage.

37. According to the passage, all of the following
are organic substances EXCEPT
  a. cementum.
  b. dentine.
  c. dahllite.
  d. ameloblasts.

38. As used in line 73, *netsukes* are most likely
  f. honed animal teeth.
  g. small statues.
  h. large statues.
  j. pieces of furniture.

39. According to the passage, how can natural ivory be authenticated?

   a. by ultraviolet light

   b. by gamma rays

   c. by physical observation

   d. by osmosis

40. According to the passage, which statement is NOT true of enamel?

   f. It is an organic substance.

   g. It is the hardest of animal tissues.

   h. It should never be exposed to ultraviolet light.

   j. Its structure is prismatic.

ACT Science Practice Test 3

40 Questions—35 Minutes

The passages in this test are followed by several questions. After reading each passage, choose the best answer to each question. You may refer back to the passages as often as necessary. You are *not* permitted to use a calculator on this test.

Passage I—Research Summary

The forces affecting an object on an inclined plane are F_G, the force due to gravity; F_N, the normal force of the plane against the object; F_F, the force due to friction between the object and the plane; and any other external forces applied. For the purpose of calculating the effects of these forces, it is usually necessary to analyze F_G as two forces: F_P the force directed down the plane, and F_P, the force perpendicular to the plane opposing the normal force. Note that F_F always works against the motion of the object. If the object is sliding down the plane, friction will tend to hold it up. If the object is being pulled up the plane, friction will tend to hold it down.

Figure 1 is a free body diagram illustrating the forces that act on an inclined plane.

These experiments were to test and calibrate a tow rope that is used to pull skiers up a ski slope. The skiers hold the rope and are pulled up the slope by a

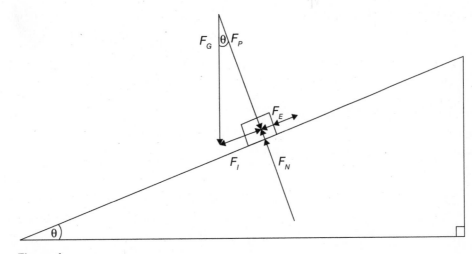

Figure 1

motorized pulley system. Skiers can hold on to or release the tow rope at any desired point on the slope. Figure 2 illustrates the tow rope mechanism and shows the mass of four skiers (including all clothing and equipment), who participated in these experiments. As shown, their masses total 420 kg.

The pulley engine must exert a tension force of 5,000 N (newtons) on the rope to balance the weight of the rope when no skiers are being towed. This is F_S, the force of the system. The total tension force applied by the pulley engine on the rope is F_T.

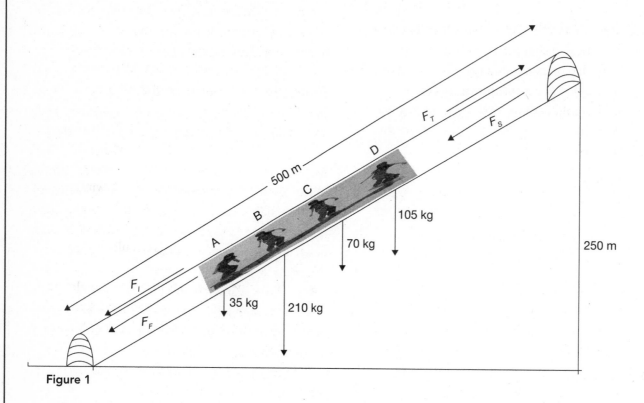

Figure 1

Each skier is affected by F_T, the tension force of the rope; F_G; and F_F. F_G is the vector sum of F_P and F_I according to the third formula given here.

The six formulas for the various forces are as follows:

1. $F_I = F_G[\sin(\theta)]$
2. $F_P = F_G[\cos(\theta)] = -F_N$
3. $F_G = \text{mass}(-10.0 \text{ m/s}^2)$, where F_G is in newtons, mass in kg
4. $F_F = \mu F_P$ where μ is the coefficient of friction
5. $F_S = -5,000 \text{ N}$
6. $F_{NET} = F_T + F_I + F_F + F_S$

Note that the downward direction is indicated as negative and the upward as positive. Acceleration due to gravity, F_G, F_P, F_F, and F_S, are negative. The only upward force exerted on the skiers is F_T, the tension force applied by the rope.

The tow rope is expected to be able to tow any number of skiers from 0 to 40, up to a maximum mass of 4,200 kg at a constant velocity of 1.0 m/s. The total mass of all of the skiers on the rope can be treated as a single mass.

To maintain a constant velocity, F_{NET}, the net force on the skiers, must be zero. To speed up to the target velocity, there must be a net force heading up the slope. To slow down to the target velocity, there must be a net force headed down the slope.

Experiment 1

To determine what force the pulley engine must be able to apply, we must determine the highest coefficient of friction that the mechanism will have to deal with.

The pulley system is equipped with monitoring and regulating equipment that tracks both the velocity of the rope and the force of tension (F_T) applied by the rope. It also adjusts F_T as necessary to maintain a constant velocity. Table 1 is a record of the results of trials on three kinds of snow towing a total skier mass of 420 kg. In each case, the highest F_T for each type of snow was recorded when the tow rope was moving at a constant rate of 1.0 m/s.

Experiment 2

Once a coefficient of friction has been determined for each of the types of snow and it is determined which type of snow requires the greatest force, experiments are conducted with a fully loaded tow rope system to determine how closely the force actually applied to maintain the target velocity agrees with the calculated force required. Table 2 indicates the F_T calculated to be required to maintain the full 4,200 kg of skiers at a constant velocity and the actual F_T recorded in four different trials when they were being towed at a constant 1.0 m/s.

1. Which Table 1 column values are either determined by the design of the experiment or calculated from the determined values?
   a. F_S, F_G, and F_I
   b. F_S, F_G, F_P, and $F_I + F_S$
   c. F_P, $F_I + F_S$, and F_F
   d. F_T and F_F

2. Which Table 1 columns contain the recorded results of the experimental trials, and which contain values calculated from the results and the predetermined values?
   f. F_T is recorded by the towing device. F_F and μ are calculated from it.
   g. F_T and μ are recorded by the towing device.
   h. F_S and F_T are recorded by the towing device. F_F and μ are calculated from them.
   j. F_P, the force along the slope, is measured by the towing device. F_T is calculated from it.

3. Which value of μ must be used to calculate the minimum F_T that the tow rope mechanism must be able to generate?
   a. 0.25
   b. 0.17
   c. 0.03
   d. The total of a, b, and c is required to accommodate all conditions.

Tension

TABLE 1						
SNOW	F_S	F_G	$F_I + F_S$	F_T	F_F	μ
powder	−5,000	−42,000	−36,414	−83,414	92,508	0.25
crust	−5,000	−42,000	−36,414	−83,414	89,703	0.17
icy	−5,000	−42,000	−36,414	−83,414	84,507	0.03

TABLE 2				
	TRIAL 1	TRIAL 2	TRIAL 3	TRIAL 4
calculated	460,080	460,080	460,080	460,080
actual	491,325	452,021	470,332	501,515
% deviation	6.4	−1.8	2.2	8.3

4. What units are the values in Table 1 reported in?

  f. kg

  g. m/s^2

  h. newtons

  j. Nm/s^2

5. Keeping in mind the calculations included in Table 1, what is the easiest way to determine the calculated value in Table 2 that is compared to the experiment 2 results?

  a. $F_T = -(F_G[\sin(\theta)] + \mu F_G[\cos(\theta) + 5{,}000\ N]$, based on $F_G = 420{,}000\ N$.

  b. $10(F_I + F_F) + F_S$, where F_P, F_F, and F_S are taken from the correct row of Table 1.

  c. $10(F_T)$, where F_T is taken from the correct row of Table 1.

  d. Multiply the average of the three F_T's in Table 1 by 10.

6. The effect of force on acceleration is given by the formula $F = ma$, which is stated as force = mass × acceleration. The tow rope mechanism must be able to accelerate at a rate of 0.5 m/s^2 to maintain the desired velocity of 1.0 m/s. Assuming that the only force required due to the rope mechanism itself is the already identified F_S, how much capacity, beyond the requirement of maintaining a constant velocity, is required to accelerate 4,200 kg of skiers at 0.5 m/s^2?

  f. 4,200 N

  g. $\cos(\theta) \times 2{,}400\ N$

  h. $\sin(\theta) \times 2{,}400\ N$

  j. 2,400 N

Passage II—Data Representation

Tsunamis are among the most dangerous natural disasters known in history. Figure 1 illustrates how tsunamis are created.

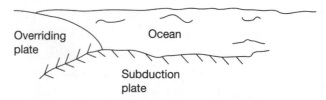

Figure 1a   Over time the subduction plate strains the overriding plate by forcing it upward.

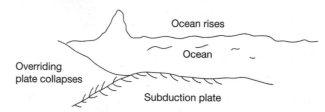

Figure 1b   An underwater earthquake occurs when the overriding plate collapses downward, causing an upsurge of water.

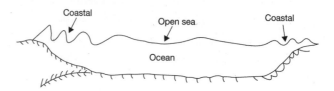

Figure 1c   The tsunami moves away from the earthquake site both toward the shore and out to sea.

Approaching the shallow coastal water, the tsunami waves can be 2 to 10 meters or more high with wavelengths in the 100 meter range. In deep ocean water, they can be 10 cm to 1 m high with wavelengths of hundreds of kilometers.

A tsunami traveling on the high seas is a stealthy killer. Much effort has been applied to developing means of detecting tsunami activity and forecasting what kind of impact one will have when it strikes land.

Factors that must be taken into account for tsunami forecasting include the force and location of the initiating event, the ocean depth at all points affected by the tsunami or in its path, and the interaction between the tsunami and the normal astronomical tides at all relevant points.

Figures 2a and 2b illustrate the influence on tides of the two most significant factors. Figure 2a shows the effect of the moon's gravity, and Figure 2b shows the effect of the sun's. The earth rotates daily relative to both the sun and the moon, but the daily, or diurnal, tidal cycles do not coincide precisely with a day. The moon also revolves in an approximately 28-day cycle around the earth, and the earth revolves in an approximately 365-day cycle around the sun. These and many other factors, most of which are ignored by Figures 2a and 2b, operate together to account for the day-to-day variations, even in the normal tidal cycles. Figure 2c illustrates the lunar and solar effects working in combination.

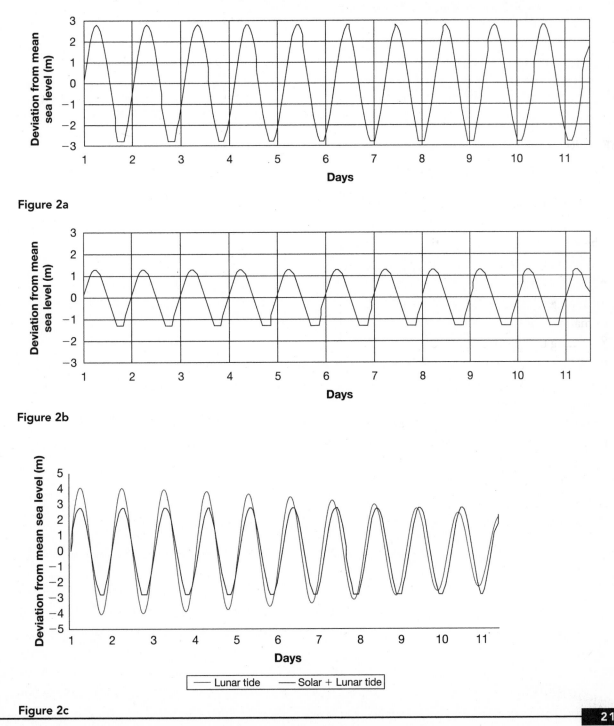

Figure 2a

Figure 2b

Figure 2c

To forecast the impact of a tsunami, a mathematical model of the tsunami's pattern of action must be superimposed on a model of the underlying activity patterns of the sea due to tides and other factors. Figure 3 illustrates how this is done for two four-hour slices of the 11-day period illustrated in Figure 2. Figure 3a shows a typical tsunami pattern, beginning with a sharp decline in sea level and withdrawal of water from coastal areas, followed by a series of incoming and outgoing waves until the tsunami energy dies out. Figures 3b and 3c are simply blowups of the lunar and solar tide cycles shown in Figures 1a and 1b for the four-hour period beginning day 1, hour 4. Figures 3d and 3e model what this tsunami would look like for two different time frames. Figure 3d models the tsunami striking at day 1, hour 4. Figure 3e models it striking at day 11, hour 0.

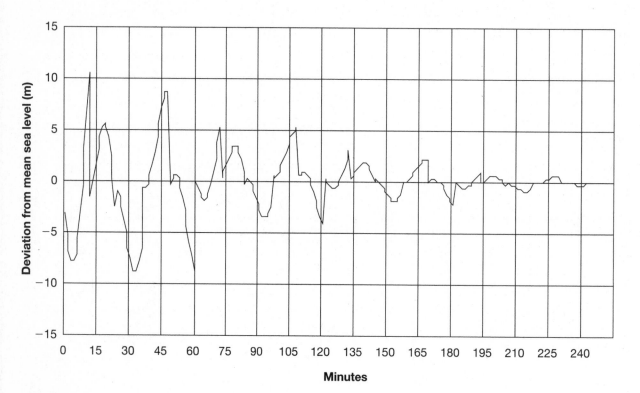

Figure 3a

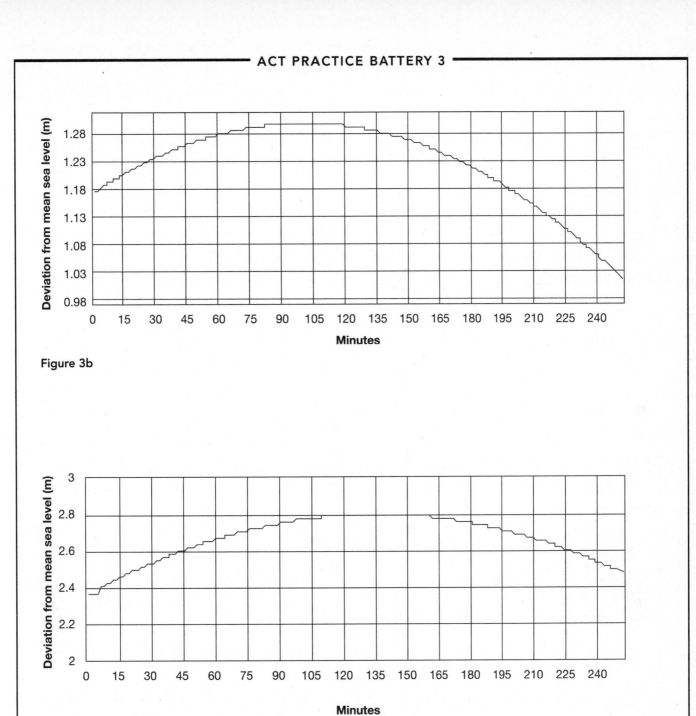

Figure 3b

Figure 3c

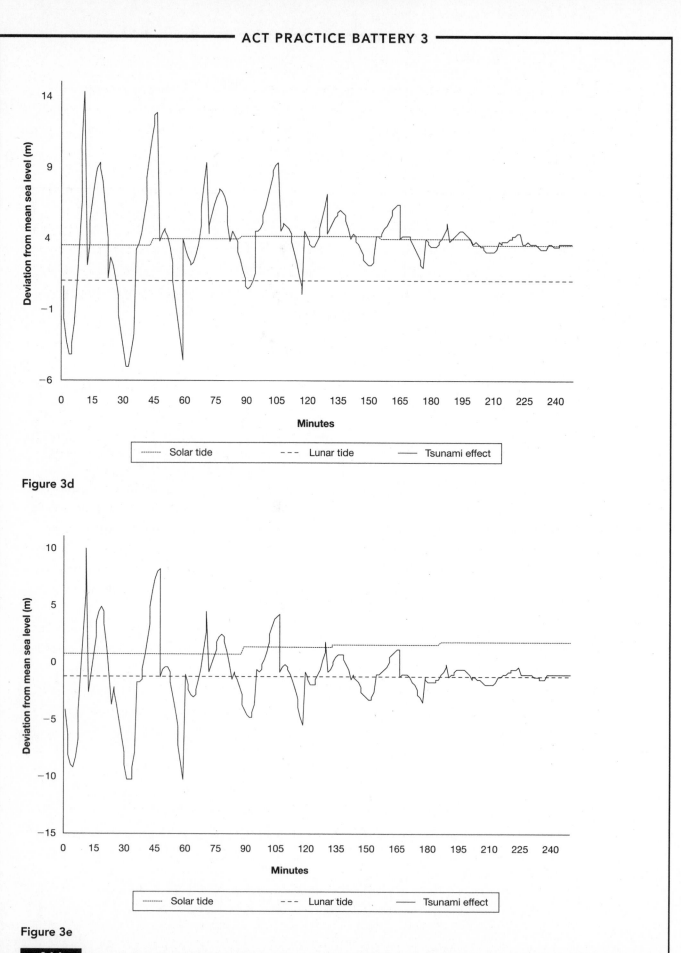

Figure 3d

Figure 3e

7. Look at the simplified model of the normal tides in Figure 2. What in Figures 2a and 2b, which illustrate the lunar and solar influences, accounts for the marked decline over the 11-day period shown in the strength of the cumulative tides illustrated in Figure 2c?

　a. At the beginning of day 1, the peaks and troughs of Figures 2a and 2b coincide, but the lunar cycle has a shorter wavelength, so that by day 9 the solar cycle's trough is almost simultaneous with the lunar cycle's peak.

　b. At the beginning of day 1, the peaks and troughs of Figures 2a and 2b coincide, but the lunar cycle has a longer wavelength, so that by day 9 the solar cycle's trough is almost simultaneous with the lunar cycle's peak.

　c. The moon and sun each move closer and further away from the earth.

　d. The tilt of the earth toward the sun changes day by day.

8. Look at the graphs in Figure 3. In Figures 3d and 3e, the line labeled "Solar tide" indicates the level of the solar tide. The line labeled "Lunar tide" indicates the combined effect of the solar and lunar tides, and the "Tsunami effect" line indicates the cumulative effect of all three. For the four-hour periods illustrated, which factor has the greatest impact on the cumulative changes in sea level illustrated by Figures 3d and 3e?

　f. tsunami effect

　g. lunar tide

　h. solar tide

　j. The strongest individual factor cannot be determined.

9. Refer to Figure 2. What is the difference between the tsunami curves in Figures 3d and 3e and how is that related to the time at which these models begin?

　a. The curve in Figure 3d shows the tsunami occurring almost entirely above mean sea level, but the curve in 3e is largely below mean sea level. This is because at day 1, hour 4, the solar and lunar tidal influences are both reaching their peak levels, but at day 11, hour 0, they are both near the bottom of a trough.

　b. The height of the curve in Figure 3e is less than that in Figure 3d because 3e begins at the highest tidal peak in the 11-day period, and 3e begins at the lowest tidal trough.

　c. The height of the curve in Figure 3e is less than that in Figure 3d because 3d begins at the highest tidal peak in the 11-day period, and 3e begins at a tidal trough.

　d. The curve in Figure 3d shows the tsunami occurring almost entirely above mean sea level, but the curve in 3e is largely below mean sea level. This is because the lunar and solar tidal influences shown in Figures 2a and 2b are moving in opposite directions.

10. Look at the amplitudes of the lunar and solar tidal influences illustrated in Figures 2a and 2b. If the graph in Figure 2c were continued beyond day 11, approximately what would be the lowest peak height above mean sea level shown?

　f. zero

　g. 1.5 meters

　h. 2.0 meters

　j. 4.1 meters

11. Based on Figure 3a and the description of a tsunami provided in the passage, what is occurring on shore as the curve goes up and down?

    a. At minute 0, water recedes from the shore. After several minutes, it begins steadily returning for about 10 minutes, when it reaches a peak of 10 meters above normal sea level. It then steadily recedes and returns in approximately 30-minute cycles for almost four hours as the high and low sea levels gradually decrease.

    b. Every 30 minutes a huge wave breaks on the shore and then recedes.

    c. At minute 0, water recedes from the shore. After several minutes, it begins returning for about 10 minutes, when it reaches a peak of 10 meters above normal sea level. It then recedes and returns in approximately 30-minute cycles, with some minor ups and downs along the way, for almost four hours as the high and low sea levels gradually decrease.

    d. The water level drops and falls but never goes much above or below mean sea level.

Passage III—Research Summary

Photosynthesis is one of the most important biochemical reactions known. The inputs and the results of photosynthesis have long been understood to be that 6 moles of carbon dioxide plus 12 moles of water, in the presence of light and chloroplasts, produces 1 mole of glucose, 6 moles of oxygen, and 6 moles of water. Chloroplasts are the complex structures containing chlorophyll found in green plant cells. Glucose is a leading storehouse of energy, not only for plants but for animals that feed on plants and for processes that use it as an energy source in abiotic reactions. The chemical formula is as follows:

$$6CO_2 + 12H_2O \xrightarrow[\text{chloroplasts}]{\text{light energy}} C_6H_{12}O_6 + 6O_2 + 6H_2O$$

It was also known that in between the input and output, there are many complex steps. One of these is named the Hill reaction, after its discoverer, Robert Hill. His experiments proved that oxygen is released directly from water, in the presence of chloroplasts and light, without any CO_2 involvement at all, and without necessarily occurring in living cells.

The chemical formula for the Hill reaction is as follows:

$$2H_2O + 2A \xrightarrow[\text{chloroplasts}]{\text{light energy}} 2AH_2 + O_2$$

In this formula, A can be any suitable electron acceptor. Within a plant cell, this would normally be adenosine diphosphate (ADP). The hydrogen and oxygen in water (H_2O) are bound together because the single excess electrons orbiting each hydrogen nucleus fill the two electron places that are available in oxygen's outer orbit. The Hill reaction requires an electron acceptor to replace oxygen's role in relation to the two hydrogen atoms and free it up to combine with other oxygen atoms, forming the normal oxygen gas molecule, O_2.

Experiment 1

These experiments are based on using 2,6-dichlorophenol-indophenol (DCPIP) as an electron accepter to free oxygen from water. DCPIP is a convenient electron acceptor to use because it changes color as the reaction occurs. In its normal oxidized form, it is blue, but when it is reduced (by giving up its oxygen and accepting electrons from hydrogen) it turns colorless. One drawback is that it quickly takes on oxygen and regains its color, which makes truly accurate readings very difficult.

The main ingredient for the experiments is a slurry of chloroplasts extracted from green leaves. The objective is to compare how the Hill reaction proceeds under differing circumstances, so it is essential that slurry from the same batch of chloroplasts, preserved by refrigeration in between trials, is used for each experiment.

For each experiment, three different preparations of extracted chloroplasts and DCPIP are tested. They all include a 1 cc mixture of chloroplast extract and distilled water and 3 cc of DCPIP.

For experiment 1, all trials are conducted under identical lighting with the test mixture at a temperature of 20°C. The difference is in the concentration of chloroplast extract. Table 1 shows characteristics of each trial for experiments 1 and 2.

TABLE 1		
Experiment/Trial	cc's Chloroplast: Distilled Water	Light Intensity
1-A	1:0	100%
1-B	0.5:0.5	100%
1-C	0:1	100%
2-A	1:0	0%
2-B	1:0	50%
2-C	1:0	100%

Each trial consists of testing the prepared test tube with a colorimeter immediately after the mixture is produced, and every two minutes thereafter until the color stabilizes. Each color measure is given an index value of 5 on a scale of 5 to 0, where 5 is the first measure, before the DCPIP has begun to fade, and 0 is totally colorless. Table 2 shows the results of the trials for both experiments.

TABLE 2						
Minute	Trial 1-A	Trial 1-B	Trial 1-C	Trial 2-A	Trial 2-B	Trial 2-C
0	5.0	5.0	5.0	5.0	5.0	5.0
2	4.2	4.5	5.0		4.6	4.4
4	3.4	4.1	5.0		4.1	3.5
6	2.7	3.7	5.0		3.8	2.8
8	2.0	3.3	5.0		3.4	2.2
10	1.3	2.8	5.0	4.8	3.0	1.4
12	1.2	2.4	5.0		2.6	1.3
14	1.1	2.1	4.9		2.2	1.3
16	1.2	1.8	4.9		1.8	1.2
18	1.2	1.5	4.9		1.4	1.2
20	1.1	1.2	4.9	4.8	1.0	0.9

Experiment 2

For experiment 2, the same concentration of chloroplast extract is used in each case, and the temperature is maintained at 20°. The difference is in the intensity of lighting, as shown in Table 1. Trial A is sealed in foil to prevent all light from entering. In order to maintain it in as close to total darkness as possible, the colorimeter reading is made only once every 10 minutes.

12. Experiment 1 and experiment 2 each measure the progress of the Hill reaction. Based on Table 1 and the other material presented, which aspect of the reaction is tested by experiment 1, and which by experiment 2?
    f. They test the relationship between chloroplast concentration and light.
    g. Experiment 1 tests the effect of chloroplast concentration on the reaction. Experiment 2 tests the effect of light.
    h. Experiment 1 tests the effect of light on the reaction. Experiment 2 tests the effect of chloroplast.
    j. They test the rate at which oxygen is produced.

13. Look at the photosynthesis and the Hill reaction formulas given in this passage in light of the overall description of photosynthesis given. What element is present in photosynthesis, but not the Hill reaction?
    a. carbon (C)
    b. A
    c. hydrogen (H)
    d. oxygen (O)

14. Which of the following are NOT either inputs or results of photosynthesis and the Hill reaction?
    f. oxygen (O)
    g. carbon (C)
    h. hydrogen (H)
    j. light and chloroplasts

15. Examine Tables 1 and 2 along with the formula for the Hill reaction given in the passage. What is the most accurate statement about the role of light and chloroplasts in the Hill reaction?
    a. They are present, but play no real role.
    b. One or the other must be present or the reaction will be very slow.
    c. The Hill reaction is enhanced by the presence of light and chloroplasts and does not occur in the absence of either of them.
    d. They are actually the only important elements of the reaction.

16. Based on Tables 1 and 2, what best describes the way in which light and chloroplasts affect the Hill reaction in these trials?
    f. They increase the rate at which the reaction occurs but have little effect on its ultimate outcome.
    g. They speed up the reaction and increase the overall production of oxygen.
    h. They moderate the production of oxygen.
    j. Chloroplasts play a much more significant role than light in enhancing the reaction.

17. In light of what the description of experiment 1 says about the role of DCPIP, what is most directly measured by the decline in colorimeter readings seen in these experiments?
    a. The activity of the chloroplasts.
    b. The release of oxygen from the water which combines with the DCPIP.
    c. DCPIP's loss of color from losing its oxygen.
    d. DCPIP's loss of color as it combines with hydrogen.

Passage IV—Research Summary

The earth is surrounded by a magnetic field. It is measured from the vicinity of the earth's surface through three primary parameters: north or south directionality, angle of inclination or dip up or down, and intensity. Figure 1 illustrates how this works. The earth has north and south magnetic poles, which are close to, but not identical with, the north and south geographical poles. By convention, what is called the north pole of a magnet is the end that points towards the earth's North Magnetic Pole. Opposites attract, so the North Pole is actually a magnetic south pole, and the South Pole is actually a magnetic north pole.

At the north magnetic pole, a magnet's north pole will point straight down toward the magnetic pole. As the magnet moves toward the equator, it will continue to point upwards toward the North Magnetic Pole at a decreasing angle, until it becomes horizontal near the equator. Then it will incline upwards until, at the South Magnetic Pole, it points straight up away from the pole.

For thousands of years, human beings have used magnetic compasses to navigate. In the mid-nineteenth century, evidence began to accumulate that many other creatures also use the magnetic field to find their way around.

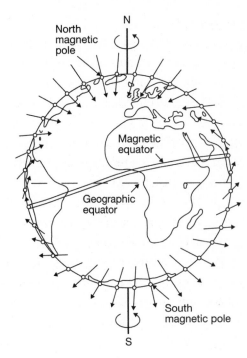

Figure 1

Experiment 1

It is known that European robins migrate northward in the spring and southward in the fall. Caged robins that cannot join in the migration tend to gather at the side of the cage facing in the desired direction of migration.

In this experiment, an artificial magnetic field is introduced that shifts the magnetic north experienced by the caged birds. Figure 2a indicates the way the birds gather under the natural geomagnetic field and Figures 2b and 2c indicate this under two artificial magnetic fields. For each environment, the direction of magnetic north (mN) and the inclination are given. The dots indicate where each bird placed itself. The vector arrow drawn from the center of each circle indicates the direction and intensity of the birds' consensus on the direction of migration.

Experiment 2

In this experiment, rather than changing the direction of magnetic north, the birds are exposed to artificial magnetic fields with reversed inclinations by reversing either the polarity or the direction of inclination. As illustrated in Figure 1, magnetic field lines are roughly horizontal near the equator but incline downward toward the north in the northern hemisphere and upward toward the south in the southern hemisphere. Figure 3 illustrates the experimental fields. This studies a spring migration of birds that remain in one hemisphere. Their pattern is to migrate toward the pole of their hemisphere where it will be cooler in summer. The two left-hand diagrams represent magnetic fields as they exist in the northern and southern hemispheres. The two right-hand diagrams represent magnetic field lines that occur only artificially.

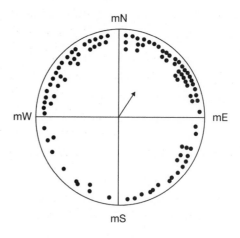

mN = 360°, 66° inclination

Figure 2a

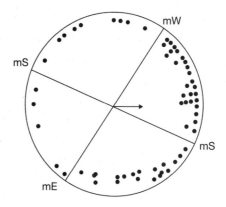

mN = 120°, 42° inclination

Figure 2b

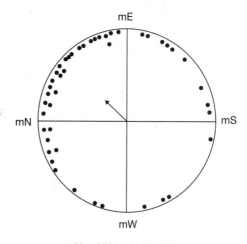

mN = 270°, 37° inclination

Figure 2c

N = geographic north
S = geographic south
p = poleward
e = equatorward
 = direction faced by birds
⟶ = the direction the north pole of a compass will point

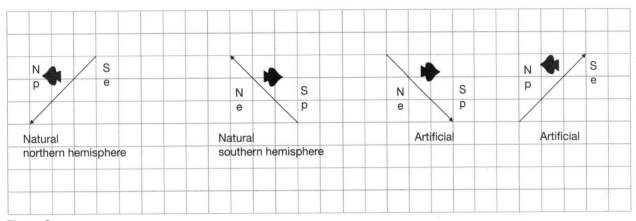

Figure 3

18. Figure 1 illustrates the direction the north pole of a compass will point at various latitudes on the earth. Which answer best describes the importance of Figure 1 in understanding this passage?

f. The compass can point north, south, east, west, or toward the points of the compass in between them.

g. The inclination of the compass changes from pointing straight up at the south magnetic pole to horizontal and northward at the equator, to straight down at the north magnetic pole.

h. The compass points north in the northern hemisphere and south in the southern hemisphere.

j. The geographical and geomagnetic North and South Poles are different.

19. What is the preferred migration direction of the robins shown in Figures 2a, 2b, and 2c and the apparent magnetic directions based on magnetic north?

a. Figure 2a: slightly east of magnetic north; Figure 2b: slightly west of magnetic north; Figure 2c: slightly east of magnetic north

b. Figure 2a: slightly east of magnetic north; Figure 2b: east; Figure 2c: slightly north of west

c. Figure 2a: magnetic north; Figure 2b: magnetic north; Figure 2c: magnetic north

d. Figure 2a: slightly east of magnetic north; Figure 2b: slightly east of magnetic north; Figure 2c: slightly west of magnetic north

20. Based on Figure 3, what magnetic field inclination and direction will induce robins to migrate northward in the springtime?

   f. downward and northward, upward and southward

   g. downward and northward, upward and northward

   h. downward and southward, upward and northward

   j. only downward and northward

21. Look at Figure 3. What is the same about both of the magnetic fields in which the birds tend to migrate northward?

   a. The magnetic field points to the north.

   b. The magnetic field points downward.

   c. The slope of the magnetic field is inclined downward toward the north in all cases where the birds migrate north.

   d. The magnetic field inclines upward.

22. Examine Figure 3 in light of the model of the geomagnetic field presented in Figure 1. Which answer is the best statement of the difference in the polarity of the apparent geomagnetic fields represented in the first and third diagrams?

   f. They are the same.

   g. In the first (leftmost) diagram the apparent magnetic north is in the same direction as geographic north. In the third diagram the apparent magnetic polarity of the North and South Poles has been reversed so that a compass needle will point south, not north. The inclination is down toward the pole in both cases.

   h. The polarity is the same, but in the first diagram the field lines incline upward and in the third they incline downward.

   j. The polarity in the first diagram is reversed from the normal geomagnetic polarity illustrated in the third diagram.

23. Based on the report in this passage, including experiment 1 and experiment 2 and Figures 1, 2, and 3, which answer is the best summary of the implications of these experiments?

   a. Birds have an internal compass, operating on the same principle as the ones that people use, to help them fly in the direction they want to.

   b. Birds seem to be influenced by magnetic fields, but they are as likely to fly in the wrong direction as the right one when guided by magnetism.

   c. Experiment 1 seemed to demonstrate that birds fly according to an internal compass, but experiment 2 disproved that.

   d. Birds are influenced by magnetic fields, but they cannot distinguish north from south polarity. When it is time to migrate toward a pole, they tend to fly toward the direction in which magnetic field lines dip.

Passage V—Data Representation

Osteoporosis is a medical condition that involves the loss of bone mass and density, and, therefore, strength. Victims of osteoporosis are prone to bone fractures and other difficulties. It is an almost universal part of the aging process, but can be more or less severe depending on various factors. The clearest distinction is the difference between osteoporosis in males and females, as illustrated in Figures 1 and 2.

Bone Development and Loss Pattern in Males and Females

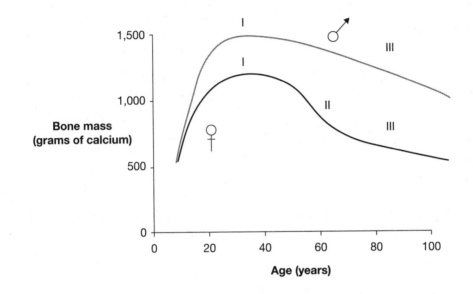

Figure 1

Age-Related Fractures

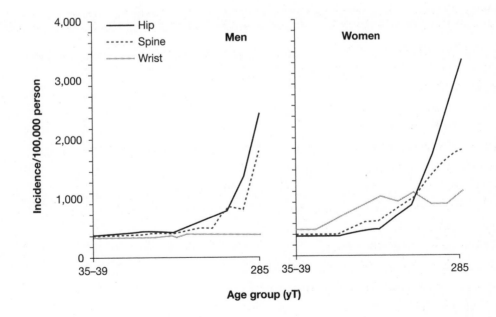

Figure 2

In recent decades it has been discovered that osteoporosis is also a hazard of long-term space flight. Figure 3 shows evidence of bone mass loss in four astronauts who were involved in space flights of different durations. Table 1 provides average monthly loss in bone mass density (BMD) for cosmonauts involved in long-term missions (between 4 and 14 months) on the MIR space station.

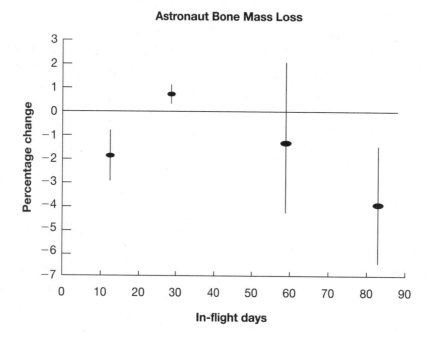

Figure 3

TABLE 1		
BONE AFFECTED	**NUMBER OF SUBJECTS**	**% AVERAGE MONTHLY BMD LOSS**
lumbar spine	18	1.06
femoral neck (hip joint)	18	1.15
trochanter (femur below hip)	18	1.56
pelvis	17	1.35
arm	17	0.04
leg	16	0.34
total body	17	0.35

24. Based on Figure 1, at approximately what age do males and females generally reach their maximum bone mass?

  f. 8 years old for both

  g. 40 for males and 60 for females

  h. 33 for both

  j. end of life

25. Based on Figure 2, what is the best statement of the differences between males and females in bone fracture rates related to advancing age?

  a. They both experience higher spine and hip fracture rates after age 60–65. Females also experience markedly higher wrist fracture rates beginning at about age 50, whereas males do not. The female hip fracture rate rises to about 40% above the male rate.

  b. They experience similar fracture rates, except that the wrist and spinal injury rates are much higher for females.

  c. The pattern of increase is similar, but the rates for females in all categories are significantly higher.

  d. They experience similar fracture rates, except that the hip fractures are much more severe in females.

26. Look at Figure 3. Each point on the chart represents only one astronaut. Which statement is supported by the data?

  f. Space flights of less than 20 days result in bone density loss. Flights of 30 to approximately 50 days result in gains, but flights of 60 days or more result in significant losses.

  g. Bone density loss does not correlate with time spent in space.

  h. Bone density loss is potentially a significant problem for space travelers.

  j. The levels of bone density loss experienced by space travelers are insignificant.

27. Without considering the relative importance of each type of bone, select the most significant line item in Table 1 from the choices given.

  a. total body

  b. trochanter

  c. arm

  d. pelvis

28. What information not included in Table 1 would be most useful in analyzing the problem of bone density loss during space flight?

  f. averages by age of each cosmonaut

  g. averages by sex of each cosmonaut

  h. actual loss per month for each bone type

  j. relative mass of each type of bone in the body

Passage VI—Conflicting Viewpoints

Scientists, including geologists, biologists, and others, generally agree that prior to approximately 3 billion years ago there was virtually no free oxygen in the earth's atmosphere or in the oceans. Early life was limited to prokaryotes (creatures that had no cellular nuclei) that processed sulfur, not oxygen, to gain energy. These early microbes are called bacteria and archaeans. Something happened to change this in the course of the 3 billion years ending about 400 million years ago. Earth now has an atmosphere consisting of 21% free oxygen, and there is enough oxygen dissolved in the seas so that respiration of oxygen to produce energy is viewed as almost synonymous with being alive. The few remaining anaerobic (non-oxygen-breathing) bacteria and archaeans reside in deep, dark underground and underwater habitats.

Two scientists present their understanding of how this occurred.

Scientist 1

About 2.5 billion years ago most existing species were killed by exposure to a dangerous gas, oxygen. The oxygen was produced by a family of bacteria, cyanobacteria, that used chlorophyll to free oxygen from water through the process of photosynthesis. Cyanobacteria had existed for about 1 billion years before this Great Oxygen Catastrophe, but the oxygen they produced was absorbed by carbon, iron, and other substances. The catastrophe occurred when the production of free oxygen exceeded the ability of the earth to absorb it. Anaerobic species largely died off, and oxygen-using (aerobic) species proliferated. This led to the development of eukaryotes (complex celled creatures) and large and complex species.

Geological evidence, including patterns of iron ore formation, demonstrates that the Great Oxygen Catastrophe increased levels of atmospheric oxygen from virtually zero to about 15%. Through a combination of gradual and not so gradual increases, this level reached about 20% approximately 400 million years ago. Cyanobacteria are still a major type of bacteria. They form huge colonies in the ocean that have been misidentified as blue-green algae, and they live inside green plant cells, where they are called chloroplasts.

Scientist 2

There was no so-called Great Oxygen Catastrophe. The cyanobacteria slowly introduced oxygen into the oceans for about 1 billion years before oxygen levels reached the vicinity of 1%. At that point, approximately 2.5 billion years ago, eukaryotes and the first multicellular creatures began to develop. The iron deposits and other evidence my colleague points to can be explained by factors other than a huge leap in free oxygen.

For about 2 billion years after the so-called Great Oxygen Catastrophe, no creatures appeared in the sea that required more than 1% to 1.5% oxygen to survive. About 550 million years ago fish several centimeters in length and other species appeared that would have required oxygen concentrations of several

percent. Then, approximately 400 million years ago, an expansion in new species types indicates a larger increase in oxygenation approaching our modern 21%. Fish species increased from several centimeters to a meter or more in length. On land, plants with complex water transport systems arose.

29. Which answer does NOT reflect Scientist 1's viewpoint?
   a. Cyanobacteria introduced the first significant levels of free oxygen to the sea and the air.
   b. About 2.5 billion years ago, atmospheric oxygen levels rose from minimal trace levels to about 15%.
   c. Oxygen eliminated the anaerobic prokaryotes and replaced them with eukaryotes.
   d. After the Great Oxygen Catastrophe, oxygen levels continued to rise to modern levels.

30. Which statement best summarizes Scientist 2's differences with Scientist 1?
   f. The iron sediment record does not accurately reflect free oxygen levels.
   g. Until about 550 million years ago, increase in oxygen levels was gradual and remained under 1.5% concentration. Two events, one 550 million years ago and another 400 million years ago, not a catastrophe 2.5 billion years ago, brought free oxygen up to modern levels.
   h. Biological, not geological, data are the only reliable record of free oxygen concentrations.
   j. Cyanobacteria played no significant role in the development of free oxygen. The increasing size of fish species and the complexity of plant species on land caused the two major oxygenation events.

31. Which statement is a point on which Scientist 1 and 2 agree?
  a. Anaerobic prokaryotes began losing their dominant role in biology approximately 2.5 billion years ago.
  b. Oxygen levels reached at least 10% 2.5 billion years ago and have subsequently increased to 21%.
  c. Oxygen levels remained under 5% until 400 million years ago.
  d. Cyanobacteria have now been replaced by photosynthetic plants.

32. Which of the following statements directly contradicts Scientist 2's hypothesis?
  f. Free oxygen was largely produced by photosynthesis, beginning with the cyanobacteria.
  g. More complex biological forms require higher levels of oxygenation.
  h. Free oxygen levels in the atmosphere might have been as high as 10% prior to 550 million years ago.
  j. none of the above

33. Which of the following statements directly contradicts Scientist 1's stated views?
  a. Archaean species became extinct in the Great Oxygen Catastrophe.
  b. Cyanobacteria have been replaced by more complex photosynthetic structures.
  c. There were major oxygenation events 550 million years ago and 400 million years ago.
  d. none of the above

34. With which statement have both Scientist 1 and Scientist 2 stated or implied their disagreement?
  f. Oxygen is a dangerous gas.
  g. Oxygen is absolutely essential to modern life.
  h. Increased oxygen levels play no role in biological evolution.
  j. Complex life may be possible without oxygen.

35. Geologists have established the following eras in the earth's history:
  Precambrian (single-cell, multicellular life): 5,000+ to 542 million years ago
  Paleozoic ("old animals"—invertebrates): 542 to 291 million years ago
  Mesozoic ("middle animals"—dinosaurs): 291 to 186 million years ago
  Cenozoic ("new animals"—mammals): 186 million years ago to the present
      How does this account of geological eras relate to the ideas of the scientific community in general, and those of Scientist 1 and Scientist 2?
  a. Scientist 2's hypothesized final significant oxygenation event occurred at the beginning of the Paleozoic era.
  b. Scientist 1's Great Oxygen Catastrophe occurred in the midst of the long Precambrian era.
  c. The increasing complexity of species correlates with the increasing free oxygen levels.
  d. All of these statements are appropriate to the scientific views reported.

Passage VII—Data Representation

The specific heat of a substance is a measure of how much heat energy is required to raise a given mass of the substance by a given temperature. Here we will measure specific heat in joules/gram/°Celsius. The heat of fusion is the quantity of heat energy required to melt a given mass of a substance when it is at its melting temperature. We will measure the heat of fusion in joules/gram. A substance at its melting temperature maintains that temperature as heat is added to it until it is completely melted.

Figure 1 shows the relationship between the joules added to 1 gram of a hypothetical solid substance as its temperature is raised, as it melts, and as the temperature of the melted liquid is raised. The first slope of rising temperature represents the solid being heated; the horizontal section of constant tem-perature represents the solid being melted; and the second slope of rising temperature represents the liq-uid being heated.

The primary formulas involved are as follows:

$$J_H = \Delta T \times SH \times m$$
$$J_M = HF \times m$$

J_H is the energy in joules required to raise m grams of a substance with specific heat SH by $\Delta T°C$. J_M is the energy in joules required to melt a substance with heat of fusion HF.

Table 1 shows the heat of fusion, the melting point (MP), and the specific heat in joules/g/°Celsius for the solid and liquid forms of four hypothetical substances. Figure 2 is a chart showing the heat energy used to heat one of those solid substances to its melting point, melt it, and heat the melted liquid.

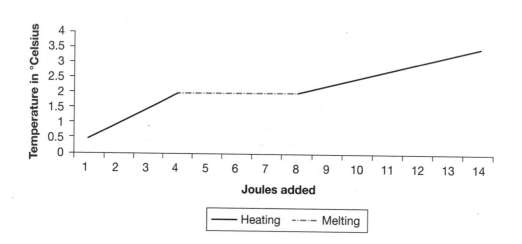

Figure 1

TABLE 1				
SUBSTANCE	*SH* SOLID	*SH* LIQUID	*HF*	MP(°C)
A	3.00	2.00	5.00	1,000
B	5.00	4.00	6.00	1,200
C	2.00	3.00	8.00	1,400
D	1.00	2.00	40.00	−20

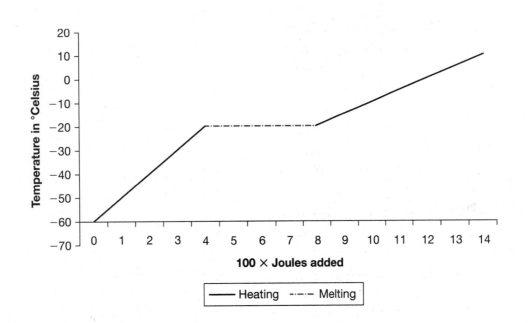

Figure 2

36. Based on the values in Table 1, how many joules of heat energy will it take to bring 1 gram of substance A from 500°C to its melting point?
  f. 1,500
  g. 500
  h. 5,000
  j. 1,000

37. Figure 2 represents one of the solid substances described in Table 1 being heated to its melting point, melted, and heated in liquid form. Which substance is it?
  a. A
  b. B
  c. C
  d. D

38. How many grams of the substance illustrated by Figure 2 are being heated?
  f. 100
  g. 1
  h. 10
  j. 1,000

39. How many joules of heat energy are required to melt 10 grams of substance B at 1,000°C?
  a. 1,060
  b. 10,060
  c. 1,600
  d. 1,160

40. What is the ratio between the heat energy required to melt 1 gram of substance C and 1 gram of substance D?
  f. 1:5
  g. 5:1
  h. 2:1
  j. 3:2

ACT Writing Practice Test 3

You have 30 minutes to complete this essay. Remember to:

- Address the specific topic and writing task.
- Create a well-organized response.
- Include developed supporting ideas and specific details.
- Use sentence variety and strong word choices.

Parents and school board members have become increasingly concerned about the use of the Internet in school. Many people report that students have either purposely visited or inadvertently been exposed to Web sites that display text and images that are inappropriate for teenagers. These people want to set up a school intranet that would allow access to only a few pre–approved Web sites. Opponents of this idea state that this is censorship and does not give students enough access to valuable information on the Internet. In your opinion, should the school create an intranet that would limit the Web sites students could visit, or do you think this is censorship that would deny students access to valuable information?

In your essay, take a position on this question. You may write about either of the two points of view given, or you may present a different point of view on the topic. Use specific reasons and examples to support your position.

Answers

ACT English Practice Test 3
Passage I—The Weekly Visit

1. c. *Typical* (choice **d**) cannot modify the verb *happened*, and choices **a**, **b**, and **d** are redundant.

2. j. Both adjectives modify the same noun— *farmhouse*—and therefore should be separated by a comma.

3. b. The conditional tense, not the present tense, is appropriate here.

4. j. Two things—in this case, *impatience* and *crippling age*—are connected simply by using *and*.

5. b. This choice has the desired meaning—circles that have the same center.

6. h. No commas are necessary, and the two colors should be connected by *and* since the metal table is a combination of white and red.

7. d. The simple past *lifted* is not appropriate here, nor is the progressive *-ing* form.

8. f. The punctuation is correct as it is.

9. d. The exclamation is properly capitalized, but the punctuation needs to be inside the quotation mark.

10. h. The *awareness* did not have a physical presence, so *laying under* is incorrect.

11. b. This provides the proper placement for the modifying phrase *during the dutiful visit*, as well as the proper comma usage.

12. g. The descriptive information makes the sentence more powerful.

13. a. Separating the conditional with commas creates an awkward structure.

14. h. This is the proper possessive form for the singular *Grandma*.

15. d. This is the most logical order.

Passage II—My Childhood

16. j. This is the proper punctuation and word choice.

17. d. This properly puts the sentence into the future.

18. h. Using the adverb creates the clearest phrasing.

19. a. No change is necessary.

20. j. This creates a parallel structure to the other verbs used in progressive form.

21. b. This properly connects two independent clauses.

22. g. This is the proper use of a semicolon between two independent clauses.

23. a. The sentence is fine as it is.

24. j. There is no need for anything additional.

25. c. The plural *siblings* end up as *babysitters*, also plural.

26. h. This is the proper parallel structure.

27. d. The simple past is the proper tense here.

28. g. The conjunction *and* properly connects the two clauses.

29. b. Sentence 6 introduces a new topic—money.

30. h. While the writer's childhood is referenced, it is in the context of thoughts on family size.

Passage III—The Internet Revolution

31. c. None of the other choices provides proper structure and grammar.

32. h. This properly connects the independent and dependent clauses.

33. d. The adjective form properly modifies the plural noun *games*.

34. j. *There's* contracts *there is*, and *limit* agrees with the singular *is*.

35. c. This is the proper placement for the necessary comma.

36. h. This eliminates the redundant part of the sentence.

37. b. There is no need for a conjunction here.

38. h. This is the proper choice of preposition.

39. d. This is the proper phrasing.

40. j. Both the *individuals* and the *opportunities* are plural.

41. c. The same object pronoun cannot be used to identify both groups. The two different groups must be distinguished—*others* are the people being bilked, and *them* refers to the scammers.

42. h. There are no specific profits previously mentioned that the definite article *the* can refer to. Instead, the possessive should be used to identify the profits.

43. c. The correct interpretation of the sentence is that the individual subscriber has an individual screen, thus the possessive *subscriber's screen*.

44. h. The verb *are* must agree with the *uses*, not the *Internet*.

45. d. Sentence 7 changes topic and begins to discuss the many uses of the Internet. This parallels the introduction and would be suitable for the beginning of a conclusion.

Passage IV—The Letter

46. h. This puts both verbs in the proper, present tense.

47. b. The scholarship, not the name, is in perpetuity.

48. f. This should be left as it is; the single fund has many sponsors.

49. c. The present progressive is the most appropriate tense here.

50. g. This correctly interprets the sentence as connecting the past with the present.

51. d. This best conveys the meaning of *particularly hesitant*, or *more hesitant than ordinary*.

52. h. This creates a proper modifying phrase properly set apart with commas.

53. b. This agrees with the singular *anyone* and the earlier *feels*.

54. h. Commas are required to separate the day from the date, the city from the state, and the date from the location.

55. a. The phrasing is correct as it is.

56. f. The structure is correct as it is.

57. d. This is an appropriate combination of an adverb and a verb.

58. g. The donation would be appreciated, not appreciative, so it must likewise be *deeply appreciated*. There is no need to repeat *would be*.

59. c. The sentence calls for the conditional tense.

60. h. The correct word is *accept* (to take in or receive), and not *except* (excluding, other than).

Passage V—The Salmon Run

61. d. The correct word is *tales*, and the sentence calls for a plural, but not possessive, *animals*.

62. h. The present tense, not the conditional or past tense, is appropriate here.

63. d. This properly retains the infinitive *to be* and properly uses the comma and coordinating conjunction.

64. h. The correct word for fish eggs is *roe*.

65. b. Although *eggs* is plural, the *trip* is singular, and it *remains* remarkable.

66. j. The verb must agree with the singular *life cycle*, not the plural *salmon*.

67. b. The proper usage is *between* this *and* that. From this *to* that is also correct, but is not a choice.

68. h. The use of *many* with *numerous* is redundant.

69. d. The semicolon is appropriate punctuation between the two independent clauses. Neither conjunction is suitable for the meaning of the sentence.

70. h. The preposition *given* is appropriate here to link with its object, the noun *classification*.

71. a. The sentence is correct as it is.

72. h. The salmon was food and nourishment, or *sustenance*, for the Indians.

73. a. The sentence is correct as it is.

74. g. The infinitive form *to leave* is appropriate in this instance.

75. b. The use of the term *in decline* is appropriate, as is the present perfect *has been* to describe an ongoing phenomenon that started in the past.

ACT Mathematics Practice Test 3

1. a. Multiply 60 by the decimal equivalent of 95% (0.95). This is $60 \times 0.95 = 57$.

2. g. The two integers that add up to 26 with the smallest product are 1 and 25.

3. a. Distribute the 4, and then isolate the variable.

4. h. Change the equation into $y = mx + b$ format, and $b = 3$.

5. b. To find the area of a parallelogram, multiply the base times the height. So, in this case, divide the area by the height to find the base.

6. k. First, $1 - \frac{1}{2} = \frac{1}{2}$. Then $\frac{2}{3}$ of $\frac{1}{2}$ is $\frac{2}{6}$. $\frac{2}{6}$ added to $\frac{1}{2}$ is $\frac{5}{6}$, so $\frac{5}{6}$ of the collection is gone, and $\frac{1}{6}$ remains.

7. d. Break up 40 into factors of 4 and 10, and then remove the square root of 4.

8. j. $-(3x + 5)^2 = -(3x + 5)(3x + 5) = -(9x^2 + 15x + 15x + 25) = -(9x^2 + 30x + 25) = -9x^2 - 30x - 25$.

9. b. The sum of the angles in a triangle is 180°, so $180 = 111 + 2x + x$. Solving for x, $x = 23$ and $2x = 46$.

10. g. Substitute the given values into the equation and solve for h.

11. c. Solve the first equation for m, then substitute the value of m in $14m$.

12. k. Isolate the absolute value sign in $|x + 7| - 8 = 14$, so $|x + 7| = 22$. Since $|22|$ and $|-22|$ both equal 22, $x + 7$ can be 22 or -22, and $x = 15$ or $x = -29$. Thus, the solution set is $\{-29, 15\}$.

13. d. Find the equation of the line containing $(2, -3)$ and $(6, 1)$. First, find the slope, which is $\frac{-3-1}{2-6}$, or $\frac{-4}{-4}$, or 1. Use trial and error to see which answer, when combined with either given point, creates a slope of 1. The correct point is $(7, 2)$.

14. j. Triangle MNP is a 5–12–13 right triangle. The height of the triangle is therefore 12, and the base is 5, so the area, found by $\frac{1}{2}bh$, is 30.

15. b. The $f[g(x)] = f(-2x - 1)$, so replace every x in $f(x)$ with $(-2x - 1)$. $f[g(x)] = 3(-2x - 1) + 2$, or $f[g(x)] = -6x - 3 + 2$, and finally $f[g(x)] = -6x - 1$.

16. h. The expression $\log_4 64$ means $4^? = 64$; $4^3 = 64$. Therefore, $\log_4 64 = 3$.

17. d. $(x - 5)$ must equal $(x + 2)$ or $-(x + 2)$. The two former terms cannot be equal, and $x = 1.5$ satisfies the second possibility.

18. h. Using the formula for circumference $= 2\pi r$, where r is the radius, find that the radius $= 8$. Now use the formula for area $= \pi r^2$, or $a = 64\pi$, which is approximately 200.

19. a. The slope of the given line is -2.5. Since parallel lines have the same slope, the slope is also -2.5, or $-\frac{5}{2}$.

20. h. Because the triangle is a 30–60–90 right triangle, the hypotenuse is twice the shorter leg, and the longer leg is therefore $x\sqrt{3}$. The perimeter is $3x + x\sqrt{3}$, and when set equal to $30 + 10\sqrt{3}$, x must be 10.

21. e. The total cost is represented by (cost per week)(# of weeks) + (cost per magazine)(# of magazines).

22. g. The length of one edge of cube Y is $\frac{1}{5}$ of 15, or 3. The volume of a cube is s^3, where $s =$ length of one edge, so the volume is 27 cubic inches.

23. e. The figure created by all points 10 units from any *single* given point on the y-axis is a circle; thus the figure created using all the points on the y-axis would be a cylinder.

24. k. While the % *increase* is found by change in price ÷ original price, % of original is found by new price ÷ original price.

25. b. Set up a proportion where $\frac{1.2}{200} = \frac{1.4}{x}$. Then, $1.2x = 280$, and $x = {\sim}233$.

26. h. To solve, divide 0.009 by 100, which is done by moving the decimal two places to the left.

27. c. Change the fractions to decimals, and the expression becomes $\frac{0.5}{0.45}$, which is $1\frac{1}{9}$.

28. f. Since the shortened sides of the rectangle are 9 and 12, the two legs of the right triangle must be 4 and 3. Thus the hypotenuse of that triangle is 5, and when added to the other sides of the polygon, the perimeter is 54.

29. b. First, $\overline{WZ} - \overline{WY} = \overline{YZ}$, so $\overline{YZ} = 17$. Then, $\overline{XZ} - \overline{YZ} = \overline{XY}$, so $\overline{XY} = 6$.

30. k. Cubic feet indicates volume, which is found by multiplying length × width × height. Divide 7,000 by (36 × 48), and the answer is just above 4.

31. b. The answer must be 1 less than a multiple of 7, and 1 less than a multiple of 6.

32. g. This is a straightforward proportion problem, where $\frac{15}{10} = \frac{12}{x}$, when x is the shortest side of the second triangle. Cross multiply and then divide both sides by 15 to solve for x.

33. e. The correct equation for a circle is $(x-h)^2 + (y-k)^2 = r^2$, where (h,k) represents the center of the circle and r is the radius.

34. g. The sine of an angle is the ratio of the opposite side to the hypotenuse, or in this case YZ to 16. Set $\frac{3}{5}$ equal to $\frac{YZ}{16}$, and solve.

35. b. Create a right triangle using the two given points and a third point of (5,0). The legs of the triangle have lengths of 4 and 5. Use the Pythagorean theorem to solve for the hypotenuse, which is the distance in question.

36. f. y^2 is a common factor of the two terms, so if y were any given value greater than 3, the square of that value would become the greatest common factor of the two terms.

37. d. Since the distance, 17.5, is 5 times as much as 3.5, the time will likewise be 5 times greater.

38. g. Any line parallel to the x-axis is also a horizontal line, and all horizontal lines have a slope of 0.

39. d. Three factors assure that the result will be even: raising the value to an even integer, multiplying the resulting value by an even integer, and adding an even integer to that total.

40. f. Plug in values to start, such as 20 and 5, for the length and width. The perimeter of this rectangle would be 50. If the lengths are tripled, to 60 and 15, the perimeter would be likewise tripled, to 150.

41. e. Trial and error, which should logically start with the largest answer, reveals that 144 and 160 are multiples of 16, so no multiple of 16 is found between 145 and 159.

42. k. Since the bases of a trapezoid are parallel, angle DCA is an alternate interior angle to angle BAC, and therefore also has a measure of 35°. Angle DCE is a straight angle, and therefore measures 180°; thus angle ACB must measure 35° $(180° - 110° - 35°)$.

43. c. The average of any odd number of consecutive integers is also the median, so the sum of the least and greatest will be the same as the double of the average.

44. j. The sum of the interior angles in any polygon is $180(n-2)$, where n is the number of sides. $180(5-2) = 540$, and then subtract 52.

45. b. Changing this expression to an exponential one would yield $4^? = 256$.

46. f. Add 9 and subtract x from both sides, and you get $2 < 0$, a statement that cannot be true, no matter the value of x.

47. e. To compare the values, use the common denominator of 12 and you get $\frac{8}{12}$ and $\frac{9}{12}$. Halfway in between would be $\frac{8.5}{12}$, which becomes $\frac{17}{24}$.

48. f. Ezra has overstated his income by $22.50 *and* understated his expenses by $22.50, thus creating an error of $45.00 extra in his balance.

49. c. First, subtract $9xb$ from both sides, creating the equation $x^2 - 9xb - 36b^2 = 0$. Factoring the left side, you get $(x - 12b)(x + 3b) = 0$. Then set each factor equal to zero and solve for x.

50. g. First, change $\tan x$ to $\frac{\sin x}{\cos x}$, and then solve.

51. d. There are nine integers with the digit zero—multiples of 10 between 10 and 90, inclusive—and there are 90 integers in all.

52. k. Use the Pythagorean theorem to solve for the diagonal of the triangle, which is also the diameter of the circle. Divide that value in half to solve for the radius, then use πr^2 to solve for the area of the circle.

53. e. Use two different laws of logarithms. First, change the equation to $2\log_a(xy)$; then change the expression to $2(\log_a x + \log_a y)$. Finally, substitute the given values into the equation.

54. g. The six integers with an average of 35 would total 210. The seven integers with an average of 41 would total 287. The difference is the seventh integer.

55. a. Plug the value $(x + y)$ in for x in the original function, square that expression, and add 3.

56. g. The total capacity of the boats would be yf, or the number of boats, y, times the capacity of each, f. Five less than that would equal the number of fishermen who were on the boats, x.

57. e. The maximum value for the sine function is 1, which occurs at 90°, or $\frac{\pi}{2}$, and then every 360° thereafter. So the minimum positive value for $2x$ is $\frac{\pi}{2}$, and the minimum positive value for x is $\frac{\pi}{4}$.

58. j. Since the radius is 15, the area of the circle is $(15)^2\pi$, or 225π. The central angle is 120°, or one-third of the circle, so the sector area is the equivalent portion of the circle, or one-third of 225π, which is 75π.

59. d. The number of dimes has no bearing on the question; the answer simply needs to be a multiple of both 7 and 8.

60. h. First add the parts of the ratio, 4 and 3, to determine that the chips are in groups of 7. Then divide 7 into 91 to find that there are 13 groups, so there must be 52 red and 39 blue chips. Adding 13 red chips creates the desired ratio.

ACT Reading Practice Test 3
Passage I—Humanities

1. c. The Lewis and Clark expedition did not have a military goal and did not have any violent encounters except the one referenced that occurred in July 1806.

2. g. Jefferson and his representatives wanted Native Americans to acknowledge American sovereignty and to see themselves as children to the Americans' role as *their fathers and friends* (line 23).

3. c. One meaning of *protocol* is a code that demands strict adherence to etiquette, which is how the word is used on this occasion.

4. j. The passage states that *Lewis and Clark sought to impose their own notions of hierarchy on Native Americans by "making chiefs" with medals, printed certificates, and gifts* (lines 44–47).

5. c. Placing a peace medal around the neck of a man killed by the expedition makes an ironic statement about the meaning of *peace*.

6. g. To the Plains Native Americans, the pipe ceremony meant that those who participated *accepted sacred obligations to share wealth, aid in war, and revenge injustice* (lines 74–76). The passage suggests that Lewis and Clark most likely did not understand the significance of the ceremony.

7. d. One meaning of *adopt* is to take by choice into a relationship. In this context, *adopt* has another meaning: to take up and practice or use.

8. j. By giving manufactured goods to Native Americans, Lewis and Clark were promoting Euro-American culture. Jefferson hoped that these *free samples* would *introduce the Native Americans to mechanized agriculture as part of his plan to "civilize and instruct" them* (lines 90–92).

9. a. The passage compares different abstract principles, or organizing principles of Euro-American society versus those of tribal societies. For example, it explores the principles of hierarchy and kinship.

10. g. Answer choice **f** is too general to be the primary purpose of the passage, whereas answer choice **h** is too specific. Answer choice **j** is not supported by the passage.

Passage II—Prose Fiction

11. d. In the first few lines, the narrator states that Miss Temple was the *superintendent of the seminary* and that the narrator received both *instruction* and *friendship* from Miss Temple, who was also like a mother to her—*she had stood me in the stead of mother.*

12. g. Combined with the earlier use of *usually*, the word *appeared* conveys a temporary state—in this case, of being disciplined and subdued. When Miss Temple departs, the narrator is left in her *natural element*, and she feels the *stirring of old emotions*, thus affirming the earlier implication.

13. a. The narrator states that with Miss Temple, *I had given in allegiance to duty and order; I was quiet; I believed I was content* (lines 18–20).

14. h. The context here suggests existence or habitation, not captivity or illness.

15. c. We can assume that the narrator would go home during vacations, but she spent all of her vacations at school because *Mrs. Reed had never sent for me to Gateshead* (lines 74–75). Thus we can infer that Mrs. Reed was her guardian, the one who sent the narrator to Lowood in the first place.

16. g. The narrator describes her experience with *school-rules* and *school-duties* (line 78) and how she *tired of the routine* (line 83) after Miss Temple left, and describes a view from her window that seemed a *prison ground, exile limits* (lines 64–65). Thus it can be inferred that Lowood is both a structured and an isolated place.

17. a. The narrator states in lines 51–54 that she *remembered that the real world was wide, and . . . awaited those who had courage to go forth.* She also looks at the road from Lowood and states, *how I longed to follow it further!* (lines 67–68)

18. j. In lines 82–90, the narrator's desire for freedom and to explore the world are evident. She longs to follow the road that leads away from Lowood and she is *half desperate* in her cry for something new, something beyond Lowood and the rules and systems she *tired of . . . in one* afternoon.

19. d. Lowood had been the narrator's home for eight years. She realizes her initial prayers were unrealistic; a *new servitude* would provide some familiar territory, and it therefore seems more attainable than *liberty or change.*

20. g. The narrator first *uttered a prayer*, then *framed a humbler supplication* (also meaning prayer), and then refers to that supplication as a *petition*, again meaning prayer.

Passage III—Social Sciences

21. c. Answer choice **d** is true, but too specific to be the author's primary purpose. Answer choices **a** and **b** are too positive.

22. f. The author contrasts the public's dismissal of the arcane practice of wearing garlic with its increasing acceptance of herbal remedies.

23. b. In this context, *conventional* refers to the established system of Western medicine or biomedicine.

24. j. Answer choice **f** is overly general and answer choice **g** is too negative to be inferred from the survey's findings. Answer choice **h** is incorrect—the author does not mention the baby boom age group, but that does not mean that the survey did not include it.

25. a. The statistic illustrates the popularity of alternative therapies without giving any specific information as to why.

26. j. The author states that Americans are not replacing conventional healthcare but are adding to or supplementing it with alternative care.

27. d. The shortcomings of conventional healthcare mentioned in lines 46–53 are the *time constraints of managed care*, *focus on technology*, and inability to *relieve symptoms associated with chronic disease*.

28. f. The author states that once *scientific investigation has confirmed their safety and efficacy* (lines 55–57), alternative therapies may be accepted by the medical establishment.

29. b. The author gives evidence of observational studies to show that garlic may be beneficial. Answer choice **d** is incorrect, however, because the author emphasizes that *these findings have not been confirmed in clinical studies* (lines 77–78).

30. h. The passage does not offer a criticism or an argument about alternative healthcare, but rather reports on the phenomenon with some playfulness.

Passage IV—Natural Sciences

31. b. *Discrete* means distinct, and as used in the passage, it is paired with *specialized*, a context clue. The other choices are all synonyms for the homophone *discreet*.

32. j. Answer choices **f** and **h**, while mentioned, are too specific to be viable titles. Answer choice **j** is broad-ranging enough to encompass the entire passage.

33. c. *Scrimshawed* means carved, as in line 17 and line 77. Because scrimshaw and enamel are waxlike substances, a less careful reader may select answer choice **b**.

34. j. According to lines 29–31 of the passage, answer choices **f**, **g**, and **h** are all parts of the physical structure of teeth. Answer choice **j**, tusk, is not a component of teeth, but rather a type of tooth found in some mammals.

35. d. From the context in lines 18–19, it can be deduced that *mastication* means the act of chewing because tusks, evolved from teeth, are described as able to go *beyond chewing*.

36. g. Lines 44–47 clearly state that dentinal tubules *are micro-canals that radiate outward through the dentine from the pulp cavity to the exterior cementum border*.

37. c. In the passage, the substances in answer choices **a**, **b**, and **d** are all described as organic substances.

38. g. Answer choices **h** and **j** are too large to be made from ivory, and answer choice **f** is discussed separately.

39. a. Lines 82–86 identify how natural ivory can be authenticated using ultraviolet light.

40. h. The statement of answer choice **h** is untrue because lines 82–86 state that ivory is commonly tested via ultraviolet light, which would indicate exposure.

ACT Science Practice Test 3
Passage I—Research Summary

1. b. All of these columns have the same value regardless of the type of snow. F_S is a feature of the tow rope mechanism and is always the same. The experiment was designed to test the same mass in each case. According to the formulas given, $F_G = \text{mass}(-10.0 \text{ m/s}^2)$ and $F_I = F_G[\sin(\theta)]$.

2. f. The description of experiment 1 explains that F_T is recorded by the towing device. F_F can be calculated based on formula 6. $F_{NET} = 0$ because the velocity is constant. Then, $F_F = -(F_T + F_I + F_S)$. The coefficient of friction (μ) is calculated from formula 4 by rearranging it and substituting $F_G[\cos(\theta)]$ (formula 2) for F_P. All of the other values are either predetermined by the experiment's design or derived from the predetermined values.

3. a. The only force not determined by the system design specifications is F_F. According to formula 2, the largest value of μ produces the largest F_F. If the system can handle the largest force necessary, it can handle the smaller ones. Do not be confused by the question calling this the minimum force required. The least this system is designed to do is to adequately handle the highest force requirements of the design specification.

4. h. The explanation for formula 3 says that F_G is given in newtons. All of the forces are derived from F_G and F_S. F_S is also given in newtons.

5. b. As formulas 1, 2, 3, 4, and 6 illustrate, all of the forces involved, except for F_S, are directly proportional to the mass of the skiers. The mass in experiment 2 is exactly 10 times the mass in experiment 1, so $F_I + F_F$ can be calculated by multiplying the Table 1 values for powder by 10. F_S is always 5,000 N, regardless of the mass of the skiers. Answer choice **a** will give the correct result, but it is not the easiest way to do that because it involves recalculating values already calculated for Table 1. Answer choices **c** and **d** mistakenly multiply F_T by 10, even though its F_S component does not increase with the mass of the skiers. Answer choice **d** makes the additional mistake of averaging the three Table 1 results instead of taking the one involving the largest F_T. The concern of this experiment is not to find the average force but the greatest force required.

6. j. $F = ma$. The mass is 4,200 kg, and the acceleration required is 0.5 m/s. The result is 2,400 kgm/s. That is the same as 2,400 N. Answer choice **f** does not multiply the mass by the acceleration. Answer choices **h** and **g** multiply by $\sin(\theta)$ and $\cos(\theta)$. $\sin(\theta)$ and $\cos(\theta)$ are used to divide a force or other vector into two perpendicular components. In this case, the force applied is in the same direction as the acceleration required, so it is not divided into components.

Passage II—Data Representation

7. b. Even though each curve has a constant wavelength and wave height, the difference between the wavelengths of the two means that the solar tide at first adds to the lunar tide but then subtracts from it. By counting the peaks on the curves in Figure 2a and 2c or examining the distance between the peaks in relation to the vertical grid lines that mark each day, it is clear that the lunar wavelength is longer, not shorter, than the solar wavelength.

8. f. The shapes of the curves in Figures 3d and 3e are almost identical to the curve in Figure 3a that shows the tsunami influence alone. The level of the tides changes the magnitude of the cumulative result, but the tsunami magnitude is closer to the result than either of the tidal influences or both tidal influences combined.

9. c. The tsunami illustrated in Figure 3d reaches a height above mean sea level of more than 14 meters. The one in Figure 3e only rises to about 8 meters. The reason is that the cumulative tidal influence, illustrated in Figure 2c, is approaching the bottom of a trough at the beginning of day 11, but is peaking at day 1, hour 4. It is important to examine each answer for all claims made. The three wrong answers all accurately report a difference between the curves in Figure 3d and 3e, but the explanations they give are incorrect. Answer choice **b** says day 11 is the lowest trough, although it is actually the shallowest trough shown. Answer choices **a** and **d** make the astute observation that the tsunami in Figure 3d occurs mostly above mean sea level and the one in 3e below. Answer choice **a** states that both the lunar and the solar cycles are approaching a trough, but the solar cycle is actually rising to a peak. Answer choice **d** states that the two tidal cycles are moving in opposite directions. That is true, but it is not the reason for the stated difference. If one were just leaving a peak and the other approaching one, they would be moving in opposite directions, but the cumulative height would be above mean sea level.

10. g. The lowest peak occurs when the lunar influence is at its peak of approximately 2.75 meters and the solar at the bottom of a trough at approximately −1.25 meters. The result is approximately 1.5 meters.

11. c. Answer choice **a** is almost correct, but the wave patterns are not steadily in or out; there are changes in speed and direction between the troughs and peaks. Answer choice **b** is the popular view of what a tsunami looks like, but the graph shows changes in sea level, not breaking waves. In fact, tsunamis generally involve smooth waves that come ashore, flooding anything in their way, without breaking. Answer choice **d** is not correct. A level 10 meters above normal sea level makes a huge difference on shore. Three-story buildings at sea level will be totally submerged. A normal, gently rising shore could be flooded hundreds of meters from the normal high-water mark.

Passage III—Research Summary

12. g. Experiment 1 uses the same light intensity for each trial and measures the difference due to different chloroplast concentrations. Experiment 2 keeps the chloroplast concentration constant and tests the differences due to different light intensities. Answer choice **f** is not correct. In each case, the relationship between the characteristics of the test mixture and the production of oxygen is being measured. Answer choice **j** is true, but it describes the Hill reaction, not an aspect of it being tested by these experiments.

13. a. Carbon dioxide is one of the most important compounds involved in photosynthesis, and glucose, which contains carbon, is one of its most important products. Answer choices **c** and **d** are not correct, because hydrogen and oxygen occur as inputs and products in both reactions. Answer choice **b** is not correct for two reasons: A is part of the Hill reaction, which is a stage in the process of photosynthesis, so it is present in photosynthesis; less importantly, it is not an element. Neither ADP, the A normally involved in photosynthesis, nor DCPIP, the A used in these experiments, is an element.

14. j. This and many other experiments have demonstrated that light and chloroplasts are necessary conditions for photosynthesis, but the role they play is to aid the reactions, rather than become incorporated as part of the results.

15. c. Trial 1-C involves no chloroplasts, and 2-A involves no light. In each case, there is virtually no change in the color of the DCPIP. The passage warns that these results lack precision, so no significance should be attached to small differences. As explained in the passage, it was necessary to allow some light in during trial 2-A to get the colorimeter reading. It is after that that the DCPIP fades slightly. Answer choice **d** is not correct because the release of oxygen from water is very important.

16. f. The difference between high and low chloroplast concentration (trials 1-A and 1-B) and high and low light (trials 2-B and 2-C) is very similar. The DCPIP fades more rapidly in the trials with more light or more chloroplasts but levels off at a color intensity very close to that achieved by the trials with less light or lower chloroplast concentration. Answer choice **g** is not correct. The passage warns that DCPIP does not give precise results. The difference between the results in trials 1-A and 2-C does not warrant making any distinction between the impact of chloroplasts and light, and answer choice **j** does. There is no means presented in the passage to compare concentrations of chloroplasts to intensities of light in any case.

17. c. The passage says that DCPIP is blue in its normal oxidized form but loses its color when it loses its oxygen. Answer choice **d** is tricky because it is true that DCPIP gives up its oxygen to combine with hydrogen, but it is the loss of oxygen, regardless of the surrounding events, that is identified as the cause of DCPIP's loss of color.

Passage IV—Research Summary

18. g. Understanding experiments 1 and 2 depends on understanding the relationship between compass direction and inclination, and that is what Figure 1 illustrates. Answer choice **h** is not true. The north pole of a compass will always point toward the North Magnetic Pole, which is a magnetic south pole. Answer choice **f** is a popular view of how a compass is used, but it is not accurate. The compass needle always points northward. Answer choice **j** is a true statement but of little importance in these experiments. It is important always to answer the question asked. The best answer is usually true, but not every true statement is a good answer.

19. a. Figure 2a has magnetic north pointed upward in the usual manner. The vector arrow points slightly to the right or east. Figure 2b has its artificial magnetic north pointing southeast. The vector arrow points slightly to its left or west. Figure 2c has its magnetic north pointing west. Its vector arrow points to its right or east. Answer choice **b** treats the figures as if magnetic north pointed up in all of them. Answer choice **c** gives the answer that is the strongest confirmation of the experimental results, but it is not accurate. Answer choice **d** confuses left and right (west and east) for Figures 2b and 2c.

20. f. The leftmost and rightmost diagrams in figure 3 are the only ones in which the birds point north. The magnetic field arrow points down and to the north in the first diagram and up and to the south in the last diagram.

21. c. The magnetic field arrows are parallel in the two diagrams in which the birds migrate northward. They are lower in the north and higher in the south, but their magnetic polarities are in opposite directions.

22. g. In the first diagram, the magnetic north arrow points toward geographic N, but in the third it points toward geographic S. In both diagrams the magnetic north arrow points toward the pole (the North Pole and the South Pole, respectively). The point of this experiment is to show that the birds respond to the magnetic inclination or dip, not the polarity. In either hemisphere, they "know" that the magnetic lines go down toward the pole, but they cannot distinguish a north magnetic pole from a south magnetic pole. Answer choice **h** reverses the inclination of the two. Answer choice **j** reverses the polarity by stating that the third diagram represents normal polarity. In fact, it shows magnetic north pointing to the geographic south, which is not the way the geomagnetic field works.

23. d. It is actually less puzzling than it seems. After all, people distinguish polarity of a magnet only if it is marked or it is placed close enough to be attracted or repelled by one that is marked. We do know, however, when something is attracted by a magnet. Answer choice **a** is wrong because humans generally use compasses to determine direction based on polarity. When inclination is measured it is almost always for geodetic purposes, not direction finding. Answer choice **b** is wrong because it was only when birds were deliberately misled by the experimental conditions that they made the wrong decision on direction. Answer choice **c** is also wrong. Experiment 2 proves that birds do not distinguish the polarity of a magnet, but it shows that they do follow magnetic fields by, in some way, sensing their inclination.

Passage V—Data Representation

24. h. The high point on the curve occurs between 30 and 40 for both males and females.

25. a. With this kind of question it is important to look at all elements of each answer. Answer choice **a**'s description is correct in everything said. The one thing it says nothing about, the different pattern of spinal fracture rates, is not highly significant because the differences are relatively small, and the rates end up at about the same level. Answer choices **b**, **c**, and **d** each contain actual errors. None of them indicate, as answer choice **a** does, that males experience no significant wrist fracture increases. Answer choice **b** says they are similar except that the wrist and spinal fracture rates are significantly higher. This is only partly true of the spinal rates, and it ignores the female hip fracture rate, which is the most dramatic difference on the chart. Answer choice **d** says nothing about the difference in wrist fracture rates.

26. h. Answer choice **h** points to the need for closer study. One subject per time period is not adequate data on which to base the conclusions of answer choice **f** or **g**. Answer choice **j** is irresponsibly incorrect. A loss of 4% bone density in 80 days is significant in itself. For trips of six months to years, a loss at that rate would mean the danger of fractures is significantly increased.

27. b. The significance of data is based on its importance in developing new knowledge or pinpointing areas where more attention is required. Bones break according to their individual density, not the average density of all bones in the body. The correct answer choice is **b** because that is the most marked indication of a problem. Answer choices **a** and **c** point to auxiliary data. The total body average is derived from the other data. It is apparently relatively low due to the insignificant loss (four parts per thousand) in the arms. Answer choice **d** refers to a significant loss but not as significant a loss as the trochanter's.

28. h. Loss per month would provide a picture of how bone mass changes over time. Averages by age and sex would be less significant additions, although monthly details divided in that way would be more interesting. We know that most cosmonauts are younger than the age at which significant bone loss begins in either males or females. Relative weight of each bone type is readily available outside this study, but the level of risk and the significance of risk to each bone type do not depend on the relative mass of each type in the body.

Passage VI—Conflicting Viewpoints

29. c. Scientist 1 did not say anaerobic prokaryotes were eliminated and replaced with eukaryotes. He said that most anaerobic prokaryote species were eliminated, and they were replaced with aerobic prokaryotes as well as eukaryotes and more complex species.

30. g. Answer choice **g** correctly states Scientist 2's overall view of the rise in oxygen levels. Answer choice **f** accurately reflects one of her statements but says nothing about the hypothesis that that statement supports. She does rely on the biological record, but she does not make a blanket statement like that of answer choice **h**. She also never makes a statement like that of answer choice **j**. She points to the increasing size and complexity of species as evidence that oxygen levels had increased, not as the cause of that increase.

31. a. Scientist 1 says that the great catastrophe killed off most anaerobic prokaryotes 2.5 billion years ago. Scientist 2 says that the eukaryotes and other complex creatures expanded their role at that time. They disagree on the rapidity of the change at that time, but they agree, as the passage says most scientists do, that the anaerobic prokaryotes lost their virtual monopoly on life beginning at that time. Scientist 2 is not specific about what oxygenation levels were 2.5 billion years ago, but she disagrees with answer choice **b**'s statement that they were *at least 10%*. Scientist 1 explicitly disagrees with answer choices **c** and **d**.

32. j. Answer choices **f** and **g** are explicitly supported by Scientist 2. Answer choice **h** may seem to contradict her views, but a careful reading reveals that she said there was no evidence of oxygen levels above several percent; she does not put a definite upper limit on the level as of 550 million years ago. Her hypothesis is that the increase was gradual, with no sudden catastrophe, until a sharp increase 550 million years ago. That leaves 2 billion years for a gradual increase from 0% to 10%.

33. b. Scientist 1 explicitly points to the important continuing role of cyanobacteria, both in the form of blue-green algae and as cytoplasts, in photosynthesis. Answer choice **a** is not true and is not a part of his theory, but it is not in direct disagreement with his reported statements. Answer choice **c** is a key part of Scientist 2's idea, but Scientist 1 never denies that oxygen levels continued to increase after the catastrophe of 2.5 billion years ago. Some kind of marked increase at the times specified by Scientist 2 does not contradict Scientist 1's theory.

34. h. With these questions it is important to keep in mind that if there is no "none of the above" or "all of the above" answer, there must be one best answer. Answer choice **h** is clearly something that both scientists disagree with. Scientist 1 says most known species were eliminated by oxygen, and Scientist 2 says oxygen was necessary for the development of more complex species. There is nothing reported indicating that either scientist disagrees with answer choice **f**, although we probably all do. Scientist 1, in fact, made an ironic statement of agreement with answer choice **f**. They both implicitly support answer choice **g**. They say nothing about answer choice **j**.

35. d. This question calls on the test taker to see how people with contradictory viewpoints may have overlapping positions. Views that conflict about part of a process may reach consensus about other parts.

Passage VII—Data Representation

36. f. The specific heat for solid A is 3 J/g/°C, and the melting point is 1,000°C. One gram must be raised 500° at 3 J/g/°C. The answer is 3×500 or 1,500 J.

37. d. The melting point appears as a horizontal (constant temperature) line in Figure 2 at −20°C. Substance D is the only one in Table 1 with that melting point.

38. h. This can be calculated by using either the heating formula on the heating segment of the graph or the melting formula on the melting segment. The melting formula is the simplest, so substitute the values shown in Figure 2 and Table 1 into the melting formula:

$$J_M = HF \times m$$
$$400\ J = 40\ J/g \times m$$
$$m = 10g$$

39. b. First 10 grams of substance B must be raised from 1,000°C to its melting point, 1,200°C. By the formula $J_H = \Delta T \times SH \times m$:

$$J_H = 200°C \times 5\ J/g/°C \times 10\ g = 10,000\ J$$

Then the 10 grams has to be melted. Using $J_M = HF \times m$:

$$J_M = 6.0\ J/g \times 10\ g = 60\ J$$

Adding the two gives us 10,060 J.

40. f. The heat required to melt a substance is shown in the *HF* (heat of fusion) column of Table 1. It is 8 for substance C and 40 for substance D; $\frac{8}{40} = \frac{1}{5}$ or 1:5.

ACT Writing Practice Test 3
Sample "Score 6" Essay

When the founding fathers of our Constitution included the Bill of Rights, they wanted to guarantee American citizens the right to free speech. Although freedom of speech is a valuable right of all American citizens, it has been abused by those who are manipulating the Constitution and its writers' intent so that they may gain fame, wealth, or attention. The only way to amend this problem is to impose censorship on these abusers. Unfortunately, the Internet has become a hotbed of abuse of free speech and needs to be censored, especially in our schools so that students are protected, education continues, and the authors of the offensive websites will eventually shut down their sites.

Use of the Internet in school has skyrocketed in the past few years. It has opened a door to an aspect of education never dreamed of before. Students and teachers can use the Internet for research, demonstration, and to learn and practice new skills. However, these benefits can occur only when the Internet is used wisely. Of all the websites available through the World Wide Web, only a small percentage is really worthwhile. Many others simply use the Web to exercise their warped version of free speech. Students must be protected from this abuse. Some students who are curious purposely go to questionable Web sites. Once there they find it difficult to turn away. As humans, we have a natural inclination toward the bizarre and even salacious. That's why it's up to schools to protect their students from themselves—and their natural curiosity—by imposing restrictions on the Internet. Other students innocently type a word into a search engine and are directed to an offensive Web site. It is well known that certain violent and sexual images become imprinted on the brain and are nearly impossible to eradicate. Again, schools should protect their students from exposure to a potential long-lasting horror.

Another reason schools should have tight control over the Internet is to ensure that education continues uninterrupted. It's too easy to become sidetracked by intriguing, but unhealthy, Web sites and games. Yes, people should exercise some self-control, but if the school is in the business of education, it should make sure that all of its accoutrements enhance education, not distract from it. It's a waste of time and energy for school administrators to try to hunt down Internet abusers. That time and energy can be saved if the school has only an intranet with preapproved sites. Schools should be educating students, not policing them.

Finally, if more schools make the decision to curb Internet access, maybe the people who create these offensive sites will be shut down. Most of these people make money off advertising on their Web sites. They promise advertisers that many people view their Web sites. If a large

percentage of computer users were suddenly not included in that calculation, maybe these abusers would find better uses of their time and talents.

An intranet is a great solution to the problem of Internet abuse. It allows students quick and easy access to preapproved, educational material. But it protects students from people who do not really understand the idea behind freedom of speech. "Censorship" is not a dirty word; it is a way to ensure that people do not abuse the right of free speech and make life more difficult for others.

Critique

This essay shows an excellent understanding of the assignment. It includes interesting ideas and insightful treatment of personal observations in connection with the assignment. The thesis statement is strong and clear. The essay contains strong supporting details that are well developed and explained throughout the essay, including three strong and logical reasons for the establishment of an intranet in the school. The essay is well organized with paragraphs appropriately broken out and good transitions between ideas. It remains focused and on topic throughout. The language used is highly sophisticated, and the essay contains few, if any, spelling, grammar, or capitalization errors.

Sample "Score 5" Essay

Members of the community are considering limiting Internet access in the schools. They believe that young people are at risk of being exposed to inappropriate material on the Internet. I disagree with this proposal for a variety of reasons.

The Internet contains a wealth of information for students. It is a valuable educational and resource tool. By using the Internet students can "visit" great places like museums and government offices. Students can get the very latest, up-to-date information on science, health, and world events. To cut students off from this wealth would be a great disservice to them. While it's true that many Web sites are offensive and inappropriate, most are not. We should not "throw out the baby with the bathwater" by completely eliminating student access to the World Wide Web.

There are some students who purposely investigate questionable Web sites. These students are usually just curious or they may be chronic offenders who need to be dealt with. However, it would be very easy to figure out who these students are and limit their access to the Internet. If every student had his or her own password and login name, this problem would be eliminated. We shouldn't punish all students for the actions of a few. Censoring the entire Internet from all students just because a few can't control themselves is a violation of the students' rights.

I think an intranet will be too limiting to be useful to students. It will take too much time and effort to research websites and then upload them one by one once they have approval. Plus doing this will cause all students doing research to have the same information from the same source. We might as well just all copy off one another and then there would be even more trouble! The point is, what's the use of doing research if we're all going to look in exactly the same place for information? The idea behind research is to find new, interesting ideas and information.

Replacing the Internet with an intranet is a bad idea. It will be too limiting and cumbersome and there are better ways to deal with the problem of inappropriate websites.

Critique

This essay shows a good understanding of the prompt and offers some specific arguments to support the idea that an intranet should not replace the Internet. The indirect thesis statement is a bit weak, but it clearly states the writer's point of view. The essay uses logical arguments and contains counterarguments in paragraphs 2 and 3. The essay shows a good command of written language but lacks the style and sophistication of a sample score 6 essay.

Sample "Score 4" Essay

Censorship is when anything that is considered offensive or harmful is limited so that people cannot have access to it. For some people that includes many things from realistic video games to certain types of music. I think censorship is not a good idea in America because that's part of what we fought for—freedom. Many people think the Internet should be under censorship, but I don't agree.

Because it was invented, the Internet has been a great thing for many people. I enjoy doing research for school on it. There are many Web sites that have great information on them. I especially like to go on Web sites that deal with science and health. But some people think the Internet should be censored. They think students will go on Internet sites that are violent or have improper content on them. Its true that some students may go to these sites. But most students don't. Also, if you censor the Internet who will decide what gets censored and what doesn't. There are things on the Internet that are fine for older students but not for younger ones.

The problem with censorship is that it means different things to everybody. I don't think there should be pornography or super violent stuff on the Internet. But I do think some stuff is ok even if it may have some questionable things on it. For example, a health website may have a picture or drawing of a naked person, but that's not pornography. Or a website about war may have violent images on it, but that's what war is about, and you can't really censor it or you don't have the truth.

I think that everyone needs to decide what is a problem for themselves and censor his own Internet instead of having the school do it. This will help teach students responsibility and make it so that all students don't have to pay for the actions of a few. Make students sign an agreement that they will not abuse the Internet at the school. A good compromise might be to block some obviously non-educational Web sites.

Critique

This essay shows a good understanding of the assignment. The writer takes a clear stand on the issue even though the thesis statement is a bit weak and undeveloped. This essay is well organized overall with some specific examples, but again, it lacks some development. The essay shows an adequate command of written language but lacks sophistication in vocabulary use and sentence structure and contains a few grammatical and spelling errors.

Sample "Score 3" Essay

The school board is thinking about cutting off the Internet and going to an intranet at the school. I think this is probably a good idea.

A lot of students waste time on the school computers. They say their doing research but their really just fooling around. They may not be playing games or anything, but they go to websites that have pretty much nothing to do with school or anything educational.

If we had an intranet we could still use the computers for research and stuff but it would be for students who are serious about it, not students who just want to waste time. Anyone who wanted to do more research outside of school could do it at home or at the public library.

School is a place for learning and not fooling around on the Internet all day. The intranet would avoid this problem and make it so that real students could do their work and the people who don't really want to use the computer seriously will think it's boring and not take up all the computers.

Critique

This essay shows an adequate understanding of the assignment. The thesis statement is a bit weak: *I think this is probably a good idea.* The rest of the essay, however, supports the thesis with some logical arguments. The essay would have been stronger with better organization and better development using specific examples. It shows some command of written language but contains some simplistic sentences with simple vocabulary and some awkward sentences. There are some spelling, grammar, and punctuation errors, but they do not make the composition very difficult to read or understand.

Sample "Score 2" Essay

Censoring the Internet at school is just another way for the school to control us. The school doesn't want people going on the Internet and seeing a bunch of stuff that they think is bad for us.

The problem is that the school thinks it knows everything about how to get us to learn things. They don't realize that the Internet is probably the most used thing that students have to learn. A lot of students who don't really learn that much in class because the books and teachers are boring will learn more on the Internet.

So what if sometimes you see something that's supposebly not appropriate. Who cares. Its not like its really anything new, most people see all that junk on tv anyway.

Leave the Internet in the schools, it's the best thing about them, I probably wouldn't even go if we didn't have computers.

Critique

This essay shows a very weak understanding of the prompt. The writer does take a stand on the issue, but the support for it is weak and repetitive. The introduction does not contain a thesis statement at all. The essay drifts a bit off track by focusing on how students learn more from the Internet than from books and teachers. It is undeveloped and shows a weak command of written language, as evidenced by the grammatical and spelling errors.

Sample "Score 1" Essay

Censorship is when peple wont let you see or watch things that they think are bad for you. Like the Internet, the school doesn't want us to have the Internet cause people are looking at things that they shouldn't be. It really doesn't matter to me what the school does with the computers cause i have one at home I use and I can just go on that one and do stuff. Most students have the same thing, so the school probally shouldn't even bother doing anything cause the students will just go on the sites at home anyways.

Critique

This essay shows a lack of understanding with regard to the assignment. The student shows some understanding about censorship, but does not take a clear stand on the issue in the prompt and does not develop the essay with specific examples. The essay drifts off topic by repeatedly stating that students can use the Internet at home. The essay is poorly developed and lacks a logical form of organization. The language used shows a serious lack of command of written language, and there are numerous spelling, grammar, punctuation, and capitalization errors.

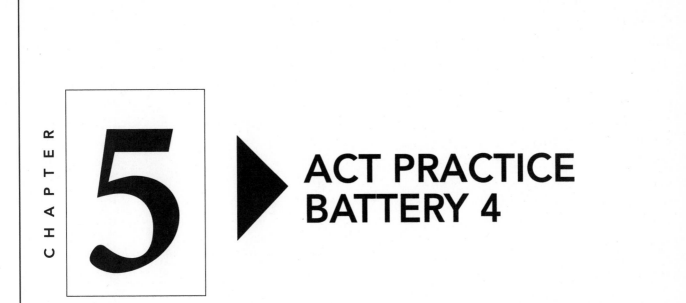

5 ▶ ACT PRACTICE BATTERY 4

This is the final practice ACT in this book. In this chapter you'll find full English, Mathematics, Reading, Science, and Writing tests. Complete answers are at the end of the chapter, and instructions on how to score these practice tests are in Chapter 6. Remember, there are four more complete practice ACTs available to you online. For details on how to access the online tests, please refer to page 337.

ACT English Practice Test 4

1.	ⓐ	ⓑ	ⓒ	ⓓ	26.	ⓕ	ⓖ	ⓗ	ⓙ	51.	ⓐ	ⓑ	ⓒ	ⓓ
2.	ⓕ	ⓖ	ⓗ	ⓙ	27.	ⓐ	ⓑ	ⓒ	ⓓ	52.	ⓕ	ⓖ	ⓗ	ⓙ
3.	ⓐ	ⓑ	ⓒ	ⓓ	28.	ⓕ	ⓖ	ⓗ	ⓙ	53.	ⓐ	ⓑ	ⓒ	ⓓ
4.	ⓕ	ⓖ	ⓗ	ⓙ	29.	ⓐ	ⓑ	ⓒ	ⓓ	54.	ⓕ	ⓖ	ⓗ	ⓙ
5.	ⓐ	ⓑ	ⓒ	ⓓ	30.	ⓕ	ⓖ	ⓗ	ⓙ	55.	ⓐ	ⓑ	ⓒ	ⓓ
6.	ⓕ	ⓖ	ⓗ	ⓙ	31.	ⓐ	ⓑ	ⓒ	ⓓ	56.	ⓕ	ⓖ	ⓗ	ⓙ
7.	ⓐ	ⓑ	ⓒ	ⓓ	32.	ⓕ	ⓖ	ⓗ	ⓙ	57.	ⓐ	ⓑ	ⓒ	ⓓ
8.	ⓕ	ⓖ	ⓗ	ⓙ	33.	ⓐ	ⓑ	ⓒ	ⓓ	58.	ⓕ	ⓖ	ⓗ	ⓙ
9.	ⓐ	ⓑ	ⓒ	ⓓ	34.	ⓕ	ⓖ	ⓗ	ⓙ	59.	ⓐ	ⓑ	ⓒ	ⓓ
10.	ⓕ	ⓖ	ⓗ	ⓙ	35.	ⓐ	ⓑ	ⓒ	ⓓ	60.	ⓕ	ⓖ	ⓗ	ⓙ
11.	ⓐ	ⓑ	ⓒ	ⓓ	36.	ⓕ	ⓖ	ⓗ	ⓙ	61.	ⓐ	ⓑ	ⓒ	ⓓ
12.	ⓕ	ⓖ	ⓗ	ⓙ	37.	ⓐ	ⓑ	ⓒ	ⓓ	62.	ⓕ	ⓖ	ⓗ	ⓙ
13.	ⓐ	ⓑ	ⓒ	ⓓ	38.	ⓕ	ⓖ	ⓗ	ⓙ	63.	ⓐ	ⓑ	ⓒ	ⓓ
14.	ⓕ	ⓖ	ⓗ	ⓙ	39.	ⓐ	ⓑ	ⓒ	ⓓ	64.	ⓕ	ⓖ	ⓗ	ⓙ
15.	ⓐ	ⓑ	ⓒ	ⓓ	40.	ⓕ	ⓖ	ⓗ	ⓙ	65.	ⓐ	ⓑ	ⓒ	ⓓ
16.	ⓕ	ⓖ	ⓗ	ⓙ	41.	ⓐ	ⓑ	ⓒ	ⓓ	66.	ⓕ	ⓖ	ⓗ	ⓙ
17.	ⓐ	ⓑ	ⓒ	ⓓ	42.	ⓕ	ⓖ	ⓗ	ⓙ	67.	ⓐ	ⓑ	ⓒ	ⓓ
18.	ⓕ	ⓖ	ⓗ	ⓙ	43.	ⓐ	ⓑ	ⓒ	ⓓ	68.	ⓕ	ⓖ	ⓗ	ⓙ
19.	ⓐ	ⓑ	ⓒ	ⓓ	44.	ⓕ	ⓖ	ⓗ	ⓙ	69.	ⓐ	ⓑ	ⓒ	ⓓ
20.	ⓕ	ⓖ	ⓗ	ⓙ	45.	ⓐ	ⓑ	ⓒ	ⓓ	70.	ⓕ	ⓖ	ⓗ	ⓙ
21.	ⓐ	ⓑ	ⓒ	ⓓ	46.	ⓕ	ⓖ	ⓗ	ⓙ	71.	ⓐ	ⓑ	ⓒ	ⓓ
22.	ⓕ	ⓖ	ⓗ	ⓙ	47.	ⓐ	ⓑ	ⓒ	ⓓ	72.	ⓕ	ⓖ	ⓗ	ⓙ
23.	ⓐ	ⓑ	ⓒ	ⓓ	48.	ⓕ	ⓖ	ⓗ	ⓙ	73.	ⓐ	ⓑ	ⓒ	ⓓ
24.	ⓕ	ⓖ	ⓗ	ⓙ	49.	ⓐ	ⓑ	ⓒ	ⓓ	74.	ⓕ	ⓖ	ⓗ	ⓙ
25.	ⓐ	ⓑ	ⓒ	ⓓ	50.	ⓕ	ⓖ	ⓗ	ⓙ	75.	ⓐ	ⓑ	ⓒ	ⓓ

ACT Mathematics Practice Test 4

1. (a) (b) (c) (d) (e)
2. (f) (g) (h) (j) (k)
3. (a) (b) (c) (d) (e)
4. (f) (g) (h) (j) (k)
5. (a) (b) (c) (d) (e)
6. (f) (g) (h) (j) (k)
7. (a) (b) (c) (d) (e)
8. (f) (g) (h) (j) (k)
9. (a) (b) (c) (d) (e)
10. (f) (g) (h) (j) (k)
11. (a) (b) (c) (d) (e)
12. (f) (g) (h) (j) (k)
13. (a) (b) (c) (d) (e)
14. (f) (g) (h) (j) (k)
15. (a) (b) (c) (d) (e)
16. (f) (g) (h) (j) (k)
17. (a) (b) (c) (d) (e)
18. (f) (g) (h) (j) (k)
19. (a) (b) (c) (d) (e)
20. (f) (g) (h) (j) (k)

21. (a) (b) (c) (d) (e)
22. (f) (g) (h) (j) (k)
23. (a) (b) (c) (d) (e)
24. (f) (g) (h) (j) (k)
25. (a) (b) (c) (d) (e)
26. (f) (g) (h) (j) (k)
27. (a) (b) (c) (d) (e)
28. (f) (g) (h) (j) (k)
29. (a) (b) (c) (d) (e)
30. (f) (g) (h) (j) (k)
31. (a) (b) (c) (d) (e)
32. (f) (g) (h) (j) (k)
33. (a) (b) (c) (d) (e)
34. (f) (g) (h) (j) (k)
35. (a) (b) (c) (d) (e)
36. (f) (g) (h) (j) (k)
37. (a) (b) (c) (d) (e)
38. (f) (g) (h) (j) (k)
39. (a) (b) (c) (d) (e)
40. (f) (g) (h) (j) (k)

41. (a) (b) (c) (d) (e)
42. (f) (g) (h) (j) (k)
43. (a) (b) (c) (d) (e)
44. (f) (g) (h) (j) (k)
45. (a) (b) (c) (d) (e)
46. (f) (g) (h) (j) (k)
47. (a) (b) (c) (d) (e)
48. (f) (g) (h) (j) (k)
49. (a) (b) (c) (d) (e)
50. (f) (g) (h) (j) (k)
51. (a) (b) (c) (d) (e)
52. (f) (g) (h) (j) (k)
53. (a) (b) (c) (d) (e)
54. (f) (g) (h) (j) (k)
55. (a) (b) (c) (d) (e)
56. (f) (g) (h) (j) (k)
57. (a) (b) (c) (d) (e)
58. (f) (g) (h) (j) (k)
59. (a) (b) (c) (d) (e)
60. (f) (g) (h) (j) (k)

ACT Reading Practice Test 4

1. (a) (b) (c) (d)
2. (f) (g) (h) (j)
3. (a) (b) (c) (d)
4. (f) (g) (h) (j)
5. (a) (b) (c) (d)
6. (f) (g) (h) (j)
7. (a) (b) (c) (d)
8. (f) (g) (h) (j)
9. (a) (b) (c) (d)
10. (f) (g) (h) (j)
11. (a) (b) (c) (d)
12. (f) (g) (h) (j)
13. (a) (b) (c) (d)
14. (f) (g) (h) (j)

15. (a) (b) (c) (d)
16. (f) (g) (h) (j)
17. (a) (b) (c) (d)
18. (f) (g) (h) (j)
19. (a) (b) (c) (d)
20. (f) (g) (h) (j)
21. (a) (b) (c) (d)
22. (f) (g) (h) (j)
23. (a) (b) (c) (d)
24. (f) (g) (h) (j)
25. (a) (b) (c) (d)
26. (f) (g) (h) (j)
27. (a) (b) (c) (d)
28. (f) (g) (h) (j)

29. (a) (b) (c) (d)
30. (f) (g) (h) (j)
31. (a) (b) (c) (d)
32. (f) (g) (h) (j)
33. (a) (b) (c) (d)
34. (f) (g) (h) (j)
35. (a) (b) (c) (d)
36. (f) (g) (h) (j)
37. (a) (b) (c) (d)
38. (f) (g) (h) (j)
39. (a) (b) (c) (d)
40. (f) (g) (h) (j)

ACT Science Practice Test 4

1. (a) (b) (c) (d)
2. (f) (g) (h) (j)
3. (a) (b) (c) (d)
4. (f) (g) (h) (j)
5. (a) (b) (c) (d)
6. (f) (g) (h) (j)
7. (a) (b) (c) (d)
8. (f) (g) (h) (j)
9. (a) (b) (c) (d)
10. (f) (g) (h) (j)
11. (a) (b) (c) (d)
12. (f) (g) (h) (j)
13. (a) (b) (c) (d)
14. (f) (g) (h) (j)

15. (a) (b) (c) (d)
16. (f) (g) (h) (j)
17. (a) (b) (c) (d)
18. (f) (g) (h) (j)
19. (a) (b) (c) (d)
20. (f) (g) (h) (j)
21. (a) (b) (c) (d)
22. (f) (g) (h) (j)
23. (a) (b) (c) (d)
24. (f) (g) (h) (j)
25. (a) (b) (c) (d)
26. (f) (g) (h) (j)
27. (a) (b) (c) (d)
28. (f) (g) (h) (j)

29. (a) (b) (c) (d)
30. (f) (g) (h) (j)
31. (a) (b) (c) (d)
32. (f) (g) (h) (j)
33. (a) (b) (c) (d)
34. (f) (g) (h) (j)
35. (a) (b) (c) (d)
36. (f) (g) (h) (j)
37. (a) (b) (c) (d)
38. (f) (g) (h) (j)
39. (a) (b) (c) (d)
40. (f) (g) (h) (j)

ACT English Practice Test 4

75 Questions—45 Minutes

Read each passage through once before you begin to answer any questions. You will see that certain words or phrases in the following five passages have been underlined and numbered. Following each passage, you will see alternatives for those underlined words or phrases. Choose the one that best expresses the idea of the passage, is the best use of standard English, or is most consistent with the tone and style of the passage. If you find the underlined part to be correct, choose "NO CHANGE." Note that to answer many of the questions you will probably need to read several sentences beyond the question. You may also find questions about a section of the passage or the passage as a whole, rather than about an underlined part.

Passage I—The Art of Lawn Tennis

This passage is taken from The Art of Lawn Tennis, *by William Tatem Tilden.*

Tennis is at once an art and a science. The game as played by such men as Norman E. Brookes and R.N. Williams is[1] art. Yet like all true art, they have their basis[2] in scientific methods that must be learned and learned thoroughly for a foundation before the artistic structure of a great tennis game can be constructed.

Every player who hopes to attain a high degree of efficiency should of had[3] a clearly defined method of development and adhere to it. He should be certain that it is based around[4] sound principles and, once assured of that, follow it, even though his progress seems slow and discouraging. I began tennis wrong.[5] My strokes were wrong and my viewpoint clouded. I did not have early training just like[6] many of our American boys have at the present time. No

one told me the importance of the fundamentals of the game, such as keeping the[7] eye on the ball or correct body position and footwork. A racquet was given to me to hit the ball.[8] Naturally, like all beginners, I acquired many very serious faults. I went along with moderate success until I graduated from school, beating some fairly good players, but losing some matches to men below my class. The year following my graduation the new captain of my alma mater's team asked me if I would aid him in developing the squad for next year. Well, "Fools rush in where angels fear to tread," so I said Yes.[9] At that point my tennis education began.

(1) Our tennis squad, comprising[10] over a dozen youngsters, all knew me well and felt at perfect liberty to ask me as many questions as they could think up. (2) Frankly, I did not know, but I answered them something at the moment and said to myself it was time I learned some fundamentals of tennis. (3) I was seized[11] with requests to explain why Jones missed a forehand drive down the sideline, or Smith couldn't serve well, or Brown failed to hit the ball at all. (4) So I began to study[12] the reasons why certain shots are missed and others made, why certain balls are hit so much faster though with less effort than others, and why some players are great while most are only good. (5) I am still studying, but my results to date have resulted in a definite system to be learned, and it is this which I hope to explain to you.

Tennis has a language all its own. The idioms of the game need to be learned, as all books on the game are written in tennis parlance. The technical terms and their counterparts in slang need to be understood to thoroughly grasp the idea in any written tennis account. I do not believe in wasting time by carefully defining each rule of the game or examining each blade of grass on a court. <u>It gets you nowhere</u>.[13] I do, however, advocate teaching the terms of the game.

1. a. NO CHANGE
   b. game as played, by such men as Norman E. Brookes and R.N. Williams is
   c. game, as played by such men as Norman E. Brookes and R.N. Williams, is
   d. game as played, by such men as Norman E. Brookes and R.N. Williams, is

2. f. NO CHANGE
   g. they have their bases
   h. it has its basis
   j. they are based

3. a. NO CHANGE
   b. should be having
   c. had
   d. should have

4. f. NO CHANGE
   g. at
   h. on
   j. over

5. a. NO CHANGE
   b. incorrect
   c. incorrectly
   d. bad

6. f. NO CHANGE
   g. the way
   h. the same as
   j. just as

7. a. NO CHANGE
   b. a
   c. you
   d. an

8. f. NO CHANGE
   g. A racquet was given to me for hitting the ball
   h. I was giving a racquet to use to hit the ball
   j. I was given a racquet to use to hit the ball

9. a. NO CHANGE
   b. so yes I said.
   c. so "Yes, I said."
   d. so I said yes.

10. f. NO CHANGE
   g. comparing
   h. reprising
   j. apprising

11. a. NO CHANGE
   b. sieged
   c. seizing
   d. besieged

12. f. NO CHANGE
   g. I begin to study
   h. I was beginning to study
   j. I had begun to study

13. a. NO CHANGE
   b. It doesn't get you anywhere
   c. It gets nothing done
   d. Omit the underlined portion.

14. The most coherent and logical order for the sentences in paragraph 3 is
   f. NO CHANGE
   g. 1, 2, 4, 3, 5
   h. 1, 3, 2, 4, 5
   j. 1, 2, 3, 5, 4

15. The author is considering adding one paragraph to the passage. The most effective placement and use of this paragraph would be
 a. as a first, introductory paragraph discussing the history of tennis.
 b. as a second paragraph discussing the artistry of tennis.
 c. as a third paragraph discussing the author's schooling and background.
 d. as a final, concluding paragraph that reiterates the central point of the introduction: that tennis is a combination of art and science.

Passage II—The Geography and Geology of Hartford, Connecticut

This passage is taken from Historic Towns of the Connecticut River Valley, *by George S. Roberts.*

The rugged hills that compose the western, and, in lesser degree, the eastern areas, are[16] formed of rocks resembling in many respects the group to which granite belongs—rocks that are very ancient, dating far back into the early history of the world. The rivers that flow among these hills have open valleys, showing that the portion of the land above the sea level has been practically unchanged for ages. But in the central portion of the state these ancient highlands sink[17] down into a broad trough running from Long Island Sound far up in to Massachusetts, and this trough is filled with rocks of much later date—who's[18] history is one of the most interesting to be found in the great book of nature.

Long before man lived upon the earth, when huge reptiles, long since utterly passed away, clambered over the hills or roamed along the muddy shores, the trough by a great lake or arm of the sea was filled.[19] Into its quiet waters ran streams from the surrounding hills, bringing down into the lake mud and sand from the land over which they flowed. These sank to the bottom and there formed beds of sand and clay. Then a strange thing happened. Somewhere in this region, which is now so peaceful, a volcano bursted[20] forth and rolled floods of molten lava over the whole area. This lava turned much of the water in the lake to steam,[21] and, spreading itself over the beds of land-waste at the bottom, there cooled and hardened into rock. Three times more has the lake lain in the trough, its bottom covered by beds of clay and sand, and three times has the lava overflowed the region, for we find now in central Connecticut three great sheets of volcanic "trap," as the rock is called, lying one above each other.[22] Each one resting[23] on beds of clay, sand, or pebbles, now hardened into rocks known respectively as shale, sandstone, and conglomerate.

Now, how can we see these three layers of lava, if they lie one above another? How is it that we can see more than the top of one, even if we should find that there is no land-waste on top of that? It is in some way such as this, long after[24] the last lava had hardened, the region was greatly disturbed and everything was tilted, so that the sheets of lava and the rocks lying between them, instead of lying horizontal, sloped strongly to the east. Since then there has been great wearing away[25] of the land caused by the weathering of the rocks, and the streams have carried away the land-waste to the sea. But the trap[26] is much harder than the sandstone and shale, so that it stands up above the country in high ridges running north and south. At the time, the rocks were tilted they were also largely broken so vast fragments[27]—miles in length—have been separated from each other in different parts of central Connecticut. But for all this, the geologist finds plainly that these fragments belong to three different sheets of lava, which marks three[28] different periods of volcanic action.

The second volcanic eruption was apparently <u>the greater one,</u>[29] for it left a sheet of lava that is in some places 500 feet thick. It is the upturned edge of this great sheet that forms the various so-called mountains of central Connecticut. Perhaps the most remarkable remains of life, those which are certainly the most famous, are the so-called Connecticut River Bird Tracks. These are footmarks left in the mud of the ancient shores by the creatures that roamed over them long ago. <u>They are found in various places, but probably the most famous localities are Turner's Falls, in Massachusetts, and the great sandstone quarries at Portland, Connecticut. But the footmarks remain intact to the present time, even though the mud has long since hardened into shale.</u>[30]

16. **f.** NO CHANGE
  g. western, and in lesser degree, the eastern areas, are
  h. western and, in lesser degree, the eastern areas are
  j. western, and in lesser degree the eastern areas, are

17. **a.** NO CHANGE
  b. sank
  c. has sunk
  d. sinks

18. **f.** NO CHANGE
  g. who
  h. whose
  j. who is

19. **a.** NO CHANGE
  b. the trough, by a great lake or arm of the sea, was filled
  c. the trough was filled by a great lake or arm of the sea
  d. the trough was filled, by a great lake or arm of the sea

20. **f.** NO CHANGE
  g. burst
  h. busted
  j. was bursting

21. **a.** NO CHANGE
  b. This lava was turning much of the water in the lake to steam
  c. This lava had been turning much of the water in the lake to steam
  d. This lava would turn much of the water in the lake to steam

22. **f.** NO CHANGE
  g. laying one above another
  h. lying one above another
  j. laying one above each other

23. **a.** NO CHANGE
  b. Each one rested
  c. Each one would rest
  d. Each one rests

24. **f.** NO CHANGE
  g. this long after
  h. this: Long after
  j. this long, after

25. All of the following would be an appropriate replacement for the underlined words EXCEPT:
  a. erosion
  b. implosion
  c. damaging
  d. decaying

26. **f.** NO CHANGE
  g. Since the trap
  h. And the trap
  j. Because the trap

27. **a.** NO CHANGE
   b. At the time the rocks were tilted they were also largely broken, so vast fragments
   c. At the time, the rocks were tilted they were also largely broken, so that vast fragments
   d. At the time, the rocks were tilted, they were also largely broken so that vast fragments

28. **f.** NO CHANGE
   g. which marked three
   h. which had marked
   j. which mark three

29. **a.** NO CHANGE
   b. the great one
   c. the greatest one
   d. a greater one

30. **f.** NO CHANGE
   g. The mud has long since hardened into shale, but the footmarks remain intact to the present time. They are found in various places, but probably the most famous localities are Turner's Falls, in Massachusetts, and the great sandstone quarries at Portland, Connecticut.
   h. They are found in various places, but probably the most famous localities are Turner's Falls, in Massachusetts, and the great sandstone quarries at Portland, Connecticut. The footmarks remain intact to the present time. The mud has long since hardened into shale.
   j. The footmarks remain intact to the present time, but the mud has long since hardened into shale. They are found in various places, but probably the most famous localities are Turner's Falls, in Massachusetts, and the great sandstone quarries at Portland, Connecticut.

Passage III—The Wonderful Magnet
By Arthur Brisbane.

Everybody knows something of the peculiarities of the magnet. As a boy you led tiny painted ducks <u>through</u>[31] the water basin, holding a magnet in your hand, or you owned a horseshoe magnet that would pick up nails and needles. You now know in a general kind of way that the magnet is <u>a very useful, as well as a somewhat mysterious thing.</u>[32] The old Greeks and Romans simply knew that some remarkable iron ore found in Lydia, near the town of Magnesia, and hence called magnet, was capable of drawing and holding pieces of metal. Ancient cultures had the wildest theories concerning the magnet, just as we have wild theories about things that are new and strange to us today. They thought that the magnet could be used in cases of sickness, could attract wood and flesh, <u>and influences</u>[33] the human brain, causing melancholy. They believed that the power of a magnet could be destroyed by rubbing garlic on it, and that the power could be brought back again by dipping the magnet in goat's blood. They believed that a magnet could be used to detect bad conduct in <u>a woman; believed</u>[34] that it would not attract iron in the presence of a diamond. <u>They believed as much other nonsense quite as ridiculous as the nonsense that we believe today.</u>[35]

The magnet was first made actually and wonderfully useful in the compass. <u>Who discovered the compass nobody knows.</u>[36] It was probably invented by the Chinese and brought to Europe through the Arabs. Anyhow, some genius found out that a small needle brought in contact with the so-called lodestone, or magnetic ore, absorbs the qualities of the lodestone, and when placed on a pivot will always point to the north.

(1) There were and still are many mysteries <u>around the magnet</u>.[37] (2) A form of perpetual motion seems to be embodied in the principle of magnetism. (3) One strange fact is <u>this; that</u>[38] the weight of the metal is exactly the same before it is magnetized and after it is magnetized. (4) <u>Early students</u>[39] thought that the magnet pointed toward some particular spot in the sky, perhaps some magnetic star. (5) This suggestion was followed by ingenious yarns to the effect that in the extreme North ships had to be built with wooden nails, instead of iron nails, as the magnetic mountains would draw the iron nails <u>out of the ship</u>.[40] (6) One genius felt sure that there must be huge mountains of lodestone near the North Pole. (7) After this came the more rational conception that our own earth is a great magnet, and that the little magnet in the compass simply obeys in pointing according to the greater force of the earth magnet.

This essay is brought about by an incident telegraphed from Vallejo, California. John Gettegg, apprentice in the Navy Yard, <u>had in his cheek embedded a flying piece of steel</u>.[41] To get it out would apparently have demanded a painful and difficult surgical operation, as the piece of steel had entered the bone. The head electrician, however, <u>simply near the wounded boy's face placed an electromagnet capable of lifting 500 pounds</u>,[42] and the sharp piece of steel instantly flew out of the cheek and attached itself to the magnet.

(1) In the great steelworks where armor plate is made, powerful magnets are used to carry the hot plates from one place to another. (2) The magnet lifts up the hot, soft metal without denting it or damaging it and drops it down where it is wanted. (3) The power that moves trolley cars through the streets is nothing in reality but an application of the force of the magnetic principle. (4) That the earth itself is a great magnet cannot be questioned. (5) And there is no doubt that each of us human beings is a compound magnet on his own account, depending for his welfare on magnetic force. (6) The millions of red corpuscles in the blood, each with its infinitesimal particles of iron, absorb <u>in</u>[43] the lungs and distribute throughout the body the electric forces on which we depend, and with which we do our work. (7) When you read of men and women dealing in a blundering kind of a way with abstract, <u>obtuse</u>[44] speculations and problems, do not laugh at them too heartily. (8) And their wild theories of today may settle down into great utility centuries from now. (9) They are no more ridiculous than the old Greeks who thought that a magnet could be regulated by garlic or goat's blood.

31. **a.** NO CHANGE
    b. over
    c. within
    d. around

32. **f.** NO CHANGE
    g. a very useful and somewhat mysterious, thing
    h. a very useful, as well as somewhat mysterious, thing
    j. a useful and mysterious thing

33. **a.** NO CHANGE
    b. and influence
    c. and could influence
    d. could influence

34. **f.** NO CHANGE
    g. a woman, and believed
    h. a woman and believed
    j. a woman, believed

35. a. NO CHANGE
   b. They believed the nonsense that we believe today as much as other nonsense quite as ridiculous.
   c. They believed the other nonsense quite as ridiculous as nonsense that we believe today as much.
   d. They believed much other nonsense quite as ridiculous as the nonsense that we believe today.

36. f. NO CHANGE
   g. Who discovered the compass, nobody knows.
   h. Nobody knows who discovered the compass?
   j. Who discovered the compass? Nobody knows.

37. a. NO CHANGE
   b. over the magnet
   c. surrounding the magnet
   d. above the magnet

38. f. NO CHANGE
   g. this, that
   h. this—it's that
   j. this—

39. a. NO CHANGE
   b. Earlier students
   c. Early on students
   d. Early, students

40. The author is considering deleting sentence 5 from the third paragraph. Should this sentence be kept or deleted?
   f. It should be deleted, because it does not add useful information to the passage.
   g. It should be deleted, because the tone is inappropriate to the passage.
   h. It should be kept, because it highlights the normalcy of foolish theories prior to the full understanding of a natural phenomenon.
   j. It should be kept, because it rightfully pokes fun at someone for having a foolish idea.

41. a. NO CHANGE
   b. had a flying piece of steel embedded in his cheek
   c. had a piece of steel flying and embedded in his cheek
   d. had embedded in his cheek a piece of steel, flying.

42. f. NO CHANGE
   g. near the wounded boy's face simply placed an electromagnet capable of lifting 500 pounds
   h. simply placed an electromagnet, capable of lifting 500 pounds, near the wounded boy's face
   j. simply placed near the wounded boy's face an electromagnet capable of lifting 500 pounds

43. a. NO CHANGE
   b. over
   c. on
   d. into

44. f. NO CHANGE
   g. acute
   h. abstruse
   j. obese

45. The author is considering a change in the closing paragraph. The most logical change would be to switch

a. sentence 2 with sentence 3.

b. sentence 4 with sentence 5.

c. sentence 6 with sentence 7.

d. sentence 8 with sentence 9.

Passage IV—The Soul of the Far East

This passage is taken from The Soul of the Far East, *by Percival Lowell.*

The belief that on the other side of our globe all things are by necessity upside down is startlingly brought back to the man when he first sets foot at Yokohama. If his initial glance does not disclose the natives in the everyday feat of standing <u>calm</u>[46] on their heads, an attitude that his <u>youthfully</u>[47] imagination conceived to be a necessary consequence of their geographical position, it does at least reveal them looking at the world as if from the standpoint of that eccentric posture. For they seem to him <u>seeing</u>[48] everything topsy-turvy. Whether it be that their antipodal situation has affected their brains, or whether it is the mind of the observer himself that has hitherto been wrong in undertaking to rectify the <u>reverted</u>[49] pictures presented by his retina, the result is undeniable. The world stands reversed, and, taking for granted his own uprightness, the stranger <u>unhesitatingly</u>[50] imputes to them an obliquity of vision.

If the inversion is not precisely of the kind he expected, it is none the less striking, and impressively more real. If personal experience has definitely convinced him that the inhabitants of that underside of our planet do not adhere to it head downwards, like flies on a ceiling (his <u>early</u>[51] a priori deduction), they still appear antipodal. Intellectually, at least, their attitude sets gravity at defiance. For to the <u>minds eye</u>[52] their world is one huge, comical antithesis of our own. What we regard intuitively in one way from our standpoint, <u>they as intuitively seen</u>[53] in a diametrically opposite manner from theirs. To speak backward, write backward, and read backward are but the ABCs of their contrariety. The inversion extends deeper than mere modes of expression, down <u>in</u>[54] the very matter of thought. Ideas of ours that we deem innate find in them no home, while methods that strike us as preposterously unnatural appear to be their birthright. <u>From the standing</u>[55] of a wet umbrella on its handle instead of its head to dry to the striking of a match away in place of toward one, there seem to be no actions of our daily lives, however trivial, that <u>does</u>[56] not find with them its appropriate reaction, equal but opposite. Indeed, to one anxious about conforming to the manners and customs of the <u>country; the</u>[57] only road to right lies in following unswervingly that course that his inherited instincts assure him to be wrong.

Yet these people are human beings; with all their <u>eccentricities, they</u>[58] are men and women like us. Physically we cannot but be cognizant of the fact, nor mentally but be conscious of it. Like us, indeed, and yet so unlike <u>were</u>[59] they that we seem, as we gaze at them, to be viewing our own humanity in some mirth-provoking mirror of the mind, a mirror that shows us our own familiar thoughts, but all turned wrong side out. Humor holds the glass, and we become the sport of our own reflections. But is it otherwise at home? Does not every one of us, looking in the mirror, conceive <u>ourself</u>[60] to be a very different-appearing person from what he or she is, forgetting that his or her right side has become the left, and vice versa? Perhaps, could we once see ourselves as others see us, our surprise in the case of foreign peoples might be less pronounced.

46. **f.** NO CHANGE
  g. calmer
  h. calmly
  j. more calmly

47. **a.** NO CHANGE
  b. youth's
  c. young
  d. youthful

48. **f.** NO CHANGE
  g. to see
  h. to have seen
  j. to be seeing

49. **a.** NO CHANGE
  b. inverted
  c. converted
  d. introverted

50. **f.** NO CHANGE
  g. unhesitatedly
  h. unhesitantly
  j. inhesitantly

51. **a.** NO CHANGE
  b. earlier
  c. prior
  d. Omit the underlined word.

52. **f.** NO CHANGE
  g. minds eyes
  h. mind eyes
  j. mind's eye

53. **a.** NO CHANGE
  b. they as intuitive see
  c. they as intuitively seen
  d. they as intuitively observe

54. **f.** NO CHANGE
  g. to
  h. into
  j. in to

55. **a.** NO CHANGE
  b. From the stand
  c. From standing
  d. From a stand

56. **f.** NO CHANGE
  g. do
  h. did
  j. could

57. **a.** NO CHANGE
  b. country. The
  c. country, the
  d. country: the

58. **f.** NO CHANGE
  g. eccentricities; they
  h. eccentricities: they
  j. eccentricities. They

59. **a.** NO CHANGE
  b. be
  c. is
  d. are

60. **f.** NO CHANGE
  g. themselves
  h. himself or herself
  j. ourselves

Passage V—Doctor Pascal

This passage is taken from Doctor Pascal, *by Emile Zola.*

In the heat of the glowing July afternoon, the room, with blinds carefully closed, <u>were</u>[61] full of a great calm. From the three windows, through the cracks of the old wooden shutters, came only a few scattered sunbeams which, in the midst of the obscurity, made a soft brightness that bathed surrounding objects in a diffused and tender light. It was cool here <u>by comparing with</u>[62] the overpowering heat that was felt outside, under the fierce rays of the sun that blazed upon the front of the house.

Standing before the press that faced the windows, <u>the paper that Dr. Pascal had come to look for remained missing.</u>[63] With doors wide open, this immense press of carved oak, adorned with strong and handsome mountings of metal, <u>dated</u>[64] from the last century, displayed within its capacious depths an extraordinary collection of papers and manuscripts of all sorts, piled up in confusion and <u>filled</u>[65] every shelf to overflowing. For more than 30 years the doctor had thrown into it every page he wrote, from brief notes to the complete texts of his great works on heredity. <u>Thus it was that</u>[66] his searches here were not always easy. He rummaged patiently among the <u>papers; and</u>[67] when he at last found the one he was looking for, he smiled.

(1) For an instant longer he remained near the bookcase, <u>reading the note</u>[68] by a golden sunbeam that came to him from the middle window. (2) In this dawnlike light, he appeared, with his snow-white hair and beard, strong and vigorous; although he was near 60, his color was so fresh, his features were so finely cut, his eyes were still so clear, and he had so youthful an air that one might have mistaken him, in his close-fitting, maroon velvet jacket, <u>as</u>[69] a young man with powdered hair.[70]

<u>"Here,"</u>[71] he said at last, "you will copy this note. Raymond would never have been able to decipher my diabolical writing." He crossed the room and <u>lied</u>[72] the paper beside the young girl, who stood working at a high desk in the embrasure of the window to the right. She did not even turn round, so engrossed was her attention with the pastel that she was at the moment rapidly sketching in with broad strokes of the crayon. Near her in a vase bloomed a stalk of hollyhocks of a singular shade of violet, striped with yellow. The profile of her small round head, with its short, fair hair, was clearly <u>distinguishable; an exquisite</u>[73] and serious profile, the straight forehead contracted in a frown of attention, the eyes of an azure blue, the nose delicately molded, the chin firm. Her bent neck, especially, of a milky whiteness, looked adorably youthful under the gold of the clustering curls. In her <u>long black blouse</u>[74] she seemed very tall, with her slight figure, slender throat, and flexible form, the flexible slenderness of the divine figures of the Renaissance. In spite of her 25 years, she still retained a <u>childish</u>[75] air and looked hardly 18.

61. **a.** NO CHANGE
   b. is
   c. was
   d. are

62. **f.** NO CHANGE
   g. by comparison to
   h. in comparison with
   j. comparing to

63. **a.** NO CHANGE
   b. the paper that Dr. Pascal had come to look for was missing.
   c. Dr. Pascal had come to look for a missing paper.
   d. there was no finding the paper that Dr. Pascal had come to look for.

64. **f.** NO CHANGE
  g. dating
  h. being dated
  j. to date

65. **a.** NO CHANGE
  b. had filled
  c. fill
  d. filling

66. All of the following would be appropriate replacements for the underlined words *except*
  f. As a result
  g. Therefore
  h. Because
  j. Consequently

67. **a.** NO CHANGE
  b. papers and
  c. papers. And,
  d. papers, and

68. **f.** NO CHANGE
  g. read the note
  h. to read
  j. having read the note

69. **a.** NO CHANGE
  b. to
  c. with
  d. for

70. The author has realized that the second sentence of the third paragraph is quite long and is considering the following change: *In this dawn-like light, he appeared strong and vigorous; although he was near 60, he had so youthful an air that one might have mistaken him to be a young man with powdered hair.* The author should
  f. make the change. The current sentence is grammatically incorrect, and the changes correct that problem.
  g. make the change. The shortened sentence makes the sentence more powerful.
  h. leave the sentence as it is, except for changing *as* to *for*. The words to be deleted add descriptive power to the sentence.
  j. leave the sentence as it is. The amended version is grammatically incorrect.

71. **a.** NO CHANGE
  b. "Here."
  c. "Here",
  d. "Here".

72. **f.** NO CHANGE
  g. lay
  h. laid
  j. lain

73. **a.** NO CHANGE
  b. distinguishable, an exquisite
  c. distinguishable, it was an exquisite
  d. distinguishable; it was an exquisite

74. **f.** NO CHANGE
  g. long-black
  h. long, black
  j. long with black

75. **a.** NO CHANGE
  b. childs
  c. immature
  d. childlike

ACT Mathematics Practice Test 4

60 Questions—60 Minutes

For each problem, choose the correct answer. You are allowed to use a calculator on this test for any problems you choose. Unless the problem states otherwise, you should assume that figures are *not* drawn to scale. For this test, all geometric figures lie in a plane, the word *line* refers to a straight line, and the word *average* refers to the arithmetic mean.

1. The lowest temperature on a winter morning was –9 degrees F. The high temperature on that same day was 22 degrees F. By how many degrees did the temperature increase?
   a. –31
   b. 21
   c. 29
   d. 31
   e. 41

2. If $6(x - 7) = 66$, then $x =$
   f. 8
   g. 14
   h. 18
   j. 22
   k. 26

3. The speed of a car exceeds twice the speed of a bus by 15 mph. If the speed of the bus is expressed by B, which of the following expresses the speed of the car?
   a. $B + 15$
   b. $2B - 15$
   c. $2B + 30$
   d. $2B + 15$
   e. $2B - 30$

4. Which of the following is a factor of the polynomial $x^2 + 3x - 18$?
   f. $x - 6$
   g. $x - 12$
   h. $x - 18$
   j. $x + 3$
   k. $x + 6$

5. $|5 - 3| - |12 - 6| =$
   a. –4
   b. –2
   c. 2
   d. 4
   e. 6

6. If Steve traveled 20 miles in four hours and Dave traveled twice as far in half the time, what was Dave's average speed, in miles per hour?
   f. 5
   g. 10
   h. 20
   j. 40
   k. 80

7. Mia ran 0.60 km on Saturday, 0.75 km on Sunday, and 1.4 km on Monday. How many kilometers did she run in total?
   a. $1\frac{1}{5}$ km
   b. $1\frac{3}{4}$ km
   c. $2\frac{1}{4}$ km
   d. $2\frac{3}{4}$ km
   e. $3\frac{1}{2}$ km

8. If 10% of x is equal to 25% of y, and $y = 16$, what is the value of x?
   f. 4
   g. 6.4
   h. 24
   j. 40
   k. 64

9. A rectangular garden has a length of x feet and a width of y feet. If the length is increased by 7 feet, and the width is decreased by 8 feet, what is the new area of the garden?

  a. $(x + 7)(y + 8)$

  b. $(x - 7)(y + 8)$

  c. $(x + 8)(y + 7)$

  d. $(x - 7)(y - 8)$

  e. $(x + 7)(y - 8)$

10. In the triangle shown, what is the measure of angle z?

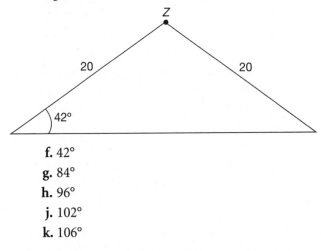

  f. $42°$

  g. $84°$

  h. $96°$

  j. $102°$

  k. $106°$

11. What number can you add to both the numerator and the denominator of $-\frac{6}{8}$ to get $\frac{2}{3}$?

  a. -4

  b. 4

  c. 12

  d. 26

  e. 34

12. What real number satisfies the equation $(3^x)(9) = 27^2$?

  f. 3

  g. 4

  h. 5

  j. 6

  k. It cannot be determined from the information provided.

13. The number p is greater than 0, a multiple of 6, and a factor of 180. How many possibilities are there for the value of p?

  a. 7

  b. 8

  c. 9

  d. 10

  e. 11

14. Lindsay grows only roses and tulips in her garden. The ratio of roses to tulips in her garden is 5:6. If there are 242 total flowers in her garden, how many of them are tulips?

  f. 22

  g. 40

  h. 110

  j. 121

  k. 132

15. A dormitory now houses 30 men and allows 42 square feet of space per man. If five more men are put into this dormitory, how much less space will each man have?

  a. 5 square feet

  b. 6 square feet

  c. 7 square feet

  d. 8 square feet

  e. 9 square feet

16. A store prices a coat at $85. During a sale, the coat is sold at 20% off. After the sale, the store raises the price of the coat 10% over its sale price. What is the price of the coat now?

  f. $18.70

  g. $61.20

  h. $68.00

  j. $74.80

  k. $93.50

17. The statement *Isabelle runs every Sunday* is always true. Which of the following statements is also true?

   a. If Isabelle does not run, then it is not Sunday.

   b. If Isabelle runs, then it is Sunday.

   c. If it is not Sunday, then Isabelle does not run.

   d. If it is Sunday, then Isabelle does not run.

   e. If it is Sunday, it is impossible to determine if Isabelle runs.

18.

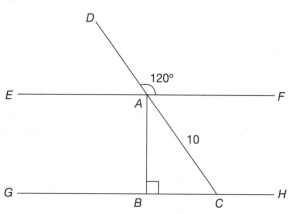

In the diagram, lines *EF* and *GH* are parallel, and line *AB* is perpendicular to lines *EF* and *GH*. What is the length of line *AB*?

   f. 5

   g. $5\sqrt{2}$

   h. $5\sqrt{3}$

   j. $10\sqrt{2}$

   k. $10\sqrt{3}$

19. How does the area of a rectangle change if both the base and the height of the original rectangle are tripled?

   a. The area is tripled.

   b. The area is six times larger.

   c. The area is nine times larger.

   d. The area remains the same.

   e. The area cannot be determined.

20.

QUANTITY	PRICE PER BALLOON
1	$1.00
10	$0.90
100	$0.75
1,000	$0.60

Balloons are sold according to the chart. If a customer buys one balloon at a time, the cost is $1.00 per balloon. If a customer buys ten balloons at a time, the cost is $0.90 per balloon. If Carlos wants to buy 2,000 balloons, how much money does he save by buying 1,000 balloons at a time rather than ten balloons at a time?

   f. $200

   g. $300

   h. $500

   j. $600

   k. $800

21. The numbers 1 through 40 are written on 40 cards, one number on each card, and stacked in a deck. The cards numbered 2, 8, 12, 16, 24, 30, and 38 are removed from the deck. If Jodi now selects a card at random from the deck, what is the probability that the card's number is both a multiple of 4 and a factor of 40?

   a. $\frac{1}{5}$

   b. $\frac{5}{33}$

   c. $\frac{1}{7}$

   d. $\frac{4}{33}$

   e. $\frac{1}{11}$

22. The function $m\#n$ is equal to $m^2 - n$. Which of the following is equivalent to $m\#(n\#m)$?

   f. $-n$

   g. $n^2 - m$

   h. $m^2 + m - n^2$

   j. $(m^2 - n)^2 - n$

   k. $(n^2 - m)^2 - m$

23. David draws a line that is 13 units long. If (−4,1) is one endpoint of the line, which of the following could be the other endpoint?

a. (1,13)

b. (9,14)

c. (3,7)

d. (3,−7)

e. (−17,−1)

24. What is the next number in the following series?

3, 16, 6, 12, 12, 8

f. 4

g. 15

h. 20

j. 24

k. 32

25. The greatest integer in a set of consecutive even integers is 22. If the sum of these integers is 102, what is the least of these integers?

a. 10

b. 12

c. 14

d. 16

e. 18

26. The area of circle A is 6.25π in.²; if the radius of the circle is doubled, what is the new area of circle A?

f. 5π in.²

g. 12.5π in.²

h. 25π in.²

j. 39.0625π in.²

k. 156.25π in.²

27. Which of the following could be the equation of the parabola shown?

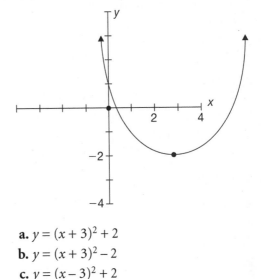

a. $y = (x + 3)^2 + 2$

b. $y = (x + 3)^2 - 2$

c. $y = (x - 3)^2 + 2$

d. $y = (x - 3)^2 - 2$

e. $y = (3x + 3)^2 - 2$

28. The equation $y = \dfrac{x + 6}{x^2 + 7x - 18}$ is undefined when $x =$

f. −9

g. −2

h. −6

j. 0

k. 9

29. If 30% of r is equal to 75% of s, what is 50% of s if r = 30?

a. 4.5

b. 6

c. 9

d. 12

e. 15

30. Line $y = \frac{2}{3}x - 5$ is perpendicular to which line?

f. $y = \frac{2}{3}x + 5$

g. $y = 5 - \frac{2}{3}x$

h. $y = -\frac{2}{3}x - 5$

j. $y = \frac{3}{2}x - 5$

k. $y = -\frac{3}{2}x + 5$

31. It takes eight people each 12 hours to clean an office. How long would it take six people to clean the office at the same rate?

   a. 9 hours

   b. 15 hours

   c. 16 hours

   d. 18 hours

   e. 24 hours

32. If the surface area of a cube is 384 cm^2, what is the volume of the cube?

   f. 64 cm^3

   g. 256 cm^3

   h. 512 cm^3

   j. 1,152 cm^3

   k. 4,096 cm^3

33. The volume of a glass of water placed in the sun decreases by 20% due to evaporation. If there are 240 mL of water in the glass now, what was the original volume of water in the glass?

   a. 192 mL

   b. 260 mL

   c. 288 mL

   d. 300 mL

   e. 360 mL

34. The figure shows two tangent circles in which the diameter of the smaller circle is equal to the radius of the larger circle. In terms of π, what is the area, in square units, of the shaded region?

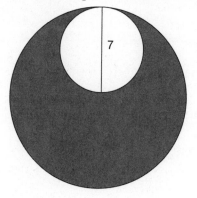

   f. 14π

   g. 22.25π

   h. 30.5π

   j. 36.75π

   k. 49π

35. For all integers x and y, let the operation $x\#y = 2xy - 4x$. If a and b are positive integers, which of the following can be equal to zero?

   I. $a\#b$

   II. $(a - b)\#b$

   III. $b\#(a - b)$

   a. I only

   b. II only

   c. III only

   d. I and II only

   e. I, II, and III

36. For the right triangle *ABC* shown, what is the value of tan *C*?

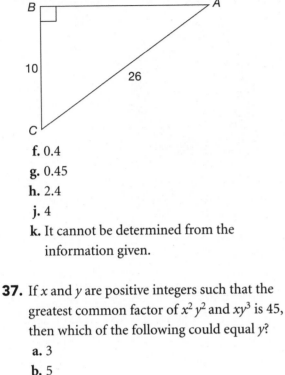

   f. 0.4

   g. 0.45

   h. 2.4

   j. 4

   k. It cannot be determined from the information given.

37. If *x* and *y* are positive integers such that the greatest common factor of $x^2 y^2$ and xy^3 is 45, then which of the following could equal *y*?

   a. 3

   b. 5

   c. 9

   d. 15

   e. 45

38. In the Smith family's household budget, 18% of the money goes toward food costs, and of that portion 25% is spent on baby food. If the Smiths spend $54 each month on baby food, what is the amount of their total budget?

   f. $216

   g. $270

   h. $1,200

   j. $1,324

   k. $2,024

39. Suppose the amount of radiation that could be received from a microwave oven varies inversely as the square of the distance from it. How many feet away must you stand to reduce your potential radiation exposure to $\frac{1}{16}$ the amount you could have received standing 1 foot away?

   a. 4

   b. 8

   c. 12

   d. 16

   e. 64

40. In the diagram shown, line *OA* is congruent to line *OB*. What is the measure of arc *CD*?

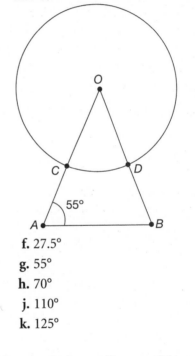

   f. 27.5°

   g. 55°

   h. 70°

   j. 110°

   k. 125°

41. What is the smallest possible positive value for *x* where $y = \sin 2x$ reaches its maximum?

   a. $\frac{\pi}{4}$

   b. $\frac{\pi}{2}$

   c. π

   d. 2π

   e. 4π

42. If $\tan A = -\frac{3}{4}$, and $90° < A° < 180°$, then $\cos A =$

  f. $-\frac{4}{5}$

  g. $-\frac{3}{5}$

  h. $\frac{3}{5}$

  j. $\frac{4}{5}$

  k. $\frac{5}{3}$

43. In the figure shown, A and B lie on circle C, which has a radius of 9. If angle ACB is 120°, what is the area of sector ACB?

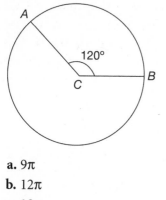

  a. 9π

  b. 12π

  c. 18π

  d. 21π

  e. 27π

44. If the function $f(x)$ is defined by $f(x) = 3(x^2 - 2)$, what is a possible value of $2x - 3$ when $f(x) = 69$?

  f. -7

  g. -5

  h. 2

  j. 5

  k. 7

45. If $w = \frac{1}{8}$, then $w^{\frac{2}{3}} =$

  a. $\frac{1}{2}$

  b. $\frac{1}{4}$

  c. $\frac{1}{8}$

  d. $\frac{1}{12}$

  e. $\frac{1}{64}$

46. The radius of the outer circle shown is 1.2 times greater than the radius of the inner circle. What is the area of the shaded region?

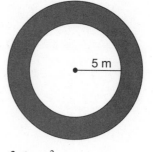

  f. 6π m^2

  g. 11π m^2

  h. 25π m^2

  j. 30π m^2

  k. 36π m^2

47. The length of the arc of a circle is equal to $\frac{1}{8}$ of the circumference of the circle. If the length of the arc is 9π inches, what is the radius, in inches, of the circle?

  a. 8

  b. 16

  c. 24

  d. 36

  e. 72

48. What are the solutions for the equation $5x^2 - 9x + 4 = 0$?

  f. $x = -\frac{4}{5}, x = 1$

  g. $x = -\frac{5}{4}, x = -1$

  h. $x = -\frac{4}{5}, x = -1$

  j. $x = \frac{4}{5}, x = 1$

  k. none of the above

49. If $\cos x = \frac{8}{9}$, what is $\sin x$?

  a. $\frac{9}{8}$

  b. $\frac{8}{5}$

  c. $\frac{\sqrt{17}}{9}$

  d. $\frac{9\sqrt{17}}{17}$

  e. It cannot be determined from the information given.

50. As shown here, a square has two diagonals and a pentagon has five diagonals. How many diagonals does the heptagon have?

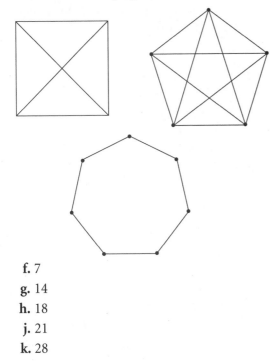

   f. 7
   g. 14
   h. 18
   j. 21
   k. 28

51. If a system of linear equations has no solutions, and the graph of one of the equations is pictured here, which of the following could be the other equation of the system?

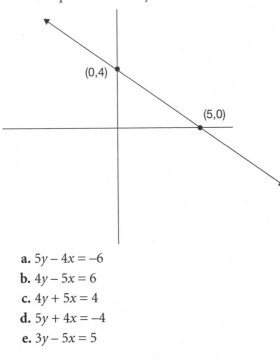

   a. $5y - 4x = -6$
   b. $4y - 5x = 6$
   c. $4y + 5x = 4$
   d. $5y + 4x = -4$
   e. $3y - 5x = 5$

52. A plane contains three distinct lines. What are the possible number of distinct regions within that plane that could be created by those three distinct lines?

   f. 3, 4, 5
   g. 3, 5, 7
   h. 4, 5, 6
   j. 4, 6, 7
   k. 5, 7, 9

53. The first term of a geometric sequence is x, and the second term of that same sequence is xy. What is the 97th term of the sequence?

   a. $(xy)^{96}$
   b. $(xy)^{97}$
   c. $x^{96}y$
   d. xy^{96}
   e. xy^{97}

54. What is the value of $\log_3 243$?

   f. 5
   g. 6
   h. 7
   j. 8
   k. 9

55. A right triangle has legs with the lengths of $2x$ inches and $5x$ inches, respectively. What is the length of the hypotenuse, in inches?

   a. $7x$
   b. $7x^2$
   c. $x\sqrt{29}$
   d. $x\sqrt{49}$
   e. $49x$

56. Greg has nine paintings. The Hickory Museum has enough space to display three of them. How many different sets of three paintings does Greg have from which to choose?

  f. 27
  g. 56
  h. 84
  j. 168
  k. 504

57. A moving company charges $50 per hour plus an additional mileage fee that varies directly with the square root of the number of miles traveled. A one-hour job that requires 25 miles of travel costs $140. What would a one-hour job that requires 36 miles of travel cost?

  a. $148
  b. $158
  c. $168
  d. $188
  e. $198

58. A line includes the point A (5,–7). If this line were to be reflected across the line $y = x$, where point A^1 is the equivalent point to point A of the original line, what would be the coordinates of A^1?

  f. (7,5)
  g. (5,7)
  h. (–5,–7)
  j. (–7,5)
  k. (–7,–5)

59. The length of an edge of a cube is equal to half the height of a cylinder that has a volume of 160π cubic units. If the radius of the cylinder is 4 units, what is the surface area of the cube?

  a. 64 square units
  b. 96 square units
  c. 100 square units
  d. 125 square units
  e. 150 square units

60. In the right triangle shown, $BC = 10$ units and $AC = 4$ units. What is the value of sin C?

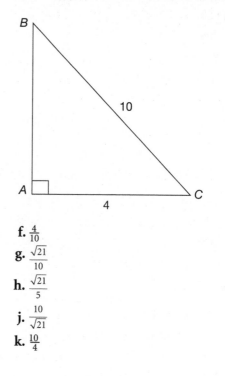

  f. $\frac{4}{10}$
  g. $\frac{\sqrt{21}}{10}$
  h. $\frac{\sqrt{21}}{5}$
  j. $\frac{10}{\sqrt{21}}$
  k. $\frac{10}{4}$

ACT Reading Practice Test 4

40 Questions—35 Minutes

In this test you will find four passages, each followed by several questions. Read each passage carefully and then select the best possible answer for each question.

Passage I—Humanities

These excerpts concern themselves with the nineteenth-century arguments made for and against women's right to vote in the United States. Excerpt 1 is from an address by Isabella Beecher Hooker before the International Council of Women in 1888. Excerpt 2 is from an 1878 report from the Senate's Committee on Privileges and Elections in response to a proposed constitutional amendment that would give women the right to vote.

Excerpt 1

1　First let me speak of the Constitution of the
2　United States, and assert that there is not a line
3　in it, nor a word, forbidding women to vote;
4　but, properly interpreted, that is, interpreted by
5　the Declaration of Independence, and by the
6　assertions of the Fathers, it actually guarantees
7　to women the right to vote in all elections, both
8　state and national. Listen to the preamble to the
9　constitution, and the preamble, you know, is
10　the key to what follows; it is the concrete, gen-
11　eral statement of the great principles which
12　subsequent articles express in detail. The pre-
13　amble says: "We the People of the United States,
14　in Order to form a more perfect Union, estab-
15　lish justice, insure domestic Tranquility, provide
16　for the common defence, promote the general
17　Welfare, and secure the Blessings of Liberty to
18　ourselves and our Posterity, do ordain and
19　establish this Constitution for the United States
20　of America."
21　　　Commit this to memory, friends; learn it
22　by heart as well as by head, and I should have

23　no need to argue the question before you of my
24　right to vote. For women are "people" surely,
25　and desire, as much as men, to say the least, to
26　establish justice and to insure domestic tran-
27　quility; and, brothers, you will never insure
28　domestic tranquility in the days to come unless
29　you allow women to vote, who pay taxes and
30　bear equally with yourselves all the burdens of
31　society; for they do not mean any longer to
32　submit patiently and quietly to such injustice,
33　and the sooner men understand this and gra-
34　ciously submit to become the political equals of
35　their mothers, wives, and daughters—aye, of
36　their grandmothers, for that is my category,
37　instead of their political masters, as they now
38　are, the sooner will this precious domestic tran-
39　quility be insured. Women are surely "people," I
40　said, and were when these words were written,
41　and were as anxious as men to establish justice
42　and promote the general welfare, and no one
43　will have the hardihood to deny that our fore-
44　mothers (have we not talked about our forefa-
45　thers alone long enough?) did their full share in
46　the work of establishing justice, providing for
47　the common defense, and promoting the gen-
48　eral welfare in all those early days.
49　　　The truth is, friends, that when liberties
50　had to be gained by the sword and protected by
51　the sword, men necessarily came to the front
52　and seemed to be the only creators and defend-
53　ers of these liberties; hence all the way down
54　women have been content to do their patriotic
55　work silently and through men, who are the
56　fighters by nature rather than themselves, until
57　the present day; but now at last, when it is
58　established that ballots instead of bullets are to
59　rule the world . . . now, it is high time that
60　women ceased to attempt to establish justice
61　and promote the general welfare, and secure the
62　blessings of liberty to themselves and their pos-
63　terity, through the votes of men.

Excerpt 2

1 This proposed amendment forbids the United
2 States or any State to deny or abridge the right
3 to vote on account of sex. If adopted, it will
4 make several millions of female voters, totally
5 inexperienced in political affairs, quite gener-
6 ally dependent upon the other sex, all incapable
7 of performing military duty and without the
8 power to enforce the laws which their numeri-
9 cal strength may enable them to make, and
10 comparatively very few of whom wish to
11 assume the irksome and responsible political
12 duties which this measure thrusts upon them.

13 An experiment so novel, a change so great,
14 should only be made slowly and in response to
15 a general public demand, of the existence of
16 which there is no evidence before your com-
17 mittee. Petitions from various parts of the
18 country, containing by estimate about 30,000
19 names, have been presented to Congress asking
20 for this legislation. They were procured through
21 the efforts of woman-suffrage societies, thor-
22 oughly organized, with active and zealous man-
23 agers. The ease with which signatures may be
24 procured to any petition is well known. The
25 small number of petitioners, when compared
26 with that of the intelligent women in the coun-
27 try, is striking evidence that there exists among
28 them no general desire to take up the heavy
29 burden of governing, which so many men seek
30 to evade. It would be unjust, unwise, and
31 impolitic to impose that burden on the great
32 mass of women throughout the country who
33 do not wish for it, to gratify the comparatively
34 few who do.

35 It has been strongly urged that without
36 the right of suffrage women are and will be
37 subjected to great oppression and injustice. But
38 everyone who has examined the subject at all
39 knows that without female suffrage, legislation
40 for years has improved and is still improving
41 the condition of women. The disabilities

42 imposed upon her by the common law have,
43 one by one, been swept away until in most of
44 the States she has the full right to her property
45 and all, or nearly all the rights which can be
46 granted without impairing or destroying the
47 marriage relation. These changes have been
48 wrought by the spirit of the age, and are not,
49 generally at least, the result of any agitation by
50 women in their own behalf.

51 Nor can women justly complain of any
52 partiality in the administration of justice. They
53 have the sympathy of judges and particularly of
54 juries to an extent which would warrant loud
55 complaint on the part of their adversaries of
56 the sterner sex. Their appeals to legislatures
57 against injustice are never unheeded, and there
58 is no doubt that when any considerable part of
59 the women of any State really wish for the right
60 to vote it will be granted without the interven-
61 tion of Congress.

62 Any State may grant the right of suffrage
63 to women. Some of them have done so to a lim-
64 ited extent, and perhaps with good results. It is
65 evident that in some States public opinion is
66 much more strongly in favor of it than it is in
67 others. Your committee regards it as unwise and
68 inexpedient to enable three-fourths in number
69 of the States, through an amendment to the
70 National Constitution, to force woman suffrage
71 upon the other fourth in which the public
72 opinion of both sexes may be strongly adverse
73 to such a change. For these reasons, your com-
74 mittee reports back said resolution with a rec-
75 ommendation that it be indefinitely postponed.

1. The author of excerpt 1 supports her argument by
   a. providing information about the educational levels achieved by women.
   b. sharing anecdotes about women who fought in the American Revolution.
   c. referring to principles already accepted by her audience.
   d. describing her personal experience as a citizen of the United States.

2. The phrase *learn it by heart as well as by head* in excerpt 1, lines 21–22 suggests
   f. an emotional and intellectual response.
   g. rote memorization.
   h. learning from experience rather than books.
   j. accepting an argument on faith.

3. Lines 53–57 of excerpt 1 portray American women as
   a. rebellious.
   b. ambitious.
   c. patriotic.
   d. uneducated.

4. Which of the following best describes the author's strategy in excerpt 2?
   f. summarizing public perceptions of the issue
   g. anticipating opposing viewpoints and then refuting them
   h. relating an incident and describing its significance
   j. persuading his audience through emotional appeal

5. As used in excerpt 2, line 13, *novel* most nearly means
   a. rare.
   b. original.
   c. untried.
   d. brilliant.

6. In the second paragraph of excerpt 2 the author characterizes the activists of the women's suffrage movement as
   f. ardent.
   g. courageous.
   h. conformist.
   j. modest.

7. The author of excerpt 2 cites the example of a woman's right to her property (lines 41–47) in order to
   a. show that women are well represented by legislation even if they cannot vote.
   b. demonstrate that if women can be responsible for property, they can be responsible voters.
   c. prove that unjust laws affect the condition of women.
   d. support the belief that political change should happen quickly.

8. Which aspect of the topic of women's voting rights is emphasized in excerpt 2, but not in excerpt 1?
   f. the interpretation of the Constitution
   g. the contributions of American women
   h. the tax-paying status of women
   j. how the judiciary treats women

9. The two authors would most likely agree with which statement?
   a. Most women do not desire the right to vote.
   b. Women are not meant to be soldiers.
   c. Voting is more of a burden than a privilege.
   d. American society is ready for female voters.

10. The approaches of the two passages to the topic differ in that only excerpt 1

    f. describes an incident from the author's personal experience.

    g. gives a point and argues its counterpoint.

    h. cites several specific examples of laws that benefit women.

    j. addresses its audience entirely in the second person.

Passage II—Prose Fiction

In excerpt 1, from Mary Shelley's Frankenstein, *Victor Frankenstein explains his motive for creating his creature. In excerpt 2, from H.G. Wells's 1896 novel* The Island of Dr. Moreau, *Dr. Moreau explains to the narrator why he has been performing experiments on animals to transform them into humans.*

Excerpt 1

1 I see by your eagerness, and the wonder and
2 hope which your eyes express, my friend, that
3 you expect to be informed of the secret with
4 which I am acquainted; that cannot be: listen
5 patiently until the end of my story, and you will
6 easily perceive why I am reserved upon that
7 subject. I will not lead you on, unguarded and
8 ardent as I then was, to your destruction and
9 infallible misery. Learn from me, if not by my
10 precepts, at least by my example, how danger-
11 ous is the acquirement of knowledge, and how
12 much happier that man is who believes his
13 native town to be the world, than he who
14 aspires to become greater than his nature
15 will allow.
16   When I found so astonishing a power
17 placed within my hand, I hesitated a long time
18 concerning the manner in which I should
19 employ it. Although I possessed the capacity of
20 bestowing animation, yet to prepare a frame for
21 the reception of it, with all its intricacies of
22 fibers, muscles, and veins, still remained a work
23 of inconceivable difficulty and labor. I doubted

24 at first whether I should attempt the creation of
25 a being like myself, or one of simpler organiza-
26 tion; but my imagination was too much exalted
27 by my first success to permit me to doubt of my
28 ability to give life to an animal as complex and
29 wonderful as man. The materials at present
30 within my command hardly appeared adequate
31 to so arduous an undertaking; but I doubted
32 not that I should ultimately succeed. I prepared
33 myself for a multitude of reverses; my opera-
34 tions might be incessantly baffled, and at last
35 my work be imperfect: yet, when I considered
36 the improvement which every day takes place in
37 science and mechanics, I was encouraged to
38 hope my present attempts would at least lay the
39 foundations of future success. Nor could I con-
40 sider the magnitude and complexity of my plan
41 as any argument of its impracticability. It was
42 with these feelings that I began the creation of
43 my human being. As the minuteness of the
44 parts formed a great hindrance to my speed, I
45 resolved, contrary to my first intention, to make
46 the being of a gigantic stature; that is to say,
47 about eight feet in height, and proportionally
48 large. After having formed this determination,
49 and having spent some months in successfully
50 collecting and arranging my materials, I began.
51   No one can conceive the variety of feelings
52 which bore me onwards, like a hurricane, in the
53 first enthusiasm of success. Life and death
54 appeared to me ideal bounds, which I should
55 first break through, and pour a torrent of light
56 into our dark world. A new species would bless
57 me as its creator and source; many happy and
58 excellent natures would owe their being to me.
59 No father could claim the gratitude of his child
60 so completely as I should deserve theirs. Pursu-
61 ing these reflections, I thought, that if I could
62 bestow animation upon lifeless matter, I might
63 in process of time (although I now found it
64 impossible) renew life where death had appar-
65 ently devoted the body to corruption.

66   These thoughts supported my spirits,
67 while I pursued my undertaking with unremit-
68 ting ardor. My cheek had grown pale with
69 study, and my person had become emaciated
70 with confinement. Sometimes, on the very
71 brink of certainty, I failed; yet still I clung to the
72 hope which the next day or the next hour
73 might realize. One secret which I alone pos-
74 sessed was the hope to which I had dedicated
75 myself; and the moon gazed on my midnight
76 labors, while, with unrelaxed and breathless
77 eagerness, I pursued nature to her hiding-
78 places. Who shall conceive the horrors of my
79 secret toil, as I dabbled among the unhallowed
80 damps of the grave, or tortured the living ani-
81 mal to animate the lifeless clay? My limbs now
82 tremble, and my eyes swim with the remem-
83 brance; but then a resistless, and almost frantic,
84 impulse urged me forward; I seemed to have
85 lost all soul or sensation but for this one
86 pursuit.

Excerpt 2

1 "Yes. These creatures you have seen are animals
2 carven and wrought into new shapes. To that—
3 to the study of the plasticity of living forms—
4 my life has been devoted. I have studied for
5 years, gaining in knowledge as I go. I see you
6 look horrified, and yet I am telling you nothing
7 new. It all lay in the surface of practical anat-
8 omy years ago, but no one had the temerity to
9 touch it. It's not simply the outward form of an
10 animal I can change. The physiology, the chem-
11 ical rhythm of the creature, may also be made
12 to undergo an enduring modification, of which
13 vaccination and other methods of inoculation
14 with living or dead matter are examples that
15 will, no doubt, be familiar to you.
16   "A similar operation is the transfusion of
17 blood, with which subject indeed I began.
18 These are all familiar cases. Less so, and proba-
19 bly far more extensive, were the operations of
20 those medieval practitioners who made dwarfs
21 and beggar cripples and show-monsters; some
22 vestiges of whose art still remain in the prelimi-
23 nary manipulation of the young mountebank
24 or contortionist. Victor Hugo gives an account
25 of them in *L'Homme qui Rit*. . . . But perhaps
26 my meaning grows plain now. You begin to see
27 that it is a possible thing to transplant tissue
28 from one part of an animal to another, or from
29 one animal to another, to alter its chemical
30 reactions and methods of growth, to modify
31 the articulations of its limbs, and indeed to
32 change it in its most intimate structure?
33   "And yet this extraordinary branch of
34 knowledge has never been sought as an end,
35 and systematically, by modern investigators,
36 until I took it up! Some such things have been
37 hit upon in the last resort of surgery; most of
38 the kindred evidence that will recur to your
39 mind has been demonstrated, as it were, by
40 accident—by tyrants, by criminals, by the
41 breeders of horses and dogs, by all kinds of
42 untrained clumsy-handed men working for
43 their own immediate ends. I was the first man
44 to take up this question armed with antiseptic
45 surgery, and with a really scientific knowledge
46 of the laws of growth.
47   "Yet one would imagine it must have been
48 practiced in secret before. Such creatures as
49 Siamese Twins. . . . And in the vaults of the
50 Inquisition. No doubt their chief aim was
51 artistic torture, but some, at least, of the
52 inquisitors must have had a touch of scientific
53 curiosity. . . ."
54   "But," said I. "These things—these ani-
55 mals *talk*!"
56   He said that was so, and proceeded to
57 point out that the possibilities of vivisection do
58 not stop at a mere physical metamorphosis. A
59 pig may be educated. The mental structure is
60 even less determinate than the bodily. In our
61 growing science of hypnotism we find the

62 promise of a possibility of replacing old inher-
63 ent instincts by new suggestions, grafting upon
64 or replacing the inherited fixed ideas. . . .
65 But I asked him why he had taken the
66 human form as a model. There seemed to me
67 then, and there still seems to me now, a strange
68 wickedness in that choice.
69 He confessed that he had chosen that
70 form by chance.
71 "I might just as well have worked to form
72 sheep into llamas, and llamas into sheep. I sup-
73 pose there is something in the human form
74 that appeals to the artistic turn of mind more
75 powerfully than any animal shape can. But I've
76 not confined myself to man-making. Once or
77 twice. . . ." He was silent, for a minute perhaps.
78 "These years! How they have slipped by! And
79 here I have wasted a day saving your life, and
80 am now wasting an hour explaining myself!"
81 "But," said I, "I still do not understand.
82 Where is your justification for inflicting all this
83 pain? The only thing that could excuse vivisec-
84 tion to me would be some application—"
85 "Precisely," said he. "But you see I am dif-
86 ferently constituted. We are on different plat-
87 forms. You are a materialist."
88 "I am *not* a materialist," I began hotly.
89 "In my view—in my view. For it is just
90 this question of pain that parts us. So long as
91 visible or audible pain turns you sick, so long as
92 your own pain drives you, so long as pain
93 underlies your propositions about sin, so long,
94 I tell you, you are an animal, thinking a little
95 less obscurely what an animal feels. This
96 pain—"
97 I gave an impatient shrug at such
98 sophistry.
99 "Oh! But it is such a little thing. A mind
100 truly open to what science has to teach must see
101 that it is a little thing."

11. In the first paragraph of excerpt 1, Frankenstein reveals that the purpose of his tale is to
a. entertain the reader.
b. explain a scientific principle.
c. teach a moral lesson.
d. share the secret of his research.

12. The word *baffled* in line 34 of excerpt 1 means
f. hindered.
g. confused.
h. puzzled.
j. eluded.

13. During the creation process, Frankenstein could best be described as
a. calm.
b. horrified.
c. evil.
d. obsessed.

14. From excerpt 2, it can be inferred that Dr. Moreau is what sort of scientist?
f. artistic
g. calculating and systematic
h. careless, haphazard
j. famous, renowned

15. *These things* that the narrator refers to in excerpt 2, line 54 are
a. Siamese twins.
b. inquisitors.
c. pigs.
d. creatures Moreau created.

16. It can be inferred from the passage that Dr. Moreau
f. does not inflict pain upon animals when he experiments on them.
g. has caused great pain to the creatures he has experimented on.
h. is unable to experience physical pain.
j. is searching for a way to eliminate physical pain.

17. Based on the information in the excerpts, Dr. Moreau is like Victor Frankenstein in that he also
   a. used dead bodies in his experiments.
   b. wanted his creations to worship him.
   c. made remarkable discoveries.
   d. kept his experiment a secret from everyone.

18. Frankenstein would be most upset by Dr. Moreau's
   f. indifference to suffering.
   g. arrogance.
   h. great achievements.
   j. education of animals.

19. As used at the end of excerpt 2, *sophistry* most closely means
   a. foolish behavior
   b. animal behavior
   c. unusual wisdom
   d. faulty reasoning

20. Which of the following best expresses Frankenstein's and Moreau's attitudes toward science?
   f. Both believe science can be dangerous.
   g. Frankenstein believes science should have a tangible application; Moreau believes scientific knowledge should be sought for its own sake.
   h. Frankenstein believes scientists should not harm living creatures in an experiment; Moreau believes it is acceptable to inflict pain on other creatures.
   j. Both men believe scientists should justify their work.

Passage III—Natural Sciences

This passage outlines the past and present use of asbestos, the potential health hazard associated with this material, and how to prevent exposure.

1   Few words in a contractor's vocabulary carry
2   more negative connotations than *asbestos*.
3   According to the Asbestos Network, "touted as
4   a miracle substance," *asbestos* is the generic
5   term for several naturally occurring mineral
6   fibers mined primarily for use as fireproof insu-
7   lation. Known for strength, flexibility, low elec-
8   trical conductivity, and resistance to heat,
9   asbestos is comprised of silicon, oxygen, hydro-
10   gen, and assorted metals. Before the public
11   knew asbestos could be harmful to one's health,
12   it was found in a variety of products to
13   strengthen them and to provide insulation and
14   fire resistance.
15   Asbestos is generally made up of fiber
16   bundles that can be broken up into long, thin
17   fibers. We now know from various studies that
18   when this friable substance is released into the
19   air and inhaled into the lungs over a period of
20   time, it can lead to a higher risk of lung cancer
21   and a condition known as *asbestosis*. Asbestosis,
22   a thickening and scarring of the lung tissue,
23   usually occurs when a person is exposed to high
24   asbestos levels over an extensive period of time.
25   Unfortunately, the symptoms do not usually
26   appear until about 20 years after initial expo-
27   sure, making it difficult to reverse or prevent. In
28   addition, smoking while exposed to asbestos
29   fibers could further increase the risk of devel-
30   oping lung cancer. When it comes to asbestos
31   exposure in the home, school, and workplace,
32   there is no safe level; any exposure is considered
33   harmful and dangerous. Prior to the 1970s
34   asbestos use was ubiquitous—many commer-
35   cial building and home insulation products
36   contained asbestos. In the home in particular,
37   there are many places where asbestos hazards

38 might be present. Building materials that may
39 contain asbestos include fireproofing material
40 (sprayed on beams), insulation material (on
41 pipes and oil and coal furnaces), and acoustical
42 or soundproofing material (sprayed onto ceil-
43 ings and walls); it is found in miscellaneous
44 materials, such as asphalt, vinyl, and cement,
45 used to make products like roofing felts, shin-
46 gles, siding, wallboard, and floor tiles.

47   We advise homeowners and concerned
48 consumers to examine material in their homes
49 if they suspect it may contain asbestos. If the
50 material is in good condition, fibers will not
51 break down and release the chemical debris
52 that may be a danger to members of the house-
53 hold. Asbestos is a powerful substance and
54 should be handled by an expert. Do not touch
55 or disturb the material—it may then become
56 damaged and release fibers. Contact local
57 health, environmental, or other appropriate
58 officials to find out proper handling and dis-
59 posal procedures, if warranted. If asbestos
60 removal or repair is needed, you should contact
61 a professional.

62   Asbestos contained in high-traffic public
63 buildings, such as schools, presents the oppor-
64 tunity for disturbance and potential exposure
65 to students and employees. To protect individu-
66 als, the Asbestos Hazard Emergency Response
67 Act (AHERA) was signed in 1986. This law
68 requires public and private nonprofit primary
69 and secondary schools to inspect their build-
70 ings for asbestos-containing building materials.
71 The Environmental Protection Agency (EPA)
72 has published regulations for schools to follow
73 in order to protect against asbestos contamina-
74 tion and provide assistance to meet the AHERA
75 requirements. These include performing an
76 original inspection and periodic reinspections
77 every three years for asbestos-containing mate-
78 rial; developing, maintaining, and updating an
79 asbestos management plan at the school;

80 providing yearly notification to parent, teacher,
81 and employee organizations regarding the
82 availability of the school's asbestos manage-
83 ment plan and any asbestos abatement actions
84 taken or planned in the school; designating a
85 contact person to ensure the responsibilities of
86 the local education agency are properly imple-
87 mented; performing periodic surveillance of
88 known or suspected asbestos-containing build-
89 ing material; and providing custodial staff with
90 asbestos awareness training.

21. In line 18 the word *friable* most nearly means
  a. able to freeze.
  b. warm or liquid.
  c. easily broken down.
  d. poisonous.

22. Which title would best describe this passage?
  f. The EPA Guide to Asbestos Protection
  g. Asbestos Protection in Public Buildings and Homes
  h. Asbestos in American Schools
  j. The AHERA—Helping Consumers Fight Asbestos-Related Disease

23. According to this passage, which statement is true?
  a. Insulation material contains asbestos fibers.
  b. Asbestos in the home should always be removed.
  c. The AHERA protects private homes against asbestos.
  d. Asbestosis usually occurs in a person exposed to high levels of asbestos.

24. As it is used in line 34, the word *ubiquitous* most nearly means
  f. sparse.
  g. universal.
  h. restricted.
  j. perilous.

25. Lung cancer and asbestosis are
   a. dangerous fibers.
   b. forms of serious lung disease.
   c. always fatal.
   d. only caused by asbestos inhalation.

26. The main purpose of this passage is to
   f. teach asbestos awareness in the home and schools.
   g. explain the specifics of the AHERA.
   h. highlight the dangers of asbestos to your health.
   j. provide a list of materials that may include asbestos.

27. The tone of this passage is best described as
   a. cautionary.
   b. apathetic.
   c. informative.
   d. admonitory.

28. For whom is the author writing this passage?
   f. professional contractors
   g. laypersons
   h. students
   j. school principals

29. As it is used in the opening of the final paragraph, *disturbance* most closely means
   a. an annoyed state.
   b. riot.
   c. being bothered by noise.
   d. fragmentation.

30. The passage mentions all of the following EPA regulations EXCEPT for
   f. inspection and reinspection.
   g. asbestos awareness training.
   h. alternatives to asbestos insulation.
   j. periodic surveillance of potential asbestos sites.

Passage IV—Social Sciences

In the following passage the author tells of public art and its functions.

1 In Manhattan's Eighth Avenue/Fourteenth
2 Street subway station, a grinning bronze alliga-
3 tor with human hands pops out of a manhole
4 cover to grab a bronze "baby" whose head is the
5 shape of a moneybag. In the Bronx General
6 Post Office, a giant 13-panel painting called
7 *Resources of America* celebrates the hard work
8 and industrialism of the country in the first
9 half of the twentieth century. And in Brooklyn's
10 MetroTech Center just over the Brooklyn
11 Bridge, several installations of art are on view at
12 any given time—such as an iron lasso resem-
13 bling a giant charm bracelet, a series of wagons
14 that play recordings of great American poems,
15 and a life-sized seeing-eye dog that looks so real
16 people are constantly stopping to pet it.
17 　　There exists in every city a symbiotic rela-
18 tionship between the city and its art. When we
19 hear the term *art*, we tend to think of private
20 art—the kind displayed in private spaces such
21 as museums, concert halls, and galleries. But
22 there is a growing interest in, and respect for,
23 public art: the kind of art created for and dis-
24 played in public spaces such as parks, building
25 lobbies, and sidewalks.
26 　　Although all art is inherently public—
27 created in order to convey an idea or emotion
28 to others—public art, as opposed to art that is
29 sequestered in museums and galleries, is art
30 specifically designed for a public arena where
31 the art will be encountered by people in their
32 normal day-to-day activities. Public art can be
33 purely ornamental or highly functional; it can
34 be as subtle as a decorative doorknob or as con-
35 spicuous as the Chicago Picasso. It is also an
36 essential element of effective urban design.
37 　　The more obvious forms of public art
38 include monuments, sculptures, fountains,

39 murals, and gardens. But public art also takes
40 the form of ornamental benches or streetlights,
41 decorative manhole covers, and mosaics on
42 trash bins. Many city dwellers would be sur-
43 prised to discover just how much public art is
44 really around them and how much art they
45 have passed by without noticing, as well as
46 how much impact public art has on their day-
47 to-day lives.

48   Public art fulfills several functions essen-
49 tial to the health of a city and its citizens. It
50 educates about history and culture—of the art-
51 ist, the neighborhood, the city, and the nation.
52 Public art is also a place-making device that
53 instantly creates memorable, experiential land-
54 marks, fashioning a unique identity for a public
55 place, personalizing it and giving it a specific
56 character. It stimulates the public, challenging
57 viewers to interpret the art and arousing their
58 emotions, and it promotes community by stim-
59 ulating interaction among viewers. In serving
60 these multiple and important functions, public
61 art beautifies the area and regenerates both the
62 place and the viewer.

63   One question often debated in public art
64 forums is whether public art should be created
65 *with* or *by* the public rather than *for* the public.
66 Increasingly, cities and artists are recognizing
67 the importance of creating works with meaning
68 for the intended audience, and this generally
69 requires direct input from the community or
70 from an artist entrenched in that community.
71 At the same time, however, art created for the
72 community by an outsider often adds fresh per-
73 spective. Thus, cities and their citizens are best
74 served by a combination of public art created
75 *by* members of the community, art created with
76 input *from* members of the community, and art
77 created by others *for* the community.

31. The primary purpose of the opening paragraph is to
   a. define public art.
   b. introduce readers to the idea of public art.
   c. show the prevalence and diversity of public art.
   d. get readers to pay more attention to public art.

32. The word *inherently* in line 26 most nearly means
   f. essentially.
   g. complicated.
   h. wealthy.
   j. snobby.

33. According to the first sentence of paragraph 2, public art is differentiated from private art mainly by
   a. the kind of ideas or emotions it aims to convey to its audience.
   b. its accessibility.
   c. its perceived value.
   d. its importance to the city.

34. The use of the word *sequestered* in line 29 suggests that the author feels
   f. private art is better than public art.
   g. private art is too isolated from the public.
   h. the admission fees for public art arenas prevent many people from experiencing the art.
   j. private art is more difficult to understand than public art.

35. According to the next to last paragraph, public art serves all of the following functions EXCEPT
   a. beautification.
   b. creation of landmarks.
   c. the fostering of community.
   d. the promotion of good citizenship.

36. Which sentence best sums up the main idea of the passage?

   f. Public art serves several important functions in the city.

   g. Public art is often in direct competition with private art.

   h. Public art should be created both by and for members of the community.

   j. In general, public art is more interesting than private art.

37. The author's goals in this passage include all of the following EXCEPT

   a. to make readers more aware of the public artworks.

   b. to explain the difference between public art and private art.

   c. to explain how public art impacts the city.

   d. to inspire readers to become public artists.

38. Which of the following does the author NOT provide in this passage?

   f. a reason why outsiders should create public art

   g. specific examples of urban art

   h. an explanation of how the city affects art

   j. a clear distinction between public and private art

39. Given the author's main purpose, which of the following would most strengthen the passage?

   a. a more detailed discussion of the differences between public and private art

   b. specific examples of art that fulfill each of the functions discussed in paragraph 5

   c. interviews with public artists about how public art should be created

   d. a specific example of public art created by a community member versus one created by an outsider to expand the final paragraph

40. The most fitting title for this passage would be

   f. Public Art and the City: A Symbiotic Relationship

   g. Public Art: The Growth of an Art Form

   h. What Is Public Art?

   j. Where to Find Public Art

ACT Science Practice Test 4

40 Questions—35 Minutes

The passages in this test are followed by several questions. After reading each passage, choose the best answer to each question. You may refer back to the passages as often as necessary. You are *not* permitted to use a calculator on this test.

Passage I—Conflicting Viewpoints

For hundreds of years, it has been known that volcanic rock is often magnetized with the same polarity found in a north-pointing compass. Accidental observation confirmed by careful experimentation has proven that many minerals or mineral-containing substances such as clay will become similarly magnetized when heated.

By the early nineteenth century, it was recognized that many volcanic rocks were magnetized with a polarity the reverse of that produced by the earth's magnetic field, which is called the geomagnetic field, and that others had polarities that diverged from normal, but were not entirely reversed.

In the 1950s and 1960s, extensive mapping of the ocean floor was undertaken using technologies developed during World War II. It was discovered that the ocean floor was magnetically striped. There were clearly measurable strips of reverse polarity in between larger strips of normal polarity.

Scientists 1 and 2 accept this general understanding of the situation, but they disagree on the cause of reversed polarity in some mineral specimens.

Scientist 1

The phenomenon of reversed polarity is too widespread to be accounted for by local peculiarities. The same phenomenon exists at many volcanic sites on land and also in widespread areas of the sea floor. Some scientists point to self-reversal of polarity, but this occurs only in limited types of rock specimens, while the reverse polarity phenomenon exists in minerals that have never been observed to self-reverse.

The magnetic stripes on the seabed occur because molten lava seeps up through large seams in the underwater crust and hardens with the polarity induced by the existing magnetic field, just as volcanic rock on dry land does. There are deep trenches on the seafloor into which seabed material sinks after spreading out from the ocean ridges, so that crust material is constantly recycled without an overall expansion of the earth's crust.

The only thing that can account for the widespread reversal in polarity is a history of reversals in the entire geomagnetic field.

Scientist 2

There is not adequate evidence to explain the phenomenon of magnetic reversal in some mineral specimens, but there is nothing unexpected in it. Volcanic rock in any given location is magnetized by the local, not the global, magnetic environment. Local magnetic fields often differ from the direction of the geomagnetic field. It is also proven that some mineral compositions undergo what is called self-reversal. They reorganize their own magnetic polarity under certain heat and other conditions. If there were a geomagnetic reversal for every magnetic stripe on the seafloor, there would have to have been hundreds, perhaps thousands, of total reversals of the planet's magnetic field in the course of its 4.5-billion-year history. Yet there is no evidence of the catastrophic disruption of all systems on the earth that would occur if the magnetic poles were reversed.

Magnetic striping on the ocean floor may be explained by ocean currents, geophysical strains on the earth's mantle beneath the crust, or other factors that must be determined. The idea that lava is constantly seeping up and spreading out over the ocean floor is absurd. If that were the case, the oceans would quickly fill up with rock and the earth would be constantly expanding and becoming hollow inside.

1. Which of these statements do Scientists 1 and 2 agree on?
   a. Molten or heated minerals are often magnetized by the magnetic field they are heated in.
   b. The earth's magnetic field periodically reverses itself.
   c. What appears to be a single geomagnetic field is actually an accumulation of magnetic fields in each locality on the planet.
   d. There is no relationship between what happens to minerals in volcanoes and what happens beneath the sea.

2. What is the major disagreement on geomagnetic reversal between Scientist 1 and Scientist 2?

  f. Scientist 1 believes that most differences in mineral polarity are caused by radical changes in the geomagnetic field. Scientist 2 believes that all minerals are magnetized with the same polarity, but that local conditions or the internal composition of minerals sometimes cause them to reverse their polarity.

  g. Scientist 1 believes that the geomagnetic field remains virtually constant. Scientist 2 believes that minerals' polarity is fixed by local conditions, which may or may not accord with the geomagnetic field.

  h. Scientist 1 believes that the geomagnetic field accounts for almost all magnetization of minerals, but that the geomagnetic field periodically changes polarity. Scientist 2 believes that the geomagnetic field has consistently had the same polarity and that local differences in the polarity of magnetized minerals are explained by local conditions.

  j. Scientist 1 believes that the geomagnetic field reorganizes the structure of hot and molten rock regardless of its orientation. Scientist 2 believes that volcanoes eject minerals in all directions, so there is no reason to believe they will be magnetized in the same direction.

3. Which of these statements would both Scientist 1 and Scientist 2 disagree with?

  a. The geomagnetic field is highly variable.

  b. There is a definite pattern to changes in the magnetic polarity on the seafloor.

  c. Heated minerals become magnetized by their magnetic environment.

  d. The geomagnetic field is uniform throughout the entire planet.

4. Improved techniques for determining the age of rock specimens demonstrate that the anomalies in polarity are consistent among specimens produced at the same time from many sites on land and beneath the sea in minerals formed anywhere from several hundreds of thousands of years to hundreds of millions of years ago. Which answer is the best statement of the impact of this new evidence on the controversy?

  f. This makes the case for Scientist 1's views on periodic geomagnetic reversal. Neither self-reversal nor any local magnetic conditions can explain polarity being reversed in almost all minerals created anywhere on the planet at a given time.

  g. This is not conclusive. There is still only a limited sampling of minerals available, and there may be some reason why the samples available for study share this characteristic.

  h. The process of mineral formation beneath the sea differs from volcanic formation on the surface. Therefore, no conclusion can be reached simply because the results beneath the sea agree with those on land.

  j. There are astronomic and other events that affect the entire planet at once. Geomagnetic reversal is not the only possible explanation for this.

5. A theory was advanced in the early twentieth century that the continents were slowly but constantly moving farther apart from each other without changing the overall size of the earth. This had been generally rejected as being based on only circumstantial evidence without any explanation of how continents could successfully slide over the ocean floor. In what way might acceptance of Scientist 1's views change the view of the theory of continental drift?

   a. If the ocean floor is spreading out from undersea ridges, the continents can be moving apart by moving with the ocean floor.

   b. If large sections of the earth's crust are moving in relation to each other, this might explain other phenomena, such as why earthquakes and volcanoes seem to occur mainly along certain established lines.

   c. The theory does explain a number of interesting things, such as why the continents seem to be shaped as if they would fit together, and how various plant and animal species developed at the same time on what are now widely separated continents.

   d. All of the above are reasonable.

6. How might Scientist 1 reasonably answer Scientist 2's objection that geomagnetic reversal would have a catastrophic effect on the earth?

   f. In fact, the earth has had a series of calamities: floods, snowball Earth, mass extinction of species, and so on, which may be explained by geomagnetic reversal.

   g. It's not clear what the overall impact of geomagnetic reversal would be, other than changing the polarity of rocks created under its influence. Most substances, biological or not, experience the intensity of a magnetic field, not its polarity. This is an issue requiring further investigation.

   h. The geomagnetic reversal affects only small portions of the earth at any given time.

   j. Since geomagnetic reversals have occurred without these calamities, we know they are not a concern.

7. The oceans have been with us since before the dawn of humans. Why was magnetic striping of the sea floor not recognized until the 1950s?

   a. This did not become an interesting question until the process of geomagnetic reversal was understood.

   b. The submarine was invented during World War II and not available for scientific use until the 1950s.

   c. Magnetic polarity is much more difficult to measure than its intensity.

   d. Technologies for measuring magnetism on the sea floor became available after World War II and were used for this purpose beginning in the 1950s.

Passage II—Research Summary

Living cells consist of various structures in the cytoplasm fluid that protects and nourishes them, surrounded by a permeable membrane. The cells are usually immersed in some kind of fluid. Single-celled plants and animals are surrounded by seawater or freshwater. Other cells are immersed in a fluid delivered to them by the organisms of which they are part. The regulation of the movement of materials between the cytoplasm and the fluid outside the cell is an important factor in the health and well-being of the cell. This transport of materials is divided into passive and active transport processes. The former are processes that cells share with nonliving fluids and membranes. The active processes are processes in which the living activity of the cell selects materials to be moved into or out of the cell.

Osmosis is the tendency of fluids to equalize their concentration across a permeable membrane. This passive transport process is one of the most important features of cell life. High-concentration solutions extract water from low-concentration solutions until they are equalized. If the fluid surrounding the cell has a higher concentration than the cytoplasm, it is hypertonic. If it has a lower concentration, it is hypotonic. If it has an equal concentration, it is isotonic. Larger differences in concentration between the fluids on either side of a membrane will cause larger osmotic pressure and faster rates of transport across the membrane. Plasmolysis is the process of extracting fluid from a cell. Deplasmolysis is the process of replenishing the fluid in a cell.

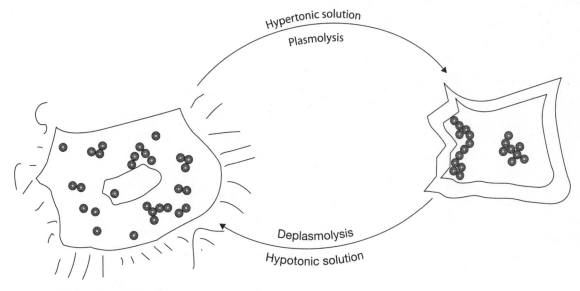

Healthy green plant cell

Figure 1

Figure 1 illustrates what happens when a cell is treated first by a hypertonic solution and then by a hypotonic solution.

Experiment 1

Test various plant cell preparations. For each preparation, transfer plant cell material to three different microscopic slides. Treat each slide with solutions of 1%, 2%, and 5% NaCl (sodium chloride).

Observe them over a 10-minute period.

Experiment 2

First, bathe a batch of plant cells having a 20% internal sucrose solution in a solution of 40% sucrose. Sucrose cannot pass through the cell membrane, but water can. After observing the result under a microscope, gently rinse the sucrose solution from the cells with distilled water. Prepare slides and observe the samples in a distilled water bath for 20 minutes.

8. What would you expect to observe in experiment 1 if the original plant cells had a 1.5% NaCl concentration?

   f. Plasmolysis in all cases. It will be quickest in the 1%, slower in the 5%, and slowest in the 2% solution.

   g. Plasmolysis in all cases. It will be faster in higher-concentration and slower in lower-concentration solutions.

   h. Deplasmolysis in the 1% solution, modest plasmolysis in the 2% solution, and rapid plasmolysis in the 5% solution.

   j. Plasmolysis in the 1% solution, modest deplasmolysis in the 2% solution, and rapid deplasmolysis in the 5% solution.

9. If the cytoplasm of the plant cell tested in experiment 1 has a 3% NaCl concentration, what would be the proper term for describing the 1%, the 2%, and the 5% test solutions?

   a. deplasmolytic, deplasmolytic, and plasmolytic

   b. hyperosmotic, hyperosmotic, and hypo-osmotic

   c. hypertonic, hypertonic, and hypotonic

   d. hypotonic, hypotonic, and hypertonic

10. If a group of plant cells were tested using a series of test solutions with the resulting plasmolysis (P) or deplasmolysis (D) as indicated, what would be the concentration of the solution in the cell's cytoplasm?

NaCl	1.0%	1.5%	2.0%	2.5%	3.0%
Result	D	D	P	P	P

   f. 1.8%

   g. 1.5%

   h. 2.0%

   j. 1.0%

11. What is the best description for the expected state of the plant cells after the first phase of experiment 2?

   a. isotonic

   b. deplasmolytic

   c. plasmolytic

   d. hypertonic

12. Which answer best describes what would be expected to occur at the beginning of the observation period of experiment 2?

   f. osmosis

   g. deplasmolysis

   h. plasmolysis

   j. isotonicism

13. What is the most reasonable prognosis for the cells in experiment 2?

   a. Deplasmolysis will continue until the mixture becomes isotonic.

   b. Plasmolysis will continue until the cells are completely shriveled.

   c. Deplasmoysis will continue until the cells burst from the pressure of the internal fluid.

   d. Deplasmolysis will continue until the osmotic pressure increases sufficiently to force a change back to plasmolysis.

Passage III—Research Summary

Coulomb's law on the strength of the electrostatic force between two objects is one of the many "inverse square" laws encountered in the study of physics. Its formula is:

$$F = \frac{k \times Q_1 \times Q_2}{d^2}$$

The force between the two objects equals a constant (k), which depends on the medium in which the charged objects are located, multiplied by the force on each object (Q_1 and Q_2), divided by the square of the distance (d) between them. The charge on either object can be positive or negative. If both charges have the same sign, their product and the calculated force (F) will be positive, which means the forces will repel the objects. If the charges have different signs, F will be negative, meaning the objects will be attracted to each other. Charged objects can be treated as if the entire charge were located at the center of charge of the object. For a spherical object, this would be the center of the sphere.

Figure 1 illustrates an apparatus that is used to demonstrate Coulomb's law. It consists of a 1-meter-high frame in the shape of a triangular prism. Two identical spheres are used. Sphere A is suspended from two equal-length dielectric (nonconducting) cords from the top ends of two of the vertical struts of the frame. Sphere B is attached to a dielectric rod that can be slid up and down the third strut and clamped into position at any height. The clamp's length is such that sphere B will be located directly above or below sphere A. The effect is that sphere B can slide toward sphere A from either above or below, and its distance above or below sphere A can always be measured. In order to avoid accidental charge or discharge of the two spheres, the entire frame, including the base it rests on, is dielectric.

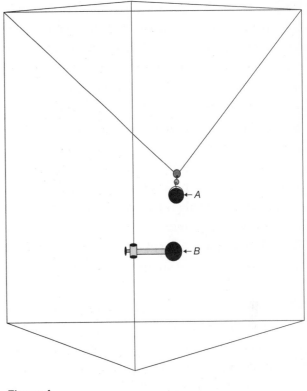

Figure 1

Experiment 1

Spheres A and B each have a mass of 1 gram. Sphere B is positioned well below sphere A, near the base of the apparatus. Both spheres are positively charged with 1 unit of charge. Sphere B is then carefully moved up toward sphere A. When sphere B reaches a distance of 10 cm from sphere A, sphere A moves.

Experiment 2

Sphere B is positioned above sphere A near the top of the apparatus. Both spheres are negatively charged with 1 unit of charge. Sphere B is moved toward Sphere A.

14. Look at the explanation of Coulomb's law and the description of experiment 1. What is the best description of why sphere A moves?

   f. The charge on sphere B pulls it down.

   g. The repulsive force between the two spheres becomes strong enough at a distance of 10 cm to overcome the force of gravity holding sphere A in place.

   h. At 10 cm, the charged spheres are close enough so that a spark is generated between them. The thermal force of the spark causes sphere A to jump.

   j. The strings prevent sphere A from moving downward, so it moves sideways.

15. Experiment 1 is repeated with each sphere negatively charged to 2 units. According to Coulomb's law, at what distance from sphere B will sphere A move?

   a. −40 cm

   b. 20 cm

   c. 40 cm

   d. 200 cm

16. Repeat experiment 1 once more with a positive charge of 1 on sphere A and a negative charge of 2 on sphere B. At what distance from sphere B will sphere A move?

   f. when sphere B touches it

   g. 10 cm

   h. $10 \times 2^{\frac{1}{2}}$ cm

   j. 20 cm

17. Consider experiment 2 based on the result reported for experiment 1. At what distance from sphere B will sphere A move in experiment 2?

   a. 10 cm

   b. never

   c. 20 cm

   d. $10 \times 3^{\frac{1}{2}}$ cm

18. Repeat experiment 2 with sphere A having a negative charge of 1 unit and sphere B having a positive charge of the same magnitude. At what distance from sphere B will sphere A move?

   f. 10 cm

   g. never

   h. 20 cm

   j. 0.1 cm

19. Repeat experiment 2 with a negative charge of 2 on sphere A and a positive charge of 3 on sphere B. At what distance from sphere B will sphere A move?

   a. 10 cm

   b. 6 cm

   c. 8 cm

   d. $10 \times 6^{\frac{1}{2}}$ cm

Passage IV—Research Summary

An earthquake is triggered by a violent disruption in the earth's crust or upper mantle, which may occur anywhere from the earth's surface to a depth of 700 km in the earth's mantle. Figure 1 illustrates the main structures of the earth. The thickness of the crust would be seen only as a boundary line at the scale of this drawing. It is approximately 10 km thick under the ocean floor and 20 km thick under the land surface.

Shock waves radiate outward in all directions from the point of origin (the epicenter) of an earthquake. Primary (P) and secondary (S) body waves travel through the earth. Surface waves, called Love or Rayleigh waves after the scientists who identified them, travel on the surface of the earth. The body waves move the fastest, but the surface waves cause the most damage because they strike where we live. P, S, Love, and Rayleigh waves emanating from an earthquake epicenter about 300 km below the surface are illustrated in Figure 1.

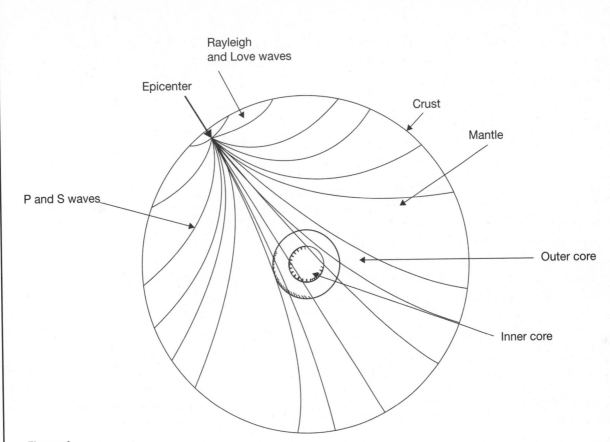

Figure 1

The velocities and frequencies of these waves vary with distance from the epicenter and with the composition of the material they are traveling through.

Our modern network of seismographs is used to track and forecast the course of an earthquake. One early warning calculation is based on the rule of thumb that in the range of 50 to 500 km from the epicenter, P waves travel at approximately 8 km/s and S waves at approximately 4 km/s.

Knowing this, we know the following:

$$T_S \approx \frac{D}{4 \text{ km/s}}$$

$$T_P \approx \frac{D}{8 \text{ km/s}}$$

$$T_S - T_P \approx \frac{D}{4 \text{ km/s}} - \frac{D}{8 \text{ km/s}}$$

$$T_S - T_P \approx \frac{D}{8 \text{ km/s}}$$

$$D \approx (T_S - T_P) \times 8 \text{ km/s}$$

T_P is the time it takes the P wave to travel from the epicenter to the recording station, and T_S is the time it takes the S wave. D is the distance to the epicenter.

Study 1

Seismographic stations A, B, and C are positioned as in Figure 2. S and P waves were recorded at each of the stations as indicated in Table 1. Using the preceding formula, the distance to the epicenter from each station is calculated, and a circle is drawn to scale at the appropriate distance to the epicenter from each station.

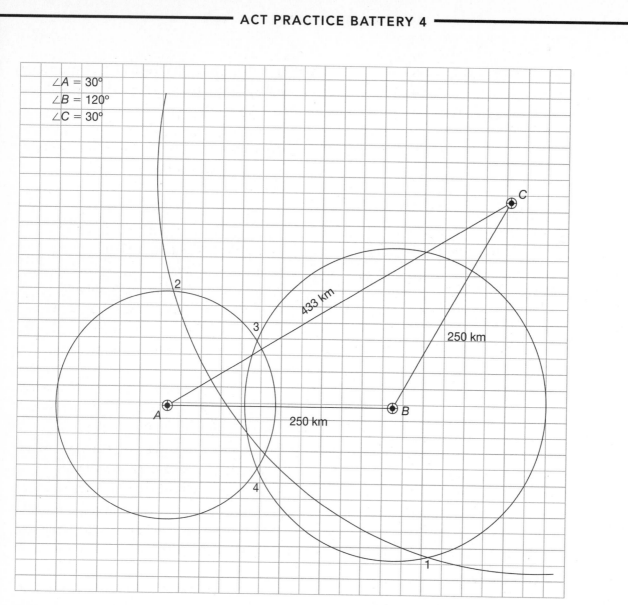

∠A = 30°
∠B = 120°
∠C = 30°

Figure 2

TABLE 1			
STATION	P WAVE	S WAVE	DIFFERENCE (SECONDS)
A	05:33:10	05:33:25	15
B	05:33:15	05:33:35	20
C	05:33:43	05:34:31	48

Study 2

On the following day, the same three stations report new evidence of earthquake shocks. The times of P and S wave arrival are reported in Table 2.

TABLE 2			
STATION	P WAVE	S WAVE	DIFFERENCE (SECONDS)
A	15:33:10	15:33:20	10
B	15:33:15	15:33:30	15
C	15:33:10	15:34:30	80

20. Look at Table 1. According to the formula described in the passage, what is the distance from station A to the epicenter?

  f. 160 km

  g. 120 km

  h. 384 km

  j. 280 km

21. Look at Figure 2. Which of the numbered points is closest to the earthquake's epicenter?

  a. 1

  b. 2

  c. 3

  d. 4

22. Look at Table 1 and the explanation in the passage regarding the speed at which P and S waves travel. At what time did the earthquake begin?

  f. 05:32:55

  g. 05:33:10

  h. 05:33:15

  j. 05:33:43

23. Look at Table 2, which is based on reports that came in the day following those analyzed in study 1. Based on the explanation in the passage of how to approximate the distance from readings of P and S waves to the epicenter of an earthquake, how far is the epicenter from station A?

  a. 120 km

  b. 160 km

  c. 80 km

  d. 360 km

24. Look at Table 2 again. Based on the explanation in the passage of how to approximate the distance from readings of P and S waves to the epicenter of an earthquake, provide a complete explanation for why these readings should be considered reliable or suspect reports of a single shock.

  f. There is no reason to question them. All of the time intervals given are correctly computed from the arrival times of the P and S waves given.

  g. The reported times are off. Station C reported the P wave at the same time as station A, but the difference between the P and S wave times was 8 times as great at station C.

  h. The reports cannot be accurate. The distance of the epicenter from station C would have to be at least 500 to 600 km. That would be on a circle outside the circles determined for both station A and station B. No single epicenter could be determined from this report.

  j. Answer choices **g** and **h** are both reasons to reassess this report.

25. Look at Table 2 again. Based on the explanation in the passage of how to approximate the distance from readings of P and S waves to the epicenter of an earthquake, how far is the epicenter from station B?

  a. greater than 640 km

  b. less than 640 km

  c. 640 km

  d. There is not enough information given to make a reliable estimate.

Passage V—Data Representation

One widely accepted definition of acids and bases is that acids are compounds that can give up a proton (hydrogen ion, chemical symbol H), and bases are compounds that can receive one. Acids and bases occur in conjugate pairs consisting of an acid and the base formed when it loses its proton. When the reaction is reversed, the base of the pair adds a proton to form the acid once more.

Table 1 shows some of the more common acid-base conjugate pairs and the reactions between them.

TABLE 1				
Compound A	+ Compound B	⟷	Compound C	+ Compound D
H_2SO_4	H_2O	⟷	HSO_4	H_3O
Cl	NH_4	⟷	HCl	NH_3
NH_3	H_2O	⟷	NH_4	OH
Cl	H_2O	⟷	HCl	OH

26. List the conjugate pairs in acid/base order in the first line of Table 1.
    f. H_2SO_4/HSO_4 and H_2O/H_3O
    g. H_2SO_4/H_2O and H_3O/HSO_4
    h. H_2SO_4/HSO_4 and H_3O/H_2O
    j. HSO_4/H_2SO_4 and H_3O/H_2O

27. Look at the third line of Table 1. If compounds A and C were reversed and compound B was not changed, what would be the resulting conjugate pairs, in acid/base order? Assume that if the number of atoms of each element in compounds A and B equals the number in compounds C and D, and if the resulting compounds appear somewhere in Table 1, that the reactions are possible.
    a. NH_4/NH_3 and H_3O/H_2O
    b. NH_4/NH_3 and H_2O/OH
    c. NH_3/H_2O and NH_4/OH
    d. NH_4/NH_3 and H_2O/H_3O

28. Examine every reaction in Table 1 and list all of the acids shown there.
    f. H_2SO_4, H_3O, NH_4, HCl
    g. H_2SO_4, H_2O, H_3O, NH_4, HCl
    h. H_2SO_4, H_3O, HCl
    j. H_2SO_4, HCl

29. List all of the bases shown in Table 1.
    a. HSO_4, H_3O, NH_3, OH
    b. HSO_4, Cl, NH_3, OH
    c. Cl, NH_3
    d. H_2O, HSO_4, Cl, NH_3, OH

30. Based on the definition of acids and bases given and an examination of Table 1, which of the following statements best characterizes this definition?

    f. It clearly distinguishes acids from bases by the nature of the ionic bonding in the compounds.

    g. Some compounds change their charge from negative to positive and can be either acids or bases.

    h. The definition is based on the way each compound functions in specific chemical reactions.

    j. It is overly dependent on the role of hydrogen.

Passage VI—Data Representation

Conditions on Earth are very much affected by the interaction between the earth's magnetic field, the sun's magnetic field, and the solar wind consisting of hot ionized plasmas constantly streaming around and through the earth's magnetic field and atmosphere. The solar wind includes storms, such as coronal mass ejections (CMEs) associated with sunspots and solar flares. Often, the earth's magnetic field is described as a dipole magnet, but there are significant differences other than its size and nearly spherical shape that distinguish the earth's so-called magnet from the ones we are familiar with handling.

    Figure 1 illustrates the magnetic field lines surrounding a typical oblong dipole magnet. Figure 2 illustrates the earth's magnetosphere in relation to the solar magnetic field and the solar wind.

    Every 11 years, the sun goes through a cycle of increasing activity and then decreasing activity, reversing magnetic polarity at the low-activity point, and then increasing activity with reversed polarity. Periods of high activity include greater density of CMEs. Figure 3 illustrates this cycle. When the curve is positive, the sun's polarity is aligned with the earth's; when the curve is negative, its polarity is opposed to the earth's.

Typical dipole magnetic field

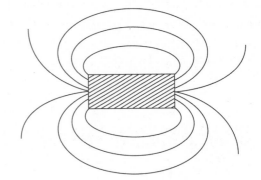

Figure 1

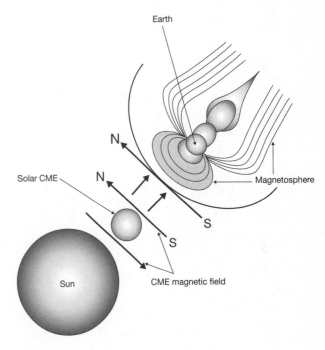

Figure 2

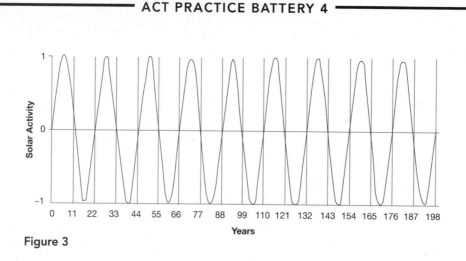

Figure 3

31. Look at Figure 1 and Figure 2. What best describes the difference in shape between the earth's magnetosphere and a typical dipole magnetic field?

  a. The earth's magnetosphere is extended horizontally more than vertically.

  b. The earth's magnetic field is much larger in comparison to the size of the earth than the dipole's is in comparison to the size of the magnet.

  c. The dipole's field is nearly symmetrical, but the earth's magnetosphere is compressed on the side closest to the sun and extended out into a long tail on the side opposite the sun.

  d. The earth's magnetic field is much stronger than the dipole's.

32. Figure 2 shows the magnetic fields of the earth, the sun, and a CME. The CMEs carry highly active ionized plasmas to the earth. The CME in Figure 2 illustrates how most CME magnetic fields orient in relation to the sun's magnetic field. At their closest points to the earth, are the solar and CME fields in Figure 2 aligned with or opposite to the earth's?

  f. They are both aligned with the earth's.

  g. They are both opposed to the earth's.

  h. The sun's is aligned with the earth's, and the CME's is opposed.

  j. The sun's is opposed to the earth's, but the CME's is aligned with it.

33. Look at Figure 3 in conjunction with Figure 2 and the description of solar cycles in the passage. If the solar cycle is approaching the 11-year mark, what is about to happen?

  a. Solar activity is increasing from its midpoint to its maximum.

  b. Solar activity is decreasing to its lowest point when the magnetic polarity of the sun will be reversed and the activity level will increase with polarity opposing the earth's.

  c. The magnetic field of the sun is rotating past the point closest to the earth.

  d. The activity level of the sun is passing from positive to negative.

34. When CME magnetic fields are aligned with the earth's, up to 20 times as many plasma ions will infiltrate the earth's magnetosphere as when the fields are opposed. As the sun's activity level is reduced and it switches from the field orientation shown in Figure 2, what can be expected?

  f. increased plasma infiltration until the low activity point is reached, then a decrease

  g. decreased plasma infiltration until the low point, then an increase to a much higher point than that reached in the last cycle

  h. decreased plasma infiltration until the cycle changes, then an increase to a lower level than the last cycle

  j. a continuous increase to the high point of the next cycle

35. The mysterious aurora borealis (northern lights), radio interference, and other electromagnetic disturbances are all phenomena associated with increased electrical activity in the magnetosphere. Ionized plasmas are much better conductors of electricity than are electrically neutral gases. Considering what has been reported in the passage about the relationship between the earth's and the sun's magnetic orientation and conditions in the earth's magnetosphere, what can be expected when the solar magnetic field points south?

    a. more spectacular aurora displays and other interference with normal electromagnetic patterns

    b. a reduced incidence of aurora displays and fewer electrical disturbances

    c. higher cancer rates

    d. a and **c**

Passage VII—Data Representation

Distilled water is a very poor conductor of electricity. However, the usual mineral and gaseous additions to water turn it into a very good conductor. An aqueous solution of electrically charged ions makes an excellent conductor. Salts, acids, and bases separate into ions when dissolved in water and are called electrolytes because they so effectively turn water into a conductor.

$$'\Omega = \frac{V}{A} \left(\text{Resistance in ohms} = \frac{\text{Electrical potential in volts}}{\text{Current flow in amperes}}\right)$$

$$S = \frac{A}{V} = \frac{1}{\Omega} = '\Omega^{-1} \ (\text{Conductivity in siemens} = \text{Inverse of resistance in ohms})$$

The conductivity of a particular electrolytic cell (see Figure 1) is called its specific conductivity. It is based on the conductivity of the electrolytic solution, the effective contact area of the electrodes, and the distance between the electrodes.

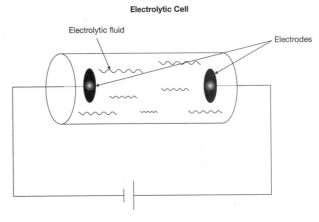

Electrolytic Cell

Electrolytic fluid

Electrodes

Figure 1

These elements are determined as follows:

The specific conductivity of the cell, mS, equals the conductivity of the solution, k, multiplied by the area of the electrodes and divided by the distance between the electrodes.

$$\textit{Formula 1: } \frac{Sm^2}{m} \text{ (or } mS) = k\left(\frac{A}{1}\right)$$

The conductivity of an electrolytic solution is proportional to the molar conductivity of the electrolyte, Λ_m, multiplied by the molar concentration, c. The molar conductivity is a measure of how much conductivity is added by each mole/liter concentration of the electrolyte in an aqueous solution:

$$\textit{Formula 2: } \Lambda_m = \frac{k}{c} \text{ or } k = \Lambda_m c$$

where c is the molar concentration of the electrolyte.

    Higher concentrations of electrolyte increase the specific conductivity. The last thing to know is that molar conductivity is not the same at all levels of concentration. Lower levels of concentration have higher molar conductivity according to this formula:

$$\textit{Formula 3: } \Lambda_m = \Lambda_m^0 - Kc^{\frac{1}{2}}$$

K is a constant specific to each electrolyte, and Λ_m^0 is the Λ_m at nearly zero concentration. This is the highest molar conductivity that that electrolyte can achieve. Thus the specific conductivity does not increase in direct proportion to the molar concentration because the rate of increase slows down as the concentration increases.

Figure 2 illustrates the way molar conductivity, Λ_m, changes with molar concentration, c.

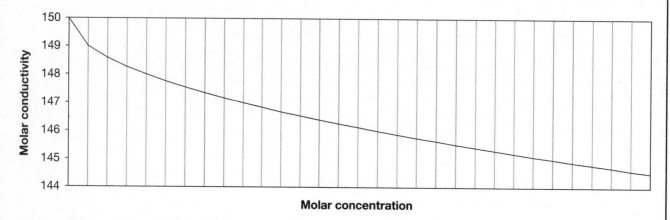

Figure 2

36. Look at formula 1. Which of the following charts best illustrates how the specific conductivity of an electrolytic cell will change as the distance between the electrodes increases?

f.

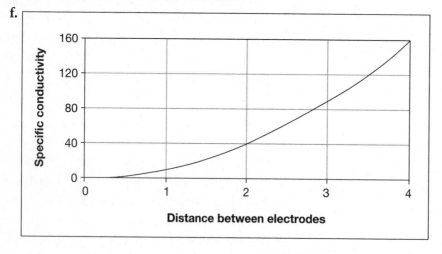

g.

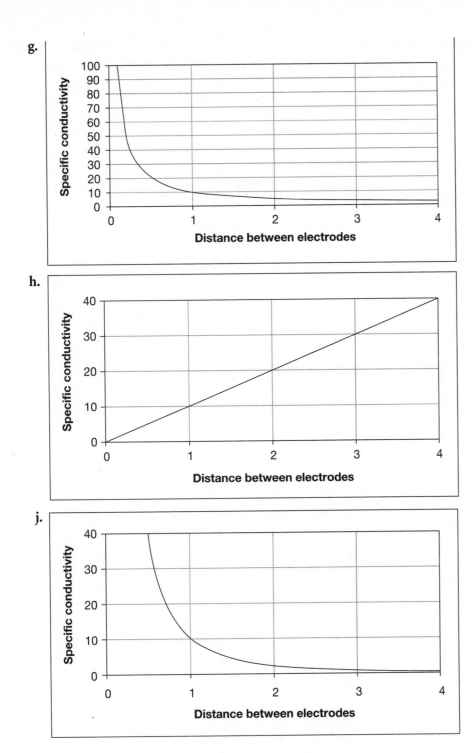

h.

j.

37. In view of the description in this passage and the illustration in Figure 2, which is the best description of what happens to the specific conductivity of an electrolytic cell as the molar concentration of electrolyte increases?

   a. It increases as the molar concentration increases, but the rate of increase decreases slightly as it does.

   b. It decreases proportionally to the square root of the molar concentration.

   c. It increases in direct proportion to the increase in molar concentration.

   d. It increases at an increasing rate in proportion to the molar concentration.

38. Based on formula 1, if an electrolytic cell has a specific conductivity of $500mS$, what would be its specific conductivity if the area of the electrodes was increased to $1,000mS$?

   f. $2,000mS$

   g. $1,000mS$

   h. $500mS$

   j. $125mS$

39. Look at formulas 1, 2, and 3. If the conductivity, k, of the electrolytic solution in an electrolytic cell is 1,200 siemens, what will it become if the distance between the electrodes is decreased from 12 to 8 cm?

   a. 1,800 siemens

   b. 800 siemens

   c. 900 siemens

   d. It will not change.

40. Refer to the opening section of the passage and formulas 1, 2, and 3. Which statement about the practical issues involved in determining the conductivity of an electrolytic solution outside of carefully controlled laboratory conditions is best supported by the passage?

   f. Everything can be calculated from the volume and molar concentration of the solution and the known Λ_m^0 and K of the electrolyte.

   g. The conductivity of the water must first be determined, and then the conductivity added by the electrolyte can be calculated.

   h. There are many variables, including the conductivity of the wide variety of minerals and gases normally dissolved in water.

   j. Accurate volume measures of the electrolytic solution are difficult to obtain outside the laboratory.

ACT Writing Practice Test 4

You have 30 minutes to complete this essay. Remember to:

- Address the specific topic and writing task.
- Create a well-organized response.
- Include developed supporting ideas and specific details.
- Use sentence variety and strong word choices.

In an effort to combat obesity and increase healthfulness among students, the school board is considering changing the cafeteria menu to avoid all junk food and provide only low-fat meals and snacks. They are also considering eliminating the soda machines. Supporters say this plan will help students slim down and have more energy for school. Opponents say this plan is unfair to students who will now have no choices in the cafeteria and the plan will cost the school a great deal of money because the soda machines generate money for the school. In your opinion, should the schools offer only low-fat meals and snacks?

In your essay, take a position on this question. You may write about either of the two points of view given, or you may present a different point of view on the topic. Use specific reasons and examples to support your position.

Answers

ACT English Practice Test 4
Passage I—The Art of Lawn Tennis

1. c. The modifying clause *as played by such men as Norman E. Brookes and R.N. Williams* should be both preceded and followed by a comma.

2. h. The game of tennis, not the men who play it, *has its basis* in science.

3. d. This form agrees with the present form of the earlier verb *hopes* and the later verb *adhere.*

4. h. In this case the proper preposition is *on.*

5. c. In order to modify the verb *began*, an adverb—in this case, *incorrectly*—must be used.

6. g. All the other choices would indicate that the author had the same training as the *American boys have at the present time*, which is counter to the intended meaning of the sentence.

7. d. The indefinite article *an* is appropriate here.

8. j. This is the proper and logical sequencing; answer choice **h** mistakenly uses *giving* instead of *given.*

9. d. The word *yes*, when used singly, is not enclosed in quotation marks except in direct discourse.

10. f. *Comprising*, or *being made up of*, is the correct word choice.

11. d. The word *besieged*, meaning *pressed with requests*, is appropriate here.

12. f. The sentence is correct as it is.

13. d. The narrator has already described the process as *wasting time*, so this sentence is unnecessary.

14. h. The sentence describing the questions (sentence 3) should precede the sentence explaining how the narrator answered them (sentence 2).

15. d. The text ends abruptly and would benefit from a paragraph that ties things together.

Passage II—The Geography and Geology of Hartford, Connecticut

16. h. The only commas needed are those required to set apart the modifying clause *in lesser degree.* The sentence would not require commas without that phrase.

17. a. The sentence is correct as is. The present verb *sink* agrees with the plurality of the *ancient highlands* and the present tense of the sentence.

18. h. The possessive form is correct here.

19. c. This option correctly connects the subject *the trough* with its verb, *was filled*, and properly places the modifying clause immediately after them.

20. g. This puts the verb *to burst* properly in the past tense.

21. a. The sentence is correct as it is.

22. h. This employs the correct verb form and the correct idiom *one above another.*

23. d. The verb form *rests*, rather than the adjective form *resting*, is required in this case.

24. h. A colon is necessary to present the explanatory statement that follows.

25. b. The word *implosion*, deriving from the verb *implode*, to burst inward, is not appropriate for this sentence.

26. f. The sentence is correct as it is.

27. b. The comma, together with the conjunction *so*, should separate the two independent clauses.

28. j. This choice creates agreement between the plural *three sheets* (not the singular *lava*) and the verb, *mark.*

29. c. Because there were three eruptions, the superlative form *greatest*, rather than the comparative form *greater*, would be correct here.

30. g. This option properly creates a logical sequence of observations: that the mud has hardened, then that the footmarks remain intact, and finally where the footmarks can be found.

Passage III—The Wonderful Magnet

31. d. This preposition correctly describes a boat's movement relative to a water basin.

32. h. This choice correctly sets apart the modifying phrase *as well as somewhat mysterious* from the rest of the sentence.

33. c. This creates the proper parallel structure within the sentence.

34. h. This properly connects the compound predicate.

35. d. This option communicates the correct information with proper sequencing—subject, verb, object, object modifier.

36. j. The two separate sentences properly present the question, and the fact that the question has no definitive answer.

37. c. The participle *surrounding* more aptly situates a mystery, rather than the preposition *around*, which is generally used to describe a physical location.

38. j. The use of the dash is appropriate to present a piece of information.

39. a. The sentence is correct as it is.

40. h. The author's ridicule is not mean-spirited but instead an attempt to make foolish theories seem quite normal.

41. b. This is the most logical order with which to present the information.

42. h. This option provides the sentence with correct structure—subject, adverb, verb, object, object modifier, and prepositional phrase.

43. d. In this case the best preposition is *into*, indicating not just a location but also the process of becoming part of something.

44. h. Whereas *obtuse* can be used to mean dull or dim-witted, *abstruse* indicates esoteric and hard to understand, and thus works with the rest of the sentence.

45. d. Sentence 9 should follow sentence 7, because it follows the admonition to *not laugh at them too heartily* by adding that the people who present such speculations *are no more ridiculous than the old Greeks*; sentence 8 should be the final sentence because it expands on sentence 9.

Passage IV—The Soul of the Far East

46. h. The adverb form is appropriate here to modify *standing*.

47. d. In this case the adjective *youthful* best modifies the noun *imagination*.

48. j. The combination of the infinitive *to be*, which completes the phrase *seem to be*, and the progressive *seeing* creates the correct meaning for the sentence.

49. b. This word, meaning *upside down* or *in opposite position*, best suits the sentence.

50. f. This is the correct form of the word.

51. d. This word *early* is redundant to the meaning of *a priori* (prior to), and therefore should be deleted.

52. j. The phrase requires the possessive form and is used with the singular *eye*.

53. d. The phrase requires the present tense in order to agree with the earlier *we regard*.

54. g. The preposition *to* correctly completes the idiom *down to*, used to describe going (all the way) down *to* a specified depth.

55. a. The sentence is correct as it is.

56. g. This option provides agreement with the present tense *seem* and the plural *actions*.

57. c. The comma properly separates the preceding dependent clause from the independent clause that follows.

58. f. The sentence is correct as it is.

59. d. This option correctly changes the verb form to the present tense.

60. h. The best way to replace *every one of us* with a reflexive pronoun is to use the phrase *himself or herself.*

Passage V—Doctor Pascal

61. c. The verb should agree with the singular *room*, not the plural *blinds.*

62. h. When using a form of the verb *to compare*, combine it with *to* in order to emphasize similarities, but combine it with *with* to emphasize differences.

63. c. The subject of the sentence, Dr. Pascal, must be introduced immediately after the modifying clause and the comma.

64. g. The appropriate expression in this case is *dating from*, meaning going back to a specified time.

65. d. The present participle of the verb—*filling*—is appropriate for the second of a tandem of verbs occurring contemporaneously, in this case *piled up* and *filling.*

66. h. The conjunction *because* by itself does not have the meaning—for this reason—necessary to the sentence.

67. d. This sentence contains two independent clauses, which need to be separated by a coordinating conjunction—in this case, *and*—and a comma.

68. f. The sentence is correct as it is.

69. d. The proper expression is *mistaken for*, not *mistaken as*; the modifying clause that is placed in between—*in his close-fitting, maroon velvet jacket*—has no bearing on this usage.

70. h. The sentence as it is structured is grammatically sound (except *as* should be *for*), and the deletion of such phrases as *snow-white hair and beard, color was so fresh, features were so finely cut,* and *close-fitting, maroon velvet jacket* would lessen the descriptive power of the sentence.

71. a. The appropriate punctuation, a comma, is properly placed inside the quotation mark.

72. h. The sentence calls for the past tense of the transitive verb *to lay* (to place down), which is *laid*, as opposed to the past tense of the intransitive verb *to lie* (to be or place oneself at rest).

73. b. A comma is appropriate to separate an independent clause from a dependent clause. In this case, everything after the comma describes (modifies) the profile mentioned in the preceding independent clause.

74. h. The two adjectives, *long* and *black*, both modify the same noun, *dress*; they are therefore coordinate adjectives and should be separated by a comma.

75. d. Her air—or general character, complexion, and appearance—was like that of a child, or *childlike.*

ACT Mathematics Practice Test 4

1. d. To find the increase, simply find the absolute value of the difference between -9 and 22, which is 31.

2. h. To solve, first distribute the 6, then add 42 to both sides. Now $6x$ equals 108, and x equals 18.

3. d. If B is the speed of the bus, then $2B$ is twice the speed, and $2B + 15$ exceeds twice the speed of a bus by 15 mph.

4. k. The numerical parts of the factors must have a product of -18 and a difference of $+3$, so the factors would be $(x + 6)$ and $(x - 3)$.

5. a. The absolute value of $(5 - 3)$ is 2, and the absolute value of $(12 - 6)$ is 6, so the value of the equation is 2 minus 6, or –4.

6. h. Dave traveled twice as far, or 40 miles, in half the time, or two hours. His average speed was $\frac{40}{2}$, or 20 miles per hour.

7. d. This is a simple addition problem, and the three distances add up to 2.75 km. The fractional equivalent of 2.75 is $2\frac{3}{4}$.

8. j. To solve, work backward from $y = 16$. Therefore, 25% of y, or $\frac{1}{4}$ of y, is 4. This is also 10%, or $\frac{1}{10}$ of x, so x must equal 40.

9. e. The area of a rectangle is found by multiplying length times width. The original length, x, is increased by 7 and becomes $(x + 7)$; the original width, y, is decreased by 8 and becomes $(y - 8)$.

10. h. Because the two sides are congruent, the triangle is an isosceles triangle, and the two base angles are also congruent. Those angles add up to 84°, and because the three angles of a triangle add up to 180°, the remaining angle must be 96°.

11. e. To solve, set up a proportion where $\frac{-6 + x}{8 + x} = \frac{2}{3}$, and solve for x. Or, use trial and error by substituting in the given answers. Adding 34 to both –6 and 8 yields the fraction $\frac{28}{42}$, which is equal to $\frac{2}{3}$.

12. g. First, convert all three bases to base 3; the equation becomes $(3^x)(3^2) = (3^3)^2$. According to the rules of exponents, this means that $x + 2 = 6$, and $x = 4$.

13. a. To solve, systematically go through the multiples of 6 to determine those that are also factors of 180. They are 6, 12, 18, 30, 36, 60, and 90.

14. k. Add the parts of the ratio (5 and 6) together. This indicates there are 11 *units* in total, and these units add up to 242, so one unit equals 22. There are six units of tulips in the garden, so multiply 6 times 22 to find the answer.

15. b. First, multiply 30 times 42 to find the total square footage in the dormitory. Then take this total (1,260) and divide it by 35 to find the new square footage per man. Subtract that figure, 36, from the original figure of 42 to find the difference.

16. j. Find 20% of $85 by multiplying 0.20 times 85. Subtract the answer, 17, from 85 to find the on-sale price of $68. Now find 10% of 68 by multiplying 0.10 times 68, and add that figure to $68 to find the final price of the coat.

17. a. The given statement can be put into if/then form by saying *If it is Sunday, then Isabelle is running*. Thus it can be definitively concluded using deductive reasoning that if Isabelle is not running, it could not be Sunday.

18. h. Since line *AB* is perpendicular to line *GH*, then angle *ABC* is a right angle. Angle *EAD* creates a linear pair with angle *DAF*, and since *DAF* equals 120°, angle *EAD* must equal 60°. Angle *BCA* is a corresponding angle to angle *EAD*, and therefore also 60°. Thus triangle *ABC* is a 30–60–90 right triangle, and side *AB* is the long leg of this triangle. By rule, the short leg is half the hypotenuse, or 5, and the long leg is equal to the short leg times $\sqrt{3}$.

19. c. Simply use x and y to represent the original dimensions. In this case, the area would equal x times y, or xy. Now triple the dimensions to become $3x$ and $3y$. The new area is $3x$ times $3y$, or $9xy$, which is 9 times larger than the original area.

20. j. The chart indicates that buying balloons 1,000 at a time costs $0.60 per balloon, or 2,000 times $0.60, which equals $1,200, for 2,000 balloons. Buying balloons 10 at a time costs $0.90 per balloon, or 2,000 times $0.90, which equals $1,800, for 2,000 balloons. The difference between $1,800 and $1,200 represents the amount saved.

21. e. Seven cards have been removed from the deck. Of the remaining cards, three numbers—4, 20, and 40—are both multiples of 4 and factors of 40. The probability of one of these cards being selected is 3 out of 33, or 1 out of 11.

22. h. First, apply the operation to the expression inside the parentheses, and you get the quantity $(n^2 - m)$. Now, again apply the operation to the expression $m\#(n^2 - m)$. The resulting expression is $m^2 - (n^2 - m)$, and distributing the negative sign yields $m^2 + m - n^2$.

23. a. Using the distance formula determines the length of the line. Simply put, this formula derives from the Pythagorean theorem by creating a right triangle between any two points. The length of each leg of this triangle can be found by finding the difference of the two x-coordinates and the difference of the two y-coordinates. Now square each of these values, add the two values together, and then take the square root of this sum. This is the distance between two points. In this case, the distance is given as 13, so the sum of the squares of the differences in the x and y coordinates must total 169. The point $(1,13)$ creates a difference of 5 in the x value and a difference of 12 in the y value; the squares of these values are 25 and 144, which add up to 169.

24. j. This sequence is actually two different sequences merged into one sequence. The odd terms are a geometric sequence with a ratio of 2. The even terms are an arithmetic sequence with a difference of –4. Since the next term would be the seventh term, simply multiply the fifth term times two.

25. b. Use trial and error to test each of the possible lowest integers offered as solutions. By starting with 12, a set of 12, 14, 16, 18, 20, and 22 is created. The sum of the elements of this set is 102.

26. h. Working backward from an area of 6.25π in.^{2} by using the formula area $= \pi r^2$, we can determine that the radius of the original circle is 2.5. Doubled, the new radius is 5, and 25π in.^{2} is the new area.

27. d. To solve, plug in the coordinates of the vertex, $(3,-2)$, into the equations provided and determine which equation is made true by these coordinates. In this case, $-2 = (3 - 3)^2 - 2$, so choice **d** is correct.

28. f. To solve, find a value for x that creates a value of zero in the denominator, and thus an undefined equation. Factor the denominator into $(x + 9)(x - 2)$, and the two solutions for x are –9 and +2.

29. b. If $r = 30$, then 30% of r is equal to 9. If 75% of s is equal to 9, then $\frac{9}{s} = \frac{75}{100}$, and by cross multiplying and then dividing by 75 we find that s is equal to 12; 50% of 12 is 6.

30. k. For a line to be perpendicular to another line, their slopes must be negative reciprocals, or when multiplied their slopes create a product of –1. Therefore, the slope of a line perpendicular to a line with a slope of $\frac{2}{3}$ must have a slope of $-\frac{3}{2}$.

31. c. If the job takes 8 people 12 hours each, then 96 hours of labor are required; thus 6 people would have to work 16 hours each.

32. h. A cube has six congruent faces, therefore each face must have an area of 384 divided by 6, or 64 cm^2. Because each face is a square, the sides of the square, and thus the cube, must be 8 cm, and the volume must be 8^3, or 512 cm^3.

33. d. If the volume has decreased by 20%, then 80% of the original volume remains, and the question is solved by the proportion $\frac{240}{x} = \frac{80}{100}$.

34. j. The area of the shaded region can be found by finding the difference between the area of the larger circle and the area of the smaller circle. The area of a circle is equal to πr^2. Using $r = 7$ for the larger circle and $r = 3.5$ (half of 7) for the smaller circle, we find their areas to be 49π and 12.25π, respectively. The difference is 36.75π.

35. e. To solve, factor $2xy - 4x$ into $2x(y - 2)$. This indicates that any time that y, or the second term, is equal to 2, the expression will have a value of 0. In all three instances given the second term can have a value of 2, so in all three instances the expression could have a value of 0.

36. h. Use the Pythagorean theorem to solve for the third side of the triangle by solving $26^2 - 10^2 = x^2$. In this case, x will equal 24, and the third side of the triangle has a measure of 24 units (you might also have recalled the Pythagorean triple of 5–12–13, which when doubled is 10–24–26). tan C is found by opposite/adjacent, or $\frac{24}{10}$, which is 2.4.

37. a. By factoring both $x^2 y^2$ and xy^3, we find the greatest common factor to be xy^2. Thus $xy^2 = 45$. The only perfect square that is a factor of 45 is 9, and y must therefore be equal to 3.

38. h. Working backward, if $54 is 25%, or $\frac{1}{4}$ of the money spent on food, then the money spent on food totals $216. Continuing, this amount represents 18% of the budget, so the entire budget, x, can be found using the proportion $\frac{18}{100} = \frac{216}{x}$. By cross multiplying and then dividing by 18, x equals 1,200, and the budget must be $1,200.

39. a. Let r = radiation and d = distance; in this case, using inverse variation we know that $rd^2 = k$, where k is a constant. When $d = 1$, r would be equal to k. If r were to be reduced by $\frac{1}{16}$, then d^2 has to equal 16 in order to keep k constant. Thus d equals 4.

40. h. First, because line OA is congruent to line OB, then angle B is congruent to angle A. These two angles total 110°, meaning the third angle of the triangle is 70°. This is the angle that intercepts the arc in question, and because it is a central angle (an angle whose vertex is the center of a circle), the measure of the intercepted arc is equal to the measure of that angle.

41. a. The maximum value of sin is 1, which is attained at an angle of 90°, so $2x$ must equal 90°, and x must equal 45°. Because a circle contains 360°, or 2π, $\frac{\pi}{4}$ is the equivalent of 45°.

42. f. tan A is found by dividing the opposite, or y, side of the triangle by the adjacent, or x, side of the triangle. Because angle A is in the second quadrant (between 90° and 180°), then cos A, found by dividing the adjacent side by the hypotenuse, would also be negative, because x is negative in the second quadrant. The third side of the right triangle in question would be 5, because it is the hypotenuse of a 3–4–5 triangle. cos A would equal the adjacent side of the angle, or –4, over the hypotenuse, or 5.

43. e. The area of the circle, πr^2, would be 81π. The area of a sector of a circle, relative to the entire area of a circle, is proportional to the ratio between the central angle that creates that sector and 360°. Because $\frac{120°}{360°}$ equals $\frac{1}{3}$, the area of the sector would be $\frac{1}{3}$ the total area.

44. k. First, substitute 69 for $f(x)$ and solve for x. If $69 = 3(x^2 - 2)$, first divide both sides by 3, and then add 2 to both sides. Thus $x^2 = 25$, and $x = 5$ or –5. Plug those values into the equation $2x - 3$. The answers are 7 or –13.

45. b. The expression $w^{\frac{2}{3}}$ can be read as "the cube root of w squared." If $w = \frac{1}{8}$, then $w^2 = \frac{1}{64}$, and the cube root of $\frac{1}{64}$ is $\frac{1}{4}$.

46. g. The area of the shaded region can be found by finding the difference between the area of the outer circle and the area of the inner circle. The outer circle has a radius of 1.2(5), or 6, and thus has an area of 36π; the area of the inner circle is 25π. The shaded region therefore has an area of 11π.

47. d. If the arc length is 9π inches, the circumference is therefore 72π inches. Since circumference, C, is equal to $2\pi r$, 72 must equal $2r$, and r equals 36.

48. j. First, use trial and error to factor the equation, keeping in mind that the first terms of the factors must be $5x$ and x, the second terms of the factors must have a product of 4, and the terms in both cases must be separated by a minus sign to produce the negative middle term of the original trinomial. The equation factors to $(5x - 4)(x - 1)$; now, set each factor equal to zero and solve for x.

49. c. cos equals adjacent/hypotenuse, so the triangle has a hypotenuse of 9 and the side adjacent to angle x has length 8. Because sin equals opposite/hypotenuse, we need to determine the length of the remaining leg. Using the Pythagorean theorem, we find that this leg has length $\sqrt{17}$. So, the sine of x is $\frac{\sqrt{17}}{9}$.

50. g. The problem can be solved two ways. First, systematically move clockwise from one vertex to the next and connect each vertex to all others. There will be 14 lines drawn. To solve this mathematically, notice the pattern from the other two polygons. Take the number of vertices and multiply that times the number of diagonals that can be drawn from each vertex; in the square, this is 4 times 1, in the pentagon this is 5 times 2. Then take the resulting product and divide by 2; for the square, the answer is 2, and for the pentagon the answer is 5. In both cases, this number represents the total number of distinct diagonals that can be drawn. For a seven-sided figure, the equation would be $\frac{7 \times 4}{2}$, which equals 14.

51. d. For a system of linear equations to have no solution, the lines must be parallel, and in order to be parallel and not be the same line they must have the same slope. The slope of a graphed line is $-\frac{4}{5}$, found by taking the change in the two y terms and dividing it by the change in the two x terms. The standard-form equation $5y + 4x = -4$, when put into slope/intercept form $y = mx + b$ (m = slope), also has a slope of $-\frac{4}{5}$.

52. j. There are four ways the lines can be drawn: as three parallel lines, as two parallel lines and a third line intersecting both, as three lines intersecting at one point, and as lines intersecting at three different points. The first case creates four regions, the next two cases each create six regions, and the final case creates seven regions.

53. d. The problem is easier than it might seem. Since the geometric sequence goes from x to xy, the common ratio between terms must be y. For each of the ensuing terms the y would simply be raised to the next power, and since the second term contains y to the first power, the 97th term would contain y to the 96th power.

54. f. Because a logarithm is the inverse operation of an exponential expression, $\log_3 243$ can be read as "3 to what power equals 243." The answer is 5.

55. c. First, apply the Pythagorean theorem to the right triangle in question. This tells us that $A^2 + B^2 = C^2$, where A and B are legs of the triangle and C is the hypotenuse. So $(2x)^2 + (5x)^2 = C^2$, and $29x^2 = C^2$. Now simply take the square root of both sides to solve for C.

56. k. This is a classic combination problem and is solved using multiplication. There are three choices to be made. The first choice would have nine possible outcomes, the second choice would then have eight possible outcomes (because one has been eliminated), and the third choice would have seven possible outcomes (because two have now been eliminated). To solve for the total possible combinations, simply multiply 9 times 8 times 7.

57. b. The cost, C, of a job would be expressed by the function $C = \$50h + k\sqrt{m}$, where h equals the number of hours of the job, k is the mileage fee, and m equals the miles traveled. We are told that a one-hour job requiring 25 miles of travel costs $140, so we know that $140 = \$50(1) + k\sqrt{25}$. Using algebra we solve for k, which equals 18. We now plug that value back into an equation to find the cost of a one-hour job requiring 36 miles of travel: $C = \$50(1) + \$18\sqrt{36}$.

58. j. The line $y = x$ starts in the third quadrant, has a slope of 1, goes through the origin, and continues into the first quadrant. Therefore, the point $(5, -7)$, which is in the fourth quadrant, would be reflected in the second quadrant, and the x and y coordinates would be reversed.

59. d. Volume of a cylinder is found with the formula $V = \pi r^2 h$, where h is the height of the cylinder. If the radius of the cylinder is 4, and we plug that value into the formula for volume, we can solve for the height, which equals 10. Because the edge of the cube is half this measure, the edge is 5, and the cube has a volume of 5^3 or 125 square units.

60. h. The measure of the missing side can be found by subtracting 4^2 from 10^2; the missing side is $\sqrt{84}$, or $2\sqrt{21}$. The value of $\sin C$ is opposite over hypotenuse, or $2\sqrt{21}$ over 10. This can be reduced to $\sqrt{21}$ over 5.

ACT Reading Practice Test 4
Passage I—Humanities

1. c. Beecher Hooker invokes the Constitution (line 1) and recites the preamble (lines 13–20) in order to appeal to and persuade her audience.

2. f. Beecher Hooker plays on the two meanings suggested by the phrase *learn it by heart as well as by head*. She asks her audience to not only memorize the Constitution's preamble, but to also use both emotion and intellect to understand its meaning.

3. c. Excerpt 1 argues that the foremothers of the nation were patriotic and *did their full share* (line 45) of contributing to the early republic.

4. g. The excerpt anticipates the arguments of those in favor of women's right to vote and attempts to refute them.

5. c. *Novel* means new and not resembling something known or used in the past. Choice **b**, *original*, could fit this definition but its connotation is too positive for the context.

6. f. Excerpt 2 describes *woman-suffrage societies* as *thoroughly organized, with active and zealous managers* (lines 21–23). Choice **b**, *courageous*, is too positive for the context of the excerpt.

7. a. Excerpt 2 states that *everyone . . . knows that without female suffrage, legislation for years has improved and is still improving the condition of women* (lines 38–41).

8. j. Excerpt 2 emphasizes how well women are served by judges. Excerpt 1 does not refer to this issue at all.

9. b. Excerpt 1 describes men as *fighters by nature* (line 56), but not women. Excerpt 2 describes women as *incapable of performing military duty* (lines 6–7).

10. j. Excerpt 1 addresses its audience in the second person, whereas Excerpt 2 does not, except for references to *your committee*. Excerpt 1 also refers to its audience as *friends* (line 21) and *brothers* (line 27).

Passage II—Prose Fiction

11. c. Frankenstein asks his listener to *[l]earn from me . . . how dangerous is the acquirement of knowledge* (lines 9–11). He is telling his tale as a warning and does not want to lead his listener into the same kind of *destruction and infallible misery* (lines 8–9).

12. f. The context reveals that Frankenstein was prepared for *a multitude of reverses* or setbacks that would hinder his operations.

13. d. Frankenstein describes himself as pursuing his *undertaking with unremitting ardor* and that his *cheek had grown pale with study, and [his] person had become emaciated with confinement* (lines 67–70). He also says that *a resistless, and almost frantic, impulse urged me forward; I seemed to have lost all soul or sensation but for this one pursuit* (lines 83–86). These are the marks of a man obsessed.

14. g. Moreau states in lines 33–36 that *this extraordinary branch of knowledge has never been sought as an end, [. . .] until I took it up!*, and later adds that he was *the first man to take up this question armed with antiseptic surgery, and with a really scientific knowledge of the laws of growth* (lines 43–46). This, and the detail with which he explains the background of his investigations, reveals that he is a calculating and systematic scientist.

15. d. Right after he says *these things*, the narrator says *these animals* to clarify that he is referring to the creatures that Moreau created. An additional context clue is provided by Moreau's response, in which he explains how animals *may be educated* so that they may talk.

16. g. The narrator asks Moreau to justify *all this pain* (lines 82–83), implying that he has inflicted great pain on the animals he has used in his experiments.

17. c. Both men make remarkable discoveries in their fields; in the other aspects the men are different. Dr. Moreau uses live animals to change their form, and there is no evidence in the passage that he wants his creatures to worship him or that he has kept his experiment a secret. Passage 2 also suggests that Moreau did not have a specific application or justification for his work; he responds to the narrator's request for a justification by philosophizing about pain.

18. f. Frankenstein confesses horror at his torture of living animals and that he trembles just remembering the pain he inflicted (excerpt 1, lines 80–83). In the next sentence he characterizes himself as having *lost all soul or sensation* in his quest; he is telling this tale as a warning. Thus it is likely that he would be most offended by Moreau's indifference to the suffering of other creatures.

19. d. Given the opposing viewpoints of the two speakers, the *shrug at such sophistry* was a shrug at a faulty way of thinking, or false reasoning.

20. g. In paragraph 3, Frankenstein cites specific goals for his pursuit of knowledge: he wanted to *pour a torrent of light into our dark world* by making important new discoveries; he wanted to create a new species that would *bless [him] as its creator and source*; and he wanted to *renew life*. Moreau, on the other hand, does not offer any application or justification; he seems motivated only by the acquisition of knowledge. He opens the excerpt by stating that he has *devoted* his life to *the study of the plasticity of living forms*, and in the final sentence of the excerpt he seems more interested in *what science has to teach* than in what can be done with that knowledge. He does not offer a justification for his experiments.

Passage III—Natural Sciences

21. c. The phrase *broken up into long, thin fibers*, used to describe asbestos bundles at the beginning of paragraph 2 and prior to the phrase *friable substance*, supports the notion that *friable* means easily broken down. All other choices are not supported in the passage.

22. g. This choice best describes the passage in its entirety, while the other choices describe individual points made within the passage.

23. d. The text notes that asbestosis *usually occurs when a person is exposed to high asbestos levels over an extensive period of time* (lines 23–24). Choice **a** is incorrect because not all insulation material contains asbestos fibers, choice **b** is incorrect because asbestos that is in good condition and not crumbled or breaking away does not need to be removed, and choice **c** is incorrect because the AHERA protects schools against asbestos exposure.

24. g. The correct choice is universal. The sentence *many commercial building and home insulation products contained asbestos* after the word *ubiquitous* shows that asbestos was commonly used.

25. b. In paragraph 2, the author explains that lung cancer and asbestosis are diseases of the lung.

26. f. While the passage does include the other choices, the overall purpose of the passage is to teach asbestos awareness in the home and school.

27. c. The tone of this passage is informative, serving to instruct the general reader about asbestos. Choices **a** and **d** (*cautionary* and *admonitory*) are synonyms and are both incorrect. *Apathetic* (choice **b**) means indifferent.

28. g. The author is writing for a layperson, such as a homeowner, parent, or student. The other choices may be interested in this information, but none of them is the specific, targeted audience.

29. d. In this case the *opportunity for disturbance*, or breaking apart, of the asbestos would create the *potential exposure to students and employees*.

30. h. While this is a reasonable consideration, it is not mentioned among the numerous EPA-published regulations that are mentioned.

Passage IV—Social Sciences

31. c. The three examples in the first paragraph show that there is a wide range of styles of public art in New York City and that public art can be found in a variety of places, including more mundane locations such as the subway and post office.

32. f. *Inherently* is an adverb that describes the essential nature of something. The context clue to answer this question is found in the same sentence. *All art is inherently public* because it is *created in order to convey an idea or emotion to others.* The author is saying that an essential characteristic of art is that it is created for others.

33. b. Paragraph 2 defines public art as *the kind of art created for and displayed in public spaces,* and lines 30–32 in paragraph 3 state that public art is *specifically designed for a public arena where the art will be encountered by people in their normal day-to-day activities.* This is in contrast to private art, which is less accessible because it is kept in specific, non-public places such as private museums and galleries.

34. g. To *sequester* is to seclude or isolate. Thus the use of this word suggests that the author feels private art is too isolated and cut off from the public.

35. d. The many functions are listed in paragraph 5: educating, place making, stimulating the public, promoting community, beautifying, and regenerating. While promoting good citizenship may be a side benefit of public art, it is not discussed in the passage.

36. f. After defining public art, the rest of the passage discusses the functions of public art and its impact on the city.

37. d. The examples in the first paragraph and the list of different kinds of public art will make readers more aware of public art; paragraphs 2 and 3 explain the difference between public and private art; paragraph 5 explains how public art affects the community; and paragraph 6 discusses how public art should be created. A few readers may be inspired to create public art after reading this passage, but that is not one of its goals.

38. h. Although the opening of paragraph 2 states that *There exists in every city a symbiotic relationship between the city and its art*, and paragraph 5 explains how public art affects the city, there is no discussion of how the city affects art.

39. b. Because the main purpose is to show what public art is and how public art affects the city, the passage would be best served by an expanded discussion of how public art fulfills each of the important functions in paragraph 5.

40. g. While the passage addresses all of the choices, the overall theme, cited at the end of paragraph 2 (*there is a growing interest in, and respect for, public art*) is the growing importance of and interest in public art.

ACT Science Practice Test 4
Passage I—Conflicting Viewpoints

1. a. They disagree on how significant local variations in magnetic field are, but their arguments indicate acceptance of the view that heated minerals are magnetized as stated. Answer choice **b** is Scientist 1's view, not Scientist 2's. Answer **c** is clearly not the view of Scientist 1. Scientist 2 says there are important local divergences from the geomagnetic field but never says there is no geomagnetic field. Answer choice **d** is opposed by Scientist 1 and neither supported nor directly opposed by Scientist 2.

2. h. Answer **f** is a partially correct description of Scientist 2's view, but Scientist 2 says that self-reversal, which is the change in magnetic polarity after the rock is magnetized by the geomagnetic field, accounts for only some of the anomalous polarities. Answer choice **g** expresses the opposite of Scientist 1's view of the changeability of the geomagnetic field. Scientist 2 does not make the statement attributed to him in answer choice **j**.

3. d. The passage states that both scientists accept the general view that had long recognized geographic differences in the effect of the geomagnetic field. The other answers all reflect the shared understanding of these scientists with the general views described.

4. f. No general condition for causing minerals to be magnetized with a particular polarity, other than the polarity of the field that it is magnetized in, has been suggested. Exceptions for self-reversing minerals and some local anomalies in the magnetic field cannot outweigh evidence from every corner of the planet over a span of hundreds of millions of years.

5. d. In fact, the theory known as tectonic plate construction of the earth's crust has been widely accepted since the 1960s for these reasons.

6. g. The question of what effect, other than reversing polarity during rock formation, geomagnetic reversal might have is to be further explored, but there is now no reason to believe the effect would be as catastrophic as Scientist 2 has asserted. Answer choice **f** is not correct because we have no evidence that these calamities are in any way associated with the geomagnetic reversals. Answer choice **h** contradicts what Scientist 1 has previously said in arguing for the geomagnetic reversal theory. His argument rested precisely on the whole earth being affected at the same time. Answer choice **j** may not be far from the truth, but answer choice **g**'s openness toward a more thorough investigation is much more reasonable.

7. d. Answer choice **d** is correct as explained in the introductory section of the passage. Answer choice **a** is incorrect because geomagnetic reversal became understood largely as a result of the magnetic mapping of the sea floor. Nothing has been said to support answer choice **b** or answer choice **c**. Actually, the submarine was invented in the late eighteenth century. Magnetic polarity, inclination, and intensity had been measured for hundreds of years prior to these investigations.

Passage II—Research Summary

8. h. The concentration in the cell is 1.5%, so it is stronger than the 1% solution and weaker than the 2% and 5% solutions. It will draw in water to balance the 1% (deplasmolysis) and lose water to balance the others (plasmolysis). Higher differentials in concentration cause higher osmotic pressure and higher rates of osmosis.

9. d. The relationship between the solution surrounding the cell and the cell is hypotonic if the surrounding fluid is lower in concentration, isotonic if it is of equal concentration, and hypertonic if it has a greater concentration. *Plasmolytic* and *deplasmolytic* (choice **a**) are terms that are not defined in the passage. They refer to the state of the cell, not the relationship of the solutions. *Hyper-* and *hypo-osmotic* were also not used in the passage. They refer to the fluid relationship from the standpoint of the internal cell fluid, not the external fluid. *Hypo-osmotic, hypo-osmotic, and hyperosmotic* is a correct definition of the cells in relation to the three test fluids, but answer choice **b** as stated is not.

10. f. The test solution causes deplasmolysis (water entering the cell) when its concentration is lower than the cell's and plasmolysis (water drawn out of the cells) when its concentration is higher. Therefore, the cell's concentration must be higher than the concentrations that cause deplasmolysis and lower than the concentrations that cause plasmolysis; 1.8% is the only possible answer.

11. c. Water would be drawn out of the cells by the surrounding hypertonic (higher-concentration) solution, resulting in plasmolysis.

12. g. The distilled water, with a solute concentration of 0%, is extremely hypotonic. Water will fill the cells. This is called deplasmolysis.

13. c. This is a case where the correct answer may seem extreme or absurd to those not familiar with the phenomenon. It is, however, the only answer consistent with the scientific principles presented. The others are all demonstrably impossible. Since sucrose cannot leave the cell, the distilled water mixture will always be hypotonic and never become isotonic as long as the cell membranes are intact. Water will be drawn into the cell until the cell walls can no longer expand. At that point they will burst. This is not merely a logical conclusion; it actually happens to cells in extremely isotonic environments. Some protozoa avoid this fate by having mechanisms to squirt out excess water. Most plant cells do not. Answer choice **a** is not correct for the reason just given. Answer choices **b** and **d** are not correct because plasmolysis can occur only when there is a higher-concentration solution outside the cell than inside.

Passage III—Research Summary

14. g. Both charges are positive, so the force between them will be repulsive, not attractive. Sphere A is held down by the force of gravity, which is approximately 10 gm/s^2. When sphere B is close enough so that the repulsive force exceeds 10 gm/s^2, sphere A moves. Answer choices **f** and **j** are incorrect because sphere B is repelling sphere A upward, not attracting it downward. Answer choice **c** is incorrect because sparks do not fly between like-charged objects.

15. b. The weight of sphere A is still 1 gram, so the same force will be required to move it. Neither F nor k have changed between experiments, so we can ignore them in this comparison. By Coulomb's law, F is proportional to $\frac{Q_1 \times Q_2}{d^2}$. In the original experiment 1, this was as follows:

$$\frac{1 \times 1}{10^2} = \frac{1}{100}$$

Now, the charge on each sphere is 2, but we do not know the distance, so we can write the following formula:

$$\frac{1}{100} = \frac{-2 \times -2}{d^2}$$
$$\frac{1}{100} = \frac{4}{d^2}$$
$$\frac{d^2}{100} = 4$$
$$d^2 = 400$$
$$d = 20$$

16. f. The charges are opposite, which means sphere A will be attracted down toward sphere B, but the strings will prevent it from moving downward until sphere B physically moves sphere A with kinetic force.

17. b. The charges are opposite, which means sphere B will push sphere A away from it downward. The strings, however, will prevent sphere A from moving.

18. f. The charge is the same magnitude as in the first version of experiment 1, but the product of the two charges is negative, not positive. That means that sphere B will pull sphere A up toward it, not push it away. The distance at which the force will overcome the gravitational force on sphere A is the same as in experiment 1.

19. d. This can be calculated as was done for question 15, but no calculation is necessary in this case. The description of experiment 1 established that if both charges = 1, the force of the charge will overcome the force of gravity at 10 cm. It is also known that the greater the charge is, the greater the force will be at any given distance. Therefore, the distance at which charges of 2 and 3 will overcome gravity must be greater than the distance for charges of 1 and 1. The only answer greater than 10 cm is choice **d**.

Passage IV—Research Summary

20. g. According to the formula, the distance to the epicenter is 15 s × 8 km/s or 120 km.

21. d. Each circle represents the approximate distance from one of the stations to the epicenter. The place where all three circles come closest to intersecting is the estimated location of the epicenter.

22. f. The other times listed are the times at which the P wave reached each seismographic station, respectively. The earthquake had to have started earlier. Specifically, the calculated distance of the epicenter from station A is 120 km. The passage states that P waves travel at approximately 8 km/s, so the earthquake started 15 seconds before the P wave reached station A, or 05:32:55.

23. c. According to the formula, the distance to the epicenter is 10 s × 8 km/s or 80 km.

24. j. The P wave is reported to arrive at the same time at stations A and C, but the S wave arrives 70 seconds later at C than A. This would, at minimum, require a very extraordinary geological situation. Also, even though the rule of thumb provided may not hold for station C, if it is anywhere close to being accurate, the distances to the epicenter computed for the three stations cannot intersect at anything close to a single point.

25. d. According to the method provided in the passage for estimating distances from a seismic reading to the epicenter, the wave velocities provided for P and S waves function only up to 500 km, but the estimate by that method would be 640 km to the epicenter. No information is given as to whether the distance should be estimated to be either greater than or less than 640 km.

Passage V—Data Representation

26. h. Compound A and compound D give up H's, so they are acids. Compounds B and C receive H's, so they are bases. Answer choice **h** correctly pairs the acid compound A with the base compound C and the acid compound D with the base compound B because those are the pairs that transform into each other by gaining or losing an H. Answer choice **f** reverses the acid/base order for the second pair. Answer choice **g** does not pair the conjugates. Answer choice **j** reverses the acid/base order for the first pair.

27. a. With the indicated changes, compound D would have to become H_3O to preserve the correct number of atoms of each element. The resulting conjugates are as in answer choice **a**. Answer choice **b** gives the correct conjugates for this line without the changes asked for. Answer choice **c** mismatches the conjugate pairs. Answer choice **d** gives the wrong acid/base order for the second pair.

28. g. Those are the compounds that give up hydrogen ions in the reactions shown.

29. d. Those are the compounds that accept hydrogen ions in the reactions shown.

30. h. This is a functional definition, not a fixed definition, based on the composition of each compound. Answer choice **f** is clearly not true. Answer choice **g** is not indicated anywhere in the passage and does not explain the different roles some compounds play. Answer choice **j** is a fair statement. In fact, some definitions of acids and bases rely entirely on the question of electrons accepted or given up. The statement does not characterize this definition, though.

Passage VI—Data Representation

31. c. As the drawing indicates, the side of the magnetosphere facing the sun follows a pattern similar to that of a normal dipole. The side away from the sun, however, sweeps away from the earth as if driven by a strong wind. That is the effect of the solar wind. Answer choice **a** is not really accurate. The lines of force, representing equivalent magnetic strength, are swept away from the sun, but the magnetosphere extends indefinitely in all directions, as does the magnetic field of the handheld dipole. Answer choice **b** is incorrect. Magnetic fields do not really have a measurable size. They become weaker and weaker as they get farther from their magnet, but there is no point at which they entirely disappear. Answer choice **d** is not directly related to shape. It is also ambiguous. As is clear from the fact that a small handheld magnet will act more forcefully on a compass needle than will the earth's magnetic field, the intensity of the earth's magnetic field is much less than that of anything we would recognize as a magnet.

32. j. The magnetic field arrow on the earth side of the sun points down, but the earth's and the earth side of the CME's point up.

33. b. The passage describes solar activity as increasing and decreasing on an 11-year cycle and reversing polarity as it reaches the low point of a cycle and begins to increase its activity level. Right before year 11, the solar cycle is ending a period of polarity aligned with the earth's and entering a period of polarity opposed to the earth's.

34. h. Figure 2 shows the CME field aligned with the earth's. If that is reversed, the level of ion infiltration in the next cycle should be lower than it was in the current cycle. Therefore, ion infiltration will decline to the low point of this cycle, then begin increasing again, but the high point of the coming cycle will be much lower than the high point of the previous cycle.

35. a. When the sun's magnetic field points south, the leading edge of CMEs approaching the earth will point north. This produces a far higher level of ionized material entering the earth's magnetic domain. This will produce a higher level of electrical activity, and auroras and other electrical disturbances are the result. There is no firm connection reported here with cancer levels.

Passage VII—Data Representation

36. g. The specific conductivity of a cell is inversely proportional to the distance between electrodes. That means it will decrease as the distance increases. Figures B and D are the only ones that meet that requirement. Then look more closely. Figure B crosses the 10 conductivity line at distance 1. At that point, the conductivity = 10/distance. It crosses the 5 conductivity line at distance 2. That is also 10/distance. At each intersection point, the ratio 10/distance holds. Figure D also crosses the 10 conductivity line at distance 1, but that is the only point at which the ratio 10/distance holds. It is clearly below 5 at distance 2 and below $\frac{1}{3}$ at distance 3.

37. a. As described by formulas 2 and 3 and illustrated by Figure 2, the specific conductivity is directly proportional to the molar conductivity, but the molar conductivity decreases slightly as the molar concentration increases. The resulting increase would be less than a direct straight-line increase.

38. g. As described by formula 1, specific conductivity is directly proportional to the area of the electrodes. If the area is doubled, specific conductivity doubles.

39. d. The distance between the electrodes affects the specific conductivity of the cell, not the conductivity of the electrolytic solution in the cell. As formulas 2 and 3 indicate, the fluid's conductivity, k, is derived from the molar concentration and the molar conductivity, not the distance between the electrodes.

40. h. The first paragraph of the passage points to some of the difficulties involved in applying the theory of electrolyte conductivity to actual electrolytic solutions. Answer choice **f** makes no mention of these problems. Answer choice **g** says nothing about how to determine the conductivity of the solution. Answer choice **j** is incorrect. Reasonably accurate volume measurements can be achieved with a wide variety of common equipment.

ACT Writing Practice Test 4
Sample "Score 6" Essay

Obesity has become a major problem in the United States. This health problem leads to other serious issues such as heart disease and diabetes. The school board is considering a plan to help students fight this problem. The new lunch program based on nutritious food and the elimination of soda machines is necessary for students to obtain nutritious food, and the program will help students become healthier, more energetic, and even smarter.

Many students in our schools have a weight problem. More and more children and teenagers are battling obesity than ever before. Much of this is due to poor food choices. At home, many families have two parents who work or even just one parent who works two jobs. This leaves little time for shopping for and preparing nutritious meals. It's simply quicker and easier to go to a fast-food restaurant or throw some macaroni and cheese into the microwave than to prepare a well-balanced meal. That's where the school comes in. At least the school can provide students with a nutritious lunch. It may be the only really nutritious food the students get. While there might be some resistance at first, students will eventually begin to eat and enjoy the new food. If students become hungry enough, they'll try it and find that they actually like it. They will begin to feel and look better. The soda machines do provide money for the school, but is the money worth the health of the students? Additionally, if we replace the soda vending machines with water vending machines, we will still make some money.

Eating healthy lunches will help students have more energy throughout the day. Students and teachers complain that many students tend to crash during the early afternoon classes. This is usually because students have eaten a lunch high in sugar and carbohydrates. This type of food gives a quick burst of energy, which the student typically uses up during the period itself, and then causes a rapid decline of energy, causing the student to feel sluggish and sleepy. Nutritious food would eliminate this problem. If students eat a meal of protein, whole grains, and vegetables, they will have a steadier supply of energy to keep them going throughout the day. Some opponents say that many students will boycott the new lunch program and not eat lunch at all, making them tired during the day. This may happen a few times, but most teenagers do not like the feeling of being hungry and tired.

They will eventually begin to eat the food, even if it's just one part of the lunch that they like.

Finally, this new lunch program will actually help students increase their academic performance. Healthy food makes people feel better and perform with more energy and alertness. This means students will pay more attention in class, have more energy to do required work, and think more clearly and creatively. This can only lead to better grades and better test scores, something students and teachers alike are always pursuing.

The new lunch program may intimidate some students. People are creatures of habit and are initially resistant to change of any kind. But much of eating is an acquired taste for certain foods. While students may miss their tacos and chocolate chip cookies, they will eventually come to appreciate and hopefully prefer grilled chicken and a nice juicy apple.

Critique

This essay shows an excellent and insightful understanding of the prompt. The writer takes a clear stand on the issue with a strong, direct thesis statement: *The new lunch program based on nutritious food and the elimination of soda machines is necessary for students to obtain nutritious food, and the program will help students become healthier, more energetic, and even smarter.* The essay is well developed with specific examples, reasons, and sound logic. It contains two counterarguments in paragraphs 2 and 3, stating that money from the soda machines should not take precedence over student health and that students who boycott the lunches will eventually begin to eat them. The essay shows excellent command of written language with sophisticated vocabulary and varied sentence structure.

Sample "Score 5" Essay

School cafeterias are not well known for gourmet food, but over the years, they've gotten better at knowing what teenagers like to eat. Now the school wants to change all that by starting a new lunch program with nutritious food and eliminating the soda machines. Doing this will actually harm the students and waste a lot of money.

Lunch is one of the most important parts of a student's day at school. It's a time when students can relax and have fun. Part of that fun is enjoying the food. Students have their likes and dislikes, but usually there's something they will eat, even if it's just the packages of chocolate chip cookies that everyone likes so much. The point is to have something in the middle of the day that will give students some energy to make it through the rest of the day. It doesn't need to be a full meal of chicken, vegetables, and whole-grain rolls. Teenagers are picky about their food and they are also a little rebellious. If the school offers only food that many teens don't like, they just won't eat it. Then many students will be trying to make it through the day without lunch. Many students do not eat breakfast, so now they will have missed two meals. This could lead to students fainting or losing a lot of weight, which could also be dangerous. If the students do eat the full meals presented in the cafeteria, this could also be a problem. The lunches we have now are light food—sandwiches, tacos. If students eat a full meal and then go right out to play gym, they could get sick.

Having a program like this will also waste a lot of money. We all know that better food costs more money to buy and takes more skill to prepare. The school will have to increase its food budget and possibly hire different people to prepare the food. All this money will go to waste because most of the students won't eat the food. Burgers and tacos may not be the healthiest foods but they also don't cost very much and teenagers will actually eat them. Eliminating the soda machines will also cost the school a lot of money. The money from those machines goes toward school supplies that benefit the students. So once again, if we have this new lunch program students are being harmed. Yes, we could replace the soda machines with water machines, but they will definitely not generate as much income and students will have to sacrifice things such as sports equipment, uniforms, or art supplies.

People will say that the school has a responsibility to provide nutritious food for the students. First of all, burgers and tacos do have nutrition; it's not like students are eating nothing but candy for lunch. Secondly, we're only talking about one meal a day; many students get very nutritious food at home. One meal is not going to make that much difference.

This new lunch program could do more harm than good. I appreciate the school trying to make students healthier, but that really is a personal choice and the responsibility of students and their parents. The school should concentrate on educating students, not trying to change their diets.

Critique

This essay shows a good understanding of the prompt, and the writer takes a strong stand on the issue. The essay is well developed with the exception of paragraph 4, which contains only a counterargument and could have been developed a bit more to make the essay more balanced. The essay gives specific examples and is logically sound. The writing shows a strong command of written language but lacks some of the sophistication of the model score 6 essay.

Sample "Score 4" Essay

To try to fight obesity and make students more healthy, the school board is thinking about changing the cafeteria menu to get rid of the junk food and have only low-fat meals and snacks. They are also thinking about getting rid of the soda machines. I think this is a good idea.

Teenagers eat way too much junk. Most of my friends don't eat breakfast or if they do, it's a doughnut or sugared cereal. Then when lunch time comes they eat a package of cookies and a soda. It's actually kind of gross. This program would force students to eat better. I know if I have a choice, I'll eat the less healthy food because I think it tastes better. But if all I had was healthy choices, I'd be eating better. I'd also probably lose some weight and so would other people. Most people I know do need to lose some weight. Some people think that the students won't eat this food, but that's not really a problem. If the teenager is overweight, skipping a meal might not be a bad idea.

Getting rid of the soda machines is also a good idea. I know the school makes some money off of them so losing the money would be bad, but not having soda around all the time would be more healthy. I had three cavities last year and I think it's mostly because I drink so much soda.

I definitely think a healthier lunch program is a good idea. It may take some getting used too but I think it will be better for everyone in the long run.

Critique

This essay shows a good understanding of the prompt, and the writer takes a strong stand on the issue. The introduction is somewhat of a restatement of the prompt, but it works. The essay lacks some development. It's only four paragraphs in length, and the writer focuses a bit too much on personal issues related to the topic (cavities due to drinking soda). The writing shows a good command of written language but lacks sophistication.

Sample "Score 3" Essay

The school board is considering changing the school lunch program so that all the food is low-fat. They are also interested in getting rid of all the soda machines. I think this is a terrible idea.

No one likes low-fat food, especially teenagers. We like to eat junk food. We have to eat enough healthy food at home, we don't need it pushed on us at school. Actually I don't even think the food at school is that unhealthy. It's not like it's fast food or anything. OK, there's burgers, but their not all greasy or anything. If we get low fat food no one will eat it. No one wants to eat whole grain pitas with tuna in them. I've tried low-fat cookies and they were terrible. They tasted like cardboard.

As far as getting rid of the soda machines, that will cause a big problem. We all like to drink soda. It's refreshing and picks us up in the afternoons. Also the soda machines make money for the school. We get supplies and stuff from that money. I think the students will probably rebel if we get rid of the soda machines or you'll have a bunch of people cutting just to get to the store to buy some soda.

This program is a bad idea. I wouldn't put it in, but if you do watch out because the students and probably even some teachers are not going to like it.

Critique

This essay shows a basic understanding of the prompt, and the writer takes a clear stand on the issue. It is undeveloped, as it is only four paragraphs. This essay focuses on the writer's personal dislike of eating healthy foods, as well as what will happen if the plan is implemented, rather than citing specific, logical reasons for not implementing the plan. The writing shows some command of written language, but it is very casual and unsophisticated.

Sample "Score 2" Essay

I think the school should maybe go into a healthier lunch plan. I also think that the soda machines should also be out.

The soda machines never work anyway. I loose so much money in them. Or if I don't loose the money I get the wrong soda. So I don't care if those go away.

The lunches are pretty bad. All we eat is hamburgers, tacos and some kids only eat chips and cookies for lunch. Thats pretty bad and I can see that a lot of people need to loose weight too. The new lunch plan might help people eat better and loose weight.

But it would be hard to always eat healthy food. Everyone likes a treat once in awhile so maybe a totally healthy lunch might not be so great.

Critique

This essay shows a weak understanding of the prompt. It does not take a very clear stand on the issue because, although the writer makes a clear statement about wanting the new lunch program in the introduction, the essay drifts off focus by discussing the fact that the writer loses money in the soda machines. In addition, in the conclusion, the writer says that the new program *might not be so great*. The essay is very undeveloped and lacks logical reasoning. The writing shows some grasp of written language, but it is very unsophisticated and contains spelling and grammatical errors that make some of the essay difficult to understand.

Sample "Score 1" Essay

There are good and bad things about the new lunch plan. Its always a good idear to eat better but ususually its not that fun. So the school should think about it before they do it.

Most kids and adults like soda. No one really likes to drink water, but they will if that's all there is so if the soda machines go out and theres only water that would be good. But if you do that the water fountains need fixing theyre always broken or actually its kind of dirty so maybe we should not use them and just go back to the soda machine.

Im not really shure what the best thing is. Well the best thing is to eat healthy and not drink soda but whose really gonna do that.

Critique

This essay shows a lack of understanding of the prompt and does not take a stand on the issue at all. The body of the essay drifts off topic by focusing on the condition of the water fountains. The writer admits in the conclusion that he or she is not sure what to think of the issue. The writing shows a poor grasp of written language, and there are many spelling and grammatical errors that make much of the essay difficult to understand.

6 ▶ SCORING YOUR ACT PRACTICE TESTS

The way that ACT reviewers arrive at your official test scores is more complicated than just adding up your correct answers. The first thing they do is take the number of correct answers on each test and then convert them to scaled scores, which allow each test, regardless of the number of questions, to have the same range, 1 being the lowest and 36 being the highest. The composite score is the average of all four multiple-choice scaled scores, rounded off to the nearest whole number. If you take the optional Writing test, you will receive two additional scores beyond what you would receive if you took only the ACT multiple-choice tests. You must take both the English and Writing tests to receive writing scores. You will receive a Writing test subscore and a combined English/Writing score, plus comments about your essay. The combined English/Writing test score is created by using a formula that weighs the English test score as two-thirds of the total and the Writing test score as one-third of the total to form a combined score. This combined score is reported on a 1–36 scale, 1 being the lowest and 36 being the highest.

If you'd like approximate ACT-like scaled scores for the individual practice tests in this book, as well as a composite score for each of the practice batteries, you can follow these simple steps. Remember, however, that the scores you earn here are only an approximation of what you might earn on your official ACT.

Scoring the Four Multiple-Choice Practice Tests

Chapters 2 through 5 in this book each contain a full battery of ACT practice tests—the four multiple-choice tests (English, Mathematics, Reading, and Science), as well as an optional Writing practice test. The first step for each practice battery is to find your individual scores on the multiple-choice tests.

You must first find your raw score for each multiple-choice test. Your raw score is simply the number of questions on each test that you answered *correctly*. Remember, on the ACT there is no penalty for guessing, so don't subtract any points for questions you answered incorrectly.

Use the following Multiple-Choice Scale Score Conversion Chart to help compute your scaled scores. You must take the raw score for a test, multiply it by 36, divide that product by the number of test questions, and then either add or subtract a specific adjustment number provided to you in the chart. If the final number you arrive at for your scaled score isn't a whole number, it be should rounded to the nearest whole number; so, for example, 34.5 should be rounded up to 35; 29.3 should be rounded down to 29.

MULTIPLE-CHOICE SCALE SCORE CONVERSION CHART

ACT PRACTICE BATTERY 1
ENGLISH PRACTICE TEST 1

Raw Score × 36 = ÷ 75 = − 2 = Scaled Score

MATHEMATICS PRACTICE TEST 1

Raw Score × 36 = ÷ 60 = + 2 = Scaled Score

READING PRACTICE TEST 1

Raw Score × 36 = ÷ 40 = + 2 = Scaled Score

SCIENCE PRACTICE TEST 1

Raw Score × 36 = ÷ 40 = − 1.5 = Scaled Score

ACT PRACTICE BATTERY 2
ENGLISH PRACTICE TEST 2

Raw Score × 36 = ÷ 75 = − 2 = Scaled Score

MATHEMATICS PRACTICE TEST 2

Raw Score × 36 = ÷ 60 = + 2 = Scaled Score

READING PRACTICE TEST 2

Raw Score × 36 = ÷ 40 = + 2 = Scaled Score

SCIENCE PRACTICE TEST 2

☐ Raw Score   × 36 =   ☐   ÷ 40 =   ☐   − 1.5 =   ☐ Scaled Score

ACT PRACTICE BATTERY 3
ENGLISH PRACTICE TEST 3

☐ Raw Score   × 36 =   ☐   ÷ 75 =   ☐   − 2 =   ☐ Scaled Score

MATHEMATICS PRACTICE TEST 3

☐ Raw Score   × 36 =   ☐   ÷ 60 =   ☐   + 2 =   ☐ Scaled Score

READING PRACTICE TEST 3

☐ Raw Score   × 36 =   ☐   ÷ 40 =   ☐   + 2 =   ☐ Scaled Score

SCIENCE PRACTICE TEST 3

☐ Raw Score   × 36 =   ☐   ÷ 40 =   ☐   − 1.5 =   ☐ Scaled Score

ACT PRACTICE BATTERY 4
ENGLISH PRACTICE TEST 4

☐ Raw Score   × 36 =   ☐   ÷ 75 =   ☐   − 2 =   ☐ Scaled Score

MATHEMATICS PRACTICE TEST 4

☐ Raw Score   × 36 =   ☐   ÷ 60 =   ☐   + 2 =   ☐ Scaled Score

READING PRACTICE TEST 4

☐ Raw Score   × 36 =   ☐   ÷ 40 =   ☐   + 2 =   ☐ Scaled Score

SCIENCE PRACTICE TEST 4

☐ Raw Score   × 36 =   ☐   ÷ 40 =   ☐   − 1.5 =   ☐ Scaled Score

Finding Your Composite Scores

The overall composite score for each of the practice batteries in this book can be calculated by finding the average of the four multiple-choice scaled scores, and rounding to the nearest whole number. The following Composite Score Chart will help you find your composite scores.

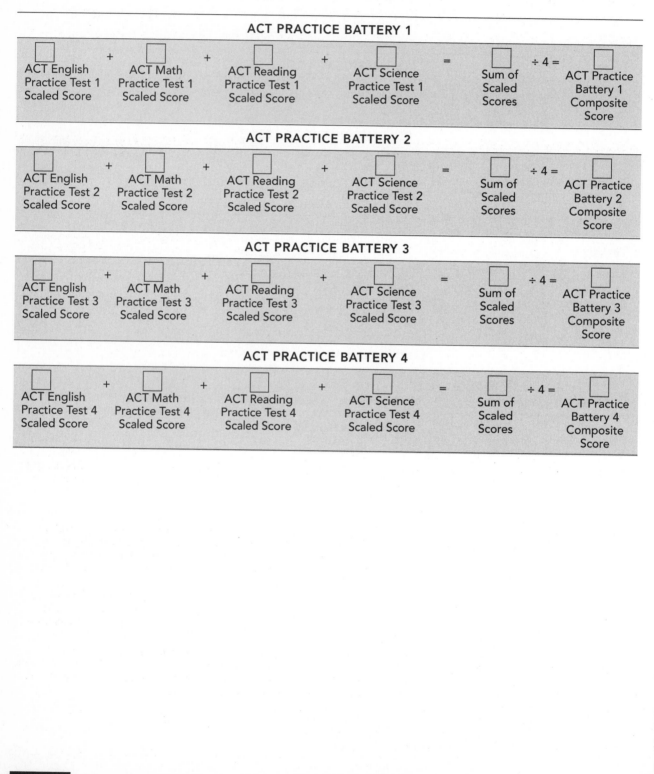

Finding Your Writing Scores

The first step toward computing your practice Writing subscores and combined English/Writing scaled scores is scoring your essays. To begin, look at the following scoring rubric. To determine your score, simply refer to the categories on the rubric to see how your writing measures up. If you have difficulty figuring out your score, ask someone knowledgeable, such as a teacher, counselor, writing coach, or college professor, to help you. If this is not an option, you can refer to the sample essays (at each ACT score level: 6, 5, 4, 3, 2, and 1) included for each practice prompt. You can use these as benchmarks to compare and contrast your writing.

Each model response at every scoring level is accompanied by a critique. The critique will help you see the strengths and weaknesses of the response. You will be able to understand what the ACT writing scorers are looking for—both pitfalls to avoid in your own response and the signs of good writing.

ACT WRITING PRACTICE TESTS SCORING RUBRIC

	6 EFFECTIVE SKILL	5 COMPETENT SKILL	4 ADEQUATE SKILL	3 DEVELOPING SKILL	2 INCONSISTENT/ WEAK SKILL	1 LITTLE OR NO SKILL
Understanding of task	Excellent and insightful understanding of assignment; provides critical context for discussion of issue; shows insight into complexities of issue; provides counterarguments	Good understanding of assignment; provides broad context for discussion of issue; shows some insight into complexities of issue; provides some counterarguments	Good understanding of assignment with some context for discussion of issue; shows recognition of complexities of issue and counterarguments	Basic understanding of assignment; takes a clear position; shows some recognition of complexities of issue and counterarguments	Weak understanding of assignment; does not take a clear position on issue; shows little recognition of complexities of issue and counterarguments	Little or no understanding of assignment; position on issue is not clear or is nonexistent
Development of Argument	Well developed with specific and interesting examples	Adequately developed with specific and appropriate examples	Some development with some specific examples	Little development; tends to be very general	Lack of development; inappropriate examples	Complete lack of development; examples are either nonexistent or completely off topic
Organization of Essay	Clear pattern of organization; uses clear logic and excellent transitions between ideas	Generally well organized; uses clear logic with good transitions between ideas	Organized with some inconsistencies; uses recognizable logic with some transitions between ideas	Inconsistent organization; uses some logic with a few transitions between ideas	Disorganized; logic is difficult to follow, and there are few transitions between ideas	No attempt at organization; argument is illogical and/or disorganized; there are few or no transitions between ideas
Language/style/ mechanics (grammar, spelling, punctuation, etc.)	Excellent command of written language with varied sentence structure and sophisticated vocabulary	Good command of written English with attempts at varying sentence structure and attempts at sophisticated vocabulary use	Adequate command of written language with some minor errors; little sentence variety and only basic vocabulary	Noticeable errors in grammar; little or no attempt at sentence variety	Many errors in grammar, making comprehension difficult	Many errors in grammar, making comprehension extremely difficult

Finding Your Writing Subscores

Your official ACT Writing Test essay will be scored by two graders using a rubric similar to one provided to you on the previous page. Each grader will assign your essay a score between 1 and 6, and those two scores are added to arrive at your Writing subscore, between 2 and 12. If you're lucky enough to have two people you trust grade your practice essays in this book using the same method, that's great; but if not, simply double the practice essay's score to arrive at an approximate subscore for each Writing practice test.

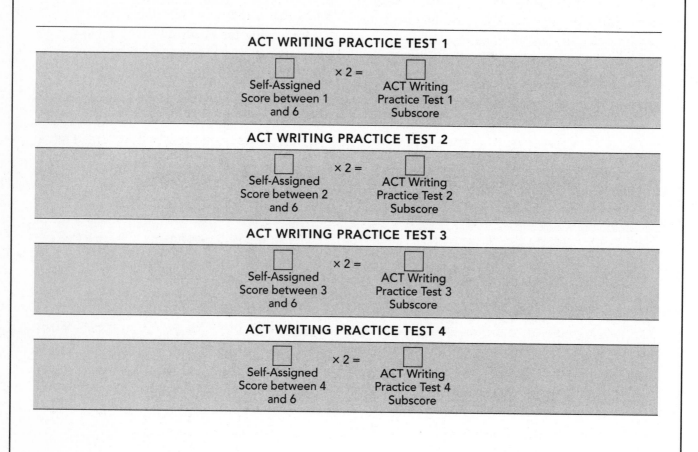

ACT WRITING PRACTICE TEST 1

☐ × 2 =
Self-Assigned
Score between 1
and 6

☐
ACT Writing
Practice Test 1
Subscore

ACT WRITING PRACTICE TEST 2

☐ × 2 =
Self-Assigned
Score between 2
and 6

☐
ACT Writing
Practice Test 2
Subscore

ACT WRITING PRACTICE TEST 3

☐ × 2 =
Self-Assigned
Score between 3
and 6

☐
ACT Writing
Practice Test 3
Subscore

ACT WRITING PRACTICE TEST 4

☐ × 2 =
Self-Assigned
Score between 4
and 6

☐
ACT Writing
Practice Test 4
Subscore

Finding Your Combined English/Writing Scaled Scores

Finally, to find your combined English/Writing scaled score for each practice battery, take the scaled score for the practice English test and the Writing subscore for the Writing practice test for a battery and use the following chart. Locate your scaled score for the English practice test in the far left column, and then locate your Writing practice test subscore in the top row. Find the box where they meet, and the number in that box is your score.

ENGLISH PRACTICE TEST SCORE	WRITING PRACTICE TEST SUBSCORE										
	2	3	4	5	6	7	8	9	10	11	12
1	1	2	3	4	5	6	7	8	9	10	11
2	2	3	4	5	6	6	7	8	9	10	11
3	2	3	4	5	6	7	8	9	10	11	12
4	3	4	5	6	7	8	9	10	11	12	13
5	4	5	6	7	8	9	10	11	12	12	13
6	5	6	7	7	8	9	10	11	12	13	14
7	5	6	7	8	9	10	11	12	13	14	15
8	6	7	8	9	10	11	12	13	14	15	16
9	7	8	9	10	11	12	13	13	14	15	16
10	8	9	9	10	11	12	13	14	15	16	17
11	8	9	10	11	12	13	14	15	16	17	18
12	9	10	11	12	13	14	15	16	17	18	19
13	10	11	12	13	14	14	15	16	17	18	19
14	10	11	12	13	14	15	16	17	18	19	20
15	11	12	13	14	15	16	17	18	19	20	21
16	12	13	14	15	16	17	18	19	20	20	21
17	13	14	15	16	16	17	18	19	20	21	22
18	13	14	15	16	17	18	19	20	21	22	23
19	14	15	16	17	18	19	20	21	22	23	24
20	15	16	17	18	19	20	21	21	22	23	24
21	16	17	17	18	19	20	21	22	23	24	25

22	16	17	18	19	20	21	22	23	24	25	26
23	17	18	19	20	21	22	23	24	25	26	27
24	18	19	20	21	22	23	23	24	25	26	27
25	18	19	20	21	22	23	24	25	26	27	28
26	19	20	21	22	23	24	25	26	27	28	29
27	20	21	22	23	24	25	26	27	28	28	29
28	21	22	23	24	24	25	26	27	28	29	30
29	21	22	23	24	25	26	27	28	29	30	31
30	22	23	24	25	26	27	28	29	30	31	32
31	23	24	25	26	27	28	29	30	30	31	32
32	24	25	25	26	27	28	29	30	31	32	33
33	24	25	26	27	28	29	30	31	32	33	34
34	25	26	27	28	29	30	31	32	33	34	35
35	26	27	28	29	30	31	31	32	33	34	35
36	26	27	28	29	30	31	32	33	34	35	36

ACCESSING YOUR FOUR ADDITIONAL ONLINE ACT PRACTICE TESTS ▶

on't forget that your purchase of *ACT: Power Practice* also gives you access to *four more* complete ACT English, Mathematics, Reading, Science, and Writing practice tests. Each test includes:

- **immediate scoring**
- **detailed answer explanations**
- **personalized recommendations for further practice and study**

Log in to the LearningExpress Practice Center by using the URL: **www.learnatest.com/practice**

This is your Access Code: **7892**

Follow the steps online to redeem your access code. After you've used your access code to register with the site, you will be prompted to create a username and password. For easy reference, record them here:

Username:_____   **Password:**_____

With your username and password, you can log in and access your additional practice tests. If you have any questions or problems, please contact LearningExpress customer service at 1-800-295-9556 ext. 2, or e-mail us at **customerservice@learningexpressllc.com.**

NOTES

NOTES

NOTES